Sociology of Mental Health

Sociology of Mental Health

GIRI RAJ GUPTA
Western Illinois University

Allyn and Bacon
Boston • London • Toronto • Sydney • Tokyo • Singapore

In memory of my parents

*The world today does not make sense,
so why should I paint pictures that do?*

Pablo Picasso

Editor-in-Chief, Social Sciences: Susan Badger
Senior Editor: Karen Hanson
Editorial Assistant: Marnie S. Greenhut
Cover Administrator: Linda Dickinson
Composition Buyer: Linda Cox
Manufacturing Buyer: Megan Cochran
Editorial–Production Service: P. M. Gordon Associates
Production Administrator: Deborah Brown

Copyright © 1993 by Allyn & Bacon
A Division of Simon & Schuster, Inc.
160 Gould Street
Needham Heights, Massachusetts 02194

All rights reserved. No part of the material protected by this copyright notice may be reproduced or utilized in any form or by any means, electronic or mechanical, including photocopying, recording, or by any information storage and retrieval system, without the written permission of the copyright owner.

Library of Congress Cataloging-in-Publication Data

Gupta, Giri Raj.
    Sociology of mental health / Giri Raj Gupta.
      p. cm.
    Includes bibliographical references and index.
    ISBN 0-205-13960-4
    1. Social psychiatry. 2. Mental illness. I. Title.
RC455.G863 1993
306.4'61—dc20   92-23282
                                                    CIP

Printed in the United States of America
10 9 8 7 6 5 4 3 2 1   97 96 95 94 93

Brief Contents

Preface   xiii

Chapter One • The Problem of Mental Disorder   1

Chapter Two • Mental Disorders: A Historical Overview   31

Chapter Three • Medical and Psychiatric Approaches to Mental Disorders   53

Chapter Four • Social and Psychological Approaches to Mental Disorders   79

Chapter Five • Anxiety, Mood, and Stress-Related Disorders   109

Chapter Six • Schizophrenia, Psychosis, and Personality Disorders   131

Chapter Seven • Substance Abuse and Mental Disorders   159

Chapter Eight • Sexuality and Mental Disorders   185

Chapter Nine • Mental Disorders: Social Class, Race, Ethnicity, and Rural and Urban Living   213

Chapter Ten • Mental Disorders: Age, Gender, Marital Status, and Religion   239

Chapter Eleven • Mental Disorders: Individual and Institutional Response   263

Chapter Twelve • Public Policy, Homelessness, and
the Law   293

Chapter Thirteen • Treatment of Mental Disorders:
Current Trends   323

References   353

Index   381

Contents

Preface   xiii

1   The Problem of Mental Disorder   1
*The Brain–Mind Controversy   2
Mental Health, Mental Illness, and Mental Disorder   3
The Extent of Mental Disorders   7
Social Forces and Mental Disorders   11
Social Reaction to Mental Disorders   13
Mental Disorders: A Cross-Cultural Perspective   18
How Sociologists Look at Mental Disorders   23
Chapter Review   29
For Further Study   30*

2   Mental Disorders: A Historical Overview   31
*Early Perceptions of Mental Disorders   31
The Middle Ages: A Period of Stagnation and Regression   37
The Age of Humanitarian Reform   39
The Renaissance: A Resurgence of Scientific Thinking   42
The Reformists   44
Emergence of Competing Models of Mental Disorders   46
Feminization and Sexualization of Mental Disorders   49
Competing Views of Mental Disorder in Contemporary Society   50
Chapter Review   51
For Further Study   52*

viii   Contents

3   **Medical and Psychiatric Approaches to Mental Disorders**   53
    Early Biological Views   54
    The Search for Brain Pathology   54
    The Medical–Biological Model   55
    Classification of Mental Disorders: A Major Controversy   57
    DSM-III-R *Classification*   58
    Organic and Biological Determinants of Mental Disorders   62
    The Biochemical Revolution and Pharmacological Advances   69
    The Psychiatric Approach: An Evaluation   73
    Does the DSM-III-R *Have Built-in Biases?*   75
    The Psychiatric Enterprise and the Power of Interest Groups   76
    Chapter Review   77
    For Further Study   78

4   **Social and Psychological Approaches to Mental Disorders**   79
    Sociological Approaches to Mental Disorders   80
    The Symbolic Interaction Perspective   81
    Social Deviance Perspective   85
    Social Reaction, Social Stress, and Social Selection Perspectives   93
    The Structural–Functional Perspective   94
    The Conflict Perspective   95
    The Social Exchange Perspective   97
    Mental Illness as Myth: The Theory of Problems of Living   99
    The Psychodynamic Perspective   101
    The Humanistic Perspective   104
    Sociopsychological Approaches to Mental Disorders: An Evaluation   105
    Chapter Review   106
    For Further Study   107

5   **Anxiety, Mood, and Stress-Related Disorders**   109
    Guilt Cultures and Shame Cultures   110
    Anxiety Disorders   111
    Panic Disorder   114
    Phobic Disorders   115
    Mood Disorders   117
    Obsessive–Compulsive Disorders   121
    Somatoform Disorders   122
    Dissociative Disorders   124
    Adjustment Disorder   126
    Posttraumatic Stress Disorder   127

Therapies and Their Outcomes 127
Chapter Review 129
For Further Study 130

6 **Schizophrenia, Psychosis, and Personality Disorders** 131
Schizophrenic Disorders 132
Psychoses 136
Explanations of Schizophrenia and Psychoses 137
Personality Disorders 145
Chapter Review 156
For Further Study 157

7 **Substance Abuse and Mental Disorders** 159
Understanding Substance Abuse 161
Typology of Substance Abuse 162
Factors That Affect Substance Abuse 163
Alcohol 166
Marijuana 170
Heroin 172
Cocaine, Crack, and "Ice" 173
Amphetamines 176
Barbiturates 177
Hallucinogenic Drugs 178
Deliriants 178
Nicotine 179
Other Addictions 179
Explanations of Substance Abuse 180
Chapter Review 182
For Further Study 182

8 **Sexuality and Mental Disorders** 185
Culture and Sexuality 185
Recreational and Procreational Sexuality 186
Changing Sexual Values 188
Sexual Variations or Deviations: The Moral Debate 188
Homosexuality 189
Sexuality and Emotions 190
Sexual Deviance and Mental Disorders 191
Sexual Disorders 192
Sexual Dysfunctions 204
AIDS and Mental Disorder 208

x   Contents

Sex Therapy Revolution   209
Chapter Review   210
For Further Study   211

9   **Mental Disorders: Social Class, Race, Ethnicity, and Rural and Urban Living**   **213**
Social Epidemiology   213
Association and Causation   214
Social Class   215
Race   222
The Double Standard in Mental Health: Class, Race, and Ethnicity   233
Ethnicity, Healing, and Mental Distress   234
Rural and Urban Living   235
Chapter Review   237
For Further Study   238

10   **Mental Disorders: Age, Gender, Marital Status, and Religion**   **239**
Data Sources: Their Strengths and Limitations   239
Age   241
Gender   245
Marital Status   248
Religion   257
Chapter Review   261
For Further Study   262

11   **Mental Disorders: Individual and Institutional Response**   **263**
The Person, Self-Feeling, and Deviance   264
Principal Diagnosis   265
Prepatient Experience   265
Career of a Mental Patient   272
The Mental Hospital: Is It a Total Institution?   275
The Ex-Mental Patient Experience   286
Chapter Review   290
For Further Study   290

12   **Public Policy, Homelessness, and the Law**   **293**
Public Policy and Mental Health   293
Community Mental Health   294

The Homeless 298
Mental Disorders and the Law 312
Chapter Review 321
For Further Study 322

13 Treatment of Mental Disorders: Current Trends 323
The Individual versus Social Environment 324
Therapies 326
The Therapy Revolution 330
Self-Help, Mutual Help, and Support Groups 331
Scientific Foundations of the Treatment of Mental Disorders 332
Modern Medicine and Therapeutic Practices 335
Psychotherapy 338
Asian Therapies 345
Conclusion 349
Chapter Review 350
For Further Study 351

References 353

Index 381

Preface

Mental health and disorder remain major concerns not only to individuals, but to the nation as a whole. This book reflects current findings while noting the usefulness of theoretical orientations and emerging sociological concepts.

The text describes the relationship between society and mental disorders. Many mental disorders are known across cultures, countries, and continents, which tells us that mental disorder or illness touches us all. We all know someone—a friend, a co-worker, a parent, or a child—who has had some kind of mental problem.

During the past five decades, research in various areas of mental health has received significant attention, and an incredible quantity of new materials has been added to aid in treating disorders. Many revolutionary changes have occurred, including the introduction of the new psychotropic drugs, new technology for scanning the brain's structure and functioning, and knowledge of sociological underpinnings that are at the base of many of our mental problems.

There are many controversies associated with the causal factors involved in mental disorders and treatment strategies. This book presents a balanced and reasonably objective view of the status of research by drawing on the contributions of the medical as well as social sciences including psychiatry, psychology, anthropology, and sociology, yet the basic orientation of the text remains sociological, particularly symbolic interactionist.

Research in mental disorders has been extremely prolific, and it is an enormous task to cull the relevant facts and integrate them into a coherent body of knowledge. Major studies sponsored by the National Institute of Mental Health on various mental disorders, including epidemiological studies and biological bases of mental disorders, require critical evaluation, rethinking, and reinterpretation of the findings. These findings, nevertheless, continue to be of significant value to sociologists, and this book incorporates a thorough updating of research developments in the field.

In an effort to place this text at the forefront of developments in the field of mental health, some of the following steps were necessary. First, within the space limitations, the book addresses major mental health topics. Second, it utilizes the *DSM-III-R* diagnostic categories for discussion purposes only and with relevant criticism. This is the only classification of mental disorders available and is used by practicing psychiatrists and other professionals. Third, it includes a chapter on the history of mental disorders for a better perspective, and a discussion of mental disorders across cultures and treatment strategies used. Fourth, rather than focusing on only one theory, several major sociological theories and approaches are discussed in the context of mental disorder. Finally, a discussion of a variety of counseling or treatment techniques is included. The latter, although generally not found in sociology of mental health texts, is for the curious student who wants to know how therapists interpret behavior to help a client.

Several features are included to facilitate student learning: The contents lists the topics of each chapter; and each chapter is highlighted by boxed material, alerting students to important issues and controversies. Real life cases of mental disorders are reported throughout the text to assist the reader in comprehending the complex nature of mental problems. To help students review, each chapter concludes with a set of study questions. A list of readings at the end of the chapter provides references for additional research along with an extensive bibliography at the end of the book. Terms, when first introduced in a chapter, are defined for clarity and consistency with clear, simple definitions that may assist students who come from various backgrounds. An Instructor's Resource Manual, written by the author, is also available and serves as an excellent reference and teaching aid.

In a constantly changing society, mental disorders, unfortunately, will continue to be part of our lives, as will be changing modes of treatment. I hope that this text provides the reader with firm knowledge of how mental disorders have been conceptualized in the past and present and with sufficient conceptual understanding to comprehend the future.

ACKNOWLEDGMENTS

Writing of this text was inspired by the thoughtful reaction of students at Western Illinois University, where special programs have also allowed me to teach the course at the graduate level to a variety of students, including law enforcement officers, counselors, case workers, and to older undergraduates through the independent home study program.

A number of people have helped me during the writing of this book. Assistance was readily available from a broad range of professionals, who are also friends, including family physicians, psychiatrists, psychologists, counselors, social workers, anthropologists, and sociologists. For extensive discussions and current psychiatric research findings I am thankful to B. K. Jhawar, S. Y. Khadri, and D. R. Chaudhari. For their encouragement, assistance, and reading the manuscript, I would like to thank professors Grant Bogue, Vernon Joy, Edward B. Kurjack, John Wade, and Rumi K. Price. The manuscript benefited from the suggestions of professors Bill Achord, Community Preservation Associates, Lincoln, NE; Angelo A. Alonzo, Ohio State University; Robert Emerick, San Diego State University; and Peter Manning, Michigan State University. I have a special debt to Norman K. Denzin, University of Illinois, and to Jack Fitzgerald, Knox College, IL, for their encouragement, valuable comments, and suggestions from the beginning of this project. Their insightful comments were usually invaluable, though at times difficult to implement. The book benefits from incisive but gentle comments from my colleague and friend Steven M. Cox, who encouraged me to write this text, and to whom I owe a great deal of gratitude. Ms. Karen Hanson, Senior Editor at Allyn & Bacon, was enthusiastic about this project from the beginning and made the process of writing a pleasant task.

Finally, this book could not have been completed without the total support of my wife Padma, daughter Sneh, and son Pankaj. They deserve special acknowledgment for their encouragement, understanding, and patience.

G. R. G.

▶ 1
The Problem of Mental Disorder

Among the disciplines that have systematically studied mental disorders, the most recent is sociology. The sociological perspective differs from dominant modes of medical (psychiatric) and psychological thought, in which illness is viewed as arising from within the individual. During the last 30 years, sociologists and representatives of allied disciplines have increasingly recognized that most of what are called mental illnesses reflect problems in personal adjustment or problems of living. Sociologists have always been intrigued with the ways people define mental problems, their causes and consequences, and strategies they use to treat such problems. Sociologists believe that most mental illnesses, unless there are physiological causes, are actually mental disorders emanating from interpersonal processes and social arrangements. For our purpose in this text, the term *mental disorder* includes mental illnesses, because in laypersons' language these terms have been used synonymously.

Cross-cultural studies suggest that mental disorders are found in all cultures. However, the way they are perceived and treatment strategies used vary from culture to culture. Klienman and Good (1985), surveying the experience of depression across cultures, reported that what are considered to be common elements in the syndrome of depression in Western societies (i.e., that the depressed person experiences an intense sense of guilt and frustration) do not appear in other cultures. Even the symptoms of depression, such as lack of pleasure, sadness, feelings of failure, loss of interest, and a sense of hopelessness, have different meanings in different societies. This finding raises some basic questions, which we hope to answer.

THE BRAIN–MIND CONTROVERSY

The issues discussed in this section are complex but are essential to understanding the conceptual confusion relating to the terms *mental illness*, *mental health*, and *mental disorder*. In other words, the way we verbalize and conceptualize determines the perception of mental illness, mental health, and mental disorder. These perceptions and the use of these terms have far-reaching consequences for everyone involved.

The Brain

The brain is a physical entity: It can be measured, observed, scanned, and operated on. It can be subjected to psychosurgery, electroconvulsive therapy (ECT), and psychotropic drugs.

Many professionals in the mental health field, especially with medical backgrounds, believe that most mental disorders are caused by biophysical, genetic, and biochemical processes that have gone askew in the brain, causing suffering to the person. The brain, as an organic part of the body, malfunctions, leading to behavioral changes in the person. This perspective, known as the *biological* or *medical* approach to mental disorders, holds that mental disorders are diseases of the brain, like cirrhosis of the liver or a stomach ulcer. From this perspective, the primary symptoms of mental disorder are manifested through a person's behavior but should be treated medically. In such a case, mental disorder is viewed as a disease of the central nervous system that is either inherited or a product of neurological or biochemical changes in the brain.

It is possible that the brain can alter the mind, but we cannot work on the mind biochemically, only relationally. Because the brain is an organic part of the body, introduction of any chemicals into it will consequently change its functioning, which may change the mental state. In this case, dysfunctioning of the brain may change the mental state or cause mental impairment or mental illness. But what about a situation in which the brain is medically healthy but a person shows signs of mental disorder?

The Mind

The mind is not a physical entity but a set of ideas, feelings, and emotions. It cannot be observed directly, cannot be scanned or operated on, but it can be amenable to medical treatment through treatment of the brain, which can change perceptions of the social world. Like the brain, the mind may be disordered but it cannot be ill in the traditional medical sense of the word. That is, the mind, although it can become disordered, cannot become diseased in a physical sense because it is not a physical entity.

To a great extent, it is still a mystery how the human mind works, but we all know that it is a product of psychosocial processes. The human mind is probably the most complex and elusive part of human nature and behavior. Most of our learning is the product of information processed by the brain, yet actions based on that process are governed by the mind. Likes and dislikes, acceptance and rejection, love and hostility, and many other individual idiosyncrasies and collective actions are thus dictated by the mind. For example, when intelligence tests are administered, we are not examining the brain but the mind. Yet brain dysfunctions may effect performance on such tests. To say "I have changed my mind" does not mean "I have changed my brain." When someone says, "I am sad due to recent tragedy in my family," *sadness* refers to the state of the mind, not the state of the brain. It is a logical and rational statement by a person who is going through some rough times. This situation may lead to depression, but again it is a mental state and not a state of the brain. Actually, the brain is healthy, allowing for a natural reaction dictated by the mind. Moreover, it is difficult at this time to ascertain a precise relationship between body and mind. Brain–mind issues are vital to our understanding because they relate to the kinds of professional help we seek.

MENTAL HEALTH, MENTAL ILLNESS, AND MENTAL DISORDER

Mental Health

When it comes to defining mental health, we are confronted with problems of conceptualization. Due to human variations, these concepts can best be viewed in relative terms. *Mental health* refers to the so-called normal state of mind of a person. On the other hand, *mental illness* relates to a condition in which a person manifests behaviors, feelings, ideas, and/or thought processes that are seemingly, and at least relatively, unusual, irrational, illogical, incoherent, unacceptable, undesirable, and serious enough to cause personal anxiety, discomfort, and problems in functioning.

To most people, problems of physical health are more real because they affect the body and its functioning, and treatment can be prescribed after the symptoms have been identified. Medical examination and testing have a certain appearance of objectivity. We have seen family members, friends, neighbors, and people we dislike or admire experiencing sickness, disability, and death. In most cases, physical illness is objectified so no one questions the validity of the person's sick role, with the anticipation that the disease will take its course or will be treated to bring the person back to normal physical health.

In contrast, mental health in many ways remains a subjective concept. As human beings, we all go through periods of high levels of anxiety as well as euphoria. Stressful periods in our lives may cause incalculable suffering, a nervous breakdown, depression or loss of interest in life, and even the intent to commit suicide.

Even today, when scientific concepts have largely been defined to connote specific meanings, the terms *mental health*, *mental illness*, and *mental disorder* remain elusive. Variations in human behavior and variations in perceptions of what may be called abnormal behavior or mental disorder lead to inconsistencies and disagreements among mental health experts as well as the lay public. One of the crucial weaknesses of these concepts is our inability to develop consensus about what constitutes normal behavior.

Mental Illness

Mental illness and mental disorder have been studied by shamans, magicians, priests, witch doctors, and quacks and currently by scientists from several distinct but closely related disciplines, such as psychiatry, psychology, and sociology. It is difficult to exclude sciences like anthropology, genetics, and biochemistry, which have significantly contributed to our understanding of human nature. Distinctions among sciences and their findings are often difficult to draw, for each discipline defines its scope of inquiry. Research findings of one science overlap others, thereby influencing the contributions in other fields. Increasingly, the understanding of current problems is not limited to the domain of one science or one distinctive perspective or theory.

Mental illness has traditionally been the province of medical science and treated as a disease, like any other disease of the human body. Currently, a special branch of medicine—psychiatry—is concerned with the study, evaluation, treatment, and prevention of mental disorder. A psychiatrist thus, by training, is a physician with an MD degree who specializes in the treatment of mental disorders. Some psychiatrists utilize, to a limited extent, psychological, social, and environmental explanations in the diagnosis of mental disorders. Thus, treatment is oriented to the diagnosis of problems in the brain and the body. Within the professional field of psychology, the special subfield of clinical psychology is concerned with the understanding, assessment, treatment, and prevention of abnormal behavior. Abnormal psychology and psychopathology of human behavior are other names that reflect varying emphasis in the study of abnormal behavior. A PhD is the terminal degree for most clinical psychologists.

Within the discipline of sociology, one of the specialty fields is sociology of mental health or mental disorders. Sociologists who study mental disorders may be known as psychiatric sociologists and, like those in other disciplines (such as clinical, abnormal, and social psychology, social work, cultural anthropology, and related disciplines), they see mental problems as consequences of interpersonal conflicts, frustrations, and failures rather than as medical problems. However, their explanations vary depending on the emphasis they place on variables that they believe may be associated with mental disorders. Recently, psychiatrists who have seen the failure or limited success of the medical model in treating mental disorders have been more inclined to look for sociological and social environmental explanations of mental disorders (Szasz, 1974, pp. 48–54).

Many mental disorders emanate from our own lives, some from encounters with unbearable circumstances such as sadness, grief, or loss of esteem. People have different levels of tolerance, fortitude, and willpower, and their ability to cope with life's problems is largely influenced by their reaction to such problems. Those who fail run the risk of having a mental disorder, sometimes severe enough to disrupt personal relationships. Seeking treatment may be the best alternative (see Table 1–1). The treatment alternatives are discussed in detail in Chapter 13.

TABLE 1–1 • Spectrum of Mental Disorders: Evolutionary Processes

Personal Situation ⟶	Reaction ⟶	Treatment
Life's problems, sadness, grief, trauma	Normal anxiety	None
Constant/free-floating anxiety	Inability to adapt or cope	Primary group support/counseling
Recurring anxiety	Depression, manic attacks (neurosis)	Counseling, psychotherapy, biochemical therapy
Overwhelmed by anxiety—emotional unrest, too little sleep or too much sleep, withdrawal, fluctuations between manic and depressive states, inability to cope with stress, delusions, hallucinations, hearing of voices, and loss of contact with reality (psychosis)	Confusion, hyperventilation, restlessness, incoherent thought process, hysteria, hostility, unpredictability, scapegoating, strained relationships, emotional outbursts	Counseling, psychotherapy Biochemical therapy, hospitalization, possible short-term institutionalization Long-term care

Mental Disorder

For our purposes, *mental disorder* refers to a state of personal distress or discomfort leading to impairment that threatens interpersonal relationships and individual well-being. It causes suffering to the individual and disrupts existing relationships due to deviation in individual behavior that is often viewed as unacceptable. Such behavior may be viewed by others as crazy, idiotic, foolish, malicious, immoral, sinful, or even criminal. Mental disorder may also be ignored as long as it does not pose a significant threat to others. Early sociological analysis of mental illness and mental disorder was influenced by deviance orientation. Mental disorders were viewed as actions or behaviors that violated social norms or institutionalized expectations shared and recognized within a social system (Cohen, 1959; Merton, 1968). The deviance orientation was followed by symbolic interactionalism. In the 1970s, theoretical works on emotions, feelings, and sentiments further advanced the understanding of mental disorders from an interactionist perspective, suggesting that the deviance framework is able to tell us only part of the story. Underpinnings of this perspective form the orientation of this book.

Becoming Mentally Ill

The process of becoming mentally disordered is complex, and research on this issue has been almost nonexistent until recently. Denzin's (1984, 1987) works are among the few that have addressed this issue. Through analysis of the psychology of emotions, he attempted to conceptualize the feelings, emotions, and behavior of people with mental disorders that lead to others perceiving them as mentally disordered. Denzin theorized that the process of becoming mentally ill is an interactive phenomenon. People with mental disorders develop a divided self (i.e., self against self), a false self-system, a self trapped in its own bad faith, a self without objective existence, a self that is torn apart internally, a self that feels emptiness. Characteristics include guilt, anger, anxiety, fear, trepidation, dread, self-despair, suspicion, self-irritation, exasperation, a loss of self-hope, a splitting of the self from the body, an inability to communicate with others, and extreme withdrawal. Everyone experiences these feelings at some point in life. But the emotionally divided self lives two lives, one that is inner and perhaps fantasy based and one that is outer and perhaps real (Denzin, 1984, p. 201). Analyzing anxiety and depression, for example, Denzin stated the following:

> Anxiety and depression are correlates of fear, anger, and resentment. They too are produced by structural and interpersonal relationships, but less so. Anxiety, in contrast to fear, arises from within the subject. There is nothing imme-

diately threatening him except his own anxiety. . . . The person can find no meaning. He turns inward, into himself. He becomes preoccupied with his current presence in the world. He is locked into present and can neither move forward or backward. He cannot give himself to a future and move into line of action that would overcome his anxiety. Anxiety moves into his inner core, leaving him weakened, and without purpose, except to be in a state of anxiety.

Such a state of the self becomes a mental disorder.

By reviewing studies of mental patients based on their autobiographies, sociology, psychology, and psychiatry, Cockerham (1990, pp. 339–350) structured a seven-phase model of becoming mentally ill. The seven phases are (1) alienation from place (inability to keep one's place in society by failing to observe rules that govern relationship with others), (2) realization of symptoms, (3) madness as a method of coping, (4) the definitive outburst (a decisive point when the observer is unable to understand the behavior of the person expressing insane behavior, such as havoc-creating behavior), (5) rendering of accounts (person with mental disorders offers tentative explanations of his or her behavior—excuses, justifications of misconduct, apologies, disclaimers, and rationalizations), (6) the paradox of normalcy (should behavior associated with mental disorder continue and that person's explanations for insane behavior are rejected by others, then others define that behavior as normal or a typical trait of that person), and (7) removal from place (an action taken by the mentally disordered person or others when it becomes clear that an insane person's behavior cannot be tolerated—the new place may be a hospital, mental institution, or residence of some empathetic relative or friend).

Becoming mentally disordered is not only a psychological or psychiatric experience. Given that, the causes of becoming insane may be rooted in the psychology and probably in the biochemistry of the individual influencing the mind, but the expression of that struggle is sociological (Cockerham, 1990, p. 348).

THE EXTENT OF MENTAL DISORDERS

The National Institute of Mental Health (NIMH) estimates that one of four or five Americans will be mentally impaired at least once in their life (NIMH, 1990a; Reynolds, 1989, p. 9A). Such disorders may vary from a mild case of depression to full-blown psychosis. In a 1988 NIMH study, it was found that 19% of American adults suffer from at least one psychiatric disorder in any given period of 6 months, and 29 to 38% have been mentally ill once in their lifetime. The study did not include patients of mental hospitals and institutions and the homeless. For various reasons,

13% of the individuals initially selected later declined to be interviewed (Thio, 1988, pp. 303–304). We cannot be certain about the reliability of these figures, because not everyone who has a mental disorder sees a psychiatrist or a mental health counselor. Furthermore, there may be thousands of people who are not aware that they have a problem. A variety of helping institutions offer services in the area of mental health, but they do not necessarily report these as mental health cases. Many cases of drug abuse, alcoholism, suicide, homicide, spousal and child abuse, and similar pathologies have their roots in mental disorders. But by labeling them as specific problems, we do not go beyond initial and superficial identification of these problems. Of course, one problem may be the cause of another problem, but we tend to treat the problem that surfaces.

According to the World Health Organization (WHO), the number of people suffering from severe mental disorders worldwide is reported to be between 40 and 100 million (Evans, 1989, p. 24). Many, if not all, are detained against their will, stripped of their civil rights, neglected, abused and made fun of.

Who Treats Mental Disorders?

Often, in their initial stages, mental disorders are not identified by the afflicted people themselves, especially if the problem has interpersonal underpinnings. They discuss the problem with trusted family members, friends, co-workers, clergy members, or a physician. If the problem does not go away or recurs, they might seek professional help.

Because of the strong impact of television, books, popular magazines, and scientific research that is influenced by biological research, our approach to mental disorders is characterized by a strong medical orientation. Underlying this orientation is a belief that all emotional and physiological maladies are medically treatable. Thus, most mental disorders are perceived to be diseases of the brain or body, although we may realize at one level that this is not the case. We prefer to focus on the individual in sorting out the origins of mental problems, not the social environment.

Contrary to the popular belief that most people with mental disorders are treated by psychiatrists and psychologists, figures from epidemiological and mental health services suggest that 50 to 60% of people with mental disorders in the United States are treated within the general medical care system (Regier et al., 1978; Shapiro et al., 1984). Only more severe disorders, such as schizophrenia, manic depressive disorder, and personality disorders, are referred to the mental health system. Even higher percentages of those with anxiety and depression are treated exclusively in the general health care system, especially for primary care, where nonmedical therapies are rarely used. A recent NIMH report based on Epidemiological Catchment Area (ECA) studies reported that over a 6-month period, 70% of people with affective disorders visited a general medical care clinic, whereas only 20% visited a mental health professional (Shapiro et al., 1984). These figures suggest that an overwhelming number of people with mental disorders are treated by physicians in general practice, professionals who are not fully equipped with the knowledge to treat mental disorders. By implication, of course, they are treating an organic disease. In addition, they might be treating an ailment that may not exist or simply be peripheral to the main complaint. One of the major problems in identifying a mental disorder is *somatization*—that is, that many mental problems are manifested in organic and physiological complaints. In addition, a host of other nonmedical therapists work with people who have mental or personal adjustment problems (see Chapter 13).

Reliability of Mental Health Figures

Although we believe that figures supplied by various agencies about the extent of mental disorders are relevant, there are some basic problems, especially concerning their accuracy. Reliable figures about the extent of mental disorders are not available for the following reasons:

1. Many people know that they have a mental problem and believe they can handle it. Often, they use means such as drinking or drugs to resolve their problems, and they are not included in mental health statistics.

2. People who have mild depression or insomnia or even suicidal tendencies sometimes consult a clergy member, a friend, or a family physician, and such cases are not entered as mental health problems.

3. Class, education, occupation, income, race, age and sex variables to an extent determine if a problem is defined as a mental problem. For example, a chief executive officer of a multimillion-dollar corporation who is suffering from constant anxiety leading to serious insomnia will be treated by a family physician for job-related stress, but a poor person suffering the stress of a dead-end job may be labeled as manic depressive. Chances are, the latter will seek help at a local hospital or mental health center and become part of the mental health figures, but not the former.

4. Those who consult a general physician, especially in a health maintenance organization (HMO), may be viewed as malingering, especially if the physician cannot find a physical cause for the person's complaints, such as chronic backaches or headaches.

5. Influential and powerful people who do not like certain individuals have a tendency to identify them with labels, such as "psycho," and "crazy." These people may have no mental problems but may be forced to seek treatment.

6. Many cases of spousal and child abuse involve elements of mental disorder. Abuse may simply be a symptom of other serious problems, but such cases are generally treated as either domestic or legal problems and rarely treated as problems of mental health.

7. The homeless, who not only have no place to live but have no money, no job, and no place to go, may be viewed as mentally disordered, though not all of them have mental problems. No one knows exactly how many homeless people there are. Since most do not seek mental health services, they do not become part of the mental health statistics.

Is it safer to say that the rates of mental disorders are on the increase? The answer must be a qualified one. Some of the reasons for this increase may be attributed to the following: (1) There is more public awareness about emotional health; (2) educational programs have sensitized people that help is available and many mental disorders are treatable; (3) the stigma associated with mental problems is gradually declining as celebrities and political leaders discuss their problems in public (i.e., Betty Ford and Kitty Dukakis for alcoholism; Mike Wallace of CBS's "60 Minutes" for depression); (4) a certain amount of narcissism has helped in seeking help ("I should not suffer anymore"); (5) the mass media, though often constrained by time and space, has generally offered reports about a variety of mental problems; and (6) psychiatric and pharmaceutical enterprise has done its best to promote its business through the propagation of knowledge of new drugs and treatments.

The introduction of psychoactive drugs in the 1960s was a promising step in that other methods of treatment of mental disorders, especially Freudian psychoanalysis, proved to be ineffective in severe cases of psychosis and varieties of schizophrenia. In 1952, medical researchers in France discovered that chlorpromazine, a drug commonly used to reduce inflammation and pain in surgery patients, was also effective in people who showed signs of schizophrenia, psychosis, manic depression, and chronic anxiety disorders. The drug was first introduced in the United States in 1954, and in the following few years several major pharmaceutical companies developed a variety of drugs intended for severe cases of depression and schizophrenia. The advent of these new drugs resulted in (1) extensive use of psychoactive drugs in the treatment of mental disorders and in strengthening the power of psychiatry, (2) an astounding decline in the number of resident patients in mental institutions based on the belief that drugs would take care of their problems, and (3) the ability of patients to live with their families. Of course, the consequences were mixed. Psychoactive drugs initially helped in controlling the symptoms of mental disorders rather than curing them, and many mental patients who might have benefited more from institutionalized treatment ended up on the streets. Even when medical attention was given, the follow-up and monitoring of drug therapy turned out to be a task. The use of drugs was no longer limited to organic brain syndromes or diseases of the brain but was extended to a vast variety of mental disorders and has been termed by Conrad and Schneider (1980) as the *medicalization of deviance*. Cable News Network reported on August 12, 1990 that 69 million prescriptions were filled for tranquilizers alone during the past year (CNN, 1990). Such treatment is one of several known as *biochemical* therapy. One of the major consequences of drug therapy has been the declining number of resident patients due to early releases. As help-seeking rates increased significantly, so did net releases (see Table 1–2).

Recent figures available from NIMH (1990) show that there were 512,501 resident patients in state and county mental hospitals at the end of 1950 compared to 110,743 in 1986. Admissions went up steadily from 152,286 in 1950 to 332,001 in 1986. Net releases were significantly up from 99,659 in 1950 to 330,912 in 1986, reaching a peak at 384,511 in 1970. The highest number of deaths in mental hospitals was in 1960 (49,748), up from 41,280 in 1950, with an impressive low at 3,503 in 1986. Deinstitutionalization was one of the major factors in the declining number of deaths in mental hospitals.

SOCIAL FORCES AND MENTAL DISORDERS

Sociologists are concerned with how various changes can influence the network of relationships in a society. Considering the increasing rates of mental disorders in American society, social analysts have attempted to

TABLE 1–2 • Percent Distribution of Patient Care Episodes in Mental Health Organizations by Type of Service in the United States, 1976–1986

	Percent Distribution				
Type of Service	1971	1975	1981	1983	1986
Inpatient	42	27	27	26	26
Outpatient	55	70	69	70	69
Partial care	3	3	4	4	5
Total number of episodes (in millions)	4.2	6.6	6.4	7.2	7.9

Adapted from National Institute of Mental Health (1990a). *Mental Health, United States*, Manderscheid, R.W. and Sonnenschein, M.A., eds. DHHS Pub. No. (ADM) 90–1708. Washington, D.C.: U.S. Government Printing Office.

find explanations, many of which originate in society itself. Like any other social issue, there are several sides to this problem. Some observers point out that American society is an affluent and probably the most healthy society in the world. We earn more, spend more, live longer, and have the highest literacy rate in the world. We are the most powerful democratic nation, with a great sense of pride, patriotism, and freedom. Yet the media often dramatizes and focuses on the negative, especially deviant acts and episodes. Others suggest that successes have their costs and that many people are simply experiencing serious problems trying to cope with the rapidity of change and keep their lives on an even keel. Technology has been transforming our lives so rapidly that the values we cherished in the past are gradually dissolving, and we find ourselves facing one crisis after another. Basic institutions that were once a haven for everyone are giving up their functions to secondary impersonal institutions. And a loss of faith is paramount. Institutions that have been the backbone of society (i.e., government, the economic system, and religion) are tarnished by greed and scandals. Sociologists believe that individual emotional instability is simply a reflection of the general disruption of society.

The Power of Interest Groups and Mental Disorders

Mental health is a huge enterprise in the United States, and in sheer economic terms it is at least an $80 billion per year industry. It involves a variety of interests groups, such as insurance; pharmaceutical and medical supply companies; hospitals, clinics and rehabilitation centers; real estate brokers and building contractors; financial institutions; politicians; physicians, psychiatrists, and other counselors; and a host of ancillary service providers. Power and money dictate the interests of these services, turning them into major business enterprises that increasingly become attuned to the goals of the business rather than the clients.

During the past three decades, we have entered a new era, the "therapy revolution," and new and innovative ways of treating mental disorders are being explored (see Box 1–1). It is a booming business. Due to the power of special interest groups, controversies in defining mental disorders have not received needed attention, while new categories of mental disorders have been added with each revision of the *Diagnostic and Statistical Manual* (*DSM*). Recently the National Institute of Mental Health (NIMH) (1990b), has addressed issues of mental problems among children leading to the expansion of the field of "infant psychiatry." For example, rumination (swallowing regurgitated food) among 4- to 6-month-olds and refusal to hold a glass by 7- to 9-month-olds may be seen as signs of early psychological disturbances. In addition, feminists were appalled by what they considered a male bias in the early drafts. Girls who were tomboys were labeled

> **BOX 1–1 • The Psychiatrist and Psychosocial Therapy**
>
> Most ethnographers consider Californians, though predominantly Anglo-American, a distinct subculture. Dr. Boyce, MD, a psychiatrist, is well known in California, and most of his clients come from towns in the area. He lives in an affluent, intellectual town, located between rolling green hills and the San Francisco Bay. His clients' expectations are raised by his impressive office, a new steel and glass building, richly furnished and carpeted. Decorations in his office bespeak his success, refinement, and intelligence. His office is located adjacent to the Stanford Medical Center, and the eminence of this prestigious institution spills over into his clients' expectations. Whenever hospitalization is needed, it is carried out in the Stanford Medical Center.
>
> Dr. Boyce was trained at a leading psychiatric center on the East Coast and then went to Europe, where he studied briefly with one of Freud's leading disciples. His colleagues regard him as being well trained in the classical psychiatric tradition. All his credentials, framed and neatly hung on the wall, attest to his accomplishments.
>
> Dr. Boyce's outstanding personal qualities are his self-confidence and his professional manner. His patients share a common world view about what is wrong—they have been made ill by bad childhood experiences. In their childhood, the clients had pathological relationships, which in turn infected their adult relationships. Often, the offending adult is either the father or mother or some other authority figure. Interestingly, when these early relationships are explored, the clients get well.
>
> A distinctive-looking man, Dr. Boyce is almost 6 feet tall, with heavy glasses and a full beard. He is not orthodox in his demeanor or dress, but he usually dresses in a suit. His fee is $90 for each visit, whether or not the client gets well. Dr. Boyce has an aura of mystery in handling his clients that the clients find attractive.

From Torrey, 1986, pp. 128–131.

as victims of "gender-identity disorder of childhood." The American Psychiatric Association's (APA's) Committee on Women had the specific clause rewritten to give tomboys a clean bill of mental health (Eitzen & Zinn, 1992, p. 522). Thomas Szasz, a practicing psychiatrist and an ardent social advocate with a professional career of over 45 years, has repeatedly warned that what actually are "problems of living," and not medical problems, are being treated by medical means.

SOCIAL REACTION TO MENTAL DISORDERS

Perception of mental disorder depends largely on social reaction to a certain pattern of behavior, which is seen as intolerable and sometimes dangerous to the person as well as to others. For example, in New Haven, Connecticut, Hollingshead and Redlich (1953, 1958) found that members of the lower class were more inclined to tolerate high levels of abnormal behavior and to attribute their problems to bad luck, laziness, discrimination, scarcity, or physical ailments; while the affluent believed that their problems were the consequences of frustration, rejection, unhappiness, and other psychological difficulties. Interestingly, there are two kinds of processes involved here: (1) the social judgment about oneself, one's feelings, and behavior; and (2) the social reaction of others—their judgments as to whether the behavior is extremely abnormal and needs attention. However, in some circumstances, the severely mentally disordered may lose touch with reality but may not be aware of the disorder at all. This raises another valid question: Do we have objective criteria for making these social judgments? At best, the criteria for defining mental disorders remain vague, fuzzy, unreliable, and unobjective and vary depending on social class, ethnicity, audience, and situation, among other factors. That is, behavior is viewed in the context of a person and his or her attributes (physical-social characteristics) by an audience in a certain situation (at a certain time and in a certain place). Behavior in itself is not the sole determinant of mental disorders.

Culture also plays a significant role in defining a mental disorder. In Southeast Asia, a woman possessed by the spirit of a deity may be viewed as a perfectly normal person who has earned respect because she is one of the chosen ones, while the same phenomena in North America may be viewed with skepticism and as a case of hysteria. Within a culture, subgroups or subcultures may interpret the same behavior differently. For example, becoming hysterical during church services may be viewed by one group as a mark of great devotion to God, while another group may see it as a symptom of neurosis. If a poor minority teenager steals a pair of pantyhose, she is considered a common criminal. Yet if a rich woman steals the same pantyhose, she might be considered mentally ill—a kleptomaniac.

Sex biases also play a major role in defining mental disorder. Boys are not supposed to be shy. If they are shy, there is a problem; maybe they have internalized feminine characteristics. Even color choices have meanings. Boys, if they are to be masculine, should not prefer bright, light, gaudy, or so-called feminine colors. If they do, they may be suspected of being less than masculine or gay. If a woman is sexually promiscuous, she may be considered a nymphomaniac, yet a man exhibiting the same behavior may be positively labeled, at least by other males—"Don Juan," "Casanova," "stud," or "swinger." Another example is a college student who behaves well most of the time and is known to be likable, responsible, and obedient during the week, but on Saturday afternoons in the fall drinks to excess, yells profanities at authorities, and even participates in the destruction of property. Is his behavior weird? No, because his actions are within limits and are acceptable for football fans. But what if he behaved similarly at his work or when attending a concert (Eitzen & Zinn, 1992, p. 520)? The context in which this behavior is manifested is crucial. Similarly, a nagging, complaining, and sharp-tongued wife has greater chances of being declared mentally disordered than an authoritarian, inconsiderate, alcoholic, and abusing husband. Historically, too, homosexuality was considered not only deviant behavior but a sin and a criminal act manifesting mental disorder, especially during the period of the Inquisition (see Chapter 8). It was only in 1973 that the American Psychiatric Association declared that homosexuality should no longer be listed as a mental disorder (*Diagnostic and Statistical Manual, DSM-II*).

Social Stigma

Mental illness or mental disorder is often misunderstood, and its consequences are greatly underestimated. Most people believe it happens only to other people. The impact of mental disorder is not only limited to the person who is suffering, but also his or her family, relatives, community, and the nation at large. The stigma of mental disorder has tremendous potential to ruin not only personal and family life, but one's career. In the presidential race of 1972, when vice-presidential candidate Thomas Eagleton, a running mate of presidential candidate George McGovern, was rumored to have been consulting a psychiatrist for depression, he was forced out of the race, though he served as a senator from Missouri for several more years. Michael Dukakis, a Democratic party presidential candidate in 1988 and governor of the state of Massachusetts, also was accused of having mental problems. He was forced to make a statement to clear his name. Having one's name associated with mental disorder is obviously more dangerous to one's self-esteem, prestige, career, and future than having cancer or any incurable disease. (We will discuss the subject of stigma later in this chapter.)

Referring to a recent survey by The National Alliance for the Mentally Ill (one of the major advocacy organizations for the mentally ill), Dr. Lewis Judd, Director of the National Institute of Mental Health, stated that 71% of the respondents felt that mental illnesses were due to emotional weakness. Approximately one third felt that mental illnesses might be due to sinful behavior. About 40% said that they were brought on by the patients themselves and that patients could will them away if they wished (Reynolds, 1989, p. 9A). Incidentally, these findings contradict the commonly held belief that mental disorder is a disease of the brain. The stigma discredits anyone who has sought help for mental health problems and continues to play its disparaging role today. Many people do not understand mental disorders as they do other problems. Most diseases do not result in lasting stigma as do mental disorders. Part of the problem is that mental disorders directly influence our relationships, roles, and self-esteem and generate a degree of uncertainty about the behavior of those who are known or perceived to have mental disorders. We often use stigmatic terms to show our displeasure, frustration, and aggravation. Thus, stigma can be extremely destructive for the person against whom it is used.

Let us examine the significance of stigma. Erving Goffman (1963b) defined the term *stigma* as "an attribute that is deeply discrediting." Unfortunately, stigmatizing an individual not only discriminates against, discredits, and brings disrepute, but it also excludes, disheartens, and demoralizes, and in the long run may reduce life chances (see Box 1–2).

BOX 1–2 • Myths about People with Mental Disorders

Myths about people with mental disorders are widespread and are perpetuated by ignorance, indifference, and misinformation. The National Institute of Mental Health (1985a) listed 14 such myths:

1. A person who has been mentally ill can never be normal.
2. Even if some mentally ill persons return to normal, chronically mentally ill remain different—in fact crazy.
3. If people with other handicaps can cope on their own, recovered mental patients should be able to do so, too.
4. Persons with mental illness are unpredictable.
5. Those with "split personalities" must remain unpredictable.
6. Mentally ill people are dangerous.
7. Recovered mental patients are surely potentially dangerous; they could go berserk at any time.
8. Anyone who has had shock treatment must really be in a bad way.
9. When you learn that a person has been mentally ill, you have learned the most important thing about his or her personality.
10. You can't talk to someone who has been mentally ill.
11. If a former mental patient has a really bad history, there is not much hope.
12. A former mental patient is bound to make a second-rate employee.
13. Perhaps recovered mental patients can work successfully at low-level jobs, but they are not suited for really important or responsible positions.
14. Recovered mental patients have a tough row to hoe, but there is not much that can be done about it.

National Institute of Mental Health, 1985a.

Causes of Stigma

Mental disorders are surrounded by so many negative stereotypes that even the scientific information is often discarded as meaningless. Some of these stereotypes are based on rare cases or images created by mass media; others are so deep-rooted and entrenched in culture that they persist today. Major negative stereotypes associated with stigma are as follows.

1. *Dangerousness:* People believe that those suffering from mental disorders are dangerous, though this belief is largely inaccurate. The mentally disordered are viewed as having "lost their minds" and therefore capable of committing any type of perilous act (images often come to mind of the Son of Sam, a notorious New York City murderer, and John Hinckley, who attempted to assassinate former President Ronald Reagan).

2. *Contagiousness:* The belief that real estate values will go down if mentally disordered people live in a neighborhood is based on the fear of contagiousness of the disorder. Some believe that mentally disordered people can influence or, worse yet, infect the young minds in a neighborhood and disrupt "healthy" families.

3. *Social failures:* A common fallacy is that those who have mental problems could not succeed or failed to meet the challenges of life, or slipped into misery because they could not combat day-to-day problems or handle crises. Such failures are believed to be bad role models in a family or community.

4. *Potential abusers:* Research shows that the so-called normal person is on an average more dangerous than the average mentally impaired. A most misunderstood fact is that mental disorder does not make a person more likely to hurt someone or endanger anyone's life. Sensationalized media reports of unusual and rare cases indirectly or subtly terrorize people more than the actual action of the mentally disordered.

5. *Uncertainty:* We all know stories of idiotic, whimsical, grandiose, paranoid, or in some ways "weird" people. Like any other problem or disease, a mental problem can recur. Some people, depending on the severity of their problems, may need prolonged attention and care, and the process of rehabilitation never ends for them; but most people are able to overcome their problems. Most mentally impaired do not need hospitalization, but we are never certain.

6. *Unpredictability:* There is an ongoing debate about the predictability of individual behavior, and it has not been possible yet for any science to predict such behavior objectively. However, information provided by these sciences is fairly accurate if predictions are based on social groups. Findings based on large statistical studies indicate that mentally disordered people are no more likely to commit unacceptable acts than the rest of the population.

Potential consequences of stigma, which are often ignored but which keep even mildly mentally impaired people away from the mainstream, result from zoning laws, restricted housing, and public and private facilities. Interests groups, such as banks, real estate brokers, affluent and influential people in the community, members of community boards, and city councils, who fear backlash from their patrons and electorate, continue to follow restrictive laws to keep the mentally disordered outside the community life. Such covenants restrict the possibility of allowing the mentally impaired to share in community life, which could help in their rehabilitation. However, many myths about people with mental disorders persist (see Box 1–2). Throughout the remainder of this text, you may want to reconsider any myths you subscribe to.

MENTAL DISORDERS: A CROSS-CULTURAL PERSPECTIVE

What constitutes mental illness or mental disorder is defined in a cultural setting. Considering the wide variety of cultural systems throughout the world, definitions of the terms we are accustomed to and accept routinely may not carry the same meaning elsewhere. Attempts have been made to find similarities and differences in cultural systems to add to our understanding of human behavior and often to understand ourselves better.

There are many variations in the treatment of people with mental disorders. For example, in Switzerland a person with a mental disorder can be detained against his or her will if considered "a danger to public morals." In India, such a person is ignored until his or her actions are deemed to be apparently violent. Suspicious or immoral behavior is deemed valid ground for detention in Iraq. Japan has 350,000 people in mental hospitals, one of the highest per capita figures in the world. It is easier in Japan for relatives to place and detain people in mental institutions, which are privately owned. In the former U.S.S.R., mentally disordered people and political dissidents were forcibly subjected to treatment with psychotropic drugs. Far worse situations are found in many nations of Asia, Africa, and South America. The WHO predicts a 72% increase in rates of mental disorders, a 20% growth between 1975 and 2000 (Evans, 1989, p. 25). What is known as mental disorder has a cultural perspective about which sociologists and psychiatrists sometimes do not agree. Some disorders are cultural-specific (see Table 1–3).

Using indigenous healers (shamans, witch-doctors, and faith healers) for physical as well as mental problems has occurred in almost all cultural systems, but it is more popular in developing societies. Often, a mental problem is not perceived as a problem in isolation, apart from conflicts in

TABLE 1–3 • Culture-Specific Mental Disorders

Name of Disorder	Culture/Geographical Area	Characteristic Symptoms
Amok	Some parts of Africa, Malaya, Java, and the Philippines	The onset of this disorder, usually found in males, shows signs of withdrawal, quietness, and loss of interest in the immediate environment; and then a phase of brooding follows. Gradually, the person manifests loss of reality, ideas of persecution, and general anger. The person in a full-blown stage of the disorder yells, jumps, and attacks people, sometimes with objects that may be handily available. *Amok*, or automatism, in its severe stage is marked by extreme aggression, sudden acts of hostility, and homicidal tendencies, which may lead to endangering lives of others. It is believed that alcohol, stress, fatigue, and extreme heat and exhaustion precipitate the disorder. After the outburst, a phase of calm and inactivity follows, which is marked by amnesia about the episodes and a slow recovery to normalcy.
Anorexia nervosa	Most of the Western world, especially North America	The disorder is characterized by a preoccupation with the body and its slender and emaciated appearance, and is found among young women, who often starve or refuse to eat. It is sometimes combined with mild *bulimia* when the sufferer believes that she may gain weight and therefore engages in fasting, self-induced vomiting, and frequent use of laxatives and diuretics.
Kitsunetsuki	Japan	More common in rural Japan, the people and families affected by this disorder believe that they are possessed by foxes, and they change their facial appearances to resemble foxes.
Koro	Southeast Asia, including Malay Archipelago	Characterized by intense anxiety and sudden onset, the person fears that his penis will withdraw into his abdomen and eventually he will die from this malady. It is believed that the person suffers from the guilt of overindulgence in sex or excessive masturbation. The fear of loss of strength and withered masculinity is suspected to be the cause of anxiety.

Continued

TABLE 1-3 • *Continued*

Name of Disorder	Culture/Geographical Area	Characteristic Symptoms
Kuru	Fore, of the Highlands of New Guinea	Believed to be a fatal mental/neurological disorder, primarily among adult women. The person is suspected to be a victim of sorcery, often leading to death. Some observers believe that the disorder is a reaction to the attempts of lechers to gain control over the lives of recalcitrant women.
Nuthkavihak	Eskimos	A disorder manifested by talking to oneself, screaming at someone who does not exist, believing that a child or husband was murdered by witchcraft when nobody else believes it, believing oneself to be an animal, refusing to eat for fear that eating will kill one, refusing to talk, getting lost, hiding in strange places, making strange grimaces, drinking urine, becoming strong and violent, killing dogs, and threatening people.
Were	Yoruba, Nigeria	A disorder in which the victim hears voices and tries to get other people to see their source, laughing when there is nothing to laugh at, talking all the time or not talking at all, asking oneself questions and answering them, piling up sticks with no goal in mind, throwing away food because it is thought to contain *juju*, a malevolent spirit, tearing off one's clothes, setting fires, defecating in public and then mushing around in feces, breaking things in a state of being stronger than normal, believing that an odor is being emitted from one's body.
Wittiko	Cree and Ojibwa Indians	A disorder, though rare, in which a person believes himself to be a cannibalistic monster, often associated with agitation and anger (variants of the same disorder are reported among Algonquin, Mahave, and Sioux Indians).

Adapted from Kiev, 1972; Kleinman, 1988; Lebra, 1976; Lehmann & Myers, 1989; Murphy, 1976; and Torrey, 1986.

the family, job, or other relationships. Not only may the problem be physiological, medical, or supernatural (spirit or demon possession), but the person is viewed in a holistic way in relation to his or her environment—ecological and social. The use of healers in most of the non-Western world is so widespread and extensive that it forms the backbone of the rural health care system. The healer, in his or her specialized role, plays a variety of other roles in the community. He or she is able to address many different aspects of the problems of living reported by a person or client and possibly suggest appropriate remedies. Such remedies may include diet changes, prohibition of the use of certain drugs, ritual practices and offerings to the deities or spirits of the ancestors, and magical rites. In many cases, the healer is the only psychotherapist a client will ever see. The healer plays a variety of roles; in addition to being a medicine man, he or she is something of a social worker, teacher, priest, even an arbitrator to settle disputes. He or she may tackle the problem, of which the patient's symptoms are only a part, with an across-the-board approach impossible to the fragmented social, penal, and medical services in the West (Pigache, 1973, pp. 45–47).

Throughout Latin America, *curanderos*, who blend religion and folk medicine in therapeutic procedures, do not distinguish between natural and supernatural causes of disorders. Often, Catholic tradition is central to the *curanderos'* treatment procedures. It is estimated that 10% of the men in northern Peru are such healers on a part-time basis (Dobkin, 1968, pp. 28–32). In Nigeria, over 80% of the rural population is treated by traditional healers (Oyebola, 1980, pp. 23–29). In Daresslaam, the capital of Tanzania, there is one traditional *mganga* (healer) for every 350 residents (Rappaport, 1977, pp. 127–132). A study of curative seance in Zululand emphasizes a close relationship between the functions of divination and therapy. Sometimes the diviner and the doctor are the same person, but more often the roles are specialized and performed by different individuals (Turner, 1972, pp. 437–444).

In many cultures of Asia, it is not uncommon that a person suffering from any kind of disorder, physical or emotional, may consult a priest, a shaman, a witch doctor, a traditional healer, or an indigenous medicine man before going to a hospital. Often, the elderly in the family know from experience that just going to the hospital may not be enough, because the allopathic or Western medicine is limited in its approach to the cure of a malady, as it does not take into account other aspects of the problem. The *Bomoh*, traditional healers in Malaysia, are so popular that half the patients who come to the psychiatric unit of the University Medical College have already consulted a *Bomoh*. There are 10 practicing *Bomohs* to every Western-trained physician. Three-fourths of the people who come to the hospitals in Indonesia have already consulted a traditional healer (Maretzki, 1981, pp. 237–256). This figure increases to 90% in Singapore and

Thailand, where it is viewed as a prudent precaution to consult traditional healers before taking other steps to find a cure (Neki, 1973, pp. 257–269).

Throughout Southern Asia, categorical differentiations between medical, psychological, and demonological are rarely clear, especially in the rural areas and to some extent in urban areas, too. The confluence of various sects of Hinduism, Islam, Sikkhism, Christianity, and other offshoots of these major belief systems presents an interesting phenomenon of seeking help for mental disorders from a variety of specialists, irrespective of one's religious affiliation. Seeking out a therapist in India is generally a family or collective affair. Advice may even be sought from unknown people who may be referred by someone else. The therapist often must listen to the family members of the patient recount their version of the illness before getting direct access to the patient. Most families, though, may not be sure about the nature of the ailment, yet almost every member tries to help in any way he or she can. Thus, the ailment receives attention from all fronts, with varying opinions and with a possibility of seeking a variety of help to ensure rapid recovery of the patient. The belief is that it is the person of the healer and not his or her particular techniques that are of decisive importance for the healing process. For example, for an unknown malady, a person may be advised to consult a *hakim* (a practitioner of the Arabic system of medicine), a *vaidya* (a physician practicing *Ayurveda*, the traditional Indian system of medicine), and a physician who follows the Western medical system. In addition, if satisfaction from the treatment is not forthcoming, the person and/or the family may decide to consult a *pir* (a Muslim wise man), a *pundit* (a Hindu wise man with the knowledge of scriptures, who is usually also well versed in astrological calculations), and a *bhopa* or a *sayana* (an oracle of smaller gods and deities who may also function as a shaman on occasion). In southern Indian villages, a survey identified a traditional healer for every 391 people (Carstairs & Kapur, 1976). Spirit possession, which refers to an external power taking control over the mind of a person for good or bad reasons, which is a sort of neurotic hysteria in Western psychiatric terminology, is one of the most common phenomena in almost all communities, including Muslims. Islam recognizes three classes of living beings higher than men—*farishta* (angels), *shaitan* (satanic beings), and *jinn* (demons or spirits). It is the latter two categories of disembodied beings who cause problems, physical as well as mental (Kakar, 1982, pp. 22–55). There is evidence that, to an extent, traditional healers are highly effective as long as the client seeking help has "problems of living."

The healers who have strong personality characteristics as therapeutic agents often share the same worldview of the client and are able to put a name on what is wrong, by rational-emotive techniques or mystical explanations and manipulation, allowing the client to gain a sense of mastery. If one healer fails to accomplish what the client wanted, there are others. The healer may advise the client to seek medical help. Intriguing though it may appear, the healers, relying primarily on the power of suggestion and hypnosis, are able to achieve the same results as Western therapists, sometimes even better (Torrey, 1986, pp. 184-194).

HOW SOCIOLOGISTS LOOK AT MENTAL DISORDERS

There is a significant difference between sociologists and other scientists in the way they view mental disorders. Within the field of sociology, there are several theoretical orientations or explanations that are commonly employed to gain insight into the causes of mental disorders. Often, causal relationships are difficult to ascertain due to the nature of human phenomena, yet it is possible to find associations between different factors that may be responsible for the onset of a mental disorder. In some cases, sociologists have viewed mental disorder as deviant behavior. In others, mental disorders are seen as products of social disorganization in society, such as high divorce or crime rates. The conflict school of thought espouses that mental disorders are nothing but the consequences of perpetual struggle between the classes, sexes, and majority and minority groups. Another school of thought theorizes that mental disorders are learned like any other behavior. All these approaches have their strengths and limitations, which we discuss in detail in Chapter 4.

The term *symbolic interaction* refers to the peculiar and distinctive behavior that takes place between human beings. Interaction conveys meanings, messages, values, or opinions. The fact that human beings interpret or "define" each other's actions instead of merely reacting to them determines the nature of the response. Responses are not made directly to the actions of one another, but instead are based on the meaning that each attaches to such actions. Thus, all our actions are mediated by the use of symbols, by interpretation, and by ascertaining the meaning of one another's actions. Such mediations become intrinsic to the interpretive process (Blumer, 1969, pp. 78-79). Many sociologists, such as Charles Horton Cooley, W. I. Thomas, Robert E. Park, E. W. Burgess, Florian Znaniecki, Ellsworth Faris, James Mickel Williams, and George Herbert Mead, have contributed to the development of symbolic interaction. Mead's analysis of human behavior suggested that human beings have a self and can be the object of their own actions. In other words, they can act toward themselves as they can act toward other people. For example, we can get angry with ourselves, argue, rebuff, or punish ourselves. By the same token, one can brag about, take pride in, or attempt to bolster one's self-image. As human beings, we sometimes act out in ways that may be extremely detrimental to our own interests, while most of the time we do things to enhance our self-image. In this way, individual actions are determined by two processes: (1) Human beings make indications to themselves of things that are part of their surroundings, of which they are conscious, like the presence of a friend or the ringing of a doorbell; and (2) their actions are based on a variety of alternatives available rather than a mere release or automated response. Such responses are beyond any conventional psychological explanations because self-indication is not a stimulus–response activity. It is a moving communicative process in which the individual consciously notes things, evaluates them, assigns them meaning, and finally decides to act on the basis of that meaning. As a result of this process, the person stands against the rest of the society or against "alters." All subsequent actions are subjected to the process of interpretation, not merely reactions.

The symbolic interaction model is based on interaction—physical or symbolic. Interaction occurs when two or more people take into account the possible actions and reactions of one another. Physical interaction involves co-presence. Symbolic interaction does not require co-presence, but mental anticipation, reflection, and rehearsal. Suppose, for example, that person A threatens person B. Person B says, "If you act in this fashion I will take action to stop you or punish you." Physical interaction has occurred. Now suppose that person A is contemplating acting rudely to person B but hasn't actually done so. Prior to physically interacting with B, A thinks about that interaction and interprets or rehearses in his mind possible responses of B. He then adjusts the planned behavior in terms of the anticipated consequences, not the actual consequences, and believes that B is "out to get him." In anticipating the reaction of B, A may come to fear that person or may become paranoid, even though no behavioral cause exists. Is the fear any less real? Is it organic? Or is it relational?

Most mental disorders are the products of interpersonal problems. They are rooted in poor self-concepts, alienation, frustration, and disenchantment. Some people believe that they deserve to suffer from such problems because there is something wrong with them or the way they feel. Others feel that it is a curse from the Almighty for their sins. Symbolic interaction theory explains that it is possible that people may "own" their mental disorders due to the personal interpretive processes involved in defining a situation. An individual's capacity to comprehend a situation may depend on one's own evaluation of oneself as an object. Initial transitory self-images derived from specific others in each interactive situation eventually become crystallized into a self-conception of oneself as a certain type of object. These self-conceptions gradually take a firmer shape, since they are mediated through a coherent and stable set of attitudes, dispositions, values, or meanings about oneself as a certain type of person. Because society is a *constructed* phenomena and not a rigid pattern of social organization, adaptive interactions are a constant phenomenon leading to high levels of unpredictability and indeterminacy of action.

Self-conceptions of individuals are reinforced by self-interpretation and reaction of others. For example, a person suffering from depression due to a high level of anxiety is not only experiencing depression as he or she sees it, but other people also impute meaning to his or her behavior and call it depression. It is possible that since the person's state of depression may evoke sufficiently strong societal reaction with mixed results of empathy, rejection, or hostility, the people may reinterpret his or her objective reality. Due to anticipatory fear of facing rejection, the individual may incorporate the elements of depressive personality, even though the factors leading to such feelings may have disappeared due to change in the social situation. When a person discovers that a new situation is acceptable to people and allows him or her to function better than before, the person accepts the new situation as a new role that is relatively less threatening to self as well as others. This view of oneself would seem to be one of the most pervasively threatening things that can happen, especially since it is likely to occur at a time when the person is sufficiently troubled to be unable to dissociate from symptoms of depression. Coupled with the person's disintegrative revaluation of self and the almost equally pervasive circumstance of attempting to interpret reactions of others, this may lead to the creation of a new self-system. Most people who are vulnerable to these kinds of situations not only suffer from their own creations of other people's perceptions, but also from the consequences of such perceptions. Often, these perceptions are culturally derived and socially ingrained and are utilized by even healthy individuals to avoid unpleasant situations. Let us look at the case of John Clark, a young man in his early twenties (author's case files).

John was born to a 16-year-old high school dropout from a lower-middle-class rural family. Her parents had strong sentiments against abortion, insisted that Debbie keep her child, and promised to help raise the child. Arguments about Debbie's irresponsible behavior caused her to believe that she was no longer wanted by the family. She ran away from home several times during pregnancy, but finally delivered John at her parents' home. John's arrival placed new demands on her as well as her parents, and often John became the center of their arguments. Her resentment of being a young mother and her parents' unhappiness about her unwed pregnancy were never resolved. She could not take care of John as an infant and cursed him for being a liability in her teen years. John grew up in an environment that was basically unhappy. Debbie, to avoid dependence on her parents, found a boyfriend and moved in with him when John was only 3 years old. John became a victim of neglect and a sort of unwanted guest in the new setting. In a few months Debbie was pregnant again, but her boyfriend told her that he could not marry her because he did not have a stable job. Unwed and pregnant, Debbie decided to seek an abortion, but her boyfriend insisted that he was opposed to abortion on religious grounds. In a few months, Debbie was a mother of two before she was even 20 years old. Money problems continued and the boyfriend moved out, leaving Debbie, John, and Eric behind. Taking care of two children with no help irritated Debbie, and whenever she lost her temper she punished John verbally and physically. She was often so exhausted and stressed that she would not care for the children for days. Abuse and neglect instilled a poor self-image and insecurity in John and caused high levels of anxiety, yet he could complain to no one. His classmates did not like him due to his timid and withdrawn personality and poor work habits. Now John is a college freshman. He rarely sees his mother but visits his grandparents and spends time with them during holidays. He complains of insomnia and mood swings and his inability to relate to people. He says he enjoys classes, but he has difficulty comprehending materials. Several times he has given serious thought to committing suicide (see Box 1–3).

Let us apply the symbolic interactionist model to John's situation. Basically, there are three elements involved here: (1) a person, (2) an audience, and (3) a situation. John, as a member of the family, interprets his mother's behavior as intolerable. He is seen by his mother, classmates, and grand-

---

BOX 1–3 • Suicide: Is It a Product of Interpersonal Crisis?

Attempts to analyze the causes of suicide can be frustrating partly because no one is able to discern what goes on in the mind of an individual who commits suicide. Durkheim (1897; 1951), in his classic study of suicide, explained this disturbing phenomena through the relationship between the individual and society. The increasing incidence of suicide among youth in the United States has become a matter of serious concern. Suicide has become the second leading cause of death among 15- to 24-year-olds. A recent study from metropolitan Pittsburgh provides some insights. The study compared cases of completed suicides to those of suicidal inpatients and found that generally, in both cases, the major factors contributing to suicide were interpersonal conflicts with parents, peers, and boy/girlfriends, compounded by external stressors such as school problems, financial problems, legal difficulties, interparental discord, abuse and neglect, and parental medical and psychiatric illness. Over 70% of those who completed suicide (parent report) and 87.5% of those who were suicidal inpatients reported interpersonal conflict. There were no significant differences between completers and suicidal inpatients by race, socioeconomic status, or living with two or nonbiological parents.

From Brent et al., 1988, pp. 581–588.

parents as unwanted, withdrawn, and socially incapable. His personal situation is that of a child who suffered the consequences of his mother's early unwed and unwanted pregnancy. John's self has been constantly hurt, causing him to believe that he is a problem for everyone. If John suffers from depression, it is a natural consequence of an unpleasant situation, audience definitions that are perceived to be unfavorable, and a resulting internalized self-concept that is basically negative. Even though his circumstances have improved, his self-concept has not. John's self-concept has been determined by his life experiences, but he is also partially responsible for that self-concept, which, we might argue, he can change if he simply has the will to do so. But is he totally free to make the necessary changes; is the remainder of his life determined totally by prior circumstances; or are both free will and determinism important factors in shaping his future?

Free Will and Determinism

The early attempts to explain various forms of deviant behavior, including mental disorders, were tested through the use of classical theory (often referred to as the *free will* approach), which emerged in Italy and England in the later half of the eighteenth century. The basic premise of the approach was that human beings exercise free will and that human behavior results from rationally calculating rewards and costs in terms of pleasure and pain. No human behavior is irrelevant. In other words, before an individual commits a specific act, he or she determines whether the consequences of the act will be pleasurable or painful. Presumably, acts that have painful consequences will be avoided (Cox & Conrad, 1987, pp. 51–53). Do people who have mental disorders calculate the costs and rewards the same way as others? Is it possible for them to calculate rationally the consequences of their behavior? Do they like to project a poor self-image of themselves? Finally, do they have control over their behavior? Many societies view people with mental disorders as deviants, demons, or spirit possessed, moonstruck, even unacceptable and unsightly. Depending on the severity of the disorder, most people with mental disorders would prefer not to act or behave like they are mentally disordered. Due to their personal situations, it is often not possible for them to make rational judgments, and they do not look at costs and rewards the same way as unimpaired people do.

Mental disorders can be caused by diseases or pathological conditions of the brain. In such cases, it is not always possible for a layperson to discern whether the problem is due to organic, physiological, or biochemical changes in the brain or is a problem of living. But each of these cases (e.g., organic brain syndromes such as syphilis of the central nervous system, intracranial infection, or dysfunctioning of the neurotransmitters in the brain) would call for medical attention. Some mental disorders may have a biological or genetic link, and some people may be vulnerable to some mental problems due to their genetic makeup. How much modern medicine or psychiatry can do to treat these problems depends on the nature and severity of these problems, and we have not yet found cures for all mental problems. Most mental disorders are not rooted in the genetic and biological makeup of people, but are basically interpersonal in nature and emanate from life situations rather than the brain. They may originate from sad or traumatic experiences, unmet expectations, loss of love and dignity, or frustrations in life and may simply be reactions to intolerable life conditions. To say that a mental disorder may be a product of a combination of factors in a given situation requires the attention of appropriate professionals. In most cases, we continue to believe that mental disorder is a disease, like any other disease of the human body, and look for treatment accordingly, without realizing that if the problem is not in the body it is unlikely to be treated successfully by a professional who is only equipped with the knowledge and training to treat the body.

Thomas Scheff (1984) observed that various afflictions labeled as mental illness have very little in common, but one common factor in all of them is the *violation* of expectations. Many such expectations may not be defined clearly, but if they are defined their transgression is readily identified and named. In addition, there are areas of *marginality* or vague and ambiguous expectations—a residue of rules of living, such as to show concern to an injured friend, to show deference to the elderly, to relate lovingly to one's spouse, or to raise children responsibly. Unfortunately, hazards to mental health are commonplace in a cultural system in which expectations are always high and unusual demands are placed on people to meet them on a regular basis.

Theoretical Orientation of This Book

Every text uses a theoretical orientation of some sort, whether explicit or implied. The sociological orientation of this text is *symbolic interactionist*, as discussed earlier in this chapter. A brief review of that orientation is in order here. Interactionists view humans as unique animals displaying enormous behavioral variations and as relying on learning rather than instincts when adjusting to the environment. The most significant difference between humans and other animals is that humans employ an open system of symbols—language—to communicate. The symbols consist of both sounds and gestures to which humans attach, by mutual agreement, meaning. In other words, we live in a world composed of symbolic rather than real objects. Symbols take on meanings of their own for each of us, and we tend to assume that these meanings are shared and understood by others.

When two or more people come together, they interact with one another. That is, they take into consideration the actions and reactions of one another in designing their own behavior. Certain actions and reactions are expected in certain situations as a result of interactional experiences over time. When others act or react as we expect them to, we regard their behavior as normal. When their actions or reactions are not those we expected, we view them as abnormal and we attach differing degrees of importance to violations of expectations depending on the nature of the audience and the importance of the behavior involved (see Chapter 4). In some cases, we view unexpected behavior as criminal (e.g., a battery on a stranger), in some cases as simply antisocial (e.g., pouting at a party), and in some cases as symptomatic of mental disorder (e.g., alternating hyperactivity and depression). Of course, sometimes we regard behavior as indicating a combination of all the aforementioned forms of abnormality.

The important point is that behavior is viewed as normal or abnormal, appropriate or inappropriate, only in terms of relationships with others. Thus, with mental disorders, as well as with other forms of behavior, the recognition and consequences of the disorders, whatever their causes (organic or nonorganic), occur in terms of relationships. Thus, mental disorders are the result of problems, both real and perceived, in interaction with others. Although various approaches to understanding mental disorders are presented and discussed in this book, our underlying assumption is that mental disorders can best be understood and treated in terms of the social context (interactional relationships) within which they occur.

Chapter 2 focuses on the history and treatment of mental disorders. It examines how people with mental disorders were treated throughout history and discusses efforts to understand and treat mental disorders along with the ongoing changes in the structure of society. It addresses the social origins of mental problems and how social processes affected the conceptualization of mental disorders, as well as what is currently being done about mental disorders and why so many social policies fail and more people now suffer from mental disorders than ever before.

CHAPTER REVIEW

1. The concepts of mental illness and mental disorder have two distinct meanings. Do you agree? Explain.

2. What is the brain–mind controversy in mental health? How does it influence the treatment of mental disorders in the United States?

3. No one knows the exact extent of mental disorders in the United States, because the figures reported are incomplete and unreliable. Why is this so?

4. Mental health and mental disorder are relative concepts determined by an audience, a situation, and variables associated with a person such as class, age, sex, ethnicity, and so on. Explain.
5. Mental health is an enterprise involving a variety of professionals, services, and agencies. Many of these are powerful groups who influence changes in public opinion, professional fads, and treatment modalities. Explain.
6. Social reaction to mental disorder is influenced by a variety of variables leading to stigma. What are the variables that play a significant role in the creation of stigma?
7. Social reaction to people with mental disorders is usually negative, surrounded by some common myths. What are the common myths leading to this negative stereotype?
8. Mental disorders are conceptualized in a cultural setting. How do people in various cultures conceptualize mental disorders and seek treatment? If these concepts differ, how?
9. Mental problems can be viewed as "problems of living" and reactions to social situations and social arrangements. How does the symbolic interactionist approach address these problems as they originate from society and influence the person in adverse ways?
10. What are the theories of free will and determinism? What consequences do they have for the mentally impaired?

FOR FURTHER STUDY

Cockerham, W. C. (1989). *Sociology of mental disorder.* Englewood Cliffs, NJ: Prentice Hall.
Foucault, M. (1973). *Madness and civilization: A history of insanity in the age of reason.* New York: Random House.
Goffman, E. (1963). *Stigma.* Englewood Cliffs, NJ: Prentice Hall.
Lehmann, A. C., & Myers, J. E. (1989). *Magic, witchcraft, and religion* (2nd ed.). Mountain View, CA: Mayfield Publishing Co.
Szasz, T. S. (1970). *The manufacture of madness.* New York: Delta Books.
Szasz, T. S. (1974). *The myth of mental illness* (rev. ed.). New York: Harper & Row.
Szasz, T. S. (1987). *Insanity: The idea and its consequences.* New York: John Wiley & Sons.
Torrey, E. F. (1986). *Witchdoctors and psychiatrists.* New York: Harper & Row.

▶ 2

Mental Disorders: A Historical Overview

Behavior that is identified as mental illness or mental disorder has been known throughout human history. People in ancient times were not sure how to react to individuals suffering from mental disorders (just as we are not sure today). Often, such people were viewed with a mixture of ignorance, fear, and revulsion. They were neglected, rejected, ill treated and persecuted, and, at times, protected. In both historical and contemporary societies, people have tried to find causes of, and treatments for, behavior that is seemingly irrational, unintelligible, and purposeless. While scientific research has challenged many historical beliefs about mental disorders, many of our current treatment approaches originate in these beliefs. In this chapter, we trace beliefs concerning mental disorders and their treatments from ancient times to the present. Progress in understanding and treating mental disorders has not been consistent, as we shall see.

EARLY PERCEPTIONS OF MENTAL DISORDERS

In ancient times, distinctions between physical and mental disorder were almost nonexistent and at best subjective and unclear, but causation and prognosis were thought to be related to the environment. Treatment of mental disorders can be traced to Stone Age cave dwellers over half a million years ago. The medicine man or shaman treated mental disorders, with ritual incantations, flogging, starvation, immersion in ice-cold water, or trephining (chipping away or drilling a hole in the skull to allow evil spirits to escape and, unintentionally, relieving pressure on the brain). It was believed that mental disorders resulted from curses by evil spirits or possession by such spirits. Durkheim suggested that societies classify such spirits in categories of good and evil, pure and impure, sacred and profane in a particular cultural context (Durkheim, 1947, pp. 16–20). In most of Africa and Asia, for example, possession was considered "good" unless the individual's symptoms indicated possession involving ghosts, witches, or evil or dissatisfied spirits. Evil possession was indicated when signs, dictums, behavior, or ideas contrary to prevalent religious beliefs were expressed and the spirit avowed to hurt the possessed person. Possession by an evil spirit indicated the withdrawal of God's protection or abandonment. The primary mode of treatment was exorcism. It was an unpleasant experience, to say the least, involving practices such as whipping, beating and torture, starving, use of purgatives, and concoctions made from feces, urine, and other defiling materials. The objective was to make the body such an unpleasant place to reside that the evil spirit would leave.

Kiev (1972) argued that etiological explanations of mental disorders are based on linking certain kinds of symptoms to certain kinds of beliefs grounded in particular cultural patterns in specific societies. Generally, curses, violations of widely shared taboos, and profaning the gods were indications to the primitive mind of harmful spirit possession.

Early Chinese, Egyptian, Hebrew, Greek, and Persian historical writings included references to mental disorders. Saul, King of Israel in the 11th century B.C., is said to have suffered from manic-depressive episodes and to have stripped off all his clothes in public during one of these episodes. Cambyses, King of Persia in the 6th century B.C., is portrayed as an incurable alcoholic who forced one sister to marry him and killed another sister who was pregnant. Hercules, a hero of Greek mythology, is described as being subject to convulsive seizures and homicidal tendencies that led him to kill two of his own children and two of his brother's children. Socrates, Alexander the Great, and Julius Caesar are also described as suffering from mental disorders. George the Third (1760–1820), King of England, was known as the "mad monarch" and suffered from periods of intense excitement and hyperactivity. The phenomenon of mental disorder is not new, and humankind has always attempted to determine its causes and to find treatments.

Mesopotamia and Egypt

Babylonia, a southwestern Asian civilization contemporaneous with predynastic Egypt in about the fourth millennium before the great pyramids were built, probably recognized mental disorders. Indications are that priest-doctors treated mental disorders, which were thought to be caused by demonic possession. Magical, astrological, and oracular practices were employed along with incantations in which water played an important role. Stars were believed to be divine, and celestial bodies were thought to exacerbate or mitigate certain diseases. Although drugs were employed as one form of treatment, the most effective treatment was thought to be incantations dominated by magic and religion. An early form of psychotherapy required the patient who had allegedly sinned to search his or her soul for causes and was believed to have a liberating effect. Sigerist, a noted medical historian, stated that "Mesopotamian medicine was psychosomatic in all its aspects" (Peterson, 1946, pp. 44–45).

Egyptian healing practices date back to about 3000 B.C. and treated the human body as a microcosm of the cosmos, governed by specific spirits and composed of four elements. The flesh and bones corresponded to earth, bodily fluids to water, the heart to sun and fire, and the breath to wind. Egyptians probably were the first to identify a disorder, later to be called *hysteria* (hysteron = uterus) by the Greeks. Its symptoms were said to be caused by a misplaced uterus, and fumigation of the vagina was employed to return the uterus to its normal position. This practice was later recommended by Hippocrates, Plato, and Galen.

The Hebrews

Early Hebrew texts and inscriptions refer to the practice of blaming others for one's own faults or sins, a practice later referred to as *projection* or *scapegoating*. During the early Christian era, Rabbi Ami recommended diversion (distracting the person from anxieties) as a treatment for mental disorders, and Rabbi Asi advocated encouraging the patient to talk freely about his or her troubles (Gold, 1957, p. 11). The heart, not the brain, was considered to be the seat of emotion and intellect. Demons were thought to be the precipitating agents. Biblical descriptions illustrate stories of famous individuals who suffered from catatonic excitement, epileptic seizures, and lycanthropy (the delusion that one is a wolf). Humanitarian concern for the mentally impaired is indicated by the fact that there was a mental hospital in Jerusalem as early as 490 A.D. (Whitwell, 1936, p. 28).

The Persians

Around the middle of the first millennium B.C., Persian influence was widespread in the Middle East. An ancient Persian work, *Venidad*, states that there are 99,999 diseases that afflict humankind, all of which are caused by demons. It refers to three types of physicians—the knife doctor, the herb doctor, and the word doctor (equivalent to the modern surgeon, internist, and psychiatrist) and emphasizes healing through the holy word.

Eastern and Far Eastern Countries

Ancient Hindu explanations of mental disorders, which originated about 25 centuries B.C., dealt with the struggle between the forces of good and evil, as described in the holy books of *Vedas* (second century A.D.) and *Susrata* (fifth century A.D.), and suggested that powerful emotions may be related to peculiar behavior (Zilboorg, 1941, p. 32). Certain personality characteristics were believed to be located in certain parts of the body—goodness in the brain, passion in the chest, ignorance in the abdomen. Brahman successors to the Vedic priests considered air, bile, and phlegm to be vital to all life processes, and a proper balance among these elements ensured good health. This "balance theory" is akin to the humor theory of Hippocrates, though it is not known how much, if any, communication existed between the Greeks and the Hindus.

The Hindu medical science, *Ayurveda*, led to perfecting of many herbal treatments designed to balance the substances in the body. *Sandhya*, a form of devotional meditation for spiritual bliss based on interpolating the external world and concentrating on the inner self also developed at this time. *Yoga*, a school of Hindu philosophy that embraces betterment of all aspects of individual life, later gained popularity in the West for its practical aspects of better mental health and relaxing effects (see Chapter 13).

Gautam Buddha, the *Enlightened One* and the founder of Buddhism, was a Hindu prince who developed a psychological technique of meditation for the purpose of arriving at the ultimate stage of *nirvana*—an acme of tranquil state devoid of all striving and passion. He advocated this psychological technique not only for those suffering from mental disorders but for all those who prefer to lead lives in a peaceful and rewarding way. Absorption within one's self—*nirvana*—remains an enigma to most Westerners today even though Buddhist precepts, and some associated superficial healing practices, have attracted occasional attention in the Western world.

Early in history, the Chinese also believed in a sort of a balance theory of five elements corresponding with joy, anger, worry, sorrow, and fear. Harmony in these elements was considered essential for a healthy life (Tseng, 1973, pp. 569–572).

The Greeks

Hippocrates (460–377 B.C.), the famous Greek physician, was the first to test the humor theory (four-element theory) developed by Empedocles (490–430

B.C.). This theory relates to four humors—blood, phlegm, yellow bile, and black bile—found in the heart, brain, liver, and spleen, respectively (see Table 2–1). Disease was thought to be caused by an imbalance in these humors and was to be treated with drugs that possessed the qualities of heat, dryness, moisture, and cold. Hippocrates, known as the father of allopathic medicine, used bloodletting and purgatives to treat patients suffering from insanity, but, like some of his Hindu predecessors, he also believed that the patient's environment was critical to his or her health. Modern psychiatry owes him a debt of gratitude for being the first to assert that the brain is the interpreter of consciousness (Peterson, 1946, pp. 45–46).

Perhaps the most significant contribution of the Greeks was the development of a more rational approach toward understanding the world. Supernatural traditions were replaced by secular beliefs. Plato (427–347

TABLE 2–1 • Explanations of Mental Disorders in Ancient Times

Civilization	Major Contributor	Explanations
Chinese	Huant Ti (about 2674 B.C., later findings place him about 700 B.C.)	Ying/Yang (a variety of balance theory) and theory of five elements: fire, earth, metal, wood, and water associated with joy, anger, worry, sorrow, and fear (Tseng, 1973). Harmony in these elements was believed to be essential for vitality and a healthy life.
Greek	Hippocrates (460–370 B.C.)	Four-humor theory: Centers on four body fluids: blood, black bile, yellow bile, and phlegm, corresponding to heat, cold, moisture, and dryness, which determine a person's emotional orientation.
Indian	Holy Books of the Vedas (3000–1500 B.C.), later systematized by Charak (second century A.D.) and Susruta (fifth century A.D.) (Basham, 1959, pp. 14–25; Kakar, 1982, p. 231)	*Tridosha* (three-disorder) theory in *Ayurveda*, the Hindu system of medicine which recognizes three proximate substances: *avta* (wind, flatulence), *pitta* (bile or gall), and *Kapha* (phlegm, mucus). When the three *doshas* are out of harmony, the person suffers from physical or mental disorders.

B.C.) was influenced by Egyptian metempsychosis (transmigration of the soul) and Indian mysticism. He also believed in a body–soul dichotomy in which the soul was the vital force, the seat of reason, and divine in origin.

The famous Greek philosopher Aristotle (384–322 B.C.), a student of Plato, continued the tradition of investigating the organic aspects of behavior. His lucid description of the five senses (touch, taste, smell, sight, and hearing) helped pave the way toward an understanding of the mind and consciousness. He categorized sensations as pleasurable or painful and speculated that humans strive to eliminate pain and attain pleasure. These assumptions are the basis of hedonistic psychology, much of Freudian psychology, and a great deal of behavioral psychology. Aristotle considered reasoning to be a divine gift, yet he proceeded to describe affective states so accurately that the descriptions can still be used by modern psychologists.

The Romans

Cicero (106–43 B.C.), a philosopher, and Soranus, a physician, demonstrated exceptional clarity of thought with respect to the mind–body relationship. Cicero stated that bodily elements could be a result of emotional factors and was probably the first psychosomatist. He rejected the black bile explanation of Hippocrates and believed that melancholia was a purely psychological condition. He recognized fundamental differences between diseases of the mind and body, stating, "though the mind in perfect health may be visited by sickness, as the body may, yet the body may be disordered without our fault, the mind cannot." (Alexander & Selesnick, 1966, pp. 46–47). This thought eventually became the foundation of modern psychotherapy, for when a person accepts and understands the psychological sources of mental disturbances, he or she may be capable of changing the conditions that led to the problem.

The concept of humane treatment of the mentally ill is identified with Soranus, an enlightened physician who wrote extensively about diseases of the mind. Although Soranus described mental disorder in terms of organic disturbances, he treated the mentally impaired through psychological means. By talking to them, he allowed them to vent their feelings of discomfort and tried to interest them in subjects of their liking, thus laying another piece of the foundation for modern psychology and psychiatry.

Galen (130–200 A.D.) was a Greek physician who lived in Rome and the greatest of the Hellenistic physicians. He made significant contributions regarding the anatomy of the nervous system and was a strong proponent of the scientific method. He classified mental disorders into mental and physical and elaborated a number of possible causes for such disorders, including head injury, menstrual changes, economic reverses, excessive use of alcohol, shock, fear, and disappointment in love.

THE MIDDLE AGES: A PERIOD OF STAGNATION AND REGRESSION

During the middle ages (roughly from 500–1500 A.D.), the theocratic wave (reawakening of the belief in a supreme being) influenced understanding of the causes and treatment of mental disorders. Care of the mentally disordered became the responsibility of monks, priests, and exorcists instead of physicians. The scientific conclusions of the Greeks and Romans lost credence, and evil spirits, demons, and devils seeking to possess unsuspecting souls were regarded again as the primary causative agents in mental disorders.

Throughout the Middle Ages, the doctrine of temperaments (the belief that four mind–body states control behavior) prevailed. *Melancholia* was the term most frequently employed to describe mental disorders, including schizophrenia. For example, Alexander of Tralles (525–605), a Byzantine physician, described a condition different from simple melancholia as a cyclical mania (now known as circular insanity, a variety of the manic-depressive disorder). Epilepsy was also frequently mentioned, perhaps because of its rather dramatic manifestations.

Avicenna (980–1037) thought that sexual disorders result from a degraded mind, a vicious nature, and bad habits. Incubus, from the Latin *in cubitum* (literally translated as "on the couch" and corresponding to the concept of "nightmare") was attributed to, among other things, a male demon attacking chaste girls, as opposed to the *succubus,* or a female spirit who molested men.

Constantitus Africanus (1020–1087), founder of a medical school near Naples, enjoyed great fame and is acknowledged for ascertaining the characteristics of melancholia—sadness (due to loss of a loved one), fear (of the unknown), withdrawal (staring into space), delusions, and intense fear and guilt in religious persons (Kaplan & Sadock, 1988, pp. 2–5). Albert the Great (1193–1280) and Thomas Aquinas (1225–1274) described psychotic symptoms, organic psychosis, mania, and epilepsy. Yet beliefs that mental disorders are caused by demons and evil spirits were again gaining popularity.

Witchcraft

Witches were those who deviated from the Christian faith and supposedly represented Satan, who gave them supernatural powers. These witches were accused of causing floods, earthquakes, epidemics, pestilence, death, destruction of crops, and numerous other disasters. In most societies at this time, those who were deviant in any way were suspected of being antireligious. The label of *witch* was attached to many such individuals. Theologians alone were seen as qualified to treat disturbances caused by the devil.

> **BOX 2–1 • Women in Asylum**
>
> The 19th and 20th centuries, although reforms were taking place, can best be called a period of transition. In some cases, whenever a man could not tolerate his wife's outspoken ways and unusual ideas, he believed and declared that she was bedeviled or had mental problems. Of course, there was also an element of challenge to his authority.
>
> Some of these women became socially withdrawn, did not care how they looked, refused to eat, and became sexually withdrawn. In many ways, their lives were filled with agony and beset with loss of interest. But at the same time they were talented, aggressive, and uncommonly stubborn. One such woman was Elizabeth Packard.
>
> In 1896, Elizabeth Packard's husband psychiatrically imprisoned her because she dared to engage in "free religious inquiry." She insisted on teaching her Bible class that human beings are born good and not evil. Her husband, a clergyman, kidnapped her against her will (although he was within his legal rights, considering the prevailing law of the land) and removed her to an asylum at Jacksonville, Illinois. He forbade her children (whose ages ranged from 18 months to 18 years) to communicate with or talk about her. He kept her own (inherited) income from her. He deprived her of clothes, books, and personal papers and misrepresented her situation to her parents. Dr. MacFarland, the psychiatrist-director of the asylum, intercepted her outgoing mail and seized her few books and smuggled in writing paper. Despite these events, Mrs. Packard never lost her "wits." She always referred to the asylum as a "prison"—and not as a "hospital." She began a secret diary of asylum events and ministered to the other inmates, most of whom she regarded as sister victims of the patriarchy. However, she still believed in marriage and in male chivalry; she never wanted a divorce and was thoroughly devoted to her children.
>
> Her account of asylum abuses is lucid and at times brilliant. She describes many female asylum suicides due to constant harassment, loneliness, and despair. It is Elizabeth Packard who first made the analogy between institutional psychiatry and the Inquisition.

From Chesler, 1973, pp. 9–11.

Witch hunts were common in the European and Anglo-Saxon world during the 15th and 16th centuries. After being labeled as witches, many individuals were tortured and killed. Witches were invariably women, perceived as the stimuli of men's licentiousness and unsavory impulses. During this period, the authority of institutions such as the church and feudalism was crumbling, and scapegoats were sought. Persecution of Jews proved insufficient, so women too became targets. "Women stirred man's passions, therefore they must be the carriers of the devil. Psychotic women, with little control over voicing their sexual fantasies and sacrilegious feelings, were the clearest example of demon possession; and in turning against them the Church increased an already mounting fear of the mentally deranged" (Alexander & Selesnick, 1966, p. 67) (see Box 2–1).

Witch sorcerers, exorcists, and witch pickers and witch finders came to be regarded as professionals. Visible witch marks, such as moles, scars, and skin blemishes, were identified as the devil's privy marks.

It appears that most witch hunts had their origins in local politics, conflicts of interests, and domination and oppression of invalids, the unemployed, women, and ethnic minorities. Slowly, as evidence of the excesses of the clergy and witch hunters became apparent, witch hunting lost most of its credibility.

Collective Madness

Mass madness or mass hysteria (irrational behavior occurring in a group of people in reaction to a real or imagined threat) has been reported periodically throughout history but appears to have been widespread in 14th- and 15th-century Europe. Screaming, raving, dancing, convulsing crowds in which people sometimes tore each others' clothes and beat each other were reported during this era. Such behavior, when it involved dancing, became known as "tarantism" in Italy and as St. Vitus's dance generally. It is probable that Black Fever (which ravished Europe during this period, killing almost half the population) was responsible for much of the hysterical behavior observed.

THE AGE OF HUMANITARIAN REFORM

Until the middle of the 16th century, treating the mentally impaired involved returning them to "sanity." Treatment techniques were crude, aggressive, and sometimes torturous and were aimed at restoring the balance between body and mind. Bleeding, powerful drugs, harsh purgatives, water treatments, and use of restraints were intended to control mental patients. As late as the 1850s, new patients were placed in straight jackets, their heads shaved, placed on special diets, and were forced to stay in dark cells. When these measures did not quiet violent, unruly, or excited patients, torture, starvation, and prolonged solitary confinement were employed.

The 17th century marked the beginning of humanitarian treatment and is sometimes referred to as the "period of confinement" because the mentally disordered were housed in institutions or hospitals. As early as 1547, the monastery of St. Mary at Bethlehem (London) had been turned into a mental hospital by Henry VIII. In 1656, Hospital General in Paris was founded, and by the middle of the 18th century similar institutions existed throughout most of Europe. Social and economic conditions in Europe certainly contributed to this new way of caring for the mentally impaired. As Cockerham (1989, pp. 17–18) stated, several factors were responsible for reform in Europe:

1. Economic recession, unemployment, and higher prices led to thousands of vagrants, whose presence on the streets caused public nuisance
2. A new concept of social welfare allowed municipal and state authorities to take care of the food and shelter of the mentally ill, which had, in the past, been primarily the responsibility of the church
3. The new notion of enlightened absolutism allowed European monarchs to assume responsibility for the safety and well-being of their subjects in return for absolute authority.

As is true of all historical developments, it is impossible to ascribe the changes in philosophy concerning the mentally disordered to any one particular cause, and the changes had both positive and negative consequences.

Confinement during this period was not limited to the mentally impaired but was also used for the homeless, poor, aged, orphans, invalids, addicts, and all those who reminded the public of neglect or abuse, thus touching their conscience. Though confinement appeared as a humane gesture, it also removed the mentally impaired from the mainstream of social life, isolating them in an environment that was often neither hospitable nor helpful to their recovery. Those who could afford private psychiatrists were not often labeled, and their prognosis was generally more favorable than those who were institutionalized. Thus, treatment on the basis of class became a reality. Those who were poor became wards of the state in municipal or state hospitals with little or no contact with the outside world. Additionally, commitment to a mental hospital was not primarily intended to provide for psychiatric care but to protect society from the unwanted and to prevent the threat of disintegration of societal institutions (Rosen, 1963, p. 233). Foucault (1967, pp. 35–40) reported that the Hospital General, a few years after its founding, housed about 6,000 people or about 1% of the population of Paris. Szasz (1970a) argued that confinement policies, although believed to result from humanitarianism, were in fact designed to assure the interests of the rich and powerful.

TABLE 2–2 • Major Early Contributors to the Explanations of Mental Disorders

Contributor	Explanation	Contribution to Modern Diagnosis and Treatments
Hippocrates (460–377 B.C.)	Stated that the brain is the central organ of intellectual activity and that mental disorders were due to brain pathology caused by disbalance in body humors.	Biochemical
Cicero (106–43 B.C.)	Stated that body aliments could be the result of emotional factors.	Psychosomatic
Constantino Africanus (1020–1087 A.D.)	Recognized symptoms that characterized melancholia due to sadness, fear, withdrawal, delusions, and intense fear and guilt.	Social/environmental
Johann Weyer (1515–1588)	Described a wide range of diagnostic entities and associated symptoms of toxic psychosis, epilepsy, senile psychoses, nightmares, hysteria, delusions, paranoia, and depression.	Physical, biochemical; social/environmental
Paracelsus (1493–1541)	Presented a dynamic view of personality and its total involvement in each mental illness, such as projection, ambivalence, unconscious self-destructive trends, and economy of the libido.	Psychotherapy
Robert Burton (1577–1640)	Elucidated the psychological and social causes of insanity—for example, jealousy, solitude, fear, poverty, unrequited love, excessive religiosity.	Sociopsychological

THE RENAISSANCE: A RESURGENCE OF SCIENTIFIC THINKING

Paracelsus, a Swiss physician/astrologist (1490–1541), did not think mental disorders were caused by demons (see Table 2–2). Rather, he felt that they were the result of disturbances within the internal substances of the body, not the result of external causes. Still, he postulated that astral influences, particularly movements of the moon, influenced the brain. The term *lunatic* is derived from the Latin word for moon, *luna*, and *moonstruck* was the term commonly employed for the mentally disordered in most of Europe during the 15th century. The belief that the moon exercises considerable influence on the brain persists in many cultures, including major religious systems such as Islam and Hinduism.

The progressive ideas of the Greeks and Romans influenced the work of Johann Weyer (1515–1588), a German physician/author. He was extremely distressed by accounts of torture, confinement, maltreatment, and the burning of people accused of demon possession and witchcraft, and he published a treatise titled *The Deception of Demons* to refute the *Malleus Maleficarum* (Hammer of Witches) and to enlighten the public. Weyer was convinced that mental disorders were neither supernatural nor sacred and attributed them to natural causes (Ehrenwald, 1956, p. 240).

Though the Renaissance marked the beginning of the period of European enlightenment, a good deal of resistance to the new ideas existed. Weyer was scorned by his peers, his works were banned by the Church, and the orthodox found his beliefs unacceptable. The tacit alliance between the Church and medical science did not encourage exploration of the human mind as opposed to the human body. Slowly, as advocates of science persisted, demonology and superstition gave ground to reason and scientific investigation. Progress in these areas is perhaps the greatest legacy of the Renaissance, and Weyer, a leader in the quest for truth and reason, is regarded by many as the founding father of psychotherapy.

Asylums, Madhouses, and Shrines

In his book, *Discovery of Witchcraft* (1584), Regiland Scot convincingly argued against the existence of the devil and other demonic spirits. Persistent advocates of science argued for humane treatment of those for whom medicine had no clear remedy. As a result, special institutions, called "madhouses," were created in the late 15th and 16th centuries. Living conditions and treatment of residents in these establishments were so deplorable that many died and others lived as if they were in concentration camps. In fact, the monastery of St. Mary of Bethlehem (1547) in London, which had been officially recognized as a mental institution by Henry VIII, was known as "bedlam" due to its inhuman conditions and practices. Public exhibition of mental patients and forcing them into the streets to beg were common practices. Nonetheless, other institutions or "asylums" began to appear around the world. Bernardino Alvares, a Mexican philanthropist, established such an institution in Mexico in 1566, probably the first in the Americas. Gradually, others emerged in Paris (1641), Moscow (1764), Williamsburg, Virginia (1773), and Vienna (1784).

In the 17th century, scientists working in different disciplines agreed that it was time to define concepts, develop nomenclatures, and classify behaviors and objects into categories to systematize advancements, and the scientific study of mental disorders was caught up in this process. During this period, Robert Burton (1577–1640) attempted to clarify the psychological and social causes of mental disorders. Among those he focused on were jealousy, solitude, fear, poverty, unrequited love, and excessive religiosity. He rejected supernatural causes of mental disorders in favor of emotional factors (Kaplan & Sadock, 1988, p. 4).

In the early 18th century, mental disorders were classified as "nosologies." This was an early forerunner of the classification scheme now found in the *Diagnostic and Statistical Manual of Mental Disorders*, published and revised periodically by the American Psychiatric Association since 1952. Phrenology, founded by Franz Josef Gall (1758–1828), postulated that mental facilities were innate and that mental disorders could be diagnosed and classified through examination of the shape of the skull, which was thought to correspond with the structure of the brain. The underlying assumptions were that mental disorders are a condition of the mind and that, since the brain is the organ of the mind, these disorders might be located in different parts of the brain. Though the explanations derived from studying cranial protuberances added little to our knowledge of mental disorders, the concept was an important forerunner to the use of brain scanning as a means of searching for abnormalities.

Mesmerism and Hypnosis: Science or Quackery?

In the late 18th century, shortly after the American revolution, Franz Anton Mesmer (1734–1815), an Austrian physician living in Paris, subscribed to the concept that the movement of the planets influenced physiological and psychological phenomena. He hypothesized that humans possess magnetic forces that can be applied to influence the distribution of magnetic fluids in others, thus producing amazing healing effects. Mesmer's therapeutic episodes were public spectacles due to his assertive, exaggerated, electrifying style of bringing mentally disordered people to hypnotically induced crises characterized by sudden fits of crying, hysterical states, and crystal vision. Treatment centered on a *baquet,* or tub, containing chemicals and "magnetized water," from which protruded magnetic rods or wands that were applied to the patient's body. The setting of a darkened room, appropriate music, Mesmer's bewitching style, and the paraphernalia he used made his therapy sessions appear to be spectacular magic shows and smacked of quackery. Mesmer, of course, claimed many successes, and his followers continued to focus on treating certain kinds of mental disorders, especially hysteria, through hypnosis.

James Braid (1795–1860) felt that Mesmer's contributions were relevant, and his studies showed that hypnotic suggestion could produce a trance-like or sleeplike state that resulted from prolonged concentration. He referred to mesmerism as *hypnosis* based on the Greek term (*hypnos*) for sleep.

Mesmer has been called the father of hypnotherapy, which recognizes psychologically caused mental disorders such as anxiety, phobias, and multiple personalities, although the scientific objectivity of hypnosis remains questionable.

THE REFORMISTS

The growth of humanitarian reform coincided with the age of enlightenment in science. Of special interest to us are several reformers in the field of mental health.

Vincent Chiarugi: Respect for the Mentally Ill

Vincent Chiarugi (1759–1820), a physician in Florence, was probably the pioneer in rejecting physical force and cruel methods of restraint in treating the mentally ill. He stated, "It is a supreme moral duty and medical obligation to respect the insane individual as a person" (Kaplan & Sadock, 1988, p. 4). He also discussed extensively both congenital and environmental causes of mental disorders.

Philippe Pinel: The Moral Treatment

French physician Philippe Pinel (1745–1826) became the superintendent of La Bicetre (a hospital for male patients) in 1792 and later of Salpetriere (for female patients). Gradually, he experimented with the idea of removing the chains from mental patients and found remarkable changes in their attitudes and functioning. He is remembered for his attempts to understand, analyze, and categorize symptoms of mental disorder and his support of moral treatment. His efforts put France in the forefront of humane treatment of the mentally impaired.

William Tuke: The Humanitarian Spirit

News of Pinel's successes in France reached an English Quaker by the name of William Tuke (1732–1822). Tuke opened a retreat facility for the mentally disordered near York. The country house provided a pleasant environment and sense of freedom to mental patients, who had previously been treated with cruelty, brutality, neglect, and ignorance. Opposition to Tuke's ideas was strong as a result of persistent beliefs in witchcraft and demonology, which were thought to be biblical. Nonetheless, the country environment, cheerful accommodations without bars, and recreational opportunities afforded the mentally disordered opportunities that were amazing for the times, and they responded well.

Benjamin Rush: Moral Management in the United States

News of the surprising successes of Pinel and Tuke in Europe gradually spread to America. Benjamin Rush (1745–1813), who is considered the founding father of American psychiatry, was working in a Pennsylvania hospital (1783) and encouraging the humane treatment of the mentally disordered. He was the first American to author a treatise on psychiatry—*Medical Inquiries and Observations Upon the Diseases of the Mind* (1812). Rush became a crusader against the inhumane treatment of the mentally disordered, slavery, alcoholism, and the death penalty. He advocated free dispensaries for the indigent, hospitals for alcoholics, and higher educational facilities for women. Though Rush was a pragmatist, he could not completely free himself from many of the beliefs and practices of his time. His lectures on mental disorders were reminiscent of ancient Arabian approaches, which required that patients change their thoughts and actions. He employed bloodletting, purgatives, and astrology as treatment strategies, thus tainting his reputation as a reformer. He invented a device called a "tranquilizer" and a circulating swing (intended to stabilize the individual) that proved less than successful. Nonetheless, his explanations of derangement of passions (fear, anger, joy, envy, love, grief, malice, and sexual appetites) were remarkably insightful. Though he could not dissociate himself from his convictions concerning the organic origin of insanity, in practice he explored psychogenic origins for many mental problems. His greatest contribution was persistence in the belief that most mentally disordered were normal people who had lost the power to reason due to excessive psychological strain and severe social stress. The impact of such stresses and strains he called "moral causes of insanity." The basic goal of moral treatment was to identify the stressors, conflicts, and frustrations underlying mental disorders and to direct the individual toward positive and purposeful activities. Moral management thus became a basis for individual and group therapy and proved to be a successful approach. Eventually, the mental hygiene movement replaced moral management as advances in biomedical science fostered the notion that mental disorders required biologically based treatment. Consequently, social and psychological explanations were later rendered largely irrelevant in the treatment of mental disorders during Rush's time.

Dorothea Dix: The Mental Hygiene Movement

A Massachusetts school teacher, Dorothea Dix (1802–1887), who was forced into early retirement due to ill health, became a crusader against the antiquated, inhuman, and pathetic conditions prevalent in mental hospitals, alms houses, and jails. She carried on a zealous campaign between 1841 and 1881, arousing awareness among the public and legislators concerning the deplorable conditions in such institutions. Her appeals resulted in millions of dollars in contributions to improve these conditions in America, the British Isles, and Canada. On October 16, 1884, in Philadelphia, at her insistence, 13 superintendents of American institutions for the insane met and founded what was to become the American Psychiatric Association.

EMERGENCE OF COMPETING MODELS OF MENTAL DISORDERS

Explanations of mental disorders are related to the religious, moral, and cultural climate of the times. More often than not, mental disorders have been defined, diagnosed, and treated by physicians believing in organic causes or clergymen believing in spiritual causes. Only since Victorian times have factors such as sex, alcohol, marital discord, industrialization, and social reform been viewed as possible causes of mental disorders.

Recently, researchers have questioned the objectivity in the psychiatric assessment of women. Newmann (1984) showed that higher rates of depression among women are due to relatively mild, if not clinically trivial, symptoms of depression (see Chapter 10).

The moral treatment model, developed by Rush, prevailed in American private hospitals and some state hospitals for some time, but most of the latter rapidly became overcrowded with criminals, alcoholics, paupers, vagrants, and the homeless. These individuals are often viewed as social failures, unable to deal with life's stresses and strains. The public (and taxpayers in particular) were somewhat sympathetic to such people, who were regarded as unfortunates as a result of misfortune, calamity, accident, or incurable disease. However, over time, these unfortunates, who pay no taxes and little or none of the cost of institutionalization, have been looked on less favorably as the burden on taxpayers has increased and has, to some extent, led to negative reaction to the moral treatment concept.

At the same time, Sigmund Freud (1856–1939), regarded by many as the most influential person in the history of Western psychology, was revolutionizing ideas about mental disorders. Beginning with his exploration of neurosis in 1886 and his studies of hysteria in 1895, Freud moved to develop the first psychoanalytic system of psychology (1900–1905). The model Freud presented became popular in the Western world, and the terms *id* (the seat of all instincts), *ego* (the rational component of mind), and *superego* (the subsystem of conscience that determines judgments about right and wrong) have become household terms. Freud's use of psychoanalytic therapy has influenced generations of therapists in their attempts to treat mental disorders. Interestingly enough, Freud's model represents the conflict over the mind–brain dilemma, since many of Freud's followers have proceeded as if the id, ego, and superego could be located if the brain were explored. However, Freud believed that this was not the case—the id, ego, and superego were part of the same mind set.

A contemporary of Freud, Emil Kraeplin (1855–1926) also attempted to identify varieties of mental disorders. He viewed mental disorders as physical diseases and hypothesized that each mental disorder is a separate disease and that the rules applying to treatment of physical illnesses should also apply to mental disorders. He referred to the process of identifying diseases by their symptoms, etiology, and outcome as "disease identity" theory. On the basis of voluminous statistical data, he proposed that each mental disorder is characterized by a cluster of symptoms (syndrome) and follows a definite, predictable, and identifiable sequence. For example, he was able to differentiate between manic-depressive psychoses and *dementia praecox* (schizophrenia). Kraeplin's insightful classification and description of mental disorders laid the foundation for current clinical classification.

Early in the 19th century, this focus began to shift to psychological and sociocultural causes. Experimental psychology was used to assess individual differences in mental processing, but Emile Durkheim (1858–1917), a French sociologist, insisted that behavior cannot be understood fully in individualistic terms; rather, it must be understood within the larger social context in which it occurs. In his studies of suicide rates in France, England, and Denmark (1897), he pointed out the influence of groups, interactive processes, and societal forces on what had traditionally been viewed as a highly personal act. Durkheim's systematic scientific work clearly demonstrated that though suicide may appear to be a personal phenomenon, it is a byproduct of the individual's relationship with his or her social environment. Durkheim's theory was better able to predict than the theories of inherited tendencies or psychological conditioning, by demonstrating that suicide rates rise or fall in conjunction with certain social and economic changes (see Box 1–3 in Chapter 1, p. 26).

At about the same time, in the United States, William Healy (1869–1963), who founded the Psychopathic Institute (later to become the Institute of Juvenile Research) in Chicago (1909), pointed out for the first time that juvenile delinquency was a symptom of the phenomena of urbanization and not necessarily the result of psychological problems.

Alfred Adler, a student of Freud's, challenged the psychoanalytic movement by rejecting Freud's explanation of inherited determinants of human behavior. He hypothesized that neuroses stemmed from feelings of inferiority resulting from social factors. Adler attributed the causes of mental disorders to the dynamics of interpersonal relationships and is acknowledged as the founder of the psychodynamic movement, which views humans as inherently social beings motivated primarily by the desire to belong to and participate in groups. His pioneering work influenced a number of modern psychotherapeutic methods—psychosomatic medicine, community psychiatry (emphasizing social factors in psychopathology), and existential psychiatry.

The impact of Freudian psychology was significant in the early part of the 20th century. Its application is generally known as *psychoanalysis*. Though Freud's ideas gained popularity, their empirical foundation was, and still is, questionable. Many psychiatrists in the United States were influenced by the ideas' novelty and alternative ways of looking at many mental problems. Freudian influence was more dramatic in psychiatry because it had become a quiescent branch of medicine. During the 1940s and 1950s, Americans found an innovative way of looking at their problems, through the analysis of dreams, childhood experiences, life events, and conflicts stemming from heterosexual attraction between generations of parents and children. Freud's efforts to look deep into the unconscious to seek the root cause of problems seemed so convincing that he gained a significant intellectual following. Of course, there were and are dissenters who question many of Freud's ideas and theories, which, they assert (based on their own research) do not apply and have little relevance cross-culturally.

By the 1950s, Freud's ideas had begun to run their course, partly due to the new findings of ethnographic, anthropological, and sociological research from all parts of the world by scholars disenchanted with the Freudian therapy (psychoanalysis), its enormous cost, lengthy sessions, and limited positive results. As alternatives, psychoactive drugs were introduced during this time for their quick therapeutic value, suggesting that use of psychoactive drugs can control the symptoms of mental disorders so as to allow those who were institutionalized to lead a relatively better life in the communities. In 1962, President John F. Kennedy initiated a nationwide community mental health program. This program was designed to meet the primary mental health needs of citizens and to allow the mentally impaired to lead a reasonable life within their own communities. The program had limited success and left much to be desired (see Chapter 12 for details).

FEMINIZATION AND SEXUALIZATION OF MENTAL DISORDERS

Although reformist movements had their successes, gender role conflicts, inherent in social structure, still have their emotional consequences, especially for women. Patriarchy condoned not only the dominance of men over women in the Middle Ages but also defined their morals, remnants of which persist today. Women were seen as a threat to existing morals of the society and their sexuality as a constant danger against the authority of men. Ideas and meanings are products of society and thus structure social reality. For example, during the Middle Ages, women who questioned the scriptures or the authority of men were labeled as witches. For women, access to knowledge was actively controlled because knowledge and power are inextricably linked (Foucault, 1973, 1979). Women asking for their rights, seeking equality and freedom, and protesting sexual exploitation were viewed as deviant and inconsistent with the role of caring mother and dedicated wife. Hence, such views were identified as symptoms of mental disorder subject to medical treatment. For women, this way of thinking was a *medicalization* of their feelings, thoughts, and aspirations, which did not call for medical treatment (Conrad & Schneider, 1980) (see Boxes 2–1, p. 38 and 2–2, p. 50).

Sigmund Freud (1856–1939) used hypnosis and the *free association* technique on female hysterical patients, unraveling their unconscious (see Chapter 4). He theorized that sexual factors play a significant role in mental disorders, which are products of intrapsychic pain among women. This explanation can be dubbed as *sexualization* of mental disorders. Women are known to repress their feelings and sexuality, and their lives are more likely than men's lives to be frustrated, unfulfilled, and unrewarding.

Studies in the 1950s, and again in the 1970s, of women in San Francisco, California's Bay Area report that the women who experienced emotional trouble due to stress and inequality in their families suffered crises leading to their hospitalization for schizophrenia. Over a period of two decades, their lives changed in various ways; however, crises caused by gender roles persisted (Sampson, Messinger & Towne, 1962; Warren, 1987). Gender role conflicts continue to be major sources of emotional stress and strain in the lives of women today (Denzin, 1983) (see Chapter 10).

> BOX 2-2 • Female Passions and Marriage Manuals
>
> As every schoolgirl knows, the people in the 19th century were afraid of sex, particularly when it manifested itself in women. Women's alleged lack of passion was epitomized, too, in the story of the English mother whose daughter asked her how to behave on her wedding night. "Lie still and think of the Empire," the mother advised. Dr. William Acton's *Functions and Disorders of the Reproductive Organs*, which went through several editions in England and the United States in the middle years of the 19th century, was the most quoted sexual advice book of the time. The book sums up medical literature on women's sexuality by saying that "the majority of women (happily for them) are not very much troubled by sexual feelings of any kind. What men are habitually, women are only exceptionally."
>
> Theophilus Parvin, an American doctor, told his medical class in 1883, "I do not believe one bride in a hundred, of delicate, educated, sensitive women, accepts matrimony from any desire for sexual gratification; when she thinks of that at all, it is with shrinking, or even with horror, rather than with desire." Ben Barker-Benfield argued that male doctors were so convinced that women had no sexual interest that when it manifested itself, drastic measures were taken to subdue it, including excision of the sexual organs. Construing the absence of sexual desire in women as normal, doctors came to see it as disease. Sexual appetite was a male quality (to be properly channeled, of course). If a woman showed it, she resembled a man.

Adapted from Degler, 1978, pp. 403–405.

COMPETING VIEWS OF MENTAL DISORDER IN CONTEMPORARY SOCIETY

In Chapters 3 and 4, we discuss in detail specific theoretical orientations and treatment approaches related to mental disorders. The *biological perspective* focuses on organic and/or chemical changes as causes of psychopathology. The *psychoanalytic perspective* emphasizes adverse childhood experiences, repression, suppression of instincts, and inner conflicts as causes of anxiety. Among proponents of the psychosocial orientation, *behaviorists* focus on defective learning; *existentialists* on problems in personal growth; *interactionists* on interpersonal relationships; *functionalists* on instability in the social system; *ethnomethodologists* on problems ingrained in culture; and *conflict theorists* on maladies caused by exploitation and oppression. In spite of these widely diverse perspectives, each may be classified as belonging to one or more of the rather distinct approaches to mental disorder that have emerged over the past half century. However, there are some popular trends. Presently, advice givers are available in many forms and styles: on TV shows and radio programs, as counselors for personal service as well as for workshops and seminars, and as promoters of self-help groups and authors of popular magazine articles and books. Many of them are having a field day.

The biochemical revolution (i.e., the discovery of new mind-altering drugs over the past 40 years) and technological advancements enabling us to map the structure and functions of the brain in finer detail have led to improved precision in diagnosis and allowed medical professionals to regain control over the treatment of mental disorders in the 1970s and 1980s.

The medical model of mental illness has served significant political, ideological, and economic functions. It reaffirms the status quo, reinforces the power of the medical enterprise, and permits the continued use of drug and shock therapy and institutionalization. There are, of course, some positive consequences of this approach. Sophisticated research on the functions and structure of the brain has revealed some crucial relationships between biology and mental disorders, such as schizophrenia.

Environmental explanations of mental disorders encompass a host of approaches (see Chapter 4), ranging from labeling to family pathology.

The notions of mental disorders have changed the history of humankind. Today, the competition among these various views remains very much alive, as we have seen, and although we have made great strides in comprehending mental disorders, much remains to be done.

CHAPTER REVIEW

1. In what ways has the concept of mental disorder been influenced by beliefs in the supernatural? By the cultural system? By economics?

2. In what ways did early civilizations contribute to current explanations of mental disorders? Be specific.

3. Why is Hippocrates known as the father of modern medicine? How did he attempt to explain mental disorders?

4. What are the fundamental similarities and differences among Chinese, Greek, and Indian theories of mental disorders? How would you differentiate their current operating principles?

5. Witchcraft had its uses and misuses in early civilizations. How was witchcraft used as an instrument of exploitation, oppression, and punishment?

6. Explain why the Middle Ages are referred to as a period of stagnation and regression with respect to the treatment of the mentally impaired.

7. What factors were responsible for mental health reforms in 17th-century Europe? How did they influence policies in the United States?
8. The Renaissance has been called the period of confinement for the mentally impaired. What factors contributed to this label?
9. The reformists are noted for their rational views regarding the treatment of the mentally disordered. In what ways did contributions of Chiarugi, Pinel, Tuke, Rush, and Dix demonstrate this enlightenment?
10. What are the differences and similarities between the philosophy of moral management and mental hygiene movements in the United States?
11. The 19th century was a period of transition, when many controversial ideas were advanced to explain the processes of the mind. How have these ideas influenced our thinking today?
12. Briefly explain the following:
    a. Trephining
    b. Mesmerism
    c. *Malleus Maleficarum*
    d. Johann Weyer
    e. Feminization of mental disorders

FOR FURTHER STUDY

Alexander, F. G., & Selesnick, S. T. (1966). *The history of psychiatry*. New York: Harper & Row.
Foucault, M. (1967). *Madness and civilization*. New York: Mentor.
Kaplan, H. I., & Sadock, B. (1988). *Comprehensive text book of psychiatry/V*. Baltimore: Williams & Wilkins.
Kiev, A. (Ed.) (1964). *Magic, faith and healing*. New York: Free Press.
Kiev, A. (1972). *Transcultural psychiatry*. New York: Free Press.
Lehmann, A. C., & Myers, J. E. (1989). *Magic, witchcraft, and religion*. Mountain View, CA: Mayfield Publishing Co.
Rosen, G. (1963). Social attitudes to irrationality and madness in 17th and 18th century Europe. *Journal of History of Medicine and Allied Sciences, 18*, 220–240.
Scheff, T. J. (1984). *Being mentally ill*. (2nd Ed.). New York: Aldine.
Szasz, T. S. (1987). *Insanity: The idea and its consequences*. New York: John Wiley & Sons.
Warren, C. A. B. (1987). *Madwives: Schizophrenic women in the 1950s*. New Brunswick, NJ: Rutgers University Press.

▶ 3
Medical and Psychiatric Approaches to Mental Disorders

Among the professionals who have studied and treated mental disorders are those with medical backgrounds, who believe that most mental problems are the product of biophysical processes. The assumption is that something has gone wrong with the human body and thereby the brain of a person so affected. This view is referred to as the *biological viewpoint* or *biological approach*. Several other terms are used to connote the same viewpoint, depending on the context, such as *medical, psychiatric, neurological, biophysical, biochemical*, and *genetic*. From a medical viewpoint, mental disorder has little to do either with psychological or psychosocial factors or conditions. Rather, disorders of the mind are viewed as diseases caused by brain pathologies.

In the search for a cure for mental disorders, mistakes have been committed. You may recall the way people suffering from mental disorders were treated in the past (Chapter 2). In some ways, things are no better today. Some of the practices continue because we cannot dissociate ourselves from the beliefs that are deeply ingrained in our culture. Other reasons include power, money, prestige, and the ability to set standards for the society by those who have vested interests. These interest groups wield so much power that they can impede the growth of scientific thinking or policies that may not be in the interests of the victims (in this case, the mentally impaired). But any change has its costs and consequences.

The more complex a phenomenon being researched, the greater the number of diverse viewpoints that emerge. Ruling out any other possible explanation of a phenomena has its own disadvantages in that it does not allow us to advance our scientific thinking and thereby our ability to solve problems. It is not always easy to discard established theories, although new scientific evidence may be contrary to such propositions. The new insights, which advance our knowledge, constitute *paradigm shifts*. Such changes are inevitable in the field of mental health.

EARLY BIOLOGICAL VIEWS

In ancient times, the mentally impaired were viewed with a lot of skepticism because victims were believed to have some kind of defect, particularly in their blood line or heredity. Public knowledge of this blemish led to stigma, which families tried to avoid. Most mental problems do not have a genetic bearing; but it was safer to call a mental problem a disease than a disorder. Mental disorder as a concept was unacceptable because it reflected a failure on the part of the loved ones or the family. No one in the family wanted to declare a loved one a demon or a witch.

The early part of the 18th century was a period of many scientific strides, which allowed scientists to identify diseases and their causes and was the first step in finding a cure. The next step was to suspect that mental disorders may have natural causes. This belief firmly established the biological model of mental disorders.

THE SEARCH FOR BRAIN PATHOLOGY

In the early 18th century, the emergence of modern experimental sciences began uncovering pathological underpinnings of physical and emotional ailments. As we have noted, organic or biological explanations of mental disorders were deeply ingrained in the evolution of medical sciences.

Albrecht von Haller (1707–1777), in 1757, suggested the exploration of the brain to explain psychic functions. A German psychiatrist, William Griesinger (1817–1868), in 1845, proposed that all mental disorders must involve some kind of brain pathology, and psychiatry should clinically look for physiological causes. The climate of the times was such that not many treatment alternatives were available, and few treatments allowed respite from emotional maladies. The medical model was not without foundation. Its contributions were significant in the treatment of diseases like general paresis, a disease that caused general paralysis and insanity and brought about the death of the afflicted person within a few years; cerebral arteriosclerosis; and senile psychosis. However, these diseases are consequences of physiological changes or abnormalities in the brain and legitimately belong to the domain of medical sciences, particularly to a specialized branch of medicine known as neurology; but whether we should call them mental disorders is open to question.

The influence of Griesinger can be seen in the Western world wherever Western medicine is practiced. An ardent follower of Griesinger, Emil Kraepelin (1856–1926) pioneered a medical system of classification of mental disorders. He noted that certain symptoms of disorders appeared with a certain degree of regularity and were identified with a specific name. Based on clinical findings, Kraepelin developed a classification that became the forerunner of the *Diagnostic and Statistical Manual of Mental Disorders*, 3rd edition, revised (*DSM-III-R*). The classification of mental disorders in itself was a major advance, but even today it is difficult to apply it cross-culturally, which raises questions about its scientific validity. If a certain mental disorder is part of a category of disorders that have a biological or physiological basis, then it should not be limited to a certain culture.

THE MEDICAL–BIOLOGICAL MODEL

Medical explanations of mental disorders view any mental impairment as a physical disease that is based in the organic structure of the human body. This approach is fundamentally akin to the idea that a malady in the body is also an indicator of a malady in behavior. Therefore, if there are symptoms of disorder in the behavior of the individual, they should be treated medically.

Although biologically based thinking has contributed to the understanding and treatment of many organic diseases, for mental disorders there is little doubt that this thinking was too widely adopted before its limitations were recognized. The assessment instruments in medical practice are oriented to look for the causes of mental disorders not in interpersonal relationships, family, class, or race, but independent of such sociological variables. Psychiatrists vary widely in their orientation and approach to mental disorders. Some follow strictly the biological approach, some psychodynamic, while others attempt to be eclectic (following the best in all approaches). There is another group that rejects the biological approach completely and believes that most mental disorders originate only from the social environment. Some have gone even further to say that mental illness is a myth, because what is labeled as mental illness is simply a person's reaction to unresolvable conflicts arising from socially unmanageable situations (Szasz, 1974a). The basic tenets of the biological model applicable to the treatment of mental disorders are discussed next.

The Psychiatric Approach

1. Major mental disorders are diseases. Psychiatrists, like other physicians, typically require a physical examination, a battery of tests to determine biophysical or pathological condition, and a detailed medical history of the person. Finally, they prescribe treatment, which may involve medication and other therapies.

2. Mental disorders are caused primarily by organic factors, and most of these factors relate to the brain and the body. To psychiatrists, the mind is simply the subjective byproduct of the brain. The mind is thus a *superorganic* entity that affects behavior. To modify behavior, the thinking of the mind must be changed, and to accomplish this, the brain should be treated.

3. Psychiatrists search for medical and biological explanations of mental disorders, such as genetic links, neuropathologies, and biochemical and brain structure abnormalities.

4. The psychiatric treatment of mental disorders is based on symptoms, as is any other disease, with the assumption that a healthy person does not have a disease. Here we are referring to physical health. Even if a person is found medically fit and in sound health but complains of, for example, a high level of anxiety or insomnia, he or she is a likely candidate for psychiatric treatment.

5. Psychiatric treatment involves *somatic therapies*. These are a group of therapies involving a variety of medications and electroconvulsive therapy (ECT).

6. Psychiatric treatment provides the management of most severely mentally impaired people for whom other therapies may not have been effective. In most cases, biological therapies do not offer cure but allow people with mental disorders to manage their lives. Sometimes psychiatric advice is used not so much for the treatment of the disorder but to alleviate socially unacceptable symptoms or subject the unruly to a mode of control.

7. From a psychiatric viewpoint, mental disorder is typically treated as a mental disease, not as a personal quirk or a consequence of free will. The person experiencing the disorder may be seen as having little or no control over the disorder and as unable to modify the disorder-causing behavior by free will. It is almost as though the objectionable behavior is a product of the person's autonomous system, over which the person exercises no control.

8. Although psychiatric treatment generally includes psychosocial therapies, it only peripherally considers the importance of the elements of social or psychological environment (e.g., poor socialization, bad parenting,

weak value system, neglect, abuse, and poverty) in the treatment of mental disorders.

Some scholars, including psychiatrists, question the rationale and relevance of this approach, suggesting that not all mental disorders have biological origins; some believe that we are attempting to treat a disease that does not exist.

CLASSIFICATION OF MENTAL DISORDERS: A MAJOR CONTROVERSY

Attempts to classify mental disorders have a long history and have generated incredible controversies. We are not in agreement with or endorsing psychiatric classification because of its built-in cultural biases, inclusion of categories that in our estimation are not mental disorders, and arbitrary inclusion and exclusion of disorders with no objective assessment of the categories (critical evaluation is discussed later in this chapter). In spite of our disagreement, however, it is important to discuss this classification scheme because it is utilized extensively for identifying and treating mental disorders. For individuals, judgments based on this classification have moral, legal, social, economic, political, and personal consequences. Many individuals, in spite of the lack of objectivity in the classification, are labeled and stigmatized, and their lives, careers, and self-esteem are adversely affected.

A classification of mental disorders was attempted for the first time in the United States in 1952, by the American Psychiatric Association, in a manual called the *Diagnostic and Statistical Manual of Mental Disorders* (*DSM-I*, 1952). It has been revised three times (1968, 1980), the most recent being the *DSM-III-R* (1987), and discussion is underway for the *DSM-IV*. There is also a classification of all diseases and disorders, both physical and mental, intended to be applicable worldwide: the *International Classification of Diseases, IX Edition, 1979* (*ICD-9*), published by the World Health Organization. Following the changes in *DSM-III*, in 1980, *ICD-9* was modified and named *ICD-9CM* (CM stands for clinical modifications). Critics charge that this is another power play of the medical and psychiatric enterprise to expand the domain and power of their profession, disregarding human variations and values. Let us turn to the classification.

The *DSM-III-R* (1987) utilizes five dimensions or *axes* to evaluate the behavior of an individual who complains of a mental problem. Each axis may be used independently as well in conjunction with others. The individual's current condition is evaluated on the first three axes, which allow the therapist to gain a broad range of information, understanding, and background of a subject's mental state and to make a diagnosis based on the following:

1. Clinical syndromes, manifesting symptoms of maladaptive patterns of behavior, such as severe manic depression and schizophrenia
2. Mental problems associated with personality disorders (usually among adults) and specific developmental disorders (such as related to reading, arithmetic, speech, and articulation)
3. Presence of medical or organic disorders
4. Severity of psychosocial stressors
5. Highest level of adaptive functioning

These categories of mental disorders are simply meant for identification purposes. In reality, a person may have a combination of mental problems. Clinicians prefer a diagnosis by identifying symptoms based on a multiaxial classification system, which is known as a *psychiatric profile*. Extent and intensity of each disorder is identified by certain qualifiers. For example, *acute* or *severe* means high intensity of the symptoms for relatively short duration, which may extend from three to six months. Disorders that are fairly prolonged and recurrent, although they may be of varying intensity, are termed *chronic*. *Episodic* disorders tend to occur with changes in situations and are often triggered by untoward and unpleasant happenings. They are generally reported among manic depressives and schizophrenics, who frequently go through mood swings. In other cases, the symptoms may be of low intensity and short duration and are referred to as *moderate* or *mild*. The revisions of DSM indicate that more psychosocial categories of mental disorders have been added.

DSM-III-R CLASSIFICATION

Axis I: Clinical Syndromes

1. *Disorders, usually first evident in infancy, childhood, or adolescence* refer to special problems related to learning, hearing, memory, and articulation that may be associated with mental retardation, autism, and several other syndromes.
2. *Organic mental disorders* refer to a group of disorders with behavioral symptoms involving gross destruction of brain tissue or malfunctioning of the brain causing depression, dementia, apathy, memory loss, and confusion. In these cases, etiology of the disorder is known or presumed. The term *organic brain syndromes*, although often used interchangeably, refers to

disorders believed to reflect brain pathology, such as dementia, delirium, and amnesia.

3. *Substance-use disorders* refer to mental disorders involving chemical substance abuse or misuse, such as drug addiction, alcoholism, and crack and cocaine abuse (see Chapter 7).

4. *Schizophrenia* relates to a cluster of psychotic disorders. It is characterized by withdrawal from reality, disturbance in emotional appropriateness, disjointed thought processes marked by delusions and hallucinations, and bizarre speech and motor symptoms (see Chapter 6).

5. *Delusional (paranoid) disorders* include a variety of symptoms. The individual who suffers from paranoid disorder feels singled out, taken advantage of, cheated, mistreated, plotted against, spied on, neglected, and unfairly treated. The person's self-disturbing thoughts, such as hostility, are denied but are projected onto others, usually in an exaggerated form, to distract oneself from one's inadequacies. The delusions, usually combined with paranoia, center on one major theme, such as becoming a millionaire, being a great inventor, being a great charmer of women, and so on.

6. *Psychotic disorders not classified elsewhere* include psychotic conditions that are generally atypical and those that are either undifferentiated or bipolar (see Chapter 6).

7. *Mood disorders* are negative and positive emotional states, called mood swings, that are prolonged enough to cause serious problems of affect and maladaptation in the functioning of the individual. Bipolar disorder is characterized by both poles of affective disorder (i.e., mania and depression). Mania is an elevated, expansive, or irritable state, while depression is a state of feeling sad, blue, or unhappy. People who experience either depression or mania are known as *unipolar* (see Chapter 5).

8. *Anxiety disorders* are patterns of behavior in which irrational, unrealistic, and disabling fear of high intensity is a predominant feature. Persistent anxiety may lead to phobia (an excessive and irrational fear) or obsessive-compulsive behavior (recurrent compulsions severe enough to cause marked distress) or both, and panic (see Chapter 5).

9. *Somatoform disorders*. *Soma* means "body." In this type of disorder, a person complains of physical problems for which no organic basis can be found or no evidence of physical injury is adequately justified (see Chapter 5).

10. *Dissociative disorders*, though rare, are characterized by the dissociation of a person from his or her core personality and emergence as a new or a set of different personalities to avoid stress, unpleasant encounters, and responsibility while at the same time seeking to gratify needs. Variants of this disorder include depersonalization, amnesia, and multiple personalities (see Chapter 5).

11. *Sexual disorders* refer to a group of disorders that include a variety of paraphilias, such as exhibitionism, fetishism, frotteurism, voyeurism, and pedophilia; and sexual dysfunctions, such as sexual desire disorders, sexual arousal disorders, and orgasmic disorders. Also included are gender identity and sexual preference disorders (see Chapter 8).

12. *Sleep disorders*. Although they may be rooted in other anxiety–related or organic disorders, sleep disorders include insomnia, dyssomnia, hyposomnia and hypersomnia, sleep–wake schedule disorders, and other disorders not classified elsewhere. They may also relate to dream anxiety, nightmares, sleep terror, sleepwalking, and other unusual behavior patterns related to sleep.

13. *Factitious disorders* are also known as *Munchausen's syndrome*, named after the legendary Baron Hieronymus von Munchausen, who wandered from city to city, tavern to tavern during the 18th century, telling tales. The essential feature of the disorder is intentional manifestation of symptoms. In some cases, intentional creation of disorder may be associated with feigning of psychological symptoms, to assume a mental patient role or to escape an unpleasant situation. Some people suffer from "nonsense syndrome," in which they talk past the point or engage in devious conversation.

14. *Impulse control disorders not classified elsewhere* are manifest by behavior in which the person seems unable to retain control over his or her impulses (e.g., spouse battering, pathological gambling, pyromania, or kleptomania).

15. *Adjustment disorders* are maladaptive reactions to identifiable psychosocial or natural stressors that occur with the expectancy of or within a few months after the onset of stressors.

16. *Psychological factors affecting physical condition*. There are mental conditions that may affect particular aspects of the body, such as migraine headaches or peptic ulcer. These were previously thought to have psychological origins and were termed *psychophysiological* or *psychosomatic disorders*.

17. *Conditions not attributable to a mental disorder that are a focus of attention or treatment*. These are conditions that do not fall in any of the major categories of mental disorders but create short-term or episodic inconvenience or aggravation. Examples include marital, academic, and job-related problems.

Axis II: Developmental Disorders and Personality Disorders

Developmental Disorders
Disorders included in Axis I may also relate to developmental disorders. The latter account for a person's lack of or disturbances in the acquisition of

cognitive, language, motor, or social skills. Generally, these manifest specific difficulties in levels of maturation, and their origins may be sociopsychological or organic or both. Their impact may range from mild to profound and partial to global (e.g., autistic disorder, motor skills disorder, and speech disorder). Controversies about this category of disorders relate to the inclusion of disabilities as mental disorders, which are effectively handled by specialists in educational settings. Many such disorders do not require psychiatric attention but have social consequences, such as stigma.

Personality Disorders

Personality disorders largely originate from improper socialization and are characterized by immature, inflexible, and warped personality development. They cause significant functional impairment due to maladaptive ways of thinking, perceiving, behaving, and relating to the environment, which leads to distress. The individual prefers acting out in ways that are contrary to prevailing social norms. The *DSM-III-R* classification presents three clusters of personality disorders: (1) paranoid, schizoid, and schizotypal; (2) antisocial, borderline histrionic, and narcissistic; and (3) avoidant, dependent, obsessive compulsive, and passive aggressive. Of course, there are personality disorders that are undifferentiated. Often, personality disorders are responsible for sexual assaults, alcoholism, spouse and child abuse, pathological gambling, and a variety of criminal acts.

Axis III: Physical Disorders and Conditions

Axis III is intended to evaluate any physical disease or condition that occurs with a mental disorder, whether or not the two are interrelated. Some physical diseases may precipitate certain mental disorders, and certain mental states may cause physical problems (e.g., psychogenic or somatoform disorders).

Axis IV: Severity of Psychosocial Stressors

Most mental disorders reflect the role of life experiences and situations. Stress is a reaction to demands placed on the mind and body in a given situation, leading to physical and/or behavioral problems. The severity of stress may vary from none to catastrophic levels and may involve complex patterns of responses. The Axis IV scale is generally utilized in conjunction with Axis I to ascertain the influence of stressors on certain categories of disorders. An example is the *adjustment disorder*, which refers to a maladaptive reaction to psychosocial stressors (such as death of a loved one, divorce, loss of job), impairing a person's functioning for an extended period of time following the episode. Another example is *posttraumatic stress disorder*, a condition in which a person reexperiences traumatic events and persistent, intrusive, distressing thoughts and dreams continue to adversely affect emotional state and functioning (see Chapter 4).

Axis V: Global Assessment of Functioning

Axis V is devised to evaluate the highest level of adaptive functioning during the past year (a year being a reasonable length of time), especially in the context of the quality of the person's relationships rated on a 90-point scale. This scale ranges from good in all areas (90 points) to persistent danger, the lowest functioning level (10). As we look at axes IV and V, we find that in *DSM-III-R* considerable attention has been given to social and psychological factors in the diagnosis of mental disorders. Such diagnosis, based on social and psychological attributes, offers supplemental information that is not without hazards. One of the major criticisms leveled against such assessment is that it assumes that all people are alike and should be functioning effectively in most areas of their personal and social lives.

ORGANIC AND BIOLOGICAL DETERMINANTS OF MENTAL DISORDERS

One of the biological factors considered responsible for mental disorders is the genetic link (biological inheritance), and any traits thus organically inherited through genes and chromosomes are called genetic markers. Not all studies based on this theory are free from problems (especially the controls) and therefore are not the final word in explaining mental disorders.

Genetic Factors

People have long believed that mental problems run in families. But are such problems inherited or learned? If they are inherited, then they are caused by genetic transmission. Cesare Lombroso became known for the theory of the "born criminal," suggesting that criminality is inherited. Although Lombroso's theory has long been rejected in criminology, it has yet to be tested fully in the field of mental health.

It is known that heredity is the major determining factor in certain physical attributes and physiological conditions (e.g., color blindness, diabetes mellitus, hemophylia, and certain heart diseases).

The nature (heredity)–nurture (environment) controversy has plagued the scientific world for a long time. Those who come from the field of biology focus on the contributions of nature, while those who belong to the domain of social sciences assert the role of the environment. Some believe, like the eminent geneticist William Bateson, that natural genetic distinctions differentiate people into types—artists, actors, farmers, musicians, poets, scientists, servants, etc. At the other extreme, J. B. Watson, the founder of behaviorism, made the proud boast that given a dozen healthy infants and the freedom to shape their environment, he could produce any kind of specialist—doctor, lawyer, merchant, artist, etc. (Connolly, 1987, pp. 284–286). The current status of the findings is that genetic as well as environmental contributions are essential, though the degree of contributions made by each depends on the characteristics in question. For example, attempts have been made to explore the relationship of mood with the food we consume (see Box 3–1).

The Role of Genes and Chromosomes

Each of us has six million genes in our bodies, which are carried on chromosomes in the nuclei of our body cells, and we receive half of them from each of our parents. Human cells contain elongated microscopic substances called *chromosomes*. Each chromosome is composed of thousands of jellylike parts called *genes*. There are two types of genes—dominant and recessive. Which characteristics will actually be derived from genetic inheritance depends on their quality of manifestation. Some genes are *dominant* and powerful enough that they clearly make a mark on the individual and overwhelm lesser genes if they form heterozygous pairs. The *recessive genes* do not manifest themselves unless they are paired with the same recessive genes. Mental disorders are suspected to be associated with recessive genes and will not show their impact unless the person has a combination of homozygous genes. With the exception of the male sperm and the female ovum, each cell contains 23 pairs of chromosomes. Genetic transmission controls, in a significant way, our looks, skin color, height, weight, and perhaps our basic personalities and general abilities. Genetic makeup turns each of us into a unique individual and generally sets the tone for the physical attributes that affect our personalities. Thus, each one of us is born with a genetic program that interacts with nongenetic factors and determines our likes and dislikes, preferences and apprehensions. Beyond the process of genetic transmission, some studies have focused on the pathology of chromosomes contributing to the phenomena of mental disorders. Recent technological advances have made the study of chromosomes more precise through *karyotypes*, or pictures of chromosomes. Diseases like mongolism or Down's Syndrome, characterized by intellectual deficit, short stature, protruding tongue, epicanthic fold in the eyes (almond eyes), and general

> **BOX 3-1 • The Food–Mood Link**
>
> Do you believe that having dinner at a high-priced restaurant gives you a feeling of spending a pleasant evening, or is it the quality of food or the bill you paid? People have suspected for centuries that the kind of food we consume determines our emotional states. Many cultures have incorporated food prohibitions in their religious practices. For example, the followers of Buddhism and Hinduism have complex rules governing food consumption, suggesting that food has an impact on one's soul as well as the body. In recent years, a new science called clinical ecology or environmental medicine has grown up around the controversial theory that certain foods or chemicals may be linked to an array of symptoms, including behavior disorders, depression, chronic fatigue, and hypertension. Dr. Wayne Callaway, an endocrinologist and nutritionist at the Mayo Clinic in Rochester, Minnesota, says, "There is no argument that diet affects mood. The big argument is *how* does it do it." Dr. Bonnie Spring found a link between high carbohydrate/low protein diets and drowsiness that, in turn, causes impaired performance. But what about a protein-rich diet? It may keep you alert, but excess protein may cause insomnia, hyperactivity, or even aggression. Psychologist Bernard Lyman of the University of British Columbia found that people experiencing different emotional states preferred different kinds of food. Generally, they preferred hearty, full-course meals when they were feeling happy and self-confident, and junk foods when they were depressed. It has been found that obese people crave carbohydrates because they make them feel less anxious and depressed. Harris Lieberman noted that carbohydrates eaten alone increase the brain's uptake of the amino acid tryptophan. In turn, the tryptophan stimulates production of serotonin, a neurotransmitter that has a hypnotic effect. Dr. Norman Rosenthal, of the NIMH, who popularized the concept of seasonal affective disorder (the "winter blues") found that some of his winter-depressed people craved carbohydrates. He said, "Foods are chemicals, and some people may be medicating themselves with food because it makes them feel better." Researchers complain that the medical establishment is bent on debunking the claims instead of devising new means to test them. The field is wide open.

Adapted from Gelman et al., 1985.

mental retardation, seem to be associated with the presence of three chromosomes in one of the sets in affected people instead of the normal two (Lejeune, Turpin, & Gautie, 1959). Critics charge that rather than being a cause, the presence of the third chromosome may be one of the many symptoms of Down's syndrome.

The normal male carries an XY set of chromosomes and the normal woman an XX set. Occasionally, though rarely, an extra Y chromosome appears in men (XYY), which is believed to cause behavioral aberrations. Probability of this defect increases with the age of the mother after 40, and to a lesser extent with the age of the father. Richard Speck, who murdered eight nurses and was eventually convicted, was found to have an XYY combination.

Anomalies have also been reported that may predispose a person to develop mental disorder. Klinefelter's syndrome, found in men, also involves 47 chromosomes instead of 46, but in this case the extra chromosome is X. These men appear like men, but they are usually infertile and suffer from gender identity confusion and generally have run-ins with the law (Wright, Schaefer, & Solomons, 1979). It is estimated that in the United States 0.5% of newborns have chromosomal abnormalities. Much of the evidence at this point is sketchy but suggests that an extra chromosome may be a culprit in mental disorders.

Family History Studies

To find out if a mental disorder has been caused by genetic transmission, family studies over several generations provide the most direct way of studying the mode of inheritance of a characteristic. Tracing the incidence of a trait down a family line can reveal the dominance and recessiveness of genes. Recent research suggests that the defect causing Huntington's disease is carried on a gene on chromosome 4 and Alzheimer's disease on chromosome 21. There are some indications that manic-depressive psychosis is associated with a gene carried on chromosome 11. But this last finding has not been confirmed by other researchers (Torrey, 1988b, p. 144). The limitation of this research is that conclusions are based on diagnosed cases and have not been supported by research on general populations.

Studies of Twins

Another way of deciphering the causes of mental disorder (probably in a more precise way) is through the study of twins. Twins are either *identical* (monozygotic, MZ) or *fraternal* (dizygotic, DZ). Identical twins share exactly the same genetic material, derived from the splitting of a single fertilized egg, whereas fraternal twins derive from the fertilization of two eggs by two sperms. The DZ twins are no more alike than ordinary siblings, but since they share a common prenatal environment and usually grow up together, they tend to be more alike than siblings born at different times. Differences within MZ pairs arise only from the environment. The rate of agreement between a pair of twins with respect to the likelihood of developing a disorder is known as the *concordance rate*. For example, if 100 pairs of twins are studied and only 75 share a certain trait, the concordance rate is 75%; the remaining 25 who do not share the same trait are discordant, or there is a 25% *discordance rate*. When we look at the studies of twins for mental disorders like schizophrenia (which is known to be one of the most severe and complicated disorders), the findings are mixed but interesting. It is commonly believed that schizophrenia runs in families. Research in Belgium, Denmark, and the United States over the past several decades provides us with some understanding of the relevance of genetic transmission of mental disorders (Torrey, 1988a, pp. 144-146).

The child of nonschizophrenic parents has a 1% chance of developing schizophrenia; if one parent is schizophrenic there is a 13% chance; and if both parents are schizophrenic there is a 46% chance. Studies of fraternal (nonidentical) twins suggest that the twin of a schizophrenic has only a 10 to 15% chance of being schizophrenic (slightly higher than for other siblings), whereas the identical twin has a 35 to 50% chance. It is important to note that not all identical twins develop schizophrenia when one does (Andreasen, 1984, pp. 227-230; Torrey, 1988a, pp. 144-146). Such studies suggest that genetic inheritance cannot be the only cause of this mental disorder. But what about the role of social environment? Critics are quick to point out that twin studies do not give us a true picture of the separation of nature and nurture, because the twins generally grow up in the same environment and may model themselves after the same significant others or after one another, partly because of being twins. To isolate the influence of environment, scientists introduced a creative research design by studying the children of schizophrenic mothers who were adopted by normal families.

Adoption Studies

Studies done in Denmark, Finland, Israel, and the United States on children of schizophrenic parents who were adopted by other families at birth, and follow-up studies in their adulthood, suggest that the children retained their schizophrenic tendencies despite the change in their social environment due to adoption. A recent report on Danish samples of 71 subjects with mood disorders matched normal control adoptees with close biological and adoptive relatives who were evaluated for psychiatric status. Unipolar depression was reported to be more likely among the biological relatives of the depressed subjects under study, compared with control cases. The likelihood of suicide was 15 times higher among biological relatives (Wender et al., 1986).

Heston (1966) studied cases of children of schizophrenic mothers and reported that they were more likely to be diagnosed as schizophrenic (16.6%), mentally retarded, neurotic, and psychopathic. Chances of their being involved in criminal activity were significantly higher, leading to time spent in penal institutions. Heston's findings suggest that children born to schizophrenic mothers, even though reared without contact with them, were more likely to suffer not only from mental disorders but also from various other kinds of personal problems. A noteworthy finding is that women who have schizophrenic tendencies may find men with criminal and antisocial tendencies to be preferable mates, thus compounding the adverse impact of genetic contribution to their offspring (Mednick, 1978). Many of these studies tell us that symptoms of mental disorder in offspring may not be the same as those found in one or both parents. They may vary, such as mild schizophrenia, borderline states, uncertain schizophrenia, schizoid, and "inadequate" personality disorder (Rosenthal, 1970; Rosenthal et al., 1971; Wender et al., 1986). Some of these studies provide evidence of genetic transmission of mental disorders along family lines. Nonetheless, these findings have not gone unchallenged.

Some of the major criticisms are not only based on ideological grounds but also on reinterpretation of the same studies, such as the following: First, schizophrenia is a vague concept at best because of the variety of characteristics found among those who suffer from this disorder. Second, in most adoption studies, controls have not been adequately used (e.g., the normal families were assumed to be normal because they did not report any mental inadequacy). Sarbin and Mancuso (1980) noted that data reported contain a fair amount of anomalies, that children originally surveyed have had low rates of schizophrenic breakdown, while the relatives, including the adoptive ones and those biologically related to control adoptees, have had high rates of symptomatic schizophrenia identified. Third, the schizophrenic adoptee/biological relative concordance rate has been most pronounced among half siblings (siblings sharing only one parent in common) of schizophrenic adoptees and not in parents or full siblings who were also evaluated. These findings are so peculiar that it makes the genetic transmission principle weak and inconclusive (Benjamin, 1976). Fourth, adoption in most of these cases was forced due to the abuse and mistreatment found in biological families. It is not uncommon to expect high levels of disturbance in these families, and this disturbance may have caused emotional trauma to many members due to constant battering and abuse. Fifth, in cases where adoption was handled by carefully scrutinizing families for foster child placement, few of the adopted children manifested any signs of schizophrenia or any other mental disorder. Hence, what appears to be a genetic transmission of mental disorder may have more to do with the enduring impact of neglect, abuse, and ill treatment of the person in the family or the environment in which the person has been raised.

Neuroscience

During the past several decades, the followers of the medical model realized that the best way to diagnose mental disorder is to look at it from all possible angles. This new approach does not rule out any possible cause(s), including psychological, sociological, or environmental. Neuroscience is a new science that combines approaches of several disciplines to achieve the common goal of understanding the relationship between brain structure and function and human thoughts, feelings, and behavior. Each of these disciplines focuses on a specific area: for example, neuroanatomy (the study of brain structure), neurochemistry (the study of the chemical processes that control brain function), neuroendocrinology (the study of the relationship between glandular function and brain function), neuropathology (the study of disease processes caused by disorders of brain structure), neuropharmacology (the study of the effects of drugs on the brain), and neuropsychology (the study of various psychological or mental functions and brain structure).

Our emphasis here is on the brain and its functioning and how it influences behavior. Both neurology and psychiatry are medical specialties that are closely allied, interdependent, drawing from and contributing to all the aforementioned neurosciences (Andreasen, 1984, p. 27). Since the focus is on the brain, neuroscientists generally rule out any causal factors of mental disorders that may stem from interpersonal problems unless they are unable to find a cause in the brain. If there is a problem in the brain, in its structure, or due to the effects of chemical processes, it certainly is a neurological problem and a medical problem irrespective of the probability of cure. But is it a mental disease or a neurological defect? If it is a defect, it cannot be a disease. A person may be born with it or genetically predisposed to it. And it cannot be a mental disease unless it has mental or behavioral consequences. In most cases, where precise brain pathology or abnormalities are found (such as Parkinson's disease, lesions in the brain, extensive injury to the brain, stroke, or brain tumor), these diseases are manifested by such obvious symptoms as tremor, weakness, memory loss, or paralysis of the body organs. A clear example of neurological disorder is Parkinson's disease, named after James Parkinson in 1817, who called it "shaking palsy." Its cause is known to be the loss of nerve cells in a small part of brain called the *substantia nigra*, which controls the body movements, the "motor system." Parkinson's disease is now treated with a form of dopamine known as L-dopa with some success. Although there

The Dopamine Hypothesis

The technology for measuring body chemistry has advanced significantly more recently. The neurotransmitter dopamine, one of the brain chemicals that helps in transmitting information between nerve cells, has received the most attention. The human brain is so complex that its detailed structure is only beginning to be understood. It contains ten thousand million nerve cells, and each one may make and receive several thousand contacts with other cells. The dopamine neurotransmitter has been identified because when amphetamines are introduced in the body in large doses, the dopamine level goes up and causes schizophrenia-like symptoms. And when L-dopa, a drug that the body may turn into dopamine, is given to schizophrenic patients, their condition gets worse. Therefore, the theory is that any drug that blocks the dopamine action can control the symptoms of schizophrenia, and any excess of dopamine may be associated with at least one of the causes of schizophrenia. Dopamine is broken down in the body to other compounds through the action of other enzymes. Monoamine oxidase (MAO) is suspected to be one of those enzymes, and schizophrenic people have lower amounts of MAO in their blood platelets. Generally, an excess of dopamine and a deficit of MAO are associated with serious mental disorders like schizophrenia and severe cases of manic depression. These findings are not the last word, and we expect to hear more about the possible causes of mental disorder.

Research on the brain has identified only a few neurotransmitters, such as acetylcholine, dopamine, norepinephrine, sertonin, histamine, aminobutyric acid, glycine, and glutamate, and we are not yet sure about others and their role in mental disorders. Often the research process is slow, expensive, and difficult.

THE BIOCHEMICAL REVOLUTION AND PHARMACOLOGICAL ADVANCES

Another area of biological intervention to modify maladaptive behavior is psychopharmacology. There are four types of drugs commonly used in the treatment of mental disorders, known as psychotropic drugs: (1) antipsychotic drugs, (2) antidepressants, (3) antianxiety drugs, and (4) lithium. In practice, a combination of drugs are used based on the person's symptoms. At this point, a brief note on each of these four categories of drugs is in order.

Antipsychotic Drugs

Commonly known as tranquilizers, these drug compounds not only calm a person but also alleviate pronounced psychotic symptoms, such as hallucinations and delusions. *The Indian Medical Gazette*, in 1943, reported that the root of a plant *rauwolfia* (snakeroot), which was commonly used in the Ayurvedic system of medicine in India for centuries, greatly reduced symptoms of schizophrenia and manic reaction and some other mental disorders. A derivative of this drug known as *reserpine* was introduced in the United States in early 1950s (Kline, 1954). Due to the discovery of new synthetic drugs, such as the phenothiazine family of drugs, reserpine is now used primarily in controlling hypertension. Among the new drugs is *chlorpromazine*, whose primary effect is to block dopamine receptors and to reduce psychotic symptoms. Most of these drugs have serious side-effects (see Table 3–1).

Antidepressants

Researchers also sought drugs for the treatment of a variety of disorders that are more common than psychotic disorders: (1) the monoamine oxidase (MAO) inhibitors and (2) the tricyclics, which are used to increase the concentrations of serotonin and norepinephrine neurotransmitters at relevant synaptic sites in the brain. The MAO inhibitors are toxic and must be administered with a series of dietary restrictions. Most recent research suggests that interpersonal psychotherapies (IPT) and cognitive behavior therapies (CBT) were no less effective than the popular tricyclic antidepressant, imipramine hydrocloride, administered with brief clinical management (Elkin et al., 1989, pp. 971–982). Since we do not find consistent characteristics among those who suffer from depression, it is difficult to identify which therapy is most effective. Medical therapy appears to initially reduce the impact of the adverse thought processes through rest, needed sleep, and medication. The major problem is to restrict the interference of the anxiety-causing agents that led to the depression in the first place. We have yet to prove that depression is a physical disease, and medications are not a cure—simply the means to manage the disorder, with often intolerable side-effects (see Table 3–2).

Antianxiety Drugs

The search for anxiety-relieving substances is not new, ranging from over-the-counter (OTC) drugs to yoga. Basically, there are two classes of antianxiety drugs: (1) meprobamate compounds (Miltown and Equanil), generally used to reduce muscle tension, which have a sedating effect; and (2)

TABLE 3-1 • Frequently Used Medications in the Treatment of Psychotic Symptoms

Class/Generic Name	Trade Name	Used to Treat	Side-Effects
Antipsychotic			
(a) Phenothiazines		All kinds of psychotic symptoms, including delusions (frequently absurd and multiple, idiosyncratic and persecutional, marked by grandeur). Common are poverty of content of speech, thought broadcasting, echolalia, neologism (such as Parkinsonism), overinclusion, loosening of associations, and unpredictable behavior. Other common symptoms are hallucinations, hypersensitivity, agitation, aggression, and inappropriate affect.	Side-effects include dry mouth, blurred vision, dizziness, constipation, urinary retention, memory dysfunction, hypotension, and involuntary muscle contractions. The long-term use may produce motor disturbances such as Parkinsonism, tardive dyskinesia, reflex tachycardia, and postural hypotension.
Chlorpromazine	Thorazine		
Thioridazine	Mellaril		
Promazine	Sparine		
Trifluoperazine	Stelazine		
Prochlorperazine	Compazine		
Perp!enazine	Trilafon		
Fluphenazine	Prolixin		
Triflupromazine	Stelazine Pentazine		
(b) Butyrophenones			
Droperdol	Haldol		
Haloperidol	Inapsine		
(c) Thioxanthenes			
Thiothixine	Navane		
Chlorprothixene	Taractan		
(d) Dibenzepines			
Loxipine	Loxitane		
(e) Dihydroindolones	Moban		
Molindone	Lindone		

Adapted from Flaherty, Channon, & Davis, 1988; and Goodman, Rall, & Murad, 1985.

benzodiazepines, which diminish generalized anxiety (for details, see Chapter 5).

Lithium

Commonly used for the treatment of bipolar disorders, lithium carbonate, a simple salt, is an effective as well as a highly dangerous drug. It is highly toxic and has serious side-effects, such as uncontrollable tremor, convulsions, delirium, and even death. Its dosage requires close monitoring due to its varying impact on different individuals. A recent study shows that lithium is effective in a wide range of children's behavioral disorders (DeLong, 1990, pp. 13–16). Lithium is an effective drug for the treatment of bipolar or manic-depressive disorder.

TABLE 3–2 • Frequently Used Medications in the Treatment of Depression

Class/Generic Name	Trade Name	Used to Treat	Side-Effects
Antidepressant			
(a) Tricyclics		A variety of relatively severe depressive symptoms, usually of unipolar nature and marked by manifest psychotic severity.	Many physiological changes, including drowsiness, light-headedness, blurred vision, constipation, dry mouth, increased heart rate, and urinary retention. Some of those frequently reported are skin rash, sweating, tremors, orgasmic dysfunction, and weight gain.
Imipramine	Tofranil		
Amitriptyline	Elavil		
Nortriptyline	Aventyl		
Protriptyline	Vivactil		
Doxepin	Sinequan		
Amoxabine	Surmontil		
Trimipramine Maleate	Asendin		
		Impact of medications is variable in alleviating depressive symptoms, and noticeable effects may be delayed up to 3 weeks.	
(b) Monoamine oxidase (MAO) inhibitors			
Isocarboxazid	Marplan		
Phenelzine	Nardil		
Tranylcypromine	Parnate		

Adapted from Flaherty, Channon, & Davis, 1988; and Goodman, Rall, & Murad, 1985.

Electroconvulsive Therapy

In 1938, researchers in Italy introduced electroshock therapy (EST), later known as electroconvulsive therapy (ECT). The basic premise of this therapy was to activate those parts of the brain that, for some reason, were not functioning properly. Electroconvulsive therapy, which involves passing an electric current (not more than 170 volts) by placing electrodes around the brain for less than 1 second, produces a condition like seizures. Though it is not yet clearly known how ECT works, it is believed that the electric shock releases norepinephrine in the brain, and this antidepressant relieves the person from depression. Another explanation relates to the loss of consciousness due to ECT, resulting in confusion, short-lived amnesia, and elimination of thought processes responsible for depression. After the therapy, individuals also complain of stiffness of muscles and/or headache and some memory loss. In one study, those who had undergone ECT, 81% said that their trip to the dentist was more distressing than their positive experience with ECT (Papolos & Papolos, 1988, p. 118). But ECT is not for everyone; it is used only when other treatments fail. The use of ECT in the presence of other physiological complications can be harmful simply because the adverse impact of its working is unknown.

Currently, psychiatric treatments include several kinds of therapies, and pharmacological advancements have reduced the severity and chronicity of many mental disorders. Most fundamental advancements have been in controlling the symptoms of mental disorders rather than curing them. To an extent, the new medications have helped individuals manage their impairments. Extended periods of hospitalization and institutionalization are now limited to the severely impaired, and even in those cases conditions have changed significantly, from restraints and locked wards to a more flexible, open, and favorable climate of rehabilitation. But these changes are not across the board. Complete reliance on drug therapy with little or no effective monitoring or reasonable follow-up has created another set of problems: homelessness, crime, and a persistent sense of fear and insecurity among the public. All psychotropic drugs, though they may help in some ways, have limitations and often cause other physiological complications and undesirable side-effects. Drugs are not the most appropriate alternative to allow the individual to confront reality. They do not resolve problems or change situations that are the cause of maladaptive behavior. Critics charge that the psychiatric approach generally disregards psychological and sociological factors in the treatment of disorders, although the latter are used for diagnostic purposes.

THE PSYCHIATRIC APPROACH: AN EVALUATION

Neurosurgeons are now implanting new tissues in the brain, and scientists are looking into the brain with PET (positron emission tomography) scanners to tune into tiny radio signals given off by the molecules that comprise brain tissue, using magnetic resonance imaging (MRI). Scientists are finding ways to enhance memory, and sophisticated scanners are helping map the parts of the brain involved in hearing, seeing, speaking, and thinking. Neuroscientist Richard Masland exclaimed, "We are going to be able to create from birth a person who is tall, has blue eyes and an IQ of 400. The technology is going to do that. . . . The Pandora's box will be open" (Kotulak, 1989, p. 20). In this process of searching for the cure of mental disorders, we have far too long neglected the healing power of the mind, and there is evidence that the mind can, if put to work in a proper way, cure some of the diseases once thought to be incurable. This new field, which deals with the healing power of the mind, is called *psychoneuroimmunology* (see Box 3-2).

There have been so many advances in the field of mental health that it is difficult to say which particular one is going to set a trend in the next century. We know that psychiatric modes of treatment of mental disorders are, if not gaining ground, here to stay. Despite the advances, our basic

> **BOX 3–2 • Can Our Mind Heal Our Body?**
>
> For centuries, people have believed that one's mind has the capability to control and regulate one's body. The Eastern religions, especially Hinduism and Buddhism, have long propagated that the mind is the driving force behind all of our activities and therefore has the power of healing as well as destruction. In a recent PBS documentary, *Mysteries of Mind*, scientists were surprised to see that a man in his sixties, probably a mystic equipped with the knowledge of self-control techniques, could survive, with no ostensible discomfort and with little use of oxygen, for several hours in an enclosed glass chamber. How could he do it? His apparent explanation was that his mind controlled his vital signs. This may have appeared far fetched some years ago, but no longer.
>
> Leonard Borden, 40, a cancer patient, should have been dead by now, because he has a rare form of kidney cancer and modern medicine has little to cure it. His cancerous kidney was removed in July 1986, and his doctors were encouraged that they had found no signs that the disease had spread. That hope faded a few weeks later when X-rays showed cancer in his lungs, a virtual death sentence. With nowhere else to turn, Borden mobilized his brain to do the job it had been failing at. Although there are many skeptics who do not believe in this mysterious process, some people call it "mind over body," "positive thinking," or "behavioral medicine." This rediscovered field is attracting increasing attention, and speculations range from the brain's communication to the immune system to the thymus's ability to boost immunity in people who are depressed or under stress. We don't know whether Borden's white cells went out and killed cancer cells. What *is* known is that a month after his tumor had spread, it began to recede and is now in complete remission, with no evidence of cancer in his body. Dr. John M. Merrill, a Northwestern University cancer specialist who is working with Borden, is surprised at his remission and frankly admits that he was not very hopeful that Borden would survive.

Adapted from Kotulak, 1989, pp. 8–15.

knowledge about the causation of many mental disorders and their treatment remains limited. Many such treatments, especially the extensive use of psychotropic drugs, have serious side-effects leading to other medical and functional problems. However, in the process of refining the tools of diagnosis, we may lose the meaning of being human. The traditional medical, and sometimes psychiatric, view leaves little room for human deviation, which is vital for human ingenuity, creativity, and innovation. Anyone who is deviant in one or more aspects of life, according to this approach, will be identified as mentally ill (Merton, 1968, p. 824).

Although the psychiatric approach is based on the principles of science, the elements of objectivity and explanation that are basic elements of science often appear to be overlooked. For instance, if a psychiatric diagnosis is based on objective facts, explanation should be possible and prediction should be accurate (as in other sciences such as physics and chemistry), but that is not the case. What appears to be missing is the understanding that humans, unlike molecules and atoms, experience emotions, feelings, and sentiments and are affected by all relationships, including the therapist–patient relationship. Thus, while psychotropic medications may help a person have better control over a situation, they may not address the underlying problems. In fact, recent research at the Mayo Clinic in Rochester, Minnesota, and research on depression at the NIMH shows that people with a range of mental disorders often can be effectively managed with behavioral techniques that do address underlying problems (Black & Bruce, 1989, pp. 1152–1157; Elkin et al., 1989).

DOES THE *DSM-III-R* HAVE BUILT-IN BIASES?

The *DSM* is widely used, but it has serious shortcomings. There are critics of *DSM-III-R* on substantive, philosophical, as well as technical grounds, including psychiatrists and neuroscientists. Our focus here is the bias reflected in the assessment by using *DSM-III-R*. Space limitations do not permit us to go into details, but let us consider the following: First, among the disruptive behavior disorders, a category of conduct disorder is included. The question is, Who decides what conduct is appropriate considering vast human variations? Further, is it a disease or a discipline problem? Second, anorexia nervosa is primarily found in the Western world. If it is a disease, why is it not found in other affluent parts of the world? Third, a catch-all category is adjustment disorder—if someone exhibits anxious or depressed mood or disturbance of emotions or conduct, it may simply be a reaction to a situation or person. By calling that reaction a disorder, we are misusing or abusing psychiatry. Fourth, although some conditions (such as bad grades in school, marital hassles, problems at work, and bereavement) are not attributed to mental problems, they are considered worth psychiatric attention according to *DSM-III-R*. If these are not psychiatric problems, why do psychiatrists try to treat them? Fifth, psychiatric assessment ignores individual variations based on gender, race, ethnicity, class, religious affiliation, and similar other variables and may lead to inaccurate diagnosis. Sixth, psychiatrists often do not agree about their diagnosis (e.g., the case of Patricia Hearst). Often, their evaluation is influenced by their own values and orientations. This list can go on. In a multiculture, multiethnic, and class-based society such as the United States, psychiatric evaluation has a high likelihood of being colored by personal biases and values, making its scientific contribution questionable at best.

The arbitrariness in determining what is mental disorder and what is not is apparent from dropping and adding new categories capriciously during the revisions of the classification. The American Psychiatric Association yielded to the power of the interest and pressure groups, adding new categories of mental disorders that were previously assumed to be human problems and not mental disorders. Any problem that may cause mental distress now has a place in the classification irrespective of its origins (e.g., cigarette smoking, coffee drinking, etc.). While in some ways this has put psychiatry on "trial" and raises questions about its credibility, in the other ways it has been dubbed as "psychiatric imperialism" (Szasz, 1974a).

THE PSYCHIATRIC ENTERPRISE AND THE POWER OF INTEREST GROUPS

The psychiatric enterprise, a medical specialty, is not free from business interests, because it provides employment to millions of people. In turn, it is also cultivated by interest groups, who lobby to boost their own interests or those of the enterprise. Such interests groups include politicians (who vote on mental health policy issues and funding), insurance companies (who would prefer to reduce the number of disorders so they will make more profits and compensate for only recognized disorders), pharmaceutical companies (to push their psychoactive products), banks (to finance safely in private mental health facilities and offices), and real estate and construction agencies (to make commissions or profit in new resortlike, corporate-run facilities), to name a few. Gradually, psychiatric enterprise has designated even the most trivial behaviors as mental disorders, thus advising that to be "normal" we should be treated.

The *DSM* has been expanding with each of its revisions. Feminists, for example, were appalled by what they considered a male bias in the early drafts. Girls who were "tomboys" were labeled as victims of "gender-identity disorder of childhood." The APA's Committee on Women had the specific clause rewritten to give tomboys a clean bill of mental health (Eitzen & Zinn, 1992, p. 522).

The critical evaluation of medical and psychiatric views of mental disorders is not meant to imply that mental disorders do not exist and medical and psychiatric treatment does not serve a purpose. Society is not devoid of people with mental disorders or emotional problems, and some of these have organic causes. The issues raised here relate to the definition of mental disorders, research findings about their causes, treatment, accuracy of diagnosis, and the role of the interest groups. In Chapter 4, social and psychological approaches to mental disorders are addressed. Depending on the theoretician's or therapist's orientation, they are viewed as complementary or adversary to medical and psychiatric views, as we shall see.

CHAPTER REVIEW

1. What are the essential medical and psychiatric views of mental disorders? Why has this approach been so influential in defining and treating mental disorders?

2. What is the relationship between brain pathology and mental disorders? Is it possible that one may suffer from a mental disorder and may not have brain pathology?

3. The psychiatric approach to mental disorders significantly differs from other approaches. Explain the basic components of the psychiatric approach.

4. The *DSM-III-R* utilizes dimensions or axes to evaluate the mental state of a person. List and explain the axes and their relevance in psychiatric evaluation.

5. The *DSM-III-R* classification lists mental disorders and their characteristics. Explain the limitations and strengths of this classification.

6. To what extent is genetic link associated with the probability of mental disorders?

7. To ascertain the role of family environment in mental disorders, family history studies have been conducted in various settings. To what extent have these studies been relevant in determining the impact of family environment on mental disorders?

8. During the past few decades, advances in neuroscience research have contributed to our understanding of mental disorders. What are these new findings?

9. What do we mean by "biochemical revolution in mental health"? How has this revolution dramatically changed the treatment strategies of mental disorders? What are its unanticipated consequences?

10. In what ways has pharmacological research changed the field of mental health? Critics charge that drugs are simply treating the symptoms and not the disease. What is your opinion?

11. The psychiatric approach to mental disorders has been criticized on several fronts. Do you think such criticism is valid?

12. Identify the following:
    a. Somatic therapies
    b. Concordance rate
    c. The dopamine hypothesis
    d. Electroconvulsive therapy
    e. Psychoneuroimmunology

FOR FURTHER STUDY

Andreasen, N. (1984). *The broken brain.* New York: Harper & Row.
Gregory, R. L. (1987). *The Oxford companion to mind.* New York: Oxford University Press.
Kotulak, R. (1989). Inside the brain. *Chicago Tribune* (special series May 8–15), pp. 1–20.
National Institute of Mental Health. (1989). *The neuroscience of mental health.* Rockville, MD: U.S. Department of Health and Human Services.
Papolos, D. F., & Papolos, J. (1988). *Overcoming depression.* New York: Harper & Row.
Shore, D. (Ed.). (1987). *Schizophrenia.* Rockville, MD: National Institute of Mental Health.
Szasz, T. S. (1987). *Insanity: The idea and its consequences.* New York: John Wiley & Sons.

▶ 4

Social and Psychological Approaches to Mental Disorders

The sociological approach to mental health is a relatively new field of inquiry. Generally, sociological studies are categorized by the level of their analysis. For example, *macrosociology* concentrates on large-scale analysis of civilizations, phenomena, and societies. Thus, epidemiological studies—the studies that relate to the extent and distribution of mental disorders throughout the United States, hospital admission rates in the United States, and the extent of schizophrenia in the United States, the former Soviet Union, and Japan are examples of macrosociology or macro-level approach in sociology. *Microsociology* or micro-level approach in sociology, stresses studies of small groups and utilizes experimental methods, and in some cases controlled situations in laboratories. Examples include studies of asylums and relationships between doctor, patient and hospital staff. Sociological writings and research have advanced our understanding in some crucial areas and determined the following (Brown, 1985; Dohrenwend & Dohrenwend, 1974b; Foucault, 1973; Scheff, 1984; Szasz, 1987):

1. Rates of mental disorder are associated with the degrees of social solidarity in a society.
2. When the level of tolerance for social deviance or different people and groups declines, the rates of mental disorder are likely to increase.

3. Most mental disorders, unless there is clear evidence of a medical problem, originate in personal as well as interpersonal conflicts.
4. Societies that are subjected to rapid change and transformation of values show a greater propensity to increases in mental disorders.
5. Societies in which personal aspiration levels are high but means of goal attainment fail to fulfill those aspirations generally reflect high rates of mental disorders.
6. Placing high value on economic and class enhancement as the only indicator of personal success contributes to higher rates of mental disorders.
7. Where the legal system requires greater adherence to certain values, any deviant form of behavior can be labeled as mental disorder.
8. The label of "mentally ill" allows people in power to maintain their authority and to seek obedience from those who are identified as inferior or subordinate.
9. Mental health as a concept is used by those who claim to be the champions of a better society to promote their business interests, claiming the prevalence of new kinds of mental disorders and finding revolutionary ways of treating them.
10. In the process of defining mental disorders, elements of discrimination (such as age, sex, class, ethnicity, religious association, and lifestyles) are ignored or overlooked because doing so serves the interests of the guardians of society.

Theoretical approaches to the studies of mental disorders are (1) person centered, and (2) system centered (studies of large aggregates, institutions, communities, and national or cross-national studies). Both of these approaches have relevance depending on the objectives of research. The treatment of a manic-depressive person by a therapist in his or her office will be a person-centered approach, while the studies of manic depressives in all or several selected state mental institutions across the United States will be called system centered.

SOCIOLOGICAL APPROACHES TO MENTAL DISORDERS

When we talk about any behavioral disorder, we are primarily considering social behavior. We know from the terms and concepts used in identifying mental disorders that many entities in psychiatric nomenclature are dependent on sociological manifestations for their detection and definition. Theoretical explanations of mental disorders are diverse and often seem competing; however, each has some merits and limitations in the sense that it is grounded in substantive social facts. We discuss some of the major theoretical perspectives or models in this chapter.

THE SYMBOLIC INTERACTION PERSPECTIVE

People, Emotions, and Social Situations

As people interact, their conduct is governed by certain normative requirements and their actions are judged by themselves as well as by others. Most such judgments involve what is considered morally right and appropriate or necessary in a given situation. Whereas many conceptions of right and wrong are deeply ingrained in society, it is not necessary for everyone to internalize them to conform in a literal sense. Often, violations of normative standards give rise to intense feelings of guilt, and people may react with a sense of outrage. For example, the same religious preachers or evangelists, politicians and corporate business leaders who talk of strengthening our morals, rooting out corruption, helping the poor and distraught, and uplifting the society act in ways that are diametrically opposed to what they say. Their actions lead to confusion and loss of faith and confidence among the trusting people. The relationship between what people do and what they feel and say and what they ought to do is complex (Deutscher, 1973). When someone acts in ways that others find strange, unacceptable, or threatening, means of social control (such as indifference, criticism, ostracizing from the group, and labeling the person as deviant) are put to work. Such actions have emotional consequences. At the heart of most mental problems are self-feelings that are the basis of emotions.

Role of Emotions in Mental Disorders

What is emotion? "*Emotions are* self-feelings. *Emotionality*, the process of being emotional, locates the person in the world of social interaction. *Self-feelings* are sequences of lived emotionality, often involving the feeling and experiencing of more than one specific, named emotion. Such experiences always have self-referents; that is, they refer back to the self of the person who feels them" (Denzin, 1984, p. 3). Further, Denzin stated that *moods* are emotional states of mind that transcend specific situational experiences, and *feelings* are sensations of the lived body. All emotions refer back to the person who feels, defines, and experiences them (Denzin, 1984, p. 3). Contrary to the views of many theorists and the sociological position we take in this book, Freud (1965b) saw emotions outside of consciousness, in the unconscious, the hidden layers of the conscious that surprise, paralyze, and cause grief as well as joy to individuals. Emotions are not simply cognitive responses to physiological, cultural, and structural factors or forces but are interactive processes as social acts involving interactions with others. A person's self is usually the manager of feelings, the emotional experience (Denzin, 1984, p. 50). Thus emotions reflect our feelings, sentiments, and expressions of like, dislike, love, hate, jealousy, anger, frustration, and fear, among others. Sometimes when people become excessively emotional, we say they are "irrational" or "out of their mind." For instance, at the death of a loved one, each member of the family may manifest different degrees of grief. For some the grief may be overwhelming and unbearable, causing anxiety or depression. Emotions form the foundation of many of our mental disorders.

Thomas Scheff (1979, p. 49) theorized that emotions are states of bodily tension produced by stress, and if not impeded by appropriate learning, socialization, or interactive processes, these emotions are instantaneously discharged. For example, these may include crying hysterically or being in a state of frenzy due to a breakup of a romantic relationship or death of a loved one. Like Freud, Scheff considered physical tension caused by emotions but explained them in behavioral terms. Scheff classified emotional states into two categories: (1) emotional distress (grief, fear, anger, and boredom), which, in the absence of intervention and loss of controls, may be displayed in a variety of states leading to emotional outbursts; and (2) emotional discharge, which may be expressed spontaneously or through *catharsis*—purging of the repressed emotions, through rage, shivering, weeping, and storming (Scheff, 1979, p. 49). This idea of catharsis eventually became the guiding principle of *rational-emotive therapy*, developed by Albert Ellis. Ellis felt that humans are self-talking, self-imagining, and self-evaluating. He viewed emotions at the center of irrational thinking and behaving. Ellis contended that irrational thinking is a natural human phenomena and afflicts all of us to some degree. However, a person's emotional disturbance (anxiety disorder, depression, or psychosis) consists of mistaken, illogical, and often unproven negative feelings in which the person believes and emotes, and often acts, to his or her own defeat (Ellis, 1967, 1984; see also Chapter 13).

Do emotions have physical and physiological consequences? The fear of something untoward occurring may increase respiration, heartbeat, and restlessness and lead to hyperventilation, insomnia, and other problems that may not have any physiological basis. Failing to overcome grief is associated with inability to sleep and concentrate, withdrawal, uneasiness, and sometimes mood swings. Emotions have physiological components. A group of mental disorders, known as somatoform disorders, are generally manifested in physical symptoms for which there are no verifiable organic or physiological evidence. Some observers believe that the same intense responses characterize all emotions and self-labeling (Thoits, 1985). It is the label that differentiates them from others (Kemper, 1981, pp. 336–362).

When someone's expression of emotions becomes intolerable, disruptive, dysfunctional, or severe enough to demand attention, we tend to label that behavior (for example, "He is a maniac"). People evaluate the person so labeled and adapt their interactions and responses accordingly. Our behavior is shaped by labels, such as "He is really weird, acts like a psycho," or "She is a very nice person." The emotional experience thus involves self-objectification as much as any other personal or social experience. Often, such experiences are identified and labeled as mental disorders.

What do we mean by *situation*? We speak of a social situation as an occasion, a social phenomenon, an activity located in space as well as in time. It is an intersection of *meaningful* time and space in which people act and to which they sometimes refer in objective terms. We frequently use the expression, "I don't know how he got into that situation." So a situation may have a past and a future. We experience a situation in a place that has a social context, meaning, and perspective(s) that exist within it and from which social reality is constructed (Hewitt, 1984, pp. 139–146). Often, it is a problematic situation that receives our attention and for which a resolution is sought. Any socially relevant behavior occurs in specific, concrete, and usually known circumstances that allow us to understand a familiar configuration of acts and objects, which is known as the *definition of the situation*. From the symbolic interactionist perspective, human conduct consists of people's actions in relation to definition of the situation.

Situations can be classified in two categories: (1) routine and (2) problematic. Most of our life is spent in *routine* activities, such as going to work. These are familiar to us and are generally not disruptive or threatening. In contrast, some situations are *problematic* or become *problematic* when the definition of the situation becomes unclear and uncertain. It is not so much that a problem situation exists, but that it upsets the routine. The importance individuals impute to a situation means that the individuals consider that situation real and consider the consequences real. For example, a minority woman who believes that she has been discriminated against everywhere may decide not to look for work anymore. The *self-fulfilling prophecy*, as a concept and theory, holds that if someone defines a situation as real, it tends to become real in its consequences (Thomas, 1923).

Social Construction of Mental Disorders

The symbolic interactionist analysis of human behavior has its roots in the philosophy of pragmatism (practicality). This philosophical tradition, which is identified with intellectuals such as Charles Pierce, William James, John Dewey, Charles Horton Cooley, and George Herbert Mead, provides us with the understanding that living things make practical adjustments to their surroundings. Human conduct is thus not only a social reaction but an adjustment to the environment. The study of human conduct allows us to examine the social processes by which mental disorders are conceptualized:

1. Mind and conduct are inescapably liked together, and the origins of the human mind lie in human society.

2. Human conduct is so varied, complex, and culturally diverse that it cannot be explained by instincts but by mental events and can be made accessible to observation. We report our inner experiences, and in this way they become observable.

3. People use symbols, gestures, and language to communicate and to establish interactive processes. We are not only attuned to overt bodily movements (also called body language) of others and ourselves, but also to a variety of verbalizations that accompany individual acts. More frequently, we mentally rehearse our actions in advance in relation to a particular situation based on our experiences. A person thus interprets the situation and constructs an appropriate response. This process allows the person to attain *control* over his or her conduct. Failure to have control over one's situation is often labeled as a mental disorder.

4. People's control over their own conduct gives them a form of consciousness of the *self*. Individuals have the capacity to employ symbols in imagining responses of others to their own acts, which in turn gives them the capacity to be conscious of themselves (Cooley, 1902, p. 152). Most human responses are not perfect and demand various levels of understanding, tolerance, and communication skills. When the responses do not meet expectations, the self is disenchanted, frustrated, angered, and sometimes withdrawn. Many mental disorders reflect such agonizing experiences that relate to self and disagreeable responses of others.

5. Ongoing human experiences in different situations lead to a set of expectations about how people in such situations should behave. These sets of expectations may be called *roles*, which relate to *positions* (father, son, doctor, bus driver, etc.). Roles have a normative component (i.e., they tell us how people normally or usually behave in different types of positions). When behavior fails to meet these expectations, we regard the behavior as deviant and attach labels to the individuals who faltered.

6. Role identities are crucial to our social existence, and once ascertained their meanings for us are established. Identifications in terms of broad social categories like military ranks (private, corporal, sergeant, and lieutenant) yield a person's *social identity* as opposed to *personal identity*, which is derived by identifying the person in terms of a set categories referring to unique individuals (Goffman, 1963), such as George Washington, the first president of the United States. Personal identities serve as the coaster

on which social identities can move up or down. If an individual could not be recognized from one occasion to another as the same person, no stable relationships could be constructed. It is especially important to note that when a person is identified as mentally impaired, the person is regarded as different from a mentally healthy person. Efforts are made to manage by the use of a variety of therapies, including drug therapy, those behaviors of individuals that are identified as mental disorders (see Box 4–1).

SOCIAL DEVIANCE PERSPECTIVE

Deviance is a term that is invariably used for many different kinds of behavior. It may range from not paying one's bills to manslaughter. At a group level, it may range from street-corner gangs to corruption at the highest level of government. *Social deviance* is behavior that violates the standards of conduct or institutionalized expectations shared by a group or society (Dentler & Erikson, 1959, p. 98; Wickman, 1991, pp. 85–87).

Another way of looking at deviance is that it refers to behavior to which the group responds with feelings of danger, embarrassment, and indignation and brings special sanctions to bear against the person in question. Erikson stated that deviance is not a property *inherent* in any particular kind of behavior; it is a property *conferred* on that behavior by the people who come in direct contact with it (Erikson, 1966, p. 6). For example, parents may tolerate or even admire the hyperactivity of their child at home, but teachers may call the same activity a behavior disorder and may ask the parents' cooperation to seek treatment for the child. Mental disorder is ascribed to people as a function of the definition given to certain types of acts by certain audiences (Spitzer & Denzin, 1968, p. vi). Due to the threatening nature of deviance, the consequent societal response of punishment or maltreatment is usually morally uplifting for society and sets more demanding standards of conduct (Durkheim, 1938, pp. 68–69; Matza, 1969, p. 13).

Deviance can only be understood in its social context. For example, a woman may be occasionally obnoxious to her husband in their home, but the same behavior in a department store may be seen as deviant. Often, we do not notice the differences among subcultures and view some practices as deviant from our own standards. Among Hispanic people, it is acceptable that a man carry a macho image and wield his authority as head of the household, and a wife is supposed to accept a subservient position in the family. This may be seen as deviant from white, middle-class standards.

Deviance, then, is a highly relative phenomenon. Social reaction to mental disorders is colored by ignorance, indifference, discrimination, exclusion, exploitation, control, and various other forms of neglect and

> **BOX 4–1 • Managing Mental Disorders**
>
> In our search for quick remedies to our problems, prescription drugs have taken a new place in our lives. An estimated 15 million Americans are diagnosed as suffering from clinical depression, and antidepressants are a booming business. No one knows quite how these drugs relieve depression. However, a few things *are* known. They bolster the action of serotonin and norepinephrine, two of the chemicals that transmit impulses through the nervous system. The trycyclics (Elavil and Tofranil) work by blocking reabsorption of these messengers by the nerve cells that release them, and monoamine oxidase inhibitors (MAOIs), such as Nardil and Parnate, interfere with enzymes that break the messengers down.
>
> Prozac (Fluoxetine), a new wonder drug for depression, hit the market in late 1987. Sales reached $125 million in 1988, soared to $350 million, and were expected to pull $500 million in 1990 and to top $1 billion by 1995. Over 650,000 prescriptions are filled every month. What we don't know is whether any wonder drug can treat depression if it arises from a job-related problem, a marital discord, or an argument with a nasty neighbor. Further, even if depression is associated with cancer, hypothyroidism, or AIDS, depression itself is not a clinical diagnosis; it is probably a consequence of the morbid nature of the physical ailments. In either case, as you may have surmised, prozac or one of the other antidepressants are the likely drugs to be prescribed. All such drugs have side-effects (some known and many unknown and some fatal), including headache, upset stomach, nervousness, blurred vision, urinary retention, constipation, dry mouth, drowsiness, dizziness, insomnia, sexual dysfunction, and continuous erection. Yet they help the person to feel better. However, the problem remains. Even the best of drugs, such as prozac, are effective in treating symptoms in only 60% of the cases of depression. However, the recent negative publicity that prozac has driven people to commit suicide or murder has received international attention and costly law suits against the pharmaceutical company, manufacturer of prozac.
>
> In short, in the absence of any quick remedies and due to our inability to resolve our personal and interpersonal conflicts, we are increasingly finding solace in the use of psychotropic drugs. These drugs have become our best friends, healers, and therapeutic agents to combat our personal consternation and to help us in managing our problems.

Adapted from Cowley et al., 1990, pp. 38–44.

punishment. Table 4–1 presents a comparison of major conceptual approaches to mental disorders. A brief discussion of each of several explanations of mental disorder within the framework of the deviance perspective follows.

TABLE 4–1 • Major Conceptual Approaches to Mental Disorders

Approach	Conceptual Framework	Treatment Strategies
Medical	Mental disorder is a disease of the brain, should be treated as any other illness of the body, and is culture free (i.e., like any other disease it can occur in diverse cultural settings).	Psychopharmocology (drug therapy), electroshock therapy (EST), psychosurgery (brain surgery), and psychotherapy (commonly known as "talk therapy")
Social deviance	Any act or pattern of behavior may be called deviant because it constitutes the infraction of group norms and is consequently labeled as deviant. Such violations visible to the public may include mental disorders, and labeling them as deviance is inherently stigmatizing and dehumanizing.	Avoid labeling; it leads to a self-fulfilling prophecy; educate society to develop greater tolerance of residual rule breakers, because rule breaking is usually a reaction to societal conditions and strained interrelationships. Develop awareness of the areas of conflict, and seek solutions.
Mental illness as myth	Mental illness is not the same thing as disease of the brain, which is a neurological defect. Individual traits or behaviors that deviate from what society considers morally or socially normal are not mental disease. They are caused by problems in living—by unmet needs and interpersonal conflicts.	Reduce and possibly eliminate situations that cause problems, and educate society to tolerate human variations in personality traits and behaviors. Traditional psychiatric treatment harms people and robs them of their potentialities by controlling and labeling them.

Labeling Theory

Labeling is an act of an audience by which it assigns a label to an individual based on inferred or observable facts. In fact, labeling is simply an explanation. Further refinement of this concept, with emphasis on status and class variables, gave rise to *social reaction theory, social stress theory*, and *social selection theory*. Whenever a person deviates from the group norms, a *label* is attached to the person. The label represents the quality of people's responses to an act and is not a characteristic of the act itself. The behavior labeled as deviant identifies such people as "outsiders" (e.g., the young men who resisted the draft in the 1960s, during the Vietnam War were labeled as "dope heads," "antiestablishment," "freaks," and "unpatriotic") because those who follow the group norms strengthen the integrity of the group or status quo and are treated as insiders. Thus deviance is not the quality of the act a person commits, but rather a consequence of the application by others of rules and sanctions. The deviant person is one to whom that label has been successfully applied (Becker, 1963). The label may lead to a deviant career. *Primary deviance* is the rule breaking that occurs prior to labeling. *Secondary deviance* is the behavior resulting from the labeling process (Lemert, 1967, pp. 42–43).

At least four interactive processes are involved in the labeling process: (1) A person acts in ways that are viewed as deviant by the normative standards of a group to which he or she belongs (primary deviance); (2) the group labels the individual as deviant (e.g., an eccentric, a sex addict, an alcoholic, a psychopath) and modifies its relationship with the person accordingly; (3) the individual's perception of the group's response reinforces the deviant identity ("This is the way they want me to be and that is what I will be, since I don't have better alternatives at the moment"); and (4) the person's subsequent reaction to the group response further reaffirms deviant identity (secondary deviance). A 42-year-old accounts executive in a brokerage firm seeks treatment at his wife's insistence. She is fed up with their marriage; she can no longer tolerate his emotional coldness, rigid demands, sexual disinterest, offensive temper and bullying behavior, long hours of work at office, and frequent business meetings and trips. This person feels no dissatisfaction and distress in his marriage. He agreed to consultation with a therapist only to humor his wife.

He is known as a hard-driving member of a hard-driving brokerage firm. He is famous for enlisting hundreds of new clients, however, finds himself increasingly unable to keep up. He has had five or six assistants a year for sixteen years. No one can tolerate working for him for very long because he is so critical of any mistakes made by others. He loves his three children but treats them as if they were mechanical dolls. He is punctilious in his dress, ponderous in his speech, dry and humorless, with a stubborn determination to get his point across. He has been very successful at work and made a great deal of money. He says he loves his wife but has trouble understanding why she is dissatisfied. In this case, the psychotherapists diagnose this man, because of his excessive devotion to work and success, as suffering from a prototype of obsessive-compulsive personality disorder. For his wife, friends, co-workers, and subordinates he is a rule breaker. Becker (1963) argued that the distinction between rule breaking and deviance is important. Following Becker, Scheff (1984, p. 36) pointed out that because identification of mental illness is based on "symptomatic behavior," it involves (1) rule breaking and (2) deviance. *Rule breaking* refers to a class of acts or behavior that involves the violation of group norms, which may or may not be formalized into law.

Most psychiatric symptoms are instances of *residual rule breaking* or *residual deviance*. The culture plays a significant role in defining the severity of norm violations, such as homicide, robbery, prostitution, obscenity, and ill manners. These categories include only specified acts and violations but leave out a residue of most diverse kinds of violations for which culture provides no explicit label. Level of tolerance of cultural diversity, rationality, and personal beliefs in each group determine the definition of norms and reality but provide no way of handling of violations of the group's expectations. For instance, an affluent local bank president who worships demons and communicates with other spirits to find ways to enhance his business fortunes, a Catholic priest who offers communion to people who admittedly commit adultery, and a woman who believes that she has been told by a higher spirit that her newborn child is an incarnation of Satan represent unthinkable violations for most people. Such violations are diverse, unnamed, and lumped together into a residual category. Although society tries to define residual behavior, it finds it undefinable and therefore uses labels, such as "mentally ill" (a vague category at best), to reconcile with residual deviance.

Goffman (1969b) examined residual behavior in public places and illustrated how normal people are perceived to show their presence by their "involvement," and how withdrawal and hallucinations are regarded as violations of residual rules. People who are seen in public loitering or hanging about are viewed as breaking residual rules (due to lack of socially approved involvement) because our norms center around the expectation that a person appearing in public should be involved in and/or doing something. We expect, in our busy life, that someone who can afford the luxury of frittering away time must be either a saint or "out of his mind." To prove our sanity, we like to appear engaged and involved, and we use cover for our disengagement and reverie, often by culturally accepted solitary activities such as craft work, painting, fishing, and sun tanning. But a homeless person walking down the sidewalk or sleeping on the park bench is suspected of being mentally ill. Thus, lack of involvement means breaking a residual rule and attachment of an unwarranted and stigmatic label.

The label of "mentally ill" has other serious personal consequences. Once a person is labeled as mentally ill, the person is robbed of his or her sanity and ability to make rational and meaningful decisions about self and the rest of the society. Kai Erikson (1962) developed a scenario—a ceremony that deviants typically go through. First, the person is taken as incompetent to make any rational decision. Second, the person is apprehended (though he or she may not have committed any crime). Third, the person is taken to a public facility (police station, Salvation Army, hospital, a shelter, or to a mental institution for a short-term stay). Fourth, psychotropic drugs may be administered. Fifth, the person is released. Chances are that the person will again be on the streets and will repeat this ceremony. The labeling perspective, though insightful, has some flaws, which are discussed at the end of this chapter.

Attributional Theory

Another explanation parallel to labeling theory is *attributional theory*. It is compatible with the assumptions of symbolical interactionism and deviance. According to attributional theory (Jones & Davis, 1965; Kelly, 1983), reality construction is a symbolic process and centers on the organization of experiences and perception of events. Thus, perceptions of and about friends, neighbors, racial and ethnic minorities, and mentally impaired people originate from the attribution process. Rather than looking for a cause (which to attribution theorists is not relevant because it cannot be objectively verified) the concern is to examine how events are organized. For example, a homeless person squatting on the sidewalk in Washington, DC will not only prompt the imagery of a skid-row bum but also of a poor, unskilled, unemployed, unhealthy, and possibly mentally impaired person. Attribution is a much wider process and may lead to labeling. A teenager from a minority broken home who frequently runs into discipline problems at school is viewed as a person raised in a "bad home environment." Such explanation, whether based on personal qualities or environmental factors or both, has a great deal of bearing on the decisions and actions of the observer(s).

Social Learning Theory

People learn from what they experience in their social environment. In general, psychologists place greater emphasis on principles of conditioning and reinforcement, while sociologists place greater emphasis on the socialization process. In psychology, the behavioristic view is organized around one central theme—the role of learning in human behavior. It is tied to experimental work on the form of learning known as *conditioning*. The Russian physiologist Pavlov discovered the *conditioned reflex* and demonstrated that a dog would learn to salivate to nonfood stimuli, such as a bell, after the stimuli had been regularly accompanied by the presence of food. Later this came to be known as *classical* or *respondent conditioning*. James B. Watson (1878–1958), an American psychologist, advanced Pavlov's discovery and applied it to human behavior. For psychology to become a true science, he argued, it must abandon the subjectivity of inner sensations and other mental events and focus on behavior. Watson reasoned that systematic changes in behavior can be brought about by rearranging stimulus conditions. This entails modification of behavior and replacing a negative stimulus with a positive one (reconditioning). *Reinforcement* is a process of learning wherein behavior can be modified by manipulating rewards and punishments. Thus, desired or positive behavior can be strengthened, while undesired behavior can be inhibited or eliminated (Skinner, 1971). Watson challenged both psychoanalysts and biologically oriented psychologists, suggesting that abnormal behavior is the product of unfortunate earlier conditioning and could be modified through reconditioning. However, what reinforcement can do in changing behavior in animal species may not be accomplished with the same degree of certainty among humans.

Watson's stimulus–response explanation was complemented by E. L. Thorndike (1874–1949) and later by B. F. Skinner (1904–1990). Skinner argued that behavior is influenced by consequences it produces. For example, if someone is extremely aggressive in obtaining material goals, with no particular regard for the interests of others, that person may run into problems with those who helped him or her obtain such goals in the first place. They may label that person as greedy, selfish, or egocentric and may withdraw their cooperation. Many such experiences may lead to frustration, anxiety, and even interpersonal crisis.

Socialization refers to the process whereby people learn the values, norms, attitudes, and actions appropriate to individuals as members of a particular group. Learning theory is similar to labeling and symbolic interaction perspectives and centers on actual behavior, rather than subjective meanings conveyed through interaction. Behavior can be observed, measured, and interpreted in an appropriate context. Those who have utilized learning theory are known as *behaviorists*. The primary group (family or peer group) is the focal point of learning social behavior, including deviant behavior and maladaptive behavior. Mental disorders are thus viewed as consequences of the learning process in which (1) a person fails to learn adaptive behaviors or competencies, such as how to establish positive and meaningful personal relationships; (2) the learning of ineffective or maladaptive responses is involved; and (3) the learning of ineffective behaviors may be tolerated and even encouraged in one's own group, while they may be viewed as deviant by the larger society.

Cognitive Theory

Cognitive theory emphasizes mental processes and the content of one's experiences. *Cognition* refers to intuitively mapping one's environment and understanding actions and events whereby deciding the course of action. Generally, people hold a coherent, stable and nondeviant view of their world that provides them with *cognitive consistency*. But this expectation is often met with alarming deviations and contradictions. For instance, a faithful wife of over 25 years never dreamed that her loving and caring husband would have an adulterous affair. She had a difficult time accepting that it could happen to her. A person faced with two contradictory or incompatible perceptions represents a case of *cognitive dissonance* (Festinger, 1957). Often, cognitive dissonance, though it may not be as real as it is perceived, has behavioral consequences because it demands reconciling with something unreal and unanticipated, which leads to feelings of mistrust, disenchantment, and dismay.

In effect, cognition reflects consciousness or awareness, which forms "reality" for a person. The world around us does not have a logic of its own that may lead to the same cognition for everyone. A person who claims to have reached the pinnacle of spiritual attainment may be viewed as a religious freak, a schizophrenic, a devoted person, or an oddball by different people. For example, someone may see a flock of birds in the street as a scene of nature's beauty, rather than an obstacle to traffic; a chemist may see a variety of colorful bottles in his laboratory as dangerous fluids; and a photographer may see the meaning in the pictures of city decay that most of us ignore or overlook.

An individual's perception of reality usually is not photographic but highly selective, based on his or her own experiences and understanding of the social and physical world. When a person is distressed by his or her social world, social judgments are also colored by distress itself. However, Krech, Crutchfield, and Ballachey (1962) observed that for each of us "there are no impartial facts" because they are based on our own experiences.

Role Theory

A role is a set of expectations held toward the occupant of a social status or position in a social group or society (Parsons, 1951). Role theory is akin to labeling theory. The major difference is that according to role theory the person accepts the role of mentally impaired, while in labeling the person is assigned a label of mentally ill by the social agents. We all conform to roles (e.g., doctor, engineer, salesperson, father, daughter, and neighbor) with some degree of flexibility, with the objective of attaining positive sanctions, or at least approval, from those holding the expectations and avoiding negative sanctions. *Role theory* holds that most mental disorders can be considered as social roles. It is through playing the role of an insane or mentally impaired person, by breaking residual rules in social situations, that the individual in question finds a place in a group and organizes his or her behavior accordingly. In such a case, accepting the role of insane is viewed by the person as a positive and rewarding experience and reaffirmed by those who profit from it. One may ask why a normal person would accept the role of an insane person. Out of the several alternatives a\ may have been the best one, given the circumstances.

Scheff (1984, pp. 65–72) examined the social processes that lead a person to the identity and role taking of an insane person. First, people who display insight into their mental problems are rewarded, and often the psychiatrist/therapist influences the manifestation of mental disorder. Second, once the person is identified as mentally ill, returning to normal life is discouraged through discrimination and refusal to assign the person roles that are commonly assigned to normal people. Third, when the person's role of an insane individual is publicly affirmed (e.g., alcoholic, psychopath, or schizophrenic), the rule breaker begins to think in terms of insanity and organizes the behavior in the framework of mental disorder. Fourth, the role playing as insane places the person through degradation ceremonies (such as the loved one's concern that the individual seems to have a mental problem and his or her rationality is in question, going to a therapist's office, being a patient in a psychiatric ward, commitment to an institution) (Garfinkel, 1956). Fifth, the new image of the insane as lacking the ability to control his or her own actions is solidified.

Thus, the social role of the mentally ill has its consequences. The pattern of symptomatic behavior in role playing is usually in conformity with the stereotyped expectations of others, thereby becoming a part of the person's self-conception.

SOCIAL REACTION, SOCIAL STRESS, AND SOCIAL SELECTION PERSPECTIVES

Sociologists have attempted to refine and explore the particular set of variables within the framework of labeling theory that define mental disorders. One such process involves *social reaction*. Mental disorder may be viewed as a social status rather than a disease, because symptoms of mental disorder are associated with social rather than medical contingencies (Scheff, 1984, pp. 90–91). Dohrenwend and Dohrenwend (1974b) reported that there is an inverse relationship between overall rates of mental disorder and social class. What is seen as psychiatric disorder among lower classes may simply be a reaction to their social circumstances. Further, being locked in a lower class, with limited opportunities, may be a major factor in *social stress*, generating symptoms of psychiatric impairment. Another way of looking at this is through *social selection theory*—those who are members of lower classes are placed in those classes due to their psychopathology. The operative process here is social selection. These theories tell us about collective social conditions and their association with mental disorders (see Chapter 9).

THE STRUCTURAL–FUNCTIONAL PERSPECTIVE

Functionalists view society as an organism in which each part of the organism contributes to its survival. This view emphasizes the way parts of a society are structured to maintain unity and integrity. When any of the parts fails to perform its functions adequately, it can threaten the unity of the society. When we refer to instability, disorganization, disintegration, and pathology, we are talking about the degree of dysfunctionality prevalent in a society, which may in turn affect individuals and lead to a variety of problems (mental disorder may be one of them).

Emile Durkheim (1858–1917), known for his sociological explanations, saw society as a network of relationships and individuals as products of social forces that influence them. For individuals, society is the reality that provides values, norms, statuses, roles, and a general system of operational rules by which the individual is governed. In his landmark study *Suicide*, published in 1897 (based on reported episodes of suicides in France, England, and Denmark), Durkheim found that whereas England had only 67 reported suicides per million inhabitants, France had 135 per million and Denmark had 277 per million. The obvious question was, "Why did France have such low rates of suicides compared to Denmark?" Durkheim did not accept the prevailing and unproven explanations of the causation of suicides. Rather, he suggested that suicide rates are associated with the degree of cohesiveness in a society. While suicide seems like a highly personal act, it is not entirely an act of free will and personal choice of the individual. Durkheim found that suicide rates in these countries were relatively constant for years in certain groups. Protestants had much higher rates than Catholics, and the unmarried had much higher rates than married people. There were more suicides in times of peace than in times of war and revolution, and more suicides in times of economic instability and recession than in times of prosperity. Thus, Durkheim developed a theory to explain how individual behavior can be understood in social context, suggesting that what may be known as highly personal acts are in fact consequences of the influences of groups and societal forces.

These findings prompted Durkheim to suggest that suicide is a "social fact" that is observable and measurable and can only be explained through the explanation of social interactions and social factors. Durkheim's explanation of suicide still holds true, contrary to the belief that people who attempt suicide have a genetic link to suicidal tendencies or have been cursed to take their own lives by some supernatural power.

The functional perspective is not a final statement and has been criticized for its shortcomings. Some of the criticisms are that (1) the perspective places too much emphasis on the social relationships and ignores individual rationality; (2) it emphasizes the ideal of an integrated society and ignores the role of competition and conflict in improving interpersonal relations; and (3) it undermines the importance of coping mechanisms people use by manipulating the social order to their advantage to adapt, survive, and succeed.

THE CONFLICT PERSPECTIVE

In contrast to the functional perspective's emphasis on unity, stability, and consensus, the conflict perspective concentrates on the social world marked by exploitation, power relations, inequities in the system, and an ongoing struggle between classes of people—the "haves" (bourgeoisie) and the "have-nots" (proletariat). The *conflict perspective* assumes that social behavior is best understood in terms of conflict and dissensions among individuals, groups, and institutions. Conflict can take a variety of forms, which may be manifested in alienation, frustration, rebellion, and revolt. Karl Marx (1818–1883), a German philosopher, intellectual, founder of communist philosophy and economic determinism, and critic of the role of the powerful institutions of feudalism and capitalism of his time, viewed struggle between social classes as inevitable given the exploitation of workers under capitalism. Georg Simmel (1858–1918), a German sociologist, however, did not see conflict as the "driving force of history" like Marx, but considered it relevant to understand all forms of conflict and to assess their outcomes and consequences for change. Both Marx and Simmel introduced the concept of "dialectics," which denotes the inherent contradiction in all social relationships. Thus, for example, *healthy* takes on meaning in reference to its opposite, *sick*. In a society, social order is a concept that implicitly refers to *social disorder*. For Marx, all social relations inherently imply their opposite, and each *social reality* contains contradictions that will actually *generate* or *cause* their opposites. Thus, feudalism contained the contradiction that eventually "caused" capitalism, and capitalism reveals the contradictions that will result in the downfall and the emergence of communism. The dynamics of change, therefore, result from inherent contradictions in social relations, and therefore conflict is inevitable (Turner, 1978, p. 125). Marx argued that social relationships between people are determined by their relative positions in society, through their relationship with the means of economic production in that society (industries, businesses, financial institutions, real estate, etc.). Some of the relevant elements of the conflict perspective are as follows (see Turner, 1978):

1. All social relationships are influenced by conflicting interests, though they appear congenial and cooperative.
2. All social systems and networks of relationships systematically generate conflict.

3. Conflict in relationships is inevitable, pervasive, and an enduring phenomenon.
4. Conflict tends to be manifested in relationships through the bipolar opposition of interests that cannot easily be reconciled.
5. Conflict occurs most frequently over the control and distribution of scarce resources, most notably money and power, and whoever has the most resources usually dictates the terms leading to exploitation.
6. Conflict is the major source of change in a society, but the direction of change is determined by those who own resources (political and economic). For a better society, these resources should be fairly shared.
7. Most problems of human society, such as alienation, role conflict, poverty, destruction of the family, neglect of the disadvantaged, and many mental disorders, are byproducts of conflict.

At the heart of the conflict perspective is the assumption that society is stratified, and those who own the resources (economic power) control the power structure and use that power (social power) to preserve that stratification and to gain and maintain that power. Not only do they use power legitimately but also by almost all available means, in some cases in subtle ways.

The conflict perspective concentrates on the ongoing struggle between the rich, affluent, and powerful and the poor, strapped, and mightless, in which the former usually are the winner. In a sense, declaring someone mentally deranged is one of the most effective ways to seek revenge and to oppress the weak. Mental disorder is a label used by the powerful for those who disagree with them; threaten their economic prowess; ask for their legitimate rights; demand better salaries, wages, and benefits; refute exploitation; assert justice; and popularize fairness in the system to which they belong. What the powerful people do, even if it is demeaning or deviant, is seen either in a positive light or as a hallmark of their success, or is shrugged off as the show of their power and wealth. In contrast, what the poor do is seen as immoral, undignified, and antisocial. For example, if a rich person commits adultery, it may be seen as a part of success and a manifestation of personal charm and attraction, but the same act by a poor person is labeled as moral failure, abrogation of the marital code, and debauchery. The powerful play roles as the harbingers of society and maintain the status quo, which ensures their power. Therefore, they either label or exclude from full participation in society those who do not conform to their ideals. Thus, those who deviate from the Protestant work ethic, materialistic lifestyles, heterosexual relationships, idealized family forms and sex roles and who question the practices of corporate greed and business ethics, corruption, and preferential treatment in government are subjected to scrutiny on mental health grounds.

The negative label of "mentally impaired" allows the powerful to control and oppress the weak (minorities, women, teenagers, and the aged) who usually are inadequately prepared (court costs, attorney fees, loss of work and pay) to defend themselves. No wonder they show up more frequently in mental health statistics, and no wonder minorities especially are overrepresented in mental institutions. On the contrary, the powerful and the affluent, even if they have mental problems, go free from these negative labels because they are able to afford private help and are rarely reported in official statistics.

The powerless are in so many ways victims of misfortune, instability in life (high rates of divorce, single parenthood, teenage pregnancies, dependence on the public welfare system, unemployment, crime and juvenile delinquency), inadequate living conditions, and lack of skills that often these personal situations become serious problems. Powerlessness leads to high levels of stress, frustration, anger, social deviance, and sometimes, in the absence of socially acceptable alternatives, to criminal acts. Consequently, for the powerless, the choices are limited and the powerful take advantage of this by stigmatizing them.

The conflict perspective thus suggests that it is not the individual who should be blamed for his or her mental suffering but the structure of society and the dominance of the powerful (usually the rich, who are often willing to find fault with the powerless). The conflict theorist's answer to the prevention and treatment of mental disorders is radical transformation of society, because society is the source of mental problems.

Although enlightening, the conflict perspective has serious limitations: (1) Mental disorders are universal phenomena and are not uncommon in socialist societies (the former Soviet Union, and the Peoples' Republic of China) where, at least in theory, people govern themselves; (2) class conflict also has been a universal phenomenon, and we have not yet found any society, including socialist societies, where powerful interest groups have not vied for power and influence and obtained benefits that have economic value; (3) the conflict perspective also ignores that many steps taken by the powerful are not intended to exploit the powerless but to ensure protection of all members of society; and (4) the conflict perspective fails to establish a causal relationship between the extent of mental disorders and the exploitation of the poor.

THE SOCIAL EXCHANGE PERSPECTIVE

Exchange theory has received little attention in the field of mental health. The concept of exchange is not new and in some ways represents the legacy of classical economics and utilitarianism. Georg Simmel, in 1917, focused on *reciprocity* and suggested that it was the foundation of everyday life and that "all human actions should be viewed as kinds of exchanges" (Levine, Carter, & Gorman, 1976, p. 823). Early anthropological works of James Frazer, Bronislaw Malinowski, Marcel Mauss, A. R. Radcliffe–Brown, Claude Levi–Strauss, and more recent theorizing by George C. Homans (1961) and Peter M. Blau (1964) have placed the exchange theory, in its various forms (such as exchange psychologism, exchange behaviorism, and exchange structuralism), in the forefront to seek better understanding of complex human phenomena.

Exchange theory contends that all interactions among people are based on the principle of cost/investment and are most likely to occur if all participants are able to realize profit from the relationship. It is not necessary that such investments/rewards always be financial—they may be subjective, such as love, concern, emotional satisfaction, approval, and self-esteem. One of the major implications of the exchange theory is that failure to invest and to benefit or inability to obtain reward staves off reciprocity, which in turn strains and jeopardizes a relationship and may have further consequences. Thus, in a marital relationship a man and a woman exchange love and a commitment to meet each other's needs and fulfill role obligations. Disbalance in the exchange system may work for a while, but it eventually leads to problems and causes frustration, conflict, and anger. Accusations flare up, and the participants begin thinking about the causes and solutions to the problem. Here the issue of *coping* emerges. Some participants are willing to negotiate and find ways by which they bring the exchange system back on track; others fail and *disengage* and *react* through expressions of unhappiness. The person who believes that he or she has invested the most in the relationship, and it has been unrequited, may feel cheated, exploited, and frustrated. The failure of the exchange system may precipitate a personal crisis and loss of control over rational thinking (withdrawal, high levels of anxiety, indifference, and depression), which may eventually be called mental disorder. Many mental disorders are in fact the byproducts or direct consequences of the failed exchange system.

The crucial element in this analysis is that people who are at a disadvantage, though not necessarily poor, subservient, or discriminated against, have a higher likelihood of expericing feelings of anxiety, fear, insecurity, frustration, and anger. High rates of divorce, child and spouse abuse, drug addiction, and alcoholism and many somatoform disorders may simply be the symptoms of the failed exchange system.

Critics of the exchange perspective say that (1) it is simplistic to reduce the value of human emotions to the transactions of an exchange system; (2) humans do not calculate as the exchange perspective says they do, because they have higher goals that are basically subjective, such as self-satisfaction, altruism, and personal sacrifice; and (3) if exchange is to work, costs should be clearly defined with identifiable gains, and people generally do not do so.

MENTAL ILLNESS AS MYTH: THE THEORY OF PROBLEMS OF LIVING

One of the most controversial explanations of mental disorder is that it is not an illness but rather a "problem of living." Thomas Szasz, who represents a minority but the most vocal opinion among psychiatrists, holds that the metaphor *mental illness* is not an illness as defined in medical science. Most mental illnesses are in fact *problems of living*, whether they are biologic, economic, political, or sociopsychological. Szasz holds that *mental illness is a myth* whose function is to disguise and thus render more palatable the bitter pill of moral conflicts in human relations (Szasz, 1974a, p. 1).

The basic assumption in this approach relates to the brain–mind controversy (see Chapter 1). If there is a *brain disease,* such as lesions or tumor in the brain, syphilis of the brain, or delirious conditions caused by intoxication or some neurological dysfunctioning or defect, it could affect the mental state of a person, but it is not a *disease of the mind* (see Chapter 1 for details). Suppose there is no brain disease, but the person exhibits symptoms of psychosis or manic depression. Should we call it mental illness? Bodily illness is something a person *has*, whereas mental illness is really something he or she is or does. Psychiatric diagnostic terms identify the person (for instance, neurotic or psychotic), which characterizes the person but does not name the disease. When a metaphor (a figure of speech founded on resemblance, by which a word is transferred from an object to which it properly belongs to another in such a manner that a comparison is implied, such as "that man *is* a horse" as opposed to "that man is *like* a horse," which is a simile or comparison) is used, meaning is mistaken for reality and is used for social purposes and we have the makings of myth (Szasz, 1974a, 1987, pp. 135–137). Distinguishing literal diseases, such as cancer, AIDS, or heart disease, from metaphorical diseases, such as love sickness, sex addiction, and mental illness, is essential.

The term *mental illness* has gained acceptance in the public because it transfers the responsibility for the causation of mental disorder from a member of the family, friend, employer, and other agents such as attorneys and estate executioners to the medical practitioner and frees them from a sense of guilt and irresponsibility. It is easier to transfer the responsibility for interpersonal conflicts, moral inadequacies, and failure to meet our social obligations to the domain of mental illness and seek treatment, because "illness" is an acceptable concept. The responsibility for the disorder is individualized, because it is personally and socially acceptable to stigmatize the person in question rather than a group of people, such as family, community, employer, and society. Szasz (1987, pp. 38–42) did not rule out the possibility of brain disease but was concerned about the people who are different, vocal and independent in their opinions, who are labeled as mentally ill. His major criticism centers on the medical model, in which mental problems are defined and conceptualized in sociopsychological terms that ignore sociopsychological factors.

Issues have been raised over the years on the analogy of mental illness to physical illness. There are significant differences.

1. *Onset*: Mental disorders often begin gradually, are triggered by certain episodes such as loss of self-esteem, sadness, grief or stress, and in many cases are disguised by other unusual or distinctive personality characteristics.

2. *Etiology*: Mental disorders are manufactured and molded, to a significant extent, by one's location in the social order, interpersonal experiences and crises, influence of significant people and situations, and social institutions.

3. *Symptomatology*: Indicators are often imprecise, questionable, and subject to various interpretations unless the person in question has acted out in ways that are readily identified as bizarre or at least unacceptable.

4. *Impact*: Mental disorder impinges on a person generally in a more profound and sweeping way and affects emotional, intellectual, perceptual, judgmental, motor, familial, interpersonal, and occupational functioning.

5. *Treatment*: Various kinds of therapies are utilized, but psychiatric treatment is most common. The treatment does not usually address the causes of the problem. There is no certainty that the treatment will work.

6. *Cure*: Most mental disorders are "managed" and "controlled," rather than cured, through medical treatment (Szasz, 1970a, 1974a, 1987).

The criticism by the adherents of medical model centers on one issue: that those who criticize the medical model do not offer any viable alternative treatments. Those who espouse sociological explanations criticize the business side of the psychiatric enterprise, maintenance of the status quo, and oppression of the victims, who include minorities, the poor, and women (see Box 4–2). There is some evidence in cases of severe mental disorders (such as schizophrenia) that genetic inheritance or biological causes may be responsible (Torrey, 1988a, pp. 144–145). Sometimes, critics of the medical model have been grudgingly rebuffed. Seymour Kety, a former Harvard psychiatrist, said, "If schizophrenia is a myth, then it is a myth with a powerful genetic component" (Kety, 1974, p. 961).

> **BOX 4-2 • Insanity of Place: The Mental Institutions**
>
> One of the questions commonly asked is, Do we have an objective test for normality or for abnormality? Is it possible that psychiatric diagnosis can be fallible? David Rosenhan (1973) conducted a study to answer this question.
>
> Eight pseudopatients (which included a psychology graduate student in his twenties, three psychologists, a pediatrician, a psychiatrist, a painter, and a homemaker, for a total of five men and three women), who were given pseudonyms, volunteered to seek admission in 12 different mental hospitals in five different states on the east and west coasts. They complained of hallucinations and hearing voices. They were admitted to the hospitals. Except for name and job, no further alterations were made in their personal history or circumstances. The hospitalization ranged from 7 to 52 days, with an average of 19 days. As soon as they were admitted, they ceased simulating symptoms of abnormality but were not detected as being fakes by the hospital staff. They acted normal and followed instructions, except to swallow medications. Some of the "real" patients quickly realized that the newcomers were a bunch of shysters and remarked, "You are not crazy, you are a journalist, or a professor checking up on the hospital." The pseudopatients took notes for this research, and apparently no one cared, as this was assumed to be a symptom of their illness. The pseudopatients were told that they would get out only if they could convince the staff that they were sane. Obviously, pseudopatients had to be cooperative, and the staff reports indicated that each one of them was "friendly," "cooperative," and "exhibited no abnormal indications." All were released with a diagnosis of schizophrenia "in remission." In one private hospital, one pseudopatient was diagnosed as manic depressive; 11 out of 12 were diagnosed as schizophrenic.

Adapted from Rosenhan, 1973, pp. 250–251.

THE PSYCHODYNAMIC PERSPECTIVE

It is known that mental disorders cannot be fully understood without exploring the psychological makeup of the human personality. The most known and controversial figure who revolutionized the thinking about psychopathology is Sigmund Freud (1856–1939). His *psychoanalytical perspective* and the psychological treatment approach he developed, called *psychoanalysis*, has influenced the field of mental health for over half of the past century. Several variants and interpretations of the psychoanalytical perspective have emerged over the years that are known as *psychodynamic approaches*. Freud, a brilliant Viennese physician, was influenced by Mesmer, Liebeault, Bernheim, Jean Charcot, and Joseph Breuer. He believed that hypnosis might be the best technique to unravel the powerful mental processes that remain hidden in the inner layers of the unconscious—the portion of the mind that embodies experiences of which we are unaware. Further, Freud discovered that to know the mind fully, the subject should be allowed to express himself or herself freely, irrespective of the nature of thoughts, logic, rationality, or decency. This technique is known as *free association*, and it laid the foundation of *psychoanalysis*. Let us briefly discuss its principles and their limitations.

Id, Ego, and Superego

Freud suggested that personality is composed of three abstract subsystems—id, ego, and superego. *Id* relates to opposing instinctual drives. *Life instincts*, which are primarily sexual, refer to almost any activity that is pleasurable. They constitute the *libido*, which operates on the *pleasure principle*. The foundation of the pleasure principle is that the id is driven by instinctual demands, with no regard for social norms. *Death instincts* relate to destructive drives that might lead to death. *Ego* develops through the mediation of the id's demands and the realities of the social world. Thus, ego operates in terms of the *reality principle*. Both id and ego are governed by the *superego*, which is composed of norms, values, and moral principles and regulates the behavior of the individual. The interplay among these systems determines behavior; however, the striving for different goals by each system is often the cause of *intrapsychic conflict*.

Mental disorders are viewed as reflections of intrapsychic conflicts. The question is, Who does not have such conflicts? Jahoda put it this way: " If it is reasonable to assume that such conflicts are universal, we all are sick in different degrees. Actually, the difference between anyone and a psychotic may lie in the way he handles his conflicts" (1958, p. 13). Karl Menninger, distinguished American psychiatrist of the post-World War II era, said, "We say that all people have mental illness of different degrees at different times, and that sometimes some are much worse, or better.... Gone forever is the notion that the mentally ill person is an exception. It is now accepted that most people have some degree of mental illness at some time" (Menninger, 1963, pp. 32–33).

Anxiety, Suffering, and the Unconscious

Freud maintained that most mental disorders are associated with feelings of fear and apprehension, causing "psychic pain." He classified anxieties into three categories: (1) *Reality* anxiety stems from the dangers, as perceived by the subject, in the external world; (2) *neurotic* anxiety originates from the id's attempts to disregard ego controls that may entail a possibility of punishment; and (3) *moral* anxiety arises from actual or contemplated actions that are in conflict with the superego, causing feelings of guilt and remorse. Often, people cope with anxiety by rational measures. When they are not able to, they resort to measures that may appear illogical and irrational, called *ego-defense mechanisms*. These defense mechanisms may take a variety of forms, such as denial of reality, fantasy, repression, rationalization, projection, reaction formation, displacement, emotional insulation, intellectualization, undoing, regression, identification, overcompensation, acting out, escaping, and splitting. Consider an example of rationalization: A man uses contrived "explanations" to conceal or disguise his loss of sexual interest by using the mechanism, "The scriptures do not recommend sex for pleasure, only for procreation." Similarly, displacement occurs when pent-up feelings of resentment and hostility are discharged on objects less dangerous than those arousing the feelings: A woman who experiences harassment and frustration by the demands placed on her by her boss may run into frequent arguments with her husband at home. Statements like, "You don't seem to care about me; when was the last time you said you loved me" are symptomatic of the displacement process.

Often, resentments, frustrations, hurtful memories, and forbidden desires are *repressed*. It is like we put on a mask to conceal our real selves in ways that are socially acceptable. Freud proposed that such feelings remain in the *unconscious*, and the conscious part of the mind represents only a small area, like the tip of the iceberg. The unconscious continues to seek expression, although the person may be unaware of it, in dreams and fantasies, when ego controls are either lowered or eliminated. Psychoanalysis brings such unconscious feelings to the surface, through the analysis of dreams and fantasies, and integrates them into the ego. Until that happens, the individual acts in irrational ways.

Psychosexual Development

Freud is probably most known for his conceptualization of the psychosexual development of the human personality. Each stage is associated with a mode of (sexual) pleasure: (1) oral stage (birth to age 1); (2) anal stage (ages 2 to 3); (3) phallic stage (ages 3 to 6); (4) latency stage (ages 6 to 12); and (5) genital stage (age 12 to adulthood). Failing to graduate from one stage to another results in *fixation*. Such a fixation might lead to maladaptive behavior later in life. Among Freud's most controversial formulations are his concepts of *Oedipus complex* and *Electra complex*. Oedipus, a young boy in Greek mythology, inadvertently killed his father and married his mother. Freud hypothesized that every boy, at the phallic stage, has incestuous cravings, perceives his father as a hostile rival, and fears that the male parent may seek revenge by removing his penis. The fear causes him *castration anxiety* and represses his sexual feelings. Failing to overcome repression might lead to disturbances in his psychic makeup. The Electra complex represents the female counterpart of the Oedipus complex and *penis envy* among girls. Its appropriate resolution may determine a girl's future social and psychological adjustment. Freud did not offer any reasonable explanation similar to castration complex among girls, except that they are able to resolve their conflict when they marry and have male children—finding replacement of their father (Freud, 1966, pp. 304–338).

Over the years, Freud's contributions have received intensive scrutiny, and the introduction of psychotropic drugs in the treatment of mental disorders during the last 40 years has relegated psychoanalysis to a secondary position, for it is very time-consuming and expensive. Each theory and its application has limitations, and psychodynamic theory is no exception. Some of the criticisms are as follows:

1. Freud's conceptualization of sexual attraction patterns between people of the opposite sex within the family, and their relationship with anxiety disorders, makes him a determinist and limits exploration of other causes of anxiety.
2. The exploration of psyche through the analysis of dreams and hypnosis even today remains an art rather than a science, and its objectivity and validity are suspect.
3. The central place of psychosexual development in mental health places unusual importance on childhood experiences but discounts the importance of learning and social experience throughout one's life.
4. Freud's theories do not address the macrolevel problems per se, the large scale social phenomena in a nation or civilization such as social stress, poverty, crime, and homelessness, but see them as microlevel problems of individuals and small groups, such as the family, and as products of the aggressive and destructive instincts present in human nature.
5. Psychodynamic theory ignores cultural differences in shaping behavior.
6. Psychodynamic theory lacks scientific evidence to support many of its concepts and assumptions, even to evaluate the effectiveness of its therapy.

THE HUMANISTIC PERSPECTIVE

The humanistic perspective is not new but has been revitalized recently by William James, Gordon Allport, Abraham Maslow, and Carl Rogers, among others (see Chapter 13). American society, in the 1950s and 1960s, saw a tremendous growth in affluence and material comforts. It also faced problems of moral decline, alienation, drug addiction, alcoholism, and spiritual emptiness. The humanistic way of resolving these problems was to empower people to solve their own problems. The major thrust of the new humanistic approach is the individual's future rather than the past, focusing on optimism, personal growth, acceptance of diversity, and attainment of self-fulfillment. In essence, the humanistic approach redefined and emphasized love, hope, compassion, values, creativity, meaning, personal growth, inner strength, and self-actualization.

Mental disorders, from the humanistic view, are the byproducts of distorted personal growth and extensive use of defense mechanisms to combat failure. Consequently, the person (1) is not able to accomplish his or her full potential; (2) becomes out of touch with reality; (3) is entangled in negative and faulty learning; (4) undergoes unwarranted pain and stress; and (5) loses rationality. In the humanist view, the goal of therapy, (at whatever level a person is) is to enhance self-esteem, find constructive ways to resolve conflicts, and foster personal growth, personal fulfillment, and effective methods of coping.

Although the humanistic perspective serves its purpose, it is not without its pitfalls; it is diffuse, lacks scientific rigor, and often attracts quacks who are good at sweet talk with no substance.

SOCIOPSYCHOLOGICAL APPROACHES TO MENTAL DISORDERS: AN EVALUATION

The theoretical perspectives described in this chapter are orientations of social scientists, especially sociologists and social psychologists. These scientists have largely contributed to our understanding of a variety of human problems at micro as well as macro levels. Many utilize this knowledge in policy making, planning, rehabilitative programs, counseling, and therapy. Social scientists' empirical knowledge and theoretical orientation provide a systematic viewpoint and direction to the application of their knowledge. However, no approach is perfect, and each has certain limitations sometimes influenced by ideologies, preferences, or biases. These operate as blinders and keep these scientists from seeing other factors that may be equally important.

The sociological orientation, especially dealing with mental disorders as deviant behavior through the application of labeling theory, has received the most criticism. In short, some of these criticisms are as follows:

1. Labeling theory is not theory at all because labeling does not create behavior in the first place. It does not explain why the behavior was enacted, the explanation of which is the foundation of any theory (e.g., why and how someone becomes a schizophrenic).

2. Labeling does not necessarily lead to deviant identity. For example, people who may have been treated for an apparent mental disorder and were able to modify their behavior are not labeled. If they are labeled, that labeled identity eventually disappears. Considering the variety of people and their geographic mobility, labeling is less likely to work if the person's history is not known.

3. Labeling does not explain the label of deviant behavior in all populations because labeling is activated by person, situation, and audience. The same behavior may be interpreted differently in two different situations to the extent that some deviant behavior may be interpreted in positive terms.

4. Labeling does not inevitably produce amplification of the symptoms of deviance or disorder. For example, a person suffering from depression does not have to go through recurring episodes of depression.

5. Evidence is not conclusive that those who are labeled are punished and stigmatized when they attempt to return to conventional roles.

6. Generally, it is not the label itself but the severity of the disorder that apparently causes others to identify the person as mentally disordered; social audiences do not appear to attach labels haphazardly (Cox & Conrad, 1991, p. 75). Cockerham has questioned some of the assumptions underlying Thomas Scheff's labeling theory and suggests that it needs further refinement (Cockerham, 1979, 1990).

Another criticism leveled is that sociologists and social psychologists do not offer any treatment alternatives, except to say that the mental health system is dominated by interest groups, particularly the psychiatric enterprise, that unnecessarily treat many problems that are not mental problems.

The discussion in this chapter reveals that there are several very different ways of looking at mental disorders. These explanations have significant implications in the understanding and treatment of mental disorders. Considering the variety of mental disorders, one explanation may be more appropriate for some mental disorders than others. Finally, we are confronted with new issues, including questioning the concept of mental disorder. Following chapters will further address the issues raised in relation to specific mental disorders.

CHAPTER REVIEW

1. Explain what is meant by the sociological approach to mental disorders. Illustrate your answer with examples.

2. What is the difference between microlevel and macrolevel approaches to mental disorders? Are they interrelated? Explain.

3. Sociologists are criticized for the varieties of perspectives they follow in explaining mental disorders, which are sometimes viewed as competing approaches. How can we best address this criticism?
4. What are the basic elements of the symbolic interactionist approach to mental disorders? Do you think this approach is more appropriate than others in explaining mental disorders?
5. Sociologists often suggest that most mental disorders are manifestations of social deviance. In what ways does society contribute to the construction of mental disorders?
6. List and discuss the similarities and differences between labeling and learning theories of mental disorders.
7. Sociologists believe that a person identified with mental disorder is not only labeled but assigned a role. Explain the significance of this process in the context of role theory.
8. How does the structural–functional perspective approach mental disorders? Discuss.
9. Conflict theorists look at mental disorders as consequences of social and economic conflicts between the classes. Do you agree or disagree? Defend your position.
10. What does Thomas Szasz mean by "the myth of mental illness"? What are the arguments that strengthen his position?
11. Which are the essential ingredients of the psychodynamic approach to mental disorders? On what grounds has this approach been most criticized?
12. Explain briefly the following:
    a. Self-fulfilling prophecy
    b. Social selection theory
    c. Residual rule-breaking
    d. Attributional theory
    e. Cognitive dissonance
13. Identify and explain the following:
    a. Secondary deviance
    b. Exchange theory
    c. Psychoanalysis
    d. David L. Rosenhan
    e. Humanistic approach
    f. Regression

FOR FURTHER STUDY

Denzin, N. K. (1983). A note on emotionality, self and interaction. *American Journal of Sociology*, 89, 402–409.

Erikson, K. T. (1962). *Wayward puritans: A study in the sociology of deviance.* New York: John Wiley & Sons.

Freud, S. (1966). *Introductory lectures on psychoanalysis.* (J. Strachey, Trans., Ed.). New York: W. W. Norton.

Grusky, O., & Pollner, M. (Eds.). (1981). *The sociology of mental illness.* New York: Holt, Rinehart and Winston.

McCall, G. J., & Simmons, J. L. (1978). *Identities and interactions.* New York: Free Press.

Scheff, T. J. (1984). *Being mentally ill.* New York: Aldine.

Szasz, T. (1987). *Insanity: The idea and its consequences.* New York: John Wiley & Sons.

Warren, C. A. B. (1987). *Madwives: Schizophrenic women in the 1950s.* New Brunswick, NJ: Rutgers University Press.

▶ 5
Anxiety, Mood, and Stress-Related Disorders

Linda, who is 35 years old, has not changed for years. She has felt somewhat depressed for as long as she can remember. She never had any motivation to do anything or enough energy or concentration to complete her college degree or hold a job. When her second marriage fell apart, she was left with three small children, little income, and a lot of stress. Linda feels sad, guilty, helpless, and depressed. She sleeps and eats too much and has gained 50 pounds in the year after her divorce.

Bob, 45, is hard working, a go-getter who is always looking for social and career advancement but is disillusioned with his life, family, and job. His wife's career goals haven't helped much. Bob believes she has neglected the family and domestic chores. He feels trapped and angry and does not hold much hope for the future. Bob's only daughter has become a drug addict and hasn't seen Bob or his wife in 3 years, and their son has survived several suicide attempts. Bob cannot sleep well, has nightmares, and tries to drown his overwhelming sadness in alcohol.

Linda and Bob may be showing symptoms of depression. We all go through some rough times and are sometimes overwhelmed by anxiety-causing, temporary episodes and situations in our lives. The Englishman William Cullen, in 1769, used the term _neurosis_ for such anxieties, which he believed were caused by disordered sensations of the nervous system. However, such sensations may have been caused by the problems we face in day-to-day situations, and their origins may lie in our attitudes, values, and interpersonal relationships. People develop *comfort zones* in their social functioning, which are determined by what they have learned through socialization. They also learn how to react in certain social situations and crises, and possibly to avoid unpleasant situations as much as possible. Robert E. Park (1950, p. 249) aptly said that "a person is a mask." Just as actors present certain images, individuals present only certain features of their personalities and conceal other characteristics that are not socially desirable. Thus, in a way, we are wearing a mask when we present ourselves in everyday life. While the stage presents things that are make believe, life presents things that are real and sometimes not well rehearsed. It is in this kind of situation that individuals may experience a lowering or breakdown of integral adaptive and coping mechanisms, leading to personal and interpersonal problems and subjecting them to stressful situations. Once long-lasting damage to a person's self-concept and self-esteem has occurred, it places a person in a vulnerable position. Generally, when a person suffers from a mental problem, the problem shows a wide range of other symptoms and a series or combination of several related problems. For instance, a person who is complaining of insomnia might also exhibit symptoms of tension headaches, stomach upsets, nervousness, dizzy spells, back pains, paranoia, negative thinking, fear of "cracking up," and hostility toward loved ones. Such problems accompany serious interpersonal difficulties, and one problem leads to another, making life difficult to bear.

GUILT CULTURES AND SHAME CULTURES

Comparative studies of societies have shown that they are classified into *guilt* and *shame* cultures. Most historical societies and most cultures of Asia are regarded as shame cultures, which primarily use shame as a means of social control and conformity. The societies of Western Europe and North America rely on internal sanctions to assure conformity by creating a sense of guilt or challenging the "conscience," and they are identified as guilt cultures. These concepts are relative, as there are no absolute shame cultures or absolute guilt cultures (Piers & Singer, 1971, pp. 59–70). However, this dichotomy allows us to examine the far-reaching consequences of guilt in personality formation, goal orientation, defining success, handling personal and social problems, and in determining moral consequences of deviance and the probable nature of its punishment. Yalom (1980, pp. 276–277) suggested a distinction between *neurotic guilt* and *real guilt*. Neurotic guilt emanates from *imagined* transgressions and is an individual's emotional reaction in a disproportionately powerful manner against certain individuals, taboos, or against parental or political authority. Real guilt flows from an actual transgression. While neurotic guilt, due to the sense of badness involved, relates to the wish for punishment, real guilt must be met by actual, or symbolically appropriate, reparation. A teenager who dreams about killing one of his authoritarian parents may suffer from neurotic guilt, whereas if he has acted out his dream or fantasy, he might face the consequences of real guilt. Chances of mental disorders increase when guilt is individualized and the responsibility for guilt is not shared.

On the positive side, guilt cultures are highly individualized—there is a great emphasis on individualism, freedom, and personal success; they are capable of progressive and technological change and materialism; they are possessed by absolute moral standards that are effectively enforced by a religious conscience; and they subscribe to war to handle disputes and to embark on crusades to seek betterment of life and dignity for the individual. Shame cultures, in contrast, are characterized by diametrically opposite characteristics. It is the element of personal guilt in a culture that is believed to be the cause of many mental disorders, especially anxiety, mood, somatoform, sleep, dissociative, and adjustment disorders. It is estimated that 15 to 20 million people in the United States suffer from a variety of anxiety-related disorders (NIMH, 1985b). It is not unusual to find that in real-life situations a person may suffer from more than one mental disorder. In this chapter we discuss generalized anxiety disorders, bipolar disorders, phobic disorders, obsessive-compulsive disorders, somatoform disorders, dissociative disorders, sleep disorders, adjustment disorders, and stress-related disorders.

ANXIETY DISORDERS

Anxiety and fear are among the most common elements in many mental disorders and are characterized by feelings of apprehension, anticipation, and a sense of impending crisis or disaster that may be real or imagined. Often disabling, irrational, and unrealistic, and intense fear of something overwhelms a person. Such fear is not uncommon. But if it is chronic and persists for an extended period (6 months or more, according to DSM-III-R), it is viewed as a cause of concern and it is a mental disorder. Generally, the anxiety leads to maladaptive functioning primarily due to the failure of coping mechanisms. *Coping mechanisms* are specific, conscious, often rational psychosocial personal adjustments that allow a person to overcome unpleasant or anxiety-causing situations. Failure to cope with the anxiety renders a person helpless, and in a fervent effort the person finds solace in making excuses for inability to cope, using defense mechanisms. *Defense mechanisms* are specific, intrapsychic adjustments people make by deploying meaningful alternative strategies to resolve emotional conflict and to reduce anxiety. Such strategies, which are in the interest of protecting the self, may involve two processes: (1) to avoid the anxiety-causing situation by logically explaining the situation to others, probably to those who may influence the person's self-esteem adversely; and (2) to voluntarily find a means of escape by rationalizing ways to avoid anxiety (a healthy young person who may be a hypochondriac may castigate others for being sloppy about sanitary precautions). Most of the coping mechanisms are learned, and therefore social learning and environmental setting plays a significant role in determining the level of adaptation and survival in a given crisis. Often excessive anxiety results in somatic (related to body) manifestations, such as trembling, restlessness, shortness of breath, frequent urination, trouble falling asleep, and being keyed up or agitated. Many of these indications are misinterpreted as symptoms of physical disease. However, if a physical or medical examination of a person shows no indications of a bodily disease, chances are that the person is suffering from one of the anxiety disorders. Although anxiety might be caused by many different factors and situations, for clinical purposes the DSM-III-R categorizes seven types of anxiety disorders: panic, agoraphobia, social phobia, simple phobia, obsessive-compulsive disorder (or neurosis), posttraumatic stress disorder, and generalized anxiety disorder. There is a certain degree of overlap among these disorders. In actual life, anxiety disorder may be only one of the disorders along with several others. Thus, for example, it is possible that a person may suffer from more than one anxiety or multiple and interrelated anxieties, along with mild psychosis and adjustment disorder. Currently, most anxiety disorders are treated with psychotherapy and biochemical therapy. Drugs used in biochemical therapy have serious side-effects and sometimes cause drug dependency (see Table 5–1). In the following pages, we discuss the most common types of anxiety disorders. Precise figures about the extent of these disorders are not known.

The Extent of Anxiety-Based Disorders

The most severe mental disorders, such as schizophrenia, manic-depressive disorder, and personality disorders, are relatively easily identifiable but are found in a very small portion of the population. Many of the anxiety-based mental disorders, in their initial stage or milder form, are not easily detectable because they are not disabling, dysfunctional, and constrictive, and often the sufferers find ways to cope with them. If there is any way to estimate the frequency of such disorders (and this may or may not accurately tell us about the population at large), it is to examine the findings of the epidemiologic and mental health services.

A NIMH Epidemiologic Catchment Area (ECA) study reports that over a 6-month period, 70% of patients with affective disorders visited a general medical care clinic and only 20% visited a mental health professional

TABLE 5-1 • Frequently Used Medications in the Treatment of Anxiety Disorders

Class/Generic Name	Trade Name	Used to Treat	Side-Effects
Antianxiety (Minor tranquilizers)		Most problems in which anxiety, tension, and hyperactivity are prominent symptoms. Also used to treat obsessive-compulsive, adjustment, convulsion, and phobic disorders.	Each drug varies in achieving the intended purpose of anxiety reduction. Drowsiness, dizziness, constipation, nausea, vomiting, and general lethargy are common manifestations. Most antianxiety drugs cause dependence and toxicity and if used for extended period may lead to dangerous consequences.
(a) Propanediois meprobamate	Equanil Miltown		
(b) Benzodiazepines Diazepam Chlordiazepoxide Flurazepam Oxazepam Clorazepate Alprazolam Prazepam	Valium Librium Dalmane Serax Tranzene Xanax Centrax		

Adapted from Flaherty, Channon, & Davis, 1988; and Goodman, Rall, & Murad, 1985.

(Shapiro et al., 1984). However, not all those who suffer from mental disorders necessarily seek professional help or are admitted to a hospital. Further, in many cases, even those who have mental problems are not classified as mental patients. On the other hand, those who may not have mental problems are often classified as mental patients. About 50 to 60% of mental patients in the United States are treated exclusively within the general medical care system (Regier et al., 1978; Shapiro et al., 1984). Currently, the tussle among the physicians relates to a substantive issue: Who should treat those patients who complain of some kind of mental problem? This raises another question: Who should determine that the person has a mental problem and possibly refer the person to an appropriate care giver? It appears more of a turf battle between the primary care-giver physicians and psychiatrists. It is argued that despite the high prevalence of mental disorders in primary care patients, one third to one half of psychiatric illnesses are not accurately diagnosed by physicians because most of them are not referred to the specialists—the psychiatrists (Katon et al., 1987; Nielson & Williams, 1980; Schulberg, Saul, & McClelland, 1985). Further, should they be treated by psychologists? Or should they not be treated at all, because as soon as a person's situation changes, factors responsible for the problem may also dissipate?

One of the explanations is *somatization* of the disorder—psychological distress manifested in organic complaints. Medical attention is sought for the disorder, which may not have a physical basis. This leads to a coping style of increased health care utilization (Katon, Ries, & Kleinman, 1984). There is no question that the United States is one of the leading countries in the use and overuse of medical services, and many of the services are obtained for nonmedical problems.

Epidemiologic studies report that from 25 to 33% of primary care patients suffer from a mental disorder diagnosable on a structured psychiatric interview (Bridges & Goldberg, 1985). Whether or not amplification of chronic medical symptoms (headaches, backaches, epigastric pain, insomnia) is associated with psychophysiologic symptoms, there is, of course, a tendency to avoid the stigma of mental disorder. But we are also ignoring the "sick role." Should we also consider that a person who has a medical problem, who assumes a "sick role," might also show symptoms of mental problems because of apprehensiveness and a feeling of having no control of life situations?

Frequent utilizers of medical services are also known to have high levels of psychological distress and poorer physical health status. It is difficult to say which is the cause and which is the consequence or whether there is simply an association between the two. Considering the complexity of the issue and a significant concern about the stigma of mental disorder (see Chapter 1), it is hard to find the true extent of mental disorders, especially those that are not disabling and do not attract immediate public attention.

PANIC DISORDER

When severe anxiety occurs, it may turn into panic. *Panic disorder* is characterized by recurrent attacks, which typically begin with a sudden onset of intense apprehension, fear, or terror (Rowe, 1989, p. 376). A panic attack is characterized by shortness of breath, palpitations, sweating, dizziness, fear of dying, and/or fear of going crazy. Often a person is able to identify and recount such episodes and rationalize them as irrelevant but is unable to control them. Apparently, the person is unable to cope with extremely high levels of anxiety and fear. Though such attacks are normally unexpected because they do not appear to be directly related to identifiable elements in immediate situations, they often are triggered by stressful life situations and anticipated crises. A panic attack thus reflects the peak of the anxiety level, although it is short lived and subsides in a short time. For example, a student who had a slow start in school is overwhelmed by deadlines to complete work, and a potential danger of failing several courses and being unable to stay in school may lead to panic. In some cases, people who suffer from panic disorder begin avoiding those situations that cause anxiety. One such example is *agoraphobia*, fear of being in places or situations from which escape may be difficult (or embarrassing) or in which help may not be available in the event of a panic attack. A variety of such fears lead to phobic disorders (see Table 5–2).

Findings in studies of the epidemiology of panic disorders are not consistent in patient populations, partly due to somatization of the disorder. Panic disorder is often accompanied by avoidance behavior, multiple phobias, high psychological distress, anxiety, depression, and personality disorders. A recent study estimated that 6.5% of primary care patients showed symptoms of panic disorder alone (Katon et al., 1987). Panic disorder is significantly more common among females than males, with a ratio of 3 to 1, reflecting the tendency of females to seek health care more frequently than men (Sheehan, 1983). In clinical populations the onset age of panic disorder is 22.5, and in an ECA study the highest 6-month prevalence was in the 25 to 44 age group (Myers et al., 1984). Still, we cannot be sure about the exact extent of panic disorders in the general population since they remain unreported, underreported, and misdiagnosed.

PHOBIC DISORDERS

A *phobia* is a persistent and heightened fear of a specific situation, object, or potential happening that in actuality does not pose a great danger but is perceived by the person as dangerous. It is distinctly different from a natural dislike, aversion, or avoidance reaction. It is not a *conditioned response*, which can be identified even in nonphobic populations. Most people are able to live with mild phobia and function relatively well by avoiding objects and situations associated with the phobia, and most do not need treatment. However, it is the distress, anxiety, and interference in one's life that usually calls for appropriate action. When a phobia is identified, it presents at least four characteristics: (1) It is object or situation related; (2) it manifests exaggerated or intense fear aroused by an object or situation; (3) it involves somatic symptoms, such as excessive sweating, dizziness, hot or cold flashes, tremor, and hyperventilation; and (4) it causes a certain degree of personal distress and dysfunctionality.

Estimates are that phobias are found in 1% of the population. Most people do not discuss, report, or seek treatment for mild phobias until they become troublesome and disabling and begin interfering with everyday activities. In some cases of phobia, the exaggerated fear leads to panic attacks, which are a desperate attempt to protect oneself from distress or from the fear of humiliation and public embarrassment. There are objects

TABLE 5–2 • Phobic Disorders

Phobia	Anxiety-Causing Agent(s)	Phobia	Anxiety-Causing Agent(s)
Acrophobia	High places	Monophobia	Being alone
Ailurophobia	Cats	Mysophobia	Contamination
Algophobia	Pain	Necrophobia	Dead bodies
Aphephobia	Touch	Nyctophobia	Night/darkness
Astraphobia	Thunder/lightning	Ocholophobia	Crowds
		Odyneohobia	Pain
Aquaphobia	Water	Paraphobia	Sexual perversion
Claustrophobia	Closed places	Pathophobia	Disease
Chrematophobia	Wealth	Phonophobia	Loud noises
Coprophobia	Excrement	Photophobia	Light
Decidophobia	Making decisions	Pyrophobia	Fire
Eurotophobia	Female genitals	Sitophobia	Eating
Gamophobia	Marriage	Spermophobia	Germs
Graphophobia	Writing	Thanatophobia	Death
Gynophobia	Women	Topophobia	Fear of performing (stage fright)
Hematophobia	Blood		
Kakorrhaphiophobia	Failure/defeat		
		Uranophobia	Homosexuality
Katagelophobia	Ridicule	Xenophobia	Strangers
Lalaphobia	Speaking	Zoophobia	Animals

and situations we all fear to some extent, such as high places, closed places, darkness, fire, floods, lightning, snakes, ferocious animals, crowds, strangers, or just being alone. Generally, it is the intensity of fear that causes panic attacks. Table 5–2 lists some of the common phobias.

A person with a phobia goes through the following phases:

1. A process of learning to fear a situation or object
2. Transparent displacement (i.e., the person substitutes a less fear-inspiring object for one difficult to deal with)
3. Manipulation of escape or avoidance mechanisms (e.g., in a case of ocholophobia, fear of crowds, a person might say, "I am a very private

person; rather than being part of a crowd in a concert hall, I would better enjoy music in the serenity of my home.")
4. The reinforcement process (avoidance of objects and situations in this case), which further intensifies the fear
5. Recurrence and stabilization of phobic behavior

At the chronic stage, frequent episodes of panic attacks are triggered by the intensity of the fear.

Because phobia involves fear, it has personal and social consequences. People with phobic disorder may elicit sympathy and increased attention from those who know about their problem. This is known as *primary gain*. They also obtain some *secondary gain* (benefits and favors received from being disabled). For example, a corporate executive who has a phobia of flying will delegate responsibility to someone else if air travel is involved. Phobic disorder may be thus used in many situations to *escape* from responsibility and at the same time to gain *control* over others. It may involve unmet needs, remote objectives, dependence, exploitation, personal insecurities, and fear of failure.

Regardless of the nature of phobic behavior, it originates in culture and is influenced by the agents of socialization. For example, a phobia of ice skating or ocean surfing will not be found where ice and ocean are not available, nor will a phobia of high places if there are no skyscrapers or tall buildings. Multiple phobias are not uncommon because each may serve a purpose, although some of them may be benign.

MOOD DISORDERS

Mood disorders are the "common cold" of major mental disorders, and an estimated 20 million Americans suffer an episode of depression or mania during their lifetimes (Papolos & Papolos, 1988, p. 3). One in five families will suffer from the impact of mood disorders. In psychiatric terminology, mood disturbances are also known as *affective disorders*, because the term *affect* has been traditionally used for emotion. Those who experience highs and lows have *bipolar disorder*, or manic depression, in which they veer from states of superactivity, elation, euphoria, and grandiose schemes to periods of blues, despondency, immobility, insomnia, guilt, and inability to experience pleasure. Frustration, negativity, unwarranted hostility, and pessimism dominate their thought processes. Those who suffer from either highs or lows have *unipolar* or *nonbipolar* mood disorder, which is considerably more prevalent than bipolar disorder.

Depression is an emotional state in which a person feels sad, blue, or unhappy. Such a state may be latent, and the person may appear normal, at

> **BOX 5–1 • Self, Morals, and Depression**
>
> Mrs. Betty Hutton, 65, a former school teacher, a religious person, and a mother of three children, retired some years ago. She lived in her home in a small town of about 500 people. Her husband died a few years ago in an auto accident. One of her sons lived in the neighborhood and dropped by occasionally to see her. She adored her grandchildren, especially 6-year-old John. Betty was lonely, and memories of her husband were never lost.
>
> One day in spring, while doing chores in her yard, Don, 65, a retiree and widower who recently moved next door, came over and introduced himself. He gradually sought Betty's attention. Betty never thought of falling in love again or remarriage. She thought those who remarry are not only unfaithful to their departed spouse but sinners. She was very concerned about her upright and righteous self-image. However, she could not resist the advances of Don. Betty was frightened that if the word got out, she would be devastated because she would not be able to live with shame.
>
> One morning, John came to deliver a piece of freshly baked pie and inadvertently saw Betty and Don together in bed. John ran away, leaving the pie on the table. Betty could not forgive herself.
>
> The fear of loss of her moral image caused her to descend into depression, and she began to experience an acute ache in her back and neck. Her condition deteriorated. She appeared sad and desperate. After over 20 visits to an area physician in six months, finally she underwent extensive tests at a major medical center, including evaluation by a neurologist and a psychiatrist. No physiological causes of her condition were found. Betty has been on antidepressants for over three years and hospitalized twice. Her diagnosis: severe anxiety disorder; major depression.

Source: Author's files.

least outwardly. Feelings of sadness and discouragement may be transitory or extended for a long period of time. Because of personality variations, depression can be very elusive and its consequences tragic (see Box 5–1).

The symptoms of depression are many and varied. They may include the following:

1. Loss of interest or pleasure in almost all usual activities
2. Poor appetite or weight loss or increased appetite and weight gain
3. Insomnia or hypersomnia or other sleep disturbances
4. Psychomotor retardation or agitation
5. Decrease in sexual drive

6. Loss of energy
7. Fatigue
8. Feelings of worthlessness
9. Self-reproach or excessive and inappropriate guilt
10. Difficulty in thinking and concentrating
11. Persistent restlessness and irritability
12. Suicidal thinking and/or attempts

Persistence or frequent recurrence of the depressed mood disorder, of at least two years' duration, is known as *dysthymia*. The presence of other disorders, such as alcoholism, drug dependence, or anxiety disorder, and older age of onset significantly increase the chances of its recurrence (NIMH, 1988, pp. 2–3). For some people, seasonal changes (particularly decreased exposure to daylight) seem to affect their mood. They experience depression during the winter and often mild highs during the summer. They are thought to have *seasonal affective disorder* (SAD).

Some individuals with manic syndromes (1) are persistently high or euphoric; (2) have irritable mood states; (3) are overindulgent and show signs of increased activity; (4) are overconfident; (5) use pressured speech; (6) have racing thoughts; (7) show loss of self-control and judgment; (8) show increased sociability; (9) show increased sexual drive; (10) indicate disturbed appetite; (11) feel a decreased need for sleep; and (12) usually are overoptimistic. Their mood is typically brittle and deteriorates rapidly into irritability. Others may become more active, restless, and talkative; feel that their thoughts are racing; have an inflated sense of self-esteem; are distracted easily; and engage impulsively in activities that could have serious consequences, such as buying sprees, sexual indiscretions, violent behaviors, or foolish business investments. Thus, mania leads to devastating consequences for personal relationships and careers. Manic episodes themselves are very disruptive and increase the likelihood of psychotic (i.e., delusions and hallucinations) behavior and suicide risk (NIMH, 1988, p. 2).

About 15% of untreated or inadequately treated people with an affective disorder commit suicide. An individual hospitalized for depression at some time in life is about 30 times more likely to commit suicide than is the nondepressed person. The chances of suicide also increase with advancing age. Depression is closely associated with alarming increases in suicide among young adults. Twice as many women as men suffer from depressive disorders, and twice as many women attempt suicide. However, men are two to three times more likely to kill themselves (Sargent, 1986, p. 6). Paradoxically, many complete the plans just as depression is lifting and they feel more energized and happy (Papolos & Papolos, 1988, pp. 13–14).

We briefly discuss depression in three major age groups: childhood, adolescence, and the elderly.

Childhood Depression

Depression can strike anyone at any time. *Childhood depression* is probably as common as it is among adults but is often unrecognized. Sadness, apathy, sleeping and eating disturbances, and, in severe cases, hopelessness and despair harbor suicidal thoughts. The loss of love, belittling, humiliating, rejection, physical, sexual, and emotional abuse, prolonged absence of care and nurturance, and perpetual parental conflict may precipitate childhood depression.

Adolescent Depression

Adolescent depression is often unrecognized because the problems of adolescents are viewed as normal adjustments in the process of transition to adulthood. Many adolescents experience generational conflicts, sibling rivalries, unrequited love, poor self-image, emptiness, anxiety, loneliness, hopelessness, helplessness, guilt, loss of confidence and self-esteem, erratic sleeping and eating habits, and they frequently face potential or real failure, which they are unable to cope with or reconcile. They try to cover their depression by acting out, which may include withdrawal, acting angry, aggressive, or violent, running away, and becoming a drug abuser, delinquent, or suicidal. Parental indifference, inattention, or inability to fulfill parental responsibility is usually at the heart of the emotional problems of adolescents. Adolescents often go through mood swings. However, sometimes a quick change in mood may be an attempt to present a cheerful self while covering up the hurt. Adolescents who seem socially withdrawn, uncaring, overly impulsive, indifferent to emotional attachments, and no longer interested in activities they once enjoyed should be carefully monitored and checked for possible depressive disorder.

Elderly Depression

Societies accept an arbitrary chronological age as a determinant of being old. In the United States, currently it is sixty five and widely accepted by various agencies of government, insurance companies, employers and the public. This irreversible biological condition of being old assigns these people a *master status* of elderly. This "new status" overshadows all other conditions and generally viewed in negative terms leads to stereotyping of and discrimination against people because they are old.

Depression among the aged, though not uncommon, is difficult to diagnose, and estimates of its occurrence range from 10 to 65% of the elderly population. It can be mistaken as senility (organic brain syndrome), memory loss, apathy, feelings of worthlessness and loneliness, and confused thinking. Interestingly, most elderly people rarely admit to feelings of depression, although they often have much to be depressed about—poor health, lack of money, loneliness, loss or death of loved ones and friends. Further, many of the illnesses that afflict the elderly (such as Alzheimer's or Parkinson's disease, cancer, arthritis, and other physical disabilities), as well as the medications prescribed for physical ailments, may precipitate depression.

OBSESSIVE-COMPULSIVE DISORDERS

An *obsession* is typically an idea, a feeling, an unwanted and recurring thought that preoccupies a person and cannot be excluded from consciousness. A *compulsion* is an impulsive, irresistible, and recurring act. *Obsessive-compulsive* traits are not uncommon among people and at times may even be considered desirable because they may demonstrate a greater sense of responsibility, cleanliness, being organized, or ability to accomplish desirable tasks. Columbus persisted for 18 years in his efforts to secure financial backing for his expedition to India, and Karl Marx studied history for decades and assembled evidence before he would present his ideas on class conflict and write a treatise on communism. However, people with *obsessive-compulsive disorder* (OCD) feel compelled to think and act against their will; they may realize the irrelevance of their irrational acts but do not seem to have control over them. Obsession may center on certain thoughts and ritualistic acts with a sense of urgency and unusual frequency (five to ten times in an hour), such as washing hands, taking showers (fear of dirt and contamination), checking door or stove knobs (making sure that the door is properly locked and safe or the stove is turned off so the house won't burn down), and, in many serious cases, thoughts of suicide, committing immoral acts, or poisoning someone.

The Epidemiologic Catchment Area study indicated that, within a 6-month period, about 1.5% or 2.4 million adult Americans suffer from obsessive-compulsive disorder. Like panic disorder, it is relatively common among females (NIMH, 1985b).

Obsessive-compulsive disorder has its links with anxiety and depression and represents irrational and exaggerated thoughts and actions in the face of stressors. Symptoms include lack of self-direction, indecisiveness, feelings of inadequacy and insecurity, rigid conscience development, low self-esteem, exhaustion, sleep and hormonal disturbances, and inadequate socialization. People suffering from obsessive-compulsive disorder are highly vulnerable to threat, appear overreactive or overaroused in the face of anxiety-causing agents, and are unable to relax. Most of them are concerned about issues of control, and many feel that they do not have control or that they are controlled by someone or something else. The ritualistic acts are intended to protect the person from that control or exploitation and are an exaggerated perfectionism to avoid terrible consequences. In some cases, this disorder itself becomes an effective means of managing a high level of hostility and aggression toward others.

SOMATOFORM DISORDERS

Somatoform disorders involve a group of anxiety-based disorders with physical symptoms for which no organic basis can be found. Although no organic cause for the disorder may be found, the person so affected sincerely believes that the symptoms are real and serious and need treatment. These symptoms should not be confused with malingering (feigning physical illness).

The Process of Somatization

Somatization is displayed in the form of psychosocial distress in an idiom of physical symptomatology and is associated with amplification of chronic organic and medical symptoms as well as psychophysiologic symptoms. It includes chronic headaches, backaches, muscle spasms, loss of vitality, low appetite, epigastric pain, and insomnia, among others. It is no coincidence that when attempts to cope with mental suffering fail, they are eventually manifested in disorders of body organs. Often, those who suffer emotionally seek medical help and show patterns of increased health care utilization due to chronic conditions, often with little improvement. Part of the problem is that the stressors present in the environment are rarely understood by therapists, and primary care physicians consequently the distress remains unabated. For many mental health therapists, and general medical practitioners these cases pose frustrating challenges because of their complexity.

The findings of epidemiological studies suggest that 25 to 33% of primary care patients suffer from a mental disorder that can be identified based on a structured psychiatric interview (Bridges & Goldberg, 1985; Hoeper, Nyezi, & Cleary, 1979). Another 20% suffer from transient stress-induced symptoms or chronic subclinical symptoms that cannot be clearly identified but are nonetheless associated with the patient's suffering. Further, studies in the past two decades have found that although there is a high prevalence of mental disorders in primary care patients visiting clinics and hospitals, one third to one half of these are not accurately diagnosed (Katon et al., 1987; NIMH, 1989; Schulberg et al., 1985). The primary reason for this discrepancy is somatization.

A recent survey of 350 primary care physicians (internal medicine, family, and general practitioners) indicated that anxiety is the most common disorder seen in their clinics (Orleans, George, & Houpt, 1985). Antianxiety medications, especially benzodiazepines, have consistently been among the most frequently prescribed medications in the United States over the past two decades. Moreover, more than 80% of these prescriptions were written by primary care physicians (Hollister, 1980). Physiologic complaints may be real and may be representing a psychologic response to acute or chronic medical illness, but in the absence of a clear diagnosis they are placed in the waste-basket category of *somatization disorder*. Various such disorders are identified by their symptoms.

Somatoform pain disorder refers to severe and lasting pain (duration of at least six months) for which no apparent physical explanation is found. It is also known as *psychogenic pain*, as it is believed to be psychologically induced. It is a common disorder and more commonly diagnosed among women. In some cases, the pain may be so disabling that the person either becomes addicted to pain killers or other medications and physical therapies which rarely solve the problem. *Conversion disorder*, also known as *hysterical neurosis* or *conversion hysteria*, involves a neurotic pattern in which some physical malfunction, limitation, or loss of control is reported without any organic pathology. This may include seizures, vomiting, blindness, mutism, deafness, and paralysis of certain organs. This disorder, which constitutes only about 5% of all neurotic disorders, presents one of the most baffling and intriguing phenomena in psychopathology. Hippocrates thought that hysteria was restricted to women and was caused by sexual difficulties; he considered marriage the best remedy. Freud used the term *conversion hysteria*, believing that symptoms of the disorder were an expression of sexual repression and psychosexual conflict that eventually *converted* into organic malfunction or disturbance. The Freudian explanation has declined in its popularity due to medical advances, growing sophistication in understanding organic and other causes of mental disorders in the general population, and changing sexual morality.

Conversion disorders were relatively common among lonely and sexually frustrated wives in the past and men in the military during wars. The disorder occurred in highly stressful combat conditions among men who were otherwise viewed as stable. Conversion involved being paralyzed in the limbs or legs or caused loss of memory, enabling the soldier to avoid anxiety caused by the horror of combat.

Hypochondriasis is a disorder in which a person is preoccupied with the body and a persistent anxiety related to health matters and unrealistic fear of disease. Hypochondriacs often lead relatively isolated lives but are prone to seek frequent medical attention. Often they are disappointed when no physical problem is found. Their morbid preoccupation with the body and its care and protection keep them engrossed in reading medical articles in popular magazines. At the same time, they are critical of physicians who are unable to find a physical cause of their problem. Some turn into "food faddists," and others experiment with exotic drugs and observe certain unusual and irrational prohibitions, including interacting with people.

DISSOCIATIVE DISORDERS

Dissociative disorders are characterized by disturbance or significant alteration of the normally integrative functions of identity, memory, or consciousness. In a way, the disorder allows a person to avoid stress while gratifying needs, without taking responsibility for unacceptable, antisocial, or even criminal acts. There are several varieties of dissociative disorders: (1) psychogenic amnesia, (2) psychogenic fugue, (3) depersonalization disorder, and (4) multiple personality disorder.

Psychogenic amnesia is the partial or total inability to recall past experiences. However, in this case it is not due to an organic cause but may be a consequence of other psychological disturbances. Psychogenic amnesia can be classified into four categories: (1) *localized*—inability to recall what happened during a specific period of time, such as after a traumatic event or accident; (2) *selective*—the person cannot recall everything but only part of the event; (3) *generalized*—failure to recall everything associated with one's life; and (4) *continuous*—the person cannot recall beyond a certain point in the past. In some rare cases, a person may retreat still further and is not only amnesic but wanders away from home and assumes a new identity. This is called *psychogenic fugue*. A fugue state is a defense by flight and may last from a few hours to several years.

Depersonalization disorder refers to a mental state in which a person experiences altered identity, has feelings of unreality, altered personality, and might deny his or her own existence. In essence, the person avoids stress or the impact of any traumatic experience by escaping—dissociating from his or her core personality. Some report that their body has drastically changed, has become grotesque. Others feel that their altered state was almost like an out-of-body experience or they visited other planets. One of the explanations for this disorder is that it is associated with high anxiety-causing episodes and an acute fear of losing control. Often the condition occurs with other personality disorders and is marked by elements of psychosis.

Multiple personality disorder (MPD) is a dissociative reaction in which there are two or more personalities or personality states within the person. It is different from other mental disorders, including schizophrenia, because the person does not manifest the signs of this disorder all the time. Each state has distinct, well-developed emotional and other unique characteristics of a distinguishable personality. The person alternates from one personality to another, varying from a few minutes to several years; however, more commonly the time frame is of short duration. Generally, different personalities are not aware of each other. In some cases, however, a *core* or *dominant* personality is in control while *subpersonalities* or *co-conscious personalities* function subconsciously or in the background. In most clear-cut cases of multiple personality, no personality knows anything about the other personality. The disorder is so rare that little is known about it and its causes. Recent case reports suggest that early childhood physical and sexual abuse and parental hostility and neglect may be causes.

Multiple personality disorder, although very rare, is so dramatic that it has been sensationalized by the media and has received a great deal of attention and publicity. There are questions about whether such a disorder actually exists, because in some cases the disorder has been used to dodge responsibility for criminal acts or to obtain public attention or financial gain, such as a motion picture or book contract. The following cases illustrate this point.

In 1977, William Stanley Milligan, 22, kidnapped, robbed, and raped over a dozen women in Columbus, Ohio, and was acquitted of all his crimes on grounds of insanity. He claimed to have 10 to 24 personalities. His sensational story became the subject of a major book and numerous articles. No one seriously contested his claims, and he became the first person in U.S. history to be acquitted on the grounds that he suffered from a disease called *multiple personality*. Yet, in other similar cases, such claims have not gone unchallenged (see also Chapter 6, "Factors Associated with Antisocial Personality").

During the 1970s, Kenneth Walker Bianchi, known as the Hillside Strangler, and his cousin and accomplice Angelo Bono picked up girls on various pretexts in the states of California and Washington. They raped, tortured, and often strangled them and left their bodies on hillsides. Bianchi was suspected of killing more than 20 girls, but he claimed that he did not commit the crimes—his other personalities did. The emergence of his other personalities was attributed to his domineering mother and bad childhood. During hypnosis, he revealed four different personalities. His defense attorney argued that Kenneth Bianchi was unaware of the crimes committed by his other personalities because he suffered from multiple personality disorder. The attorney asked for acquittal on all charges. Several psychiatrists and psychologists had examined Bianchi and made videotapes of his hypnosis sessions. One of the psychiatrists suspected that Bianchi was feigning hypnosis because his behavior was not consistent with hypnotic states, and the psychiatrist questioned the existence of multiple personalities. With all other evidence mounting, Bianchi confessed that he was faking hypnosis and the existence of multiple personalities.

After an unusually protracted and expensive trial, he was sentenced to eight life terms.

However, there have been other cases and claims of multiple personalities in which suffering has been limited to the victims themselves. One of the most bizarre and publicized cases of multiple personality is Sybil, who had three major personalities and 13 co-personalities, including two male identities (Schreiber, 1973). Sybil was the only daughter of a schizophrenic mother and a passive father. She was viciously abused by her callous mother from early childhood. Sybil's mother strapped her to a piano, broke her bones, burned her body, hung her upside down, and inserted a variety of objects in her vagina, to name a few abuses. Cornelia Wilbur, Sybil's psychoanalyst, observed that the division of Sybil's personality into a number of selves served to protect her against the horrors of her childhood (Gallagher, 1987, p. 119).

Thigpen and Cleckley (1957), in their book *Three Faces of Eve*, described three personalities of a woman and stirred a good deal of professional and public interest. In 1975, Mrs. Chris Sizemore of Fairfax, Virginia, revealed that she was Eve and published her autobiography, *I'm Eve*, suggesting that in fact she had 22 personalities. Mrs. Sizemore did not offer a clear explanation of her disorder but suggested that, "It was a defense and unique coping mechanism, which created satellite persons to cope with conflicts that were unbearable" (Sizemore & Pittillo, 1977).

Judging from the history of these cases, it would appear that stresses in life and serious problems in early socialization, such as severe abuse, neglect, and emotional trauma, have played their part. It is possible, however, that people under extreme emotional pressure may contrive a "new role" and dissociate themselves from their original personality, just to escape a set of unbearable circumstances.

ADJUSTMENT DISORDER

Adjustment disorder is a maladaptive reaction to an identifiable psychosocial stressor, within three months after the onset of the stressor but persisting no longer than six months. For most of us, the chances of experiencing natural disasters or terrors of war or imprisonment are remote, but even less dramatic situations (such as an impending job transfer, divorce, or going away to college) often become stressful. The response patterns to stress may vary from person to person and may involve *cognitive response* ("It makes me nervous"); *autonomic response* ("I felt shaky"); and *behavioral response* ("I cannot put up with this"). The severity of stress determines the level of response. Many situations act as stressors, such as *routines* (working the night shift); *single events* (grandma's death); *multiple events* (divorce and auto accident); *recurrent events* (driving on ice-packed roads); and *continu-*

ous events (fear of losing a job). Stressors are present in everyday situations and are part of our life. Often we are able to cope; they do not automatically lead to adjustment disorder. Highly stressed people often turn to heavy smoking, drinking, overeating, and drug abuse to fight stress.

POSTTRAUMATIC STRESS DISORDER

Posttraumatic stress disorder (PTSD) relates to an event that is outside the range of usual human experience and that would be markedly distressing to almost anyone (Rowe, 1989, p. 95). The disorder reflects sad and life-threatening situations, such as war, a loved one dying in an accident, destruction of one's own home, or being a victim of physical or sexual assault. The person may have experienced one of these events in the past, but the memories continue to haunt and trouble the individual. Many veterans who were participants in the war continue to remain intimate with the war and continue to be tormented by frightening years after it is over. Some who suffer from PTSD live in the jungle, preferring to subsist on things as if war is still on and they are camping in the backwoods. *Bush vets,* as they have come to be known, shun virtually all human contact even after returning home to the United States.

In August 1986, Patrick Sherrill, a U.S. Postal Service worker in Edmond, Oklahoma, used a .45-caliber pistol to kill 14 of his co-workers and then himself. At first, Sherrill's motive looked like revenge against his supervisor, but there was no clue as to why others were shot. At the house in which Sherrill lived alone, investigators found an array of ham-radio antennas, military paraphernalia, copies of *Soldier of Fortune,* camouflage dungarees, limbless human silhouettes, and dozens of bull's-eye targets. Ex-marine Sherrill sometimes talked of Vietnam, but he had never been to Vietnam. He lived with the illusion of being in war in Vietnam. Imagining himself to be a Vietnam veteran, he had flashbacks of shootings in combat. To some psychiatrists, this episode of mass murder fits with what they call *factitious posttraumatic stress disorder* because, although the person may not have been a participant in a war his imagination of being in war can cause PTSD and lead to actions as if he is fighting an enemy, in this case the innocent co-workers (Witteman, 1991).

THERAPIES AND THEIR OUTCOMES

Genetic Therapy

Our knowledge of genetic transmission of mental disorders is still limited, but there is some evidence that a genetic factor is involved. Studies of identical twins show that if one of the twins has affective disorder, the other twin has a 70% likelihood of being afflicted. Even in cases of early childhood adoptions, research carried out in New York, Brussels, and Denmark suggests that individuals with depressive disorders showed higher correlations with biological parents than with the adopting families. One of the crucial flaws of the research is that it ignores the emotional impact of adoption itself on adopted children. Genetic therapy at this time is in its infancy.

Biochemical Therapy

Three types of drugs—the trycyclics, the MAO inhibitors, and lithium—are commonly used to alleviate the symptoms of mood disorders (see Table 5–1). Two of the amines—serotonin (serves inhibitory functions) and norepinephrine (released by nerve cells and involved in the maintenance of arousal, alertness, and euphoria)—are concentrated in the areas of the brain that control drives such as hunger, sex, and thirst. Research suggests that abundance or depletion of these chemicals leads to chemical imbalance in the brain.

Certain physiological changes are also associated with depression. Changes in the production of the hormone cortisol increase when a person is exposed to stressful situations, leading to sleep disturbances. Depressed people also show increased muscle tension and heart and respiration rates.

Table 5–1 lists some of the many known side-effects of drug therapy. The drugs are initially administered to reduce the severe symptoms of the disorder. A NIMH (Sargent, 1986, p. 15) study compared the efficacy of short-term (16-week) psychosocial, cognitive behavioral, and interpersonal therapies with drug therapy. It found that after initial drug therapy, individuals (including those with severe symptoms) receiving the psychosocial treatments were equally symptom free by the end of 16 weeks.

Cognitive Behavioral Therapy

Emotions and actions are determined by how individuals view the world and interpret their experiences. Depressed people think negatively; obsessive-compulsive people are uncertain about what they do and repeat certain protective acts over which they seem to have no control; phobic actions are prompted by irrational fear. In all these situations, people make faulty inferences about other people, situations, and the intentions of others. Cognitive therapy's first goal is to provide the subject with insight into the origins of the problem and then to formulate strategies to encourage the person to shed maladaptive beliefs. Another goal is to promote realistic, logical, and positive thought processes and enhance self-worth. Psychiatrist William Glasser (1965), who found poor success rates of traditional psychiatric treatment and psychoanalysis, popularized the concept of *reality therapy*, a kind of cognitive therapy, in the 1960s. The objectives of the therapy are to lead the person toward reality, toward grappling successfully with the tangible and intangible aspects of the real world.

Interpersonal therapy is based on the premise that most anxiety-based, mood, and stress-related disorders occur in the context of disturbed personal and social relationships. Symbolic meanings are misunderstood, straining relationships and thereby causing, exacerbating, or perpetuating the dysfunctional cycle. People so affected are encouraged to understand their feelings and to focus on the positive in relating with others.

Research is still inconclusive as to the effectiveness of various kinds of therapies. For example, electroconvulsive therapy is said to be effective in very severe cases of endogenous depression and mania but not in dysthymic depression (Sargent, 1986, pp. 16–17). Some people cannot tolerate or respond to drugs. The side-effects of some drugs are serious, and some people cannot take them due to medical problems. For others, a combination of treatments is most effective—medications to control symptoms and to break the cycle of disorder, and psychosocial therapies to enhance understanding of the underlying problems and to resolve them by learning adaptive ways of relating to others.

The relationship between patient and therapist is probably more important for treatment success than the form of treatment used. Various kinds of therapists are available in the marketplace, some offering quick remedies and making easy money. It is no wonder that the therapy business is booming. It is not because therapists have some kind of panacea or are the greatest healers of our time, but we are looking for something that can offer us peace and heal our wounds. Often, we are faced with a dilemma: Should we change ourselves or change others? The answer lies in the question, Who is suffering? Those who are suffering should seek help.

The mental disorders discussed in this chapter are not uncommon and are relatively less disabling than severe disorders, such as schizophrenia. Most people are either able to cope with them or recover from them after appropriate therapy. There are probably millions of Americans who do not seek any treatment for these disorders. In Chapter 6, we discuss mental disorders that are not common and that have tragic personal and social consequences.

CHAPTER REVIEW

1. What are the characteristics of guilt and shame cultures? In what ways do they relate to mental disorders?

2. Why do we consider anxiety as the root cause of many mental disorders?

3. We do not know the extent of mental disorders in the United States. Why?
4. What is the distinction between panic disorder and phobia? Illustrate your answer with examples.
5. What is depression? How can we distinguish depression from other mental disorders?
6. What is the difference between somatoform disorder and obsessive-compulsive disorder?
7. Among the dissociative disorders, multiple personality disorder, though rare, has received much attention. Why?
8. What is adjustment disorder? Explain the phenomenon of posttraumatic stress disorder in the context of adjustment disorder.
9. Briefly explain the following:
    a. Coping mechanisms
    b. Agoraphobia
    c. Conversion hysteria
    d. The Hillside Strangler
    e. Cognitive therapy

FOR FURTHER STUDY

Conrad, P., & Schneider, J. W. (1980). *Deviance in medicalization: From badness to sickness.* St. Louis, MO: Mosby.

Goffman, E. (1963). *Encounters: Two studies in the sociology of interaction.* Indianapolis, IN, Bobbs-Merrill.

Kermis, M. D. (1986). *Mental health in late life.* Boston: Jones & Bartlett.

National Institute of Mental Health. (1989). *Panic: Disorder in the medical setting.* DHHS Pub. No. (ADM) 89–1629. Washington, DC: U.S. Government Printing Office.

Papolos, D. F., & Papolos, J. (1988). *Overcoming depression.* New York: Harper & Row.

Sargent, M. (1986). *Depressive disorders: Treatments bring new hope.* Rockville, MD: National Institute of Mental Health.

Szasz, T. S. (1970). *The manufacture of madness.* New York: Delta Books.

▶ 6

Schizophrenia, Psychosis, and Personality Disorders

In 1982, Haneda Airport in Tokyo was the scene of a shocking and tragic incident. A Japanese Airlines plane descended unusually fast, crashed into an approach light, and plunged into the sea. Of 174 passengers and crew members, 24 died and 147 sustained serious injuries. The Committee for Aviation Accidents found that the chief pilot of the ill-fated plane was having hallucinations and delusions at the time of the crash. Contrary to normal procedure (which is to respond with "checked"), 7 seconds before the accident the pilot responded to an auditory hallucination, in his hometown dialect, which commanded him to "go somewhere far." He maneuvered the plane to its tragic crash. The pilot had been under treatment for depression and a psychosomatic disorder or malfunction of the autonomic nervous system since 1976. In spite of clear evidence that he was suffering from schizophrenia, he was not diagnosed a schizophrenic because that would have brought a bad name to him and his family (Munakata, 1989, p. 203). People in the United States often feel the same way about schizophrenia; it is a cruel disorder surrounded by a multitude of myths. In this chapter, we discuss schizophrenic disorders, psychotic disorders, and personality disorders. Although these three categories of disorders are distinctly different in their attributes, due to space limitations they are discussed together in this chapter.

SCHIZOPHRENIC DISORDERS

Schizophrenia refers to a group of psychotic disorders characterized by agitation, delusions of grandeur or persecution, compelling hallucinations, gross distortions of reality, fragmentation, and disturbances manifested in language and thought including perception, emotion and interaction with others, that last longer than 6 months. This disorder represents the ultimate in psychological breakdown due to its global impact on the person's thinking and behavior. It is not one disorder. Its manifestations vary widely and from person to person. Due to attention deficit, the disorder causes problems with functional capacities. In 1919, the German psychiatrist Emil Kraepelin referred to a group of dissimilar conditions that seemed to have the common element of mental deterioration among the young, beginning in the teens or early twenties, using the term *dementia praecox*, or the insanity of the young. Eugen Bleuler, a Swiss psychiatrist, introduced the term *schizophrenia* (split mind) in 1924 to identify this condition. The "splitting" did not mean multiple personalities, but a split between the intellect and emotion and intellect and external reality. Blueler's diagnostic concept was based on "four A's": (1) loosening of *associations*, (2) flatness of *affect*, (3) *ambivalence*, and (4) *autism*. This broad and inclusive definition stirred up debates because it did not help in distinguishing schizophrenia from other disabilities, and some thought it was simply a means to label deviants and to control their lives.

As we pointed out, schizophrenia is by no means a unitary process, and the diversity of signs and symptoms can sometimes result in inaccurate diagnosis and consequent problems. Schizophrenia, which sometimes develops slowly (known as *process schizophrenia*), is marked by withdrawal, seclusiveness, lack of interest in the surrounding world, daydreaming, diminished emotional responsiveness, inappropriate response, mild hallucinations, and disjointed thought processes. *Chronic or premorbid* refers to actual manifestation of schizophrenia with identifiable symptoms, which clear up in a few weeks and may reappear. In other cases, schizophrenia is precipitated by episodes turning into *acute* or *reactive schizophrenia*. In identifying the disorder, psychiatrists currently use the terms *negative symptoms* or *positive symptoms*. Negative symptoms mean absence of the characteristics of schizophrenia in a subject's behavioral repertoire. Schizophrenia can occur with other mental disorders, and subtle differences among the disorders as well as basic personality differences can complicate objective diagnosis. A disorder that does not exhibit a recurrent pattern of psychotic symptoms is now called *schizophreniform disorder* (see discussion of psychoses later in this chapter). Disorders that show symptoms such as withdrawal and disturbed thinking are now classified as *personality disorders* (*DSM-III-R*).

Symptoms of Schizophrenia

The following are the most significant characteristics common in most cases of schizophrenia:

1. *Presence of psychotic symptoms*: Prime indicators are delusions, hallucinations, agitation, fragmented thought and communication processes, loosening of associations, grossly inappropriate affect, and catatonic behavior.

2. *Noticeable impairment in daily functioning*: People in the family, at work, and in other group situations observe that the person is not the same anymore. The *DSM-III-R* uses the criterion that the disorder involves a "deterioration from previous levels of functioning." Incidentally, the term *impairment* is a vague construct. A 30-year longitudinal study, "The Vermont Study," of 118 institutionalized patients who were diagnosed schizophrenic in the 1950s, dealt with subjects who, after their release, were provided community care services. About one half to two thirds of the patients did not continue to deteriorate but actually improved (Harding, Brooks, & Ashikaga, 1987).

3. *Evidence that symptoms were present during adolescence and childhood*: In many cases, symptoms of the disorder appear quite early but are often ignored or defined as discipline problems.

4. *Self and relationship with the external world*: Schizophrenics have problems with their identity, including gender identity. Often, grandiose presentation of self relates to "cosmic" feelings that one has personal communication with a god or deity and is obligated to follow this entity's dictums. The process of withdrawal from the external world leads to inner exploration and ideational constructs with no relationship to the real world (e.g., Son of Sam used to receive commands from the neighbor's dog, in the middle of the night, to kill couples who were cruising in a nearby park).

5. *Absence of affect and volition*: The ability to experience joy or pleasure and grief or sorrow is either low or absent in cases of severe schizophrenia. "Blunting" or emotional shallowness does not allow the person to react to a situation in appropriate ways (e.g., the subject may laugh at the funeral of a loved one). Such reactions may extend beyond one sphere of life. The use of discretion, matters of taste, social sensibilities, and goal-directed activities or resource management are usually lacking.

6. *Disturbance and fragmented use of language and communication*: These symptoms indicate the "cognitive slippage" and "derailment" or "loosening" of associations. Either the subject switches over from one incomplete statement to another or matches objects and situations that do not make sense (e.g., "I must now learn to shoot, get into medical school, and start working at a gas station"). Observers believe that thoughts race so rapidly in the minds of schizophrenics that coherence in verbalizations is lost.

7. *Motor behavior and peculiarities*: Many schizophrenics exhibit agitation and excitement and unusual ritualistic acts, such as twisting hair or pulling a mustache or ear. Peculiarities of movement, especially among catatonic schizophrenics, also include grimacing, rigid posturing, and muteness. Actually, the range of motor activity is so wide that it can vary from complete withdrawal or motor inactivity to a sort of hyperactivity marked by euphoria.

Incidence of Schizophrenic Disorders

One of every hundred people in the United States will be diagnosed with schizophrenia during his or her lifetime. How many people have schizophrenia in the United States at a given time? Estimates vary depending on diagnostic definitions, admission rates, recovery rates, and mortality rates. In 1988, based on prevalence studies, there were about 1.2 million people in the United States suffering from schizophrenia. If we add those who are known to have recovered, the number reaches 1.6 million. In the United States alone, every day, 118 people are diagnosed with schizophrenia for the first time (Torrey, 1988a, p. 4). Schizophrenia is probably one of the most misunderstood disorders. Some believe that it is a case of multiple personalities, while others believe it is psychosis. Psychosis means loss of contact with reality, but it is only one of the symptoms of schizophrenia. Psychosis may also include manic-depressive syndromes (now known as bipolar disorders).

Although schizophrenia is identified by its symptoms, the diagnosis has not always been reliable. A wrong diagnosis can be dangerous for those who are overdosed, institutionalized, and whose lives and careers are shattered. For example, where British psychiatrists diagnosed bipolar disorders, American doctors tended to diagnose schizophrenia. The incorrect diagnosis worsened the condition of the people under treatment (Pope, 1983, pp. 322–327). Of course, there is a problem of underdiagnosis. People with mental disorders initially see their personal physician and seek treatment. Even those who may have identifiable mental problems are hesitant to go to a psychiatrist, to avoid stigma and possible labeling. Such cases never appear in the prevalence studies. More than half of the people who show symptoms of schizophrenia never see a psychiatrist, and most are treated by other physicians, if treated at all.

Types of Schizophrenic Disorders

There are some controversies and disagreements regarding the psychiatric classification of mental disorders, including schizophrenia. However, this is the only classification utilized in clinical settings for diagnostic purposes as well as in court settings, when psychiatrists attest to the mental state of defendants. The *DSM-III-R* classification (1987, pp. 196–198) lists five types of schizophrenic disorders: (1) catatonic, (2) disorganized, (3) paranoid, (4) undifferentiated, and (5) residual. A brief discussion of each follows.

1. *Catatonic type*: This classification reflects the severity of the disorder and manifestations of catatonia—stupor, decreased response to the environment, and decreased activity. Other characteristics include mutism, negativism, staring into space, motionlessness, rigidity of posture, excitement, and inappropriate or bizarre postures that continue for days. Catatonic people alternate between extreme stupor and extreme excitement and sometimes become violent. Some are highly suggestible and follow commands or imitate actions, voices, or words of others. During the excitement phase, which may last from days to weeks, they may shout purposelessly, scream incoherently, pace around rapidly, indulge in genital manipulation and masturbation openly, attack others, and attempt self-mutilation or suicide.

2. *Disorganized type*: Also known as *hebephrenic*, this type is less common and occurs at an early age. Incoherence, silly smiles and giggling, inappropriate affect, hallucinations, and loosening of associations are common characteristics. Delusions are marked by moral, sexual, hypochondriacal, or persecutional associations.

3. *Paranoid type*: A common theme of the paranoid type is a very high level of suspiciousness and serious difficulties in interpersonal relations. Persecutory delusions center on grandeur and unusual achievements (e.g., the person believes that he or she was a prominent politician, religious leader, or shipping tycoon). Ideas relate to impractical, absurd, illogical themes. Delusions are marked by auditory, visual, and other hallucinations that often focus on speaking to the devil or God, conspiracies by enemies, or a powerful force from somewhere unknown hurting or paralyzing the subject's body. Paranoid schizophrenics can be dangerous, erratic, and unpredictable.

4. *Undifferentiated type*: The person exhibits mixed, overlapping, and rapidly changing symptoms that do not clearly fit the criteria for catatonic, disorganized, or paranoid type.

5. *Residual type*: This is characterized by mild indications of schizophrenia after the person is regarded as having recovered or the disorder is in remission after one of the major schizophrenic episodes.

The preceding discussion deals with the diagnostic categories. However, in real life situations, the disorders may appear in combination with other disorders, such as mood or personality disorders. In the past, for example, about one half of all schizophrenic first admissions to mental institutions were of the paranoid type. Now the undifferentiated type has shown a significant increase. It is difficult to pinpoint the reasons for this change, since the classification system has also changed several times in the last three decades.

PSYCHOSES

Setting boundaries among mental disorders and neatly defining them with very specific characteristics has been one of the most difficult tasks for clinicians as well as researchers. One such disorder is psychosis. The term *psychoses* refers to a class of disorders that cannot be labeled as organic mental disorders, schizophrenia, delusional or mood disorders but share characteristics of several mental disorders. For the common person, the term carries different meanings depending on the episode. Due to the rapidly changing nature of characteristics in a subject with psychosis, it is often impossible to identify him or her as having a particular disorder. This creates confusion among clinical professionals and disbelief in the public, including the family and friends of individuals victimized by psychotics. We hear frequently, "Those psychiatrists can't agree on anything; how can you trust them?" Patricia Hearst (who joined the Simbionese Liberation Army), Kenneth Bianchi (the Hillside Strangler), and Edmund Kemper (who killed his mother, grandparents, and several female hitchhikers) are some of the classic and extensively publicized cases in which professional disagreements about the mental state of these individuals placed psychiatry on trial.

Types of Psychoses

The *DSM-III-R* lists five types of psychoses: (1) brief reactive psychosis, (2) schizophreniform disorder, (3) schizoaffective disorder, (4) induced psychotic disorder, and (5) atypical psychosis.

    1. *Brief reactive psychosis*: This reflects a sudden onset of psychotic symptoms of at least a few hours' duration shortly after a markedly stressful event(s), in which the subject exhibits bizarre, suicidal, or other aggressive tendencies. Often, it begins in adolescence or early adulthood (due to preexisting conditions) with paranoid, histrionic, narcissistic, schizotypal, or borderline disorder.

    2. *Schizophreniform disorder*: This disorder is identical with schizophrenia, except that the duration of all its phases is less than 6 months.

    3. *Schizoaffective disorder*: This features the temporal and borderline symptoms of schizophrenic and mood disorders.

4. *Induced psychotic disorder*: Popularly known as *folie à deux*, shared paranoid disorder (or communicated psychosis), although rare, has also been known as double insanity or psychosis by association. The disorder is a result of a close relationship with a person who already has a psychotic disorder with prominent delusions.

5. *Atypical psychosis*: Atypical psychosis is a residual category reserved for those psychotic tendencies that do not meet the criteria of any other psychotic disorder.

EXPLANATIONS OF SCHIZOPHRENIA AND PSYCHOSES

Currently, we know something about the factors associated with schizophrenia, but clues to its causes point in several directions. Therefore, many myths and controversies have prevailed. Recent advances in brain research technology have helped us to understand some of the biological processes involved in schizophrenia, but the etiology of this class of disorders is still unclear.

Biological Factors

These include hereditary, biochemical, neurochemical, neurophysiological, neuroanatomical, and neuropsychological factors.

Genetic Factors

It has been suspected for centuries that schizophrenia runs in families; that is, it has a genetic link. The genetic link explanation does not explain the cause, but merely the transmission of the disorder. We must know which genetic entity has the problem and what causes it. Genes, of which we each have 6 million, are carried on 46 chromosomes in the nuclei of our body cells, half of which we receive from each of our parents. Some indications are that manic-depressive psychosis is carried on chromosome 11 (Torrey, 1988a, p. 144), but we are not certain because further research has not confirmed this finding.

Researchers have suggested that schizophrenics carry "genetic markers" (genetically transmitted traits, such as abnormal eye movements) and that such markers determine whether such traits are passed on by parents to their children. A child of nonschizophrenic parents has a 1% chance of developing schizophrenia; a child of one schizophrenic parent has a 13% chance; and a child with two schizophrenic parents has a 46% chance (Torrey, 1988a, p. 144). But is this due to nature or nurture?

Twin studies have yielded some interesting answers. Identical (monozygotic) twins share exactly the same genetic material and should be exactly the same in terms of physical and anatomical characteristics.

Similarly, nonidentical twins (dizygotic) should have only a 50% "concordance rate," which is the rate of agreement between a pair of twins to develop a certain physical characteristic. The concordance rate among identical twins is only 50% and among nonidentical twins drops to 10 to 15%, suggesting that schizophrenia is only partly determined by genetic factors (Andreasen, 1984, pp. 208–209). Some have argued that genetic process determines only the "predisposition," and therefore the concordance rate could vary from person to person.

To differentiate the impact of heredity from environment, Heston (1966) studied children of schizophrenic mothers who were placed in foster homes and with relatives. Heston found that 16.6% of these children later developed schizophrenia compared to none in the control group. Some researchers (Goldstein, 1987; Kety, 1983; Mednick, 1978) noted that there is a pronounced tendency for schizophrenic women to mate with males disposed to mental and other personality problems, which in turn contribute to the compounding effect on the children of schizophrenic mothers.

While researchers have presented their case persuasively in favor of genetic causes of schizophrenia, there are skeptics who argue that (1) most of the evidence is correlational in nature; (2) in the studies of twins, the genetic link does not prove its impact conclusively; (3) adopting families and their relationships with adopted children were presumed to be normal, suggesting that adopted children had a genetic propensity to schizophrenia (Sarbin & Mancuso, 1980); (4) further reinterpretation of adoption studies data suggested anomalies, such as half siblings having a higher likelihood of schizophrenia than full siblings (Benjamin, 1976); and (5) researchers often found a "schizophrenic spectrum," which is a broad category (a sort of wastebasket category) to include those characteristics that may not provide any basis for a genetic link.

Biochemical Factors

Biochemical explanations assume a genetic basis for explaining brain malfunctions. The center of attention in the past 2 decades has been the neurotransmitter dopamine. According to the *dopamine hypothesis*, schizophrenia is a product of excess dopamine activity at certain synaptic sites in the brain. Dopamine is broken down in the body through the action of other enzymes. One such enzyme is monoamine oxidase (MAO), a lower concentration of which has been found in schizophrenic patients. Serotonin and norepinephrine, other neurotransmitters, have also been suspected.

The dopamine-blocking drugs are used extensively in various other disordered states, including organic mental disorders, psychotic symptoms, and some manias. These drugs, in other words, are not therapeutically specific for schizophrenia and certainly not a cure, raising doubts about the dopamine hypothesis.

Neurological Findings

New technology has raised hopes for a more precise understanding of brain structure and functioning. The *computerized tomography (CT) scan* is the most widely used method of producing an image of the living brain. It exposes the subject to radiation. *Magnetic resonance imaging* (MRI) is another technique that produces a three dimensional image of the brain by placing the subject in a strong magnetic field that alters the alignment of hydrogen atoms in the body. It is expensive but does not involve any radiation. *Regional cerebral blood flow* (RCBF) measurement is a technique in which the subject inhales a radioactive form of xenon gas. As it disintegrates and emits radiation, its path in the brain is tracked by detectors placed around the head to monitor the flow of blood and the intensity of brain activity in various regions of the brain. The workings of the brain can also be measured by *positron emission tomography*. The subject is given a substance, usually glucose, containing short-lived radioactive (positron-emitting) atoms that can be traced as they disintegrate, thus measuring the activity level in neurotransmitter pathways. An advanced version of electroencephalography (EEG), *brain electric activity mapping* (BEAM) records brain activity using electrodes placed around the skull and shows results on the screen to determine brain wave responses to stimuli.

Computerized tomography scans have revealed that about one third of schizophrenics have enlarged ventricles in relation to the brain, but this is not specific evidence of schizophrenia. Schizophrenics, through PET studies, show low metabolism activity in the frontal lobes of the brain, which may produce schizophrenia-like symptoms in individuals who may not be schizophrenics (see Box 6-1). BEAM experiments are not conclusive, and MRI suggests smaller brains among schizophrenics, including abnormalities in the left brain hemisphere. Taken together, explorations of the brain have been more helpful in diagnosing Alzheimer's disease and Parkinson's disease than varieties of schizophrenia. Neurological abnormalities are only one of the many factors associated with schizophrenia.

Finally, it is not known how these brain abnormalities are related to the symptoms of schizophrenia. Correlation does not establish a causal relationship. Overactivity in the brain pathways could be either a cause or a byproduct of schizophrenia (HMS-MHL, 1989a, pp. 1–3).

Psychological Factors

The psychological explanations, which include psychodynamic and psychoanalytical theories, stand in sharp contrast to the biological explanation of schizophrenia. In this case, schizophrenia is viewed as a product of a person's inability to live with dysfunctional relationships, to escape from a cruel and unbearable social world and seemingly unsolvable conflicts by

> **BOX 6–1 • Vincent Van Gogh: Was He Crazy?**
>
> The great Dutch painter Vincent Van Gogh, who sold only one painting during his lifetime (in 1987, one of his paintings, "Irises," sold at auction for $54 million), killed himself because of debilitating epilepsy and madness. His tortured, penniless life included an incident in which he cut off one of his ears and gave it to a prostitute. In May 1889, Van Gogh voluntarily committed himself to a French asylum for epileptics and lunatics. But he could not find relief from his torment.
>
> J. K. Arenberg, MD, and his colleagues studied 796 of Van Gogh's letters. They concluded that his symptoms matched those of Meniere's disease—a rare disease found among people who do fine, meticulous work that requires great concentration. Meniere's disease (also known as watchmaker's disease) causes sensorineural hearing loss and dramatic and violent attacks during which the person feels that he or the room is moving. This is accompanied by nausea, retching, and vomiting. The authors concluded that Van Gogh's rational behavior at the asylum, as well as before (as illustrated by his voluminous correspondence), suggests that he was neither epileptic nor mad (see Arenberg, Countryman, Bernstein & Shambaugh, 1990; Runyan, 1981).
>
> Unable to find relief, Van Gogh committed suicide on July 29, 1890, at age 37.

From Arenberg et al., 1990; and Runyan, W. K. 1981.

altering the inner representations of reality (Carson, Butcher, & Coleman, 1988, p. 346).

Narcissistic Tendencies, Sexual Repression, and Regression

Sigmund Freud attempted to explain the phenomena of schizophrenia through psychoanalytical theory, which holds that the disorder is symptomized by a person's regression to the early oral stage. This stage is primarily *narcissistic* and does not allow an individual to work with the real world. The premise of the theory is that the person is *fixated* at the oral stage, either due to some frustrating weaning experience or lack of affectionate caring by the mother, which left the infant's ego emotionally unfulfilled. Eventually, this experience does not allow the ego to evolve normally and causes it to regress into the id. Social withdrawal among schizophrenics thus represents regression. According to this theory, this is why the thought processes of children and schizophrenics have similarities. Although the theory has been utilized extensively in psychiatric treatments, it has been criticized for lack of empirical support.

Attachment to Trauma, Numbing, and Depletion
Early life traumatic experiences may show residual effects in later life. Although not everyone who goes through a traumatic experience will become a schizophrenic, it may be one of the contributing factors. Those who were traumatized experience a slow decline in their ability to deal with both old and new stressors and failure to integrate new experiences. Many are "fixated" to the trauma and seem to have their lives on hold. They are unable to recite the events as they occurred, and yet they remain confronted with a painful situation in which they were unable to play a satisfactory role and make a successful adaptation.

Cognitive Difficulties and Decompensation
Cognitive processes play a key role in schizophrenia. It is known that there is an association between schizophrenic symptoms and the person's inability to focus, select, and appropriately react to situations. Such individuals are likely to misinterpret information because they cannot fit it into stable categories (Andorfer, 1984, pp. 403–409). A disproportionate level of stress in normal situations is also noticeable. For example, schizophrenics have been known to experience a flare-up of symptoms or to *decompensate* for seemingly trivial reasons, such as being turned down by a date or not being able to find an article of clothing in the closet (Gerhart, 1990, p. 20).

Attention Deficit, Distorted Self, and Faulty Communication
One of the serious problems among schizophrenics is their inability to process incoming information. Either they seem to ignore or are unable to absorb it or fail to react, which in turn adversely influences their interactions with others and the development of self. Their conversation is characterized by switching from one subject to another, incoherence of thought processes, pathogenic perceptions, and obsessions. It is often difficult to say whether such symptoms are actually causes or consequences of the disorder.

Deficit in Coping Skills
Two thirds of those who display schizophrenic symptoms probably failed to learn needed skills in everyday living: grooming, shopping, budgeting, cooking meals, using public transportation, making and keeping appointments, and the like (Grinker & Harrow, 1987). Lack of such skills is typically reflected in (1) a poor sense of self-identity, inadequacy, self-devaluation, and overdependence on others; (2) personal incompetencies coupled with unwillingness to learn and experiment; (3) inaccurate understanding of reality; and (4) extensive use of illogical and irrational defense mechanisms coupled with neurotic forms of coping.

Sociological Factors

Unfortunately, research on sociological factors of schizophrenia has been sparse, especially compared with research in the medical sciences. As we have discussed (Chapter 2), social scientists have been relatively more concerned about the structural conditions that produce individual as well as social pathologies, including schizophrenia.

The Family
The family and the socialization process have received a great deal of attention in searching for the causes of mental disorders, especially schizophrenia.

Inadequate and Pathogenic Socialization. Harry S. Sullivan (1953), one of the followers of Freud, was among those who contended that behavior of family members, the person's environment, and development of mental disorder were all intimately and inextricably linked. The sociogenic explanation of mental disorders holds that origins of mental disorders are social in origin and can be found in the role parents play in raising their children, and that corrective environmental influences, or therapy, can "cure" pathology. According to this theory, often parents, instead of guiding and advising children, act irresponsibly and confuse them instead of teaching norms and values that will help them in the long run. Experiencing frustration in social encounters places the child on the path of mental problems.

Schizophrenogenic Parent–Child Relationships. Research on interactions in the families of schizophrenics has reported some intriguing patterns. Frieda Fromm–Reichman (1948) noted that many mothers appeared to be inordinately involved with their mentally impaired children. Typically, these mothers of schizophrenic children are themselves immature and generally in need of endless emotional nurturance. Most are characterized as cold, rigid, domineering, rejecting, overprotective, impervious to the needs of others, emotionally starved, and with moralistic attitudes toward sex. While they appear concerned and accepting, basically they reject the child. First they turn to their husbands for satisfaction of their needs (who are passive, uninvolved, and rejecting of their son), but when husbands do not satisfy these needs, they seek mothering from their own children, "smothering" the children with unceasing attention. Fromm–Reichman's *blame-the-mama* theory, abandoned in the 1970s, has made a comeback. Roff and Knight's (1981) carefully designed retrospective study examined clinical records of people (prepared many years before their schizophrenic breakdown) and found a mothering style involving the aforementioned characteristics. This explanation is tenable, and the pattern may be considered one of the major causal factors in schizophrenia.

Pathogenic Marital Interactions. Theodore Lidz, a psychiatrist, postulated that schizophrenia arises in families where parents are frequently in a state of marital discord, the place of the individual in the family is constantly threatened, and the children are used as weapons in the parents' struggle for power and supremacy (Lidz, 1972; Lidz & Fleck, 1985). Children are often caught in parental wars that make it clear that neither of the parents cares for or respects the other. Lidz called this divisive process between the parents *marital schism*. In addition, children were maligned for taking sides or feared following the role model of one of the parents. Apparently, this caused parental rejection of the child, which led to mental disorder as a defensive response. Due to the distortion in family relationships, members entered into collusion, where one parent or family member wielded disproportionate power and the other accepted it passively but with enormous hostility. This pattern of gross imbalance is known as *marital skew*. Considering the current condition of the family in the United States, this explanation has some relevance. However, in view of the various emerging styles and living arrangements in families, further research is needed.

Conflicting Messages and "Double Bind." Gregory Bateson (1978) contended that schizophrenic families present a pattern of conflicting and confusing messages among members. This establishes a pattern in which what is expected, when acted upon, is rejected. The person then is confused about what is right and wrong—a sort of no-win situation. Double-bind messages are a catch 22 that inhibit a person from learning ways of dealing with the world that might eventually lead to an independent, fulfilling life. Gerhart (1990, p. 239) said that double-bind messages must be delivered on three levels. The first level consists of the actual spoken content of communication. The second is partially covert in that the message is contradicted by an unspoken message through facial expressions, tone of voice, and body movements. The third-level message is covert and secret with a tacit understanding that the second-level message must never be challenged openly and discussed. Gerhart illustrated the phenomenon as follows:

> *A father tells his daughter that she may go on a date with a classmate. This is the first-level message. But his tone of voice and facial expressions clearly convey to the daughter that he is quite worried about her dating and would prefer she stay home. This is the second-level message. Now to the third level. One of the family rules is that no one must openly disagree with the father. The daughter knows that she must not challenge the contradiction between her father's spoken words and his nonverbal communication. The covert message puts the daughter in an exceedingly stressful bind that may begin by her not knowing what is real and what is not, and end up in mental illness.*

Notwithstanding the significance of this theory, such messages are intended to be means of subtle control, to avoid loss of face or open confrontation. The double-bind messages do not in themselves launch a person on the path to schizophrenia; rather the particular patterns and sequences in which the double binds occur help bring on the disorder.

Pseudomutuality and Facade of Unity. Wynne, Ryckoff, Day, and Hirsch (1958) theorized that many warring families deny the existence of perpetual strife and give an appearance of being understanding, open, and committed while they are actually stifling, patronizing, rigid, and instrumental in creating an environment conducive to the growth of mental disorders, called *pseudomutuality*. Pseudomutuality can be identified in expressions like "Every one of us is devoted to the family," or "We would not exchange anything for our happy married life." The "myths" are presented as reality to the outside world to paper over inherent dissentions, frustrations, feelings of anger, hostility, shaky marriages, and disgruntled children. The natural outcome is that the members are forced to invest a lot of energy to put up the image of the "happy family," at the cost of personal growth and stilted relationships in and outside the family. To live with the facade of a happy family, in the make-believe world of pseudomutuality, is especially difficult for sensitive and vulnerable members, who eventually take flight in the world of schizophrenia and psychoses.

Fused Ego Mass and the Pathogenic Family. Several explanations have been advanced in the recent times that have not been tested fully. Murray Bowen (1960) theorized that severe mental disorders occur when family members are constricted to develop their own identities or unable to differentiate from the rest of the family. The family members tend to think alike and act alike; their egos are fused together and they share an "undifferentiated ego." The members rarely venture away from the rigid family norms. In such a case, a person may learn conditioned fears and vulnerabilities that lead to perception of the outside world as hostile and dangerous. The inability to sustain positive interactions leads to frustration, inappropriate actions, and paranoid tendencies, often manifested in irrational expressions of grandeur (the common characteristics of schizophrenics).

Social Class

Sociological studies in the last 4 decades have tested the hypothesis that there is an inverse relationship between the extent and severity of mental disorder and one's position in a social class. That is, the lower the class association of a person, the higher the likelihood of severe mental disorder. One landmark study conducted in 1950 by August B. Hollingshead and Fredrick C. Redlich (1953) in the urban setting of New Haven, Connecticut, suggested class association of mental disorders and paved the path for scores of other studies. Several theories have been examined and reexamined, such as *social stress hypothesis, social reaction hypothesis,* and *social selection hypothesis* or *drift hypothesis* (see Chapter 9 for details). However, the findings have been criticized because most such studies have established the association of class and mental disorder, and not the cause of mental disorder. In addition, the poor and the lower classes seek help at state and local mental health facilities that gather mental health statistics, while other classes may have similar mental health problems that are not reported to appropriate agencies. Furthermore, labeling tends to be more common among lower classes.

PERSONALITY DISORDERS

People continue to learn and change throughout the life cycle and attempt to adapt to changing demands and opportunities. Even if situations are disagreeable and they are unable to change, people try to cope or learn to live with them or reject them. This process of coping and interacting in a social environment evolves a personality—a unique construct of attributes and behaviors that characterizes the individual. It is generally crystallized by the adolescent years. For certain individuals, the process of socialization, although not necessarily detrimental to their personal growth, may have led them to learn behaviors that do not allow them to become fully functional individuals. Their personalities become so maladapted and distorted that these individuals fail to meet their various role expectations, are unable to relate to people, and often react to situations in unacceptable ways. The deeply ingrained behavior patterns that interfere with their functioning eventually become personality disorders. *Personality disorders,* also known as *character disorders,* are a group of personality traits that are inflexible and maladaptive and cause either significant functional impairment or subjective distress (*DSM-III-R*, 1987, p. 335). The disturbance in the personality adversely influences rationality and judgment. Behavior may not be as dramatic as found in a psychotic, but when all the symptoms are taken together, they prevent the person from achieving satisfaction in society, at school, or at work. Moreover, individuals with personality disorders do not recognize their problems.

Personality disorders are not reactions to situations (such as a death in the family or stress on the job) or a delayed response to experiences in the past (like posttraumatic stress disorder), but they originate in the pathology of social environment. It is more clear than in any other mental disorders that personality disorders are products of the environment. Maladaption and warped personality formation is not due to the disturbed mind but the processes of learning, perceiving, and thinking that set goals, attitudes, values, and actions. It is questionable whether we should consider personality disorders as mental disorders because, as Gerhart pointed out, sociopaths and psychopaths are not mad, but bad (Gerhart, 1990, p. 17). The behaviors characteristic of personality disorders are primarily problems in which the individual irrationally and sometimes purposelessly causes difficulty, pain, and loss of life to others. In very severe cases, they pass on their own suffering to others through sadistic acts (see Table 6–1). They lead aberrant lives.

The variations in human personalities are so vast that we tend to shy away from almost anything that is different from what we are accustomed to. Class, race, and ethnicity are also associated with personal differences (e.g., a teenager raised in a broken home in a ghetto, in a neighborhood infested with gang activity, drug dealing, and other serious crimes and who has little chance for education or a job is going to relate to people differently than a middle- or upper-class youth).

The spectrum of mental disorder is significantly different from the neat theoretical boundaries we draw among mental disorders. The symptoms are key to identification, and in real-life situations a person may exhibit several different characteristics that may belong to several different disorders. Personality disorders are different in so many ways, ranging from mild to severe (e.g., from someone who is always looking for what is wrong rather than what is right in people and situations, to serial killers who satisfy their perverted needs by murdering people). However, they share some common features:

1. *A pattern of recurring problems*: The individual's behavior is viewed by others as troublesome, showing symptoms of personal pathology through frequent disruptive episodes.

2. *A configuration of disrupted relationships*: Most relationships are marked by a variety of narcissistic, dependent, passive–aggressive, paranoid, antisocial, sadistic, and schizoid traits, leaving a trail of disturbed personal relationships.

3. *A structure of pathological traits*: The maladaptive pattern reflects the traits, often not very consistent and conspicuous in the public eye, that color the personality (e.g., extraordinary stubbornness, high level of suspiciousness, severe covert hostility, deep-rooted hatred, and callous disregard for civility, prevalent values, or human life).

4. *High level of negativity*: Past and current life experiences with negative outcomes dominate the thought process. Frustration-causing personal failures, such as loss of love, job, prestige, or money, are viewed by these individuals as "somebody's fault." Criminal acts, alcoholism, or chemical addictions compound such feelings.

5. *Distorted or weak superego*: These individuals have a warped sense of grace, dignity, and self-esteem, and their behavior demonstrates that they

are unable to realize the amount of pain they cause others. Often, they earn a reputation for callous disregard for other people. Because of the disorder, they even attempt to manipulate help-givers and are difficult to treat. In essence, they have a distorted or week superego.

6. *Contradictions in personality traits*: It is highly probable that individuals with personality disorders may exhibit opposing characteristics. They might appear very charming in one situation and quite hostile in another. Thus, although there is a considerable consistency in their maladaptive behaviors, one may be surprised by the presence of contradictions. For example, people are shocked that Kenneth Bianchi, Theodore Bundy, John Gacy, and Jeffrey Dahmer were so cunning and manipulative that they could attract young men and women, whom they eventually tortured and killed. The victims could not sense the impending danger.

Most of those who are connected with a string of murders (see Table 6–1), known as serial killers, attempted to defend themselves by the use of legal technicalities including the insanity plea. Psychiatric evaluations indicated that most of them did not seem to have had any mental disorder. If this is the case, how do we explain criminal behavior with no apparent tangible motive?

7. *Resistance to change*: The personality disorders, as pointed out earlier, are so deeply ingrained in the moral structure of individuals that they neither seek to change, nor are they willing to change. This is partly because they see problems in the outside world rather than in themselves. It is no wonder that many of these individuals commit crimes and are difficult to rehabilitate.

Types of Personality Disorders

Personality disorders are among some of the most difficult mental problems to be identified, partly due to the complex nature of human phenomena. They are classified in the *DSM-III-R* into three major clusters based on their similarities and a fourth category that needs further research support. Adding to the list in *DSM-III-R* new categories of personality disorders raises many questions about the objectivity in the definitions of *normal* as well as *abnormal*, and invites criticism of the "psychiatric enterprise."

Category 1: Paranoid, Schizoid, and Schizotypal

Typically, these individuals are oversuspicious, hypersensitive, argumentative, envious, and ascribe evil motives to others. *Paranoid* individuals believe that everyone is trying to trick them, and they validate their expectations by disregarding evidence to the contrary. They are rigid, litigious, envious of superiors, and disdainful of those who seem indifferent to their ideas. *Schizoid* personalities are loners and suffer from the inability to form

TABLE 6-1 • The Random Killers: Are They Insane?

Names	Crimes	State/Area	Psychiatric Status
1. David Berkowitz (Son of Sam)	Killed at least 20 young women and often their male companions	New York	Sane
2. Kenneth Bianchi (The Hillside Strangler)	Strangled and killed over 20 young women	California, Washington	Sane
3. Theodore Bundy	Murdered at least 40 women	Washington	Sane
4. Jeffrey Dahmer	Lured 17 young men and teenagers; after drugging them dismembered their bodies; suspected of cannibalism	Ohio, Wisconsin	Sane
5. John Gacy	Strangled 33 young men and buried them in the crawl space of his house	Illinois	Sane
6. Edmund Kemper*	Stabbed, shot, and killed his mother, grandparents, and six young female hitchhikers	California	Psychotic
7. Henry Lee Lucas†	Murdered and dumped 188–360 people	24 states	Sane
8. Richard Macek (Mad Biter)	2–8 murders; left tell tale marks on victims	Wisconsin	Sane
9. Gerald Stano	Shot, stabbed, and strangled some 35 young women	Florida	Sane
10. Elmer Williams Henley	Raped, tortured, and murdered 27 teenage boys	Texas	Sane
11. Wayne Williams	Murdered about 20 black teenagers and young men	Georgia	Sane

*Kemper was a juvenile at the time of his first homicide.
†Lucas is suspected of having claimed all other murders police could not solve.

relationships. Most do not marry, and if they do, they have difficulty in sustaining the relationship. *Schizotypal* characteristics show a touch of schizophrenia and in the past were known to be identified with pseudoneurotic schizophrenia, latent, borderline, subclinical, or ambulatory schizophrenia. The distinguishing feature between schizoid and schizotypal is that the latter also involves oddities and eccentricities of thinking, perception, speech, and behavior. Many of these individuals profess to claim superior intellectual abilities, magical thinking, clairvoyance, telepathy, and ability to communicate with powers beyond the human realm.

Category 2: Histrionic, Narcissistic, Antisocial, and Borderline

A common tendency among these individuals is to be overly emotional, erratic, and dramatic, involving impulsive, forceful, and often colorful attention-seeking antisocial activities. *Histrionic* individuals show self-dramatization, excitability, emotional immaturity, and instability. Their actions are seductive and relationships are stormy and unstable. Individuals with *narcissistic* tendencies are preoccupied with an exaggerated sense of self-importance and grandiose and self-serving plans. The core element in this personality disorder is the individual's inability to respect the interests of others and a general lack of empathy and understanding of others' viewpoints. *Antisocial* personalities are incessantly involved in activities against individuals and society, showing a lack of empathy, respect, or loyalty to anyone. Some who are intelligent become successful con artists and are able to carry out their plans by effectively using their personal charm. (We discuss this category in more detail later in the section on psychopathic personality.) In *borderline personality disorder*, the common element is that along with a personality disorder the individual also shows symptoms of some of the other severe psychological problems, usually affective disorders. Behavior patterns of these individuals are characterized by drastic mood swings, impulsiveness, irritability, unpredictability, emotional outbursts, and negative outlook. Some of the behavior features involve poor money management, indiscreet sexual liaisons, gambling, drug abuse, shoplifting, and other forms of criminal behavior.

Category 3: Avoidant, Dependent, Obsessive-Compulsive, and Passive-Aggressive

Anxiety and fear are the basic components of these personality disorders, and it is often difficult to distinguish them from anxiety-based disorders. Hypersensitivity to rejection, derogation, ridicule, disparagement, and a sense of constant apprehension are common features of *avoidant* personalities. Although they do not prefer lonely lives, they are unable to relate to people, which causes them frustration and distress. *Dependents* lack self-confidence, a sense of independence, and the ability to make decisions. In spite of their competencies in certain areas of life, they cannot function alone. *Obsessive-compulsive* personality disorder is distinctly different from obsessive-compulsive disorder in that in the latter case a person suffers from the intrusion of undesired thoughts and actions that are the cause of severe anxiety. The individual is aware of the irrationality of those thoughts and consequent actions but is unable to control them. Obsessive-compulsive personalities lead a lifestyle that features overconformity, obstinacy, compulsively mechanical approach to most activities, and absence of warm feelings. They are viewed disdainfully by people due to their rigid, cold, and often pathological way of life. *Passive-aggressive* personality disorder represents opposing characteristics in the same behavior, which may appear contradictory but can be found in real-life situations. Individuals with this disorder show their resentment, disrespect, hostility, and aggression by noncompliance, procrastinating, scapegoating, and making excuses. Typically, they lack assertiveness, courage, and decisiveness and are therefore unable to confront problems directly.

Category 4: Self-Defeating Personality Disorders and Sadistic Personality Disorders

These two personality disorders have been added in the appendix in *DSM-III-R* in view of the high rates of child and spouse abuse and criminal behavior in which a motive is unclear. *Self-defeating personality disorder* refers to a persistent pattern of an individual's involvement, despite the presence of better choices, in activities and relationships that cause pain or suffering. Such individuals are drawn to self-punishing experiences. Even when they are recognized for their accomplishments, they feel guilty and depressed rather than happy. They engage in inappropriate activities to elicit negative and rejecting responses from others. A classic case is a spouse, qualified and career oriented, who is regularly abused and mistreated but is unable to seek positive alternatives. Critics charge (especially feminists) that this explanation misplaces the blame for abuse to the victims, the women, rather than the male perpetrators.

Sadistic personality disorder features a pervasive pattern of cruel, demeaning, and aggressive behavior toward other people, beginning by early adulthood. Inflicting pain on other people and deriving satisfaction from seeing them suffer is at the heart of this disorder. The sadistic personalities have a tendency to control the lives of other people and are fascinated by violence, torture, and pain.

Is There a Psychopathic Personality?

Whenever there are dramatic episodes of shooting, killing, and mysterious deaths with no apparent motive, the public generally suspects the involvement of a psychopath. Generally known as an antisocial personality, the psychopath may have been raised in an environment in which negative behaviors against individuals, groups, and society were viewed as rewarding and acceptable. Such individuals view the rest of the world with disdain and mistrust. They are characterized by a lack of moral structure, ethical values, and the inability to follow appropriate socially approved models of behavior. Absence of empathy, concern, and loyalty to anyone brings them in conflict with the rest of society. However, such conflicts often remain latent until opportunities arise or their aggression is heightened by episodes that demand their attention. They develop antisocial personalities that include a variety of types, such as child abusers; serial killers; hardened criminals and impostors; unprincipled businesspeople, lawyers, and physicians; crooked politicians and investment brokers; shyster bankers and real estate agents; immoral and greedy evangelists; drug pushers; among others. They are not confined to one occupation, class, race, ethnic group, or geographical area.

Should we call those involved in antisocial acts mentally disordered? Psychiatry is not clear on this issue. An individual with a mental disorder does not have control over his or her malady. But antisocial individuals, in most cases, are aware of their conduct. They also know that their actions are unacceptable, often illegal and criminal. Such individuals are called *psychopaths* and *sociopaths*. Generally, these terms are used synonymously, but they are vague and convey different meaning to different people. Sutherland and Cressey (1978) suggested that some 55 descriptive terms are consistently linked with the concept of psychopathy. While the term still remains ambiguous, Gough (1948) attempted to conceptualize it by suggesting that psychopathy is the individual's inability to take "the role of the other" or "the inability to identify with others." Rather than attributing a single factor and episodic behavior, Robbins (1966) attempted to explain the "syndrome" by the persistent presence of a given set of symptoms. In retrospect, 30 years later (initial work was done between 1924 and 1925 at a St. Louis Child Guidance Clinic), Robbins postulated that it is possible to identify antecedents that may eventually be shown to constitute the causes of sociopathic personality. The childhood symptoms of incorrigibility, running away, discipline problems, aggressiveness, truancy, choosing bad companions, among others were found to be prognostic of adult-stage sociopathy. Of a list of 20 major symptoms, 5 are as follows: 85% poor work history, 79% financial dependence, 81% marital problems, 75% multiple arrests, and 73% ever-incarcerated. However, these findings do not tell us much about those who did not seek assistance and those who were involved in antisocial behavior in high places.

Gallup and Maser (1977, p. 355) questioned the concept of *psychopathology*, which they believe is grossly misleading when applied to behavior in traditional ways. Pathology implies the action of pathogens, disease-causing entities usually associated with infectious microorganisms. There is no evidence that someone can be vaccinated against any mental disorder or that visitors to mental hospitals should wash their hands when they leave for fear of contracting mental disorder. In any case, although the concept appears misleading, there is no question that the individual so labeled or identified as a psychopath learned a pattern of behavior in which conscience or the superego is marked by antisocial behavior. In fact, it is possible that the operational superego is, at least in some ways, different or opposed to the superego shared by the rest of society. It would appear that sociopaths are qualitatively different from psychopaths.

Characteristics of Psychopaths and Sociopaths

Lack of Conscience and Inability to Experience Guilt. Most psychopaths either have inadequate conscience or learned ethical values that do not correspond with the values of society. Consequently, they do not experience the same feelings of guilt as others do. They may preach and glibly verbalize higher social values, but their actions are often diametrically opposite to what they say. On the other hand, sociopaths are usually aware of their wrongdoing and concerned about their reputation, but they conduct themselves cleverly. Their moralizing turns out to be a facade and they break rules to gain power, money, or prestige. John Wayne Gacy (who sodomized and killed at least 31 teenagers and young men) in this case would be identified as a psychopath, while former president Richard Nixon would be considered a sociopath.

Impulsivity. Psychopaths, having no regard for feelings of others, act out in ways, that though sometimes well planned, are prompted by impulse or compulsion. Many are thrill seekers and instant-gratification seekers who are unable to think of the consequences. Typically intelligent, they are unable to resist the temptation of doing wrong. Many believe they are smart. The case of Ted Bundy offers us a good insight. He lured innocent coeds with his charm; he tortured and killed them; and he pleaded his own defense. If he had not been sentenced to death, he probably would have been a successful attorney. Sociopaths are cautious; they plan and they are aware of moral and legal implications of wrongdoing but are often drawn into such acts for reasons of money, power, prestige, or satisfaction of other needs. An appropriate example would be Ivan Bosky, who made millions of dollars on Wall Street through insider trading (having confidential information of mergers and takeovers of companies) and was finally caught, sent to jail, and fined $100 million.

Absence of Respect for Law and Authority. Psychopaths' perceptions of gain are different from a common criminal. They do not play the usual games of crooks and criminals, but they have an intense contempt for laws and they believe they can beat them. For example, most serial killers are caught by accident and not by police prudence. Sociopaths, publicly and deliberately, in a calculated way, talk of patriotism, morality, honesty, and fairness but selectively act in exactly opposite ways. A classic example is evangelist Jim Bakker, who was suspected of sodomy and forced sexual encounters with a secretary of the ministry, and of siphoning off millions of dollars from the ministry for his own luxuries.

Lack of Meaningful Social Bonds. Psychopaths are seldom able to establish close relationships. Their actions are largely egocentric, cynical, unsympathetic, irresponsible, and remorseless. Most of their relationships involve manipulation and exploitation. They are incapable of loving anyone or receiving love from anyone. At least partially, this explains why psychopaths are able to torture and kill other people and function routinely without manifesting any guilt or remorse and leaving no clue to their crimes. Sociopaths are fairly smooth in their relationships and often willing to take responsibility for their offenses as a means of manipulation. They publicly express guilt and remorse to gain public sympathy; however, privately they attempt to shrug off public outcry with their own logic and reasoning and often ask for forgiveness.

Ability to Put Up "a Good Front." Some characteristics are common among psychopaths and sociopaths. The differences, noted earlier, may be only of degrees. Most are charming, likable, with a disarming manner that can win friends. Their uncanny ability to gain insight into people's minds allows them to exploit others. Typically, they lie, deceive, and engage in unethical practices. While a sociopath may genuinely regret and feel sorry if caught, the psychopath may express remorse but does not experience the guilt, and chances are that he or she will repeat the act. Psychopaths fail to learn from experience. Their sense of humor, confidence, and optimism is so inspiring that the people who are victimized by them often fail to foresee the shortcomings of their character.

Faulty Rationalizations and Inability to Reform. Psychopaths promise to change but rarely do so. It is hard to say if they are ever reformed. They innovatively find excuses and rationalizations for their antisocial conduct by projecting blame on someone else, such as a dominant mean mother or violent and abusive father, thereby convincing others as well as themselves they are not at fault. They talk with disdain about the courts and the penal system's failure and convince people of their innocence. Contrary to evidence, Theodore Bundy never confessed to the killings even though he was executed in 1989. Another serial killer, Henry Lee Lucas, believed that all those who were willing to hitchhike in his truck deserved death; he did not care to know their names. Psychopaths claim that given the same circumstances, they would repeat their acts. Sociopaths have potential for reform because some of their superego mechanisms might still be at work. They seek to rehabilitate themselves.

That individuals are repeatedly involved in social and legal offenses is not a sufficient justification for assuming that they are either psychopaths or sociopaths. A large number of them manage their lives without committing any serious crimes or committing crimes in ways that can be traced to them. However, their lives are filled with frequent unpleasant episodes and situations.

Factors Associated with Antisocial Personality

Most research on humans attempts to explain the causal factors determining their behavior. However, though scientists like to claim that they can explain a cluster of factors associated with a certain behavior at a group level (such as which presidential candidate is more popular at the national level), finding causes at the individual level has been difficult. This is one of the major reasons that treatment of mental disorders has had limited success. *Cause* is a deterministic term suggesting a direct link with the *outcome*. Humans do not learn or act like atoms or molecules in physical or chemical processes in the natural world. Individuals think, observe, imitate, create, innovate, and in some cases unlearn. They have emotions, feelings, personal vicissitudes, preferences, selective attention, likes, and dislikes. Scientific studies have yet to prove conclusively, in the case of mental disorders (especially personality disorders), that the causes are known. The best we can say is that there are associations between personality characteristics and biological, psychological, and sociological variables.

Explanations of Personality Disorders

The Family
Sociologist Charles H. Cooley contended that for an individual, "family is first in time and first in importance"; it is the cradle of human civilization. Perhaps this is why when it comes to the development of an antisocial personality, social scientists are quick to blame the family. The family is often attributed as a cause of the disorder because it embraces the whole personality of the individual—biological, psychological, and sociocultural.

Parental Rejection and Emotional Deprivation. Sometimes, even with the best of intentions, parents act in ways that may be detrimental to the child's emotional well-being. Parental rejection for various reasons (including the parents' own mental problems) can have serious consequences for children. Biederman, Faraone, Keenan, Knee, and Tsuang (1990) found that children who are behaviorally inhibited in childhood had increased risk of multiple anxiety, overanxious, and phobic disorders. Considering the high rates of divorce, remarriage, and single parenthood in addition to child abuse and neglect, children experience the trauma of losing a parent at an early age. Greer (1964) reported that 60% of one group of antisocial individuals had lost a parent during their childhood to some kind of family disruption.

Serial killer Edward Kemper revealed in an interview that he was compelled to brutally kill his mother to gain his sanity. Kemper's argument may not be valid, yet it explains that his rancor for his mother turned into abomination for women in general.

Parental Values, Discretions, and Models. High value is placed on success, especially financial success, in the United States. When it comes to money, values of honesty, integrity, and forthrightness are forsaken, especially among younger adults. Many mental health problems, including alcoholism and drug abuse, originate in the failure to achieve or cope.

Biogenic Factors

Researchers have often found it difficult to delineate the boundaries of various kinds of disorders, often confusing personality disorder with schizophrenia. Personality disorder is probably the most explored, but least understood, disorder due to its appearance in serious crime statistics. Biogenic cause–effect relationships are not very clear.

Most studies of the past decades do not tell us conclusively about the role of genetics in the formation of antisocial personality. Lombroso (1968) suggested that antisocial personalities were throwbacks to cave men, incapable of moral judgment or civilized self-restraint. He attempted to recognize them by slanting forehead, eyebrows that meet, and receding jaw. However, later research did not find support for this proposition (Farber, 1981). Recently, some researchers have proposed that an extra Y male chromosome (XYY) produces "supermales," who are prone to be aggressive and involved in antisocial acts. Richard Speck, tall and mentally dull, who murdered eight nurses in Chicago in 1966, was found to have the XYY combination. Only about 1% of criminals have this chromosomonal makeup, and a substantial number of males born with this combination do not become antisocial (Gallagher, 1987, pp. 132–133; Suinn, 1984, p. 87).

Psychological Underpinnings

Psychologists seek to explain the factors associated with antisocial personalities through exploring the individual's inner levels of conscience. Some of these explanations border on physiological bases.

Thrill Seeking. It is suggested that antisocial personalities operate at a low level of arousal and are deficient in autonomic variability; therefore, they seek external stimulation through rule breaking, which provides thrills to compensate for such deficiency (Eysenck, 1970). Other studies have supported findings indicating that individuals involved in mass killings, prison escapes, drug abuse, and several other serious criminal activities see these actions as ends in themselves.

Defective Cognitive Process. General lack of concern for others, lack of commitment to society's ethical and moral codes, and poor impulse control are found to be common among antisocial personalities. This lack of concern derives from fixation early in life due to frustration and parental rejection. The search for immediate gratification with no concern for consequences or the inability for postponement is dominated by fixation (pleasure principle). Such individuals are not able to develop a normal superego that can guide their behavior.

Sociocultural Setting

The development of antisocial personalities is grounded in the social environment. Variables such as neighborhood, family structure, age, class, race and ethnic affiliation, education, and occupation play their part. For example, lower socioeconomic groups are disproportionately represented in crime as well as mental health figures. Lack of opportunity compounded by breakdown of social norms (characterized by forces of disorganization, absence of desirable role models, apathy and hostility toward authority, dissociation, and alienation from the rest of society) provides a picture-perfect setting for destructive antisocial personalities. For example, in the summer of 1989, in New York City, a 28-year-old investment banker, on a late-night run through the northern end of Central Park, was raped, beaten, and left for dead. Three Harlem teenagers, who said that they were "wilding," were convicted of rape and assault. This raised fears about underclass social pathology (Turque & Underwood, 1990, p. 39). A detailed discussion on these issues is found in Chapter 9.

CHAPTER REVIEW

1. What is schizophrenia? Why is it considered a group of disorders rather than one mental disorder.

2. What are the characteristics of schizophrenic disorders? How are they different from other mental disorders? Discuss.

3. Do the studies of twins and adopted children prove conclusively that schizophrenia is genetically inherited? Does the environment play any role in causing schizophrenia? Evaluate the status of research findings.

4. In what ways has the biological revolution in psychiatry attempted to explore the workings of the brain?
5. How is schizophrenia different from psychosis? Identify their similarities and differences.
6. What do we mean when we say that symptoms of schizophrenia can be controlled by drug therapy but we do not know the cure? Explain.
7. What theories do sociologists offer to explain the causal factors involved in schizophrenia and psychosis?
8. What are the characteristics of personality disorders? Explain.
9. Is there a psychopathic personality? How do we differentiate the characteristics of psychopaths and sociopaths?
10. What are the sociological explanations of personality disorders?
11. Distinguish between
    a. Catatonic and disorganized types of schizophrenia
    b. Brief reactive psychosis and atypical psychosis
    c. Marital schism and marital skew
    d. Double-bind family interactions and a pathogenic family
12. Write a brief note on the following:
    a. Random serial killers
    b. Cognitive slippage
    c. Computed tomography (CT) scan
    d. Decompensation
    e. Blame-the-mama theory

FOR FURTHER STUDY

Andreasen, N. C. (1984). *The broken brain: The biological revolution in psychiatry.* New York: Harper and Row.
Barnes, D. M. (1987). Biological issues in schizophrenia. *Science, 235,* 430–433.
Bland, R. C., & Orn, H. (1981). Schizophrenia: Sociocultural factors. *Canadian Journal of Psychiatry, 26,* 186–188.
Carpenter, W. T. (1987). Approaches to knowledge and understanding of schizophrenia. *Schizophrenia Bulletin, 13,* 1–8.
Eaton, W. W. (1980). A formal theory of selection for schizophrenia. *American Journal of Sociology, 86,* 149–158.
Gerhart, U. C. (1990). *Caring for the chronically mentally ill.* Itasca, IL: F. E. Peacock.
Kety, S. S. (1976). Studies designed to disentangle genetic and environmental variables in schizophrenia: Some epistemological questions and answers. *American Journal of Psychiatry, 133,* 1134–1137.
National Institute of Mental Health. (1987). *Special report: Schizophrenia.* Rockville, MD: U.S. Department of Health and Human Services, Public Health Service.
Torrey, E. F. (1988b). *Surviving schizophrenia.* New York: Harper and Row.

▶ 7
Substance Abuse and Mental Disorders

A Chicago mother and businesswoman, who was brought up in a strongly religious household in southwestern Missouri where failure to believe the teachings of the Bible met with stern disapproval, became an alcoholic. She found out that her husband of 20 years was having an affair with one of her best friends. She admits she feels powerful pangs of rage toward her husband. She says, "Alcohol soothes me, allows me to overcome anger; I feel betrayed and cheated; if I don't drink I will end up killing him." A young high school valedictorian from a small town in the Midwest was raised in an ethnic background that had strict taboos against unmarried sex and drugs. After entering a major private university, he found himself uncomfortable with the relaxed standards of his college classmates. After a year of trying to conform to their lifestyle of drug and alcohol use and sexual experimentation, he committed suicide. He left a note stating that he could not live with what he was doing. Apparently, his early life teachings stayed with him, convincing him that what he was doing was morally wrong and deserved punishment. Such episodes remind us that substance abuse is a pervasive phenomenon that touches the lives of millions. Public figures and celebrities, such as Betty Ford, Kitty Dukakis, Elvis Presley, and many others, have become involved in substance abuse, sometimes with tragic results.

People have used and misused a variety of substances throughout history and across cultures, some for medicinal purposes and some for pleasure. Weddings, funerals, and other celebrations are known to be great occasions for substance consumption. However, the epidemic of substance abuse in the United States is more pervasive and dangerous. "Its source is the large and growing traffic in illegal drugs, a pharmacopoeia of poisons hiding behind street names as innocent as grass, speed, horse and angel dust. It has taken lives, wrecked careers, broken homes, invaded schools, incited crimes, tainted businesses, toppled heroes, corrupted policemen and politicians, bled billions from the economy and in some measure infected every corner of our public and private lives" (Smith, 1986, p. 15). People use substances for different reasons and in different ways. Each person may react differently to the same substance. Substance abuse not only affects the psychological and physical condition but has major adverse personal, economic, social, and health consequences for both individuals and society. The substances with which we are concerned here, by their chemical properties, have a potential for adversely affecting the organic and mental functioning of people. Substances have their utilitarian and legal contexts. For example, prescription substances improve the health of a person if taken in proper doses. Drugs can be abused if not used according to a doctor's prescription.

The issue of substance abuse and related disorders is exceedingly complex. Virtually any substance can, of course, be abused. Substances typically abused include both over-the-counter and prescription drugs and naturally occurring substances (such as peyote, tobacco, and cocoa leaves). Others include a wide variety of chemically produced substances such as alcohol, heroin, crack, cocaine, some hallucinogens, sleeping pills, glue, paint thinner, and so on. Complicating the issue is that some of these are controlled substances—that is, their manufacture, possession, distribution, and use are regulated by law. Others (e.g., glue and paint thinner) are not subject to such regulation. Further confounding the issue is that our society uses drugs (one type of substance, as the term is used here) as remedies for a variety of disorders. Drugs are used for a host of mental disorders. They are used widely to combat other disorders, ranging from headaches to irregularity. As a result, we grow up learning that drugs are readily available and can be used to treat a variety of symptoms. Unfortunately, we do not always recognize the side effects of legitimate drug use. Often it becomes difficult to separate "good drugs" from "bad drugs." It is all right to use tobacco, but not marijuana. Morphine is used to lessen physical pain, but heroin may not be used to reduce emotional pain. Alcohol and tobacco may be used by adults, but not by minors. If one aspirin is good, aren't two better? We take some drugs to counter the effects of other drugs so we can continue to take the former. All of these examples show that, often, it is not easy to determine when use becomes abuse.

UNDERSTANDING SUBSTANCE ABUSE

Substance abuse received attention in the United States only when it became problematic. Often, programs are created to solve problems and are judged by how much money is assigned to them rather than their success rates. For example, supposedly, we have better treatments for mental disorders now than four decades ago, but the number of people suffering from mental disorders has been increasing steadily. This is true for substance abuse, too. While in some areas of substance abuse the numbers have stabilized, in others the numbers are still increasing. Public concern about the substance abuse menace has led to the creation of a variety of rehabilitation programs, shelters, and halfway houses, mobilization of community mental health resources, and new drug laws.

Factors associated with substance abuse are built into the social structure. They include class structure and ethnicity, broken families, and occupational structures. When we look at the problem of substance abuse, we focus primarily on the problem itself (e.g., alcoholism). We often ignore the factors that are responsible for alcoholism and its underlying causes. If those causes are not addressed, we are missing the target.

Why People Abuse Substances

The primary objective of substance use is to change one's state of mind or body. The goal is to feel good, to enjoy, to reduce stress and anxiety, to combat fatigue, to be in better control of one's situation, to overcome inhibitions, to present oneself in the best possible manner, to think and concentrate better, or to get "bombed" for a change. Substance use disorders are divided into two categories:

1. *Psychoactive substance-induced disorders* are a variety of mental disorders resulting from ingestion of psychoactive substances. Their use leads to organic impairment of the brain due to their toxicity (such as delusional disorders as due to amphetamine use, or alcohol amnesic disorder as a result of severe alcoholism). Frequency and amount of substance use may eventually become a *syndrome*, involving a need to use the substance to function, and may cause other physiologic changes that may be irreversible (such as damage to the brain, liver, or stomach).

2. *Psychoactive substance-abuse and dependence disorders* include maladaptive behaviors and potentially hazardous behavior, such as

driving while intoxicated. Substance *dependence* involves physiological dependence on the substance, in which the person will either show greater *tolerance* for the drug to achieve the desired effect or *withdrawal* symptoms such as sweating, hyperventilation, tremor, and tension due to abstinence when the drug is unavailable. Dependence on any substance or drug may lead to addiction. *Addiction* refers to an intense craving for a substance that results from a physical and/or psychological dependence due to prolonged, heavy use. Some people become addicted to prescribed drugs. This is termed *medical addiction* and occurs when a person feels that he or she cannot function without the use of a drug. Generally, these are psychoactive drugs, such as Valium, Librium, and Xanax. Often, overprescription has resulted not only in abuse of one drug but *cross addiction*, simultaneous abuse of more than one drug (e.g., mixing alcohol with tranquilizers). Abusers do not understand the potentially fatal results of cross addiction.

In analyzing the abuse of substances, we need to consider the person, situation, and audience. The chief executive of a multibillion-dollar corporation, who is drunk every afternoon and offers drinks to his associates, is labeled as a "great guy" for he socializes. On the other hand, a man with an empty bottle squatting on the sidewalk will be shrugged off as a "skid-row bum."

TYPOLOGY OF SUBSTANCE ABUSE

Substances used by people vary in quality, quantity, form (such as a drink, a pill, snuff, etc.), and intended use. Most drugs also have unintended consequences and often serious side-effects. Erich Goode (1990, p. 95) identified four types or "circles" of drugs in use in the United States: (1) medical use, (2) legal recreational use, (3) illegal instrumental use, and (4) illegal recreational use.

1. *Medical/therapeutic use*: Drugs prescribed by physicians and intended for medical therapy are *prescription drugs*. Over-the-counter (OTC) drugs, such as Sominex and Sleep-Eze, are obtained without a doctor's prescription. About 1.5 billion prescriptions are written annually for drugs, only half of which are refills. The prescription drug business is a $30 billion a year industry, and OTC drugs total about $10 billion annually. One of six or seven prescription drugs used each year is a *psychoactive drug*, even though their use has dropped sharply compared to during the 1960s and 1970s. There are several reasons: Many drugs (such as tranquilizers and sleeping aids) with a reasonable potency are

now available over the counter, and other drugs, such as barbiturates (Amytal, Seconal, and Nembutal), amphetamines (Benzedrine, Dexedrine, and Biphetamine), and methaqualone (Quaalude and Sopor) have lost popularity and have been replaced by other drugs, such as crack and cocaine.

2. *Legal psychoactive use*: Psychoactive drugs are easily available with few restrictions and are used for achieving a change in the state of the mind. People do not think of them as drugs because they are accepted as part of our culture. Such substances include tobacco, alcohol, and caffeine. For example, the National Institute on Drug Abuse reported in 1986 that about 114 million or 60% of Americans age 12 and over had consumed an alcoholic beverage in the past month. Alcohol is a *depressant* because it slows the activity of the central nervous system.

3. *Illegal instrumental use*: These substances are available without a physician's advice for instrumental purposes, especially to get high, to get a task done, or to counteract stress by calming feelings of anxiety or nervousness. Users often do not believe that they are "abusing" the substance or that there is anything illegal about their use.

4. *Illegal psychoactive use*: Compared to other kinds of substance use, illegal recreational use is a big business and involves huge amounts of money. Over the years, the demand for narcotic substances has increased in such proportions that annual transactions are estimated to amount to half a trillion dollars, three times the value of all U.S. currency in circulation (Mills, 1987, p. 3). Although there are no reliable figures available, others have estimated the retail drug trade at around $110 billion. This is more than the yearly sales of any major corporation in the United States (Smith, 1986, p. 15).

Drug use in the United States has reached epidemic proportions during the last 4 decades. The U.S. Department of Health and Human Services survey (1988) reported that some 72.5 million or 37% of Americans admit to illegal drug use at least once in their lives, and 28 million had used in the preceding year. Of those, half had used illegal drugs in the last month (U.S. Department of Health and Human Services, 1989, p. 17). According to government estimates, Americans have $110 billion drug habit (Smith, 1986, p. 15). People resort to drugs as a means of recreation, to ease tension, or to cope with difficult personal situations.

FACTORS THAT AFFECT SUBSTANCE USE

The wave of public concern over drugs and drug-related problems cannot be underestimated. Gang activity, kidnapping, murder, suicide, auto and industrial accidents, and crimes to support drug addiction have been ever-increasing. Erich Goode (1990, p. 89) called this concern "moral panic," a widespread, explosively upsurging feeling on the part of the public that something is terribly wrong in society because of a moral failure of a specific group of individuals, a subpopulation defined as the enemy. The public's perception of the seriousness of the problem depends on how it affects the individuals personally and how the media presents the problem to the public. Often the blame is placed on someone else. For example, the U.S. government contends that if Latin American drug lords can be stopped from producing cocaine and illegally exporting it to the United States, cocaine use in the United States will drop significantly. Others believe that this policy will simply drive the price of cocaine upward. The public will pay millions of dollars more for effective law enforcement, and the cocaine users will pay a much higher price for the drug. Many Third World countries whose unstable political systems cannot find lucrative alternative ways of improving their economies find drugs to be important cash crops. Of course, as long as we have willing users of drugs in the United States, drugs will certainly find their way here. It is fruitless to search for causes of the drug problem elsewhere and ignore the factors stemming from society itself. As John A. Clausen (1976, p. 105) put it, "If substantial numbers of persons find it necessary to use drugs in order to feel comfortable, or if their lives are lacking in meaning and they therefore turn to drugs to provide it, the problem is less in the drugs than in the way of life that has been afforded them."

Let us explore some of the factors that affect substance use:

1. *Culture*: In modern technological societies, the belief that humans are to conquer and exploit nature also encourages a feeling of condescension—humans have the supreme right to enjoy life, possibly in ways no one has experienced before. For some, getting high is a supreme experience—it is fun, exhilarating, and a means of getting away from immediate stresses of life. Recreational use is a big business involving huge amounts of money. Alcohol, for example, is so embedded in our culture that it has gained legitimacy as a recreational substance.

2. *Affluence*: In societies where material life is poor and technology has not touched the masses, most people cannot afford to use drugs unless they are readily available inexpensively. The United States is an affluent nation where most people can afford to buy drugs; and drug traffickers and drug lords make the most of the opportunity. The poor sometimes get involved in drug dealing at street corners and in ghetto neighborhoods to make quick and easy money. The big fish, the drug lords who deal in big money, shy away from such areas. By the time the

drug reaches the consumer, its price has multiplied several times, with distributors at each end making a profit.

3. *Interpersonal conflicts and changing gender roles*: Changing gender roles in the family is one of the leading causes of conflict. Conventional role playing provided a degree of stability. Due to a significant increase in dual-career families, chances of conflict have increased. Inadequate functioning of the family leaves scars on every member. Emotional neglect and crises are often handled by substance abuse. For example, men are threatened by the changing status of women. They are also prone to drinking to resolve their problems and less willing to admit their problems. They are four to five times more likely to suffer from alcoholism than women (U.S. Bureau of the Census, 1988, p. 52).

4. *Rapid social and cultural change*: Western societies have moved from the industrial and postindustrial age to the "information age" during the past 5 decades. When people are unable to adapt and cope with the ongoing changes, chances of emotional instability increase. To maintain stability and to relieve stress, people sometimes turn to substance use and abuse.

5. *Competition and survival*: Modern democracies are based on competition, which spans almost every aspect of life including education, job, and family. The presence of stressors remains a constant threat to the emotional integrity of the individual. To combat these stressors, people use a variety of means, including substance abuse, to cope and perform better. For many, dreams of success never materialize and frustration and alienation take their toll.

6. *Material success*: The drug culture has its victims and benefactors. Users are victims, but drug dealers, at the other end of the chain, make huge profits. People equate success with material success. Drug trafficking is a multibillion-dollar business simply because there are buyers and sellers everywhere. Many poor and downtrodden individuals see drug dealing as the only way to success. No wonder that in ghettos of major cities, juveniles are dealing drugs and making hundreds of dollars a day. Their families ignore their involvement in crime because they see it as the only way to success. The American class structure has not changed significantly in the past 100 years, and for those who do not see many chances in life, drug dealing seems to be the most lucrative alternative.

7. *Pathogenic families*: Healthy family is a relative term. Family pathology manifests itself in a variety of forms—the discordant family, disturbed family, disrupted family, inadequate family, antisocial family, maladaptive family, and disorganized family. Since 1975 there has been one divorce for each two new marriages (Right, 1989, p. 239), and the National Center for Health Statistics estimates that about 40% of today's marriages will end in divorce. Sharon Price (1990, p. 30) suggested that

in coming decades, two thirds of new marriages may end in divorce. Remarriage of former spouses adds further to the anxieties of children, who run the risk of being aliens in the new family. Loss of trust and mixed emotions toward a new stepparent may drive some youngsters to the haven of drugs. These and multitudes of other problems lead to frustration, demoralization, despair, drug and alcohol abuse, and possible mental disorder.

8. *Narcissism versus familism*: As opposed to individualism, familism places the family above individual interests. Familism includes many responsibilities and obligations to the immediate family and to kin. Familism has both positive and negative consequences for the individual. On the positive side, sociologists have identified lower mental illness rates, lower divorce rates, increased personal happiness, and secure feelings about aging in many American families (Kephart & Jedlicka, 1991, p. 120). Narcissistic values contradict the ideals of familism. Levine (1981, p. 78) pointed out that excessive individualism has undercut the middle-class family's efforts to achieve stability and happiness. Unbridled individualism will continue to trouble and disrupt marriage and family life, and children will increasingly pay the emotional costs of negligent and inadequate parenting.

9. *Recreation*: Americans are fun-loving and adventurous people, and they are always willing to experiment and seek excitement. Many substances are used for their recreational value, to "get high" or to "feel good." However, frequent recreational use may eventually lead to addiction and other problems, because most drugs are seductive and can lower the resistance of even strong-willed people. Misconceptions about the potential adverse effects of substances used allow their continued use and sometimes abuse (see Table 7–1).

ALCOHOL

Alcohol was an early invention, dating back at least 10,000 years. It emerges from fermented sugar in fruits, grains, and other food substances. Actually, alcohol is *ethyl alcohol* or *ethanol*. Other varieties of alcohol are very toxic and not adequate for human consumption. Not only is the production process simple, but the product has remarkable magical properties to induce euphoria, sedation, intoxication, and narcosis. Alcohol is omnipresent throughout the world, from the most simple societies to the most complex, from Hinduism to Christianity, and from inner-city ghettos to the boardrooms of multinational corporations. As Robert Straus (1976, p. 184) put it, "Its great capacity for alleviating pain,

TABLE 7-1 • Commonly Abused Psychoactive Drugs

Class	Drugs	Usage
Antianxiety drugs (tranquilizers)	Equanil Lithium Miltown Valium Xanax, etc.	To reduce anxiety and restlessness and to induce sleep
Opioids (narcotics)	Opium and its derivatives: Codeine Morphine Heroin Opium Methadone (synthetic)	To combat physical pain, stress, and anxiety; to experience flight of fancy and self-absorption
Psychedelics 1. Cannabinoids 2. Hallucinogens	Hashish Marijuana LSD Mescaline (peyote) Psilocybin PCP	To experience pleasant reverie and musing mood and behavior, expansion of mind; languor and stupor
Depressants (sedatives)	Alcohol Barbiturates Benzodiazepines Meprobamate, etc.	To relax, reduce inhibitions, improve social interaction and sleep
Stimulants	Amphetamines Cocaine Crack Ice	To reduce fatigue and increase concentration, alertness, endurance, sex drive, and ability to stay awake for long periods

Note: This table does not include all drugs. Many of these drugs have legitimate therapeutic uses, but they also may be abused because they cause psychological dependence.

relieving tension and worry, and producing a pleasurable sense of well-being, relaxation, conviviality and good will toward others" makes alcohol an almost universally accepted beverage and a most agreeable psychoactive substance.

Many use alcohol as a therapeutic drug to fight nagging problems and to keep their lives from falling apart. However, alcohol is a nervous system depressant and is classified with barbiturates and antianxiety drugs (Julian, 1985). The overall impact of alcohol ingestion is not only determined by its intake but also by the biochemical makeup of the individual. Behavioral symptoms of alcohol ingestion are impaired judgment and rational processes, disorientation, amnesia, lowered self-control, poor motor coordination, blunted perception, and violent behavior. Brain cells are destroyed by heavy alcohol use, leading to serious neurological problems. Alcohol interferes with the release of norepinephrine and dopamine in the brain, affecting the same receptor sites that control the potential for addiction to alcohol and opiates (National Institute on Alcohol Abuse and Alcoholism, 1985). For women, use of alcohol during pregnancy may cause fetal alcohol syndrome, which may cause the fetus to be deformed or brain damaged. Such damage may also occur from abuse of other drugs, including opiates and cocaine; mixing of drugs or cross addiction can be fatal to the fetus.

The potency of alcoholic beverages varies by percent of *absolute alcohol* they contain. The influence of alcohol is determined not by the kind of drink itself but the amount of absolute alcohol it contains. Beer contains 4 to 5% alcohol; wine about 12%; whiskey, gin, rum, and vodka, sold under various brand names, contain about 40 to 50% alcohol or are 80 to 100 "proof." The effects of alcohol are influenced by several factors, such as size of the drinker, presence of food and water in the stomach, rate of ingestion (how many drinks in an hour), and presence of carbonation in the beverage. Finally, *blood-alcohol concentration* (BAC) or *blood-alcohol level* (BAL) reflects the percent of alcohol in one's blood that determines the alcohol-influenced condition. Four cans of beer (48 oz.) or four glasses of wine (16 oz.) ingested by a person weighing 150 pounds can raise the BAC/BAL to .10 level, which constitutes legal intoxication in most states. The Federal Aviation Administration sets a .04% BAC and prohibits pilots from flying at this level of intoxication.

Alcohol Abuse and Dependence

Over 80 million Americans drink and spend over $75 billion annually on their drinking. In 1987, per capita consumption of alcoholic beverages was 34.4 gallons of beer, 2.3 gallons of distilled spirits, and 3.4 gallons of wine (NIDA, 1989). Per capita alcohol consumption has doubled in the last 50 years. About 5% of the adult population has a serious drinking problem, and 10 to 15 million Americans have experienced episodes of abusive use of alcohol. According to the U.S. National Highway Traffic Safety Administration, in 1988, of a total of 62,237 fatal accidents, 20,208 involved drunk drivers. The highest rates were in the 25–34 age group, followed by 18–21, and 22–24 (U.S. Bureau of the Census, 1990, p. 608).

Explanations of Alcohol Abuse

Biological Explanations
Along with biochemical susceptibility, another factor responsible for alcoholism is neuropathology—neurological disorders, which may be hereditary or congenital (such as brain lesions). Increased dopamine levels in the brain, according to one theory, increase schizophrenic symptoms; alcohol acts to interfere with the release of dopamine, thereby reducing such symptoms. Excessive drinking over long periods along with a neurological condition may lead to "alcoholic psychosis."

Psychological Explanations
Psychological explanations attribute alcoholism to personality problems, character or moral disorders, and some physiological vulnerabilities. Jellinek (1960) contended that alcoholism evolves in stages: Psychological dependence follows biological dependency, leading to addiction. Although it appears logical, this theory has not been tested rigorously. Pure psychological explanations include inadequate mothering, latent homosexuality that alcoholics try to conceal, schizophrenic tendencies that are masked by alcohol abuse, suicidal tendencies that alcohol helps in averting, and inadequate personality that seeks gratification in alcohol. Researchers have not yet come up with precise characteristics for the "alcoholic personality," and most of the aforementioned explanations lack significant research support.

Sociocultural Explanations
Alcohol use and abuse varies among different groups and cultures. For example, alcoholism rates are high among Irish Americans and lower among Jewish people. The interactionist explanation implies that abusers are products of frustrations, ruined relationships, and emotional deprivations. They are engaged in a retreat from reality, to combat job-related stress or to avoid friction with authority, to relieve themselves of emptiness, intolerable situations, and feelings of inadequacy and inferiority. Unhappy families, broken homes, desertion, divorce, impoverished families, and deprived or displaced children are all part of the toll. They are all caught in the "alcohol web." The sociological way of looking at the alcoholic person focuses on changing their relationships and problems in living, as do rehabilitative efforts espoused by those adhering to this approach.

Norman K. Denzin (1987) examined alcoholism by applying principles of symbolic interactionalism. He contended that the alcoholic self is in the center of alcoholic experience. The culture dictates the attitudes attached to the drinking act and how to act under its influence. The social meanings attached to drinking are not the same among all groups within a society. If the culture encourages alcohol abuse and does not have models of controlled drinking organized around family or religious rituals, it is likely to have high rates of alcoholism. The alcoholic self lives as a divided self—the sober self and the intoxicated self. The divided self magnifies deep-seated negative emotions, which include resentment, anger, fear, self-loathing, self-pity, self-hatred, despair, anguish, remorse, guilt, and shame. Significant others of the alcoholic are caught up in the emotional turmoil and are unable to communicate effectively. The flawed interactions produce a variety of emotional problems, including anxiety and depression (Denzin 1987, p. 135). After alcoholics "hit the bottom," they may (on their own or through coercion) seek treatment to detoxify (to manage the severity of alcoholism) and begin attending meetings of Alcoholics Anonymous (AA). Alcoholics Anonymous approaches alcoholism from a holistic perspective through its 12-step program incorporating mental, physical, spiritual, and interactional aspects of the alcoholic's life. It has better success rates compared to other treatment and rehabilitation methods.

MARIJUANA

Marijuana, "pot," "grass," "weed," and "smoke," one of the most widely used illegal drug in the United States, is made of dried leaves and flowering tops of the *Cannabis sativa* or *Cannabis indica* plants. The history of cannabis use is lengthy. Hashish, commonly known as *hash*, contains only the resin and flowering tops of the plant. Although smoking is the most common mode of consumption in the United States for both psychoactive substances, in South Asian countries where its use is legal, hashish is sometimes an ingredient in milkshakes, pastry, eggrolls, and sweet dishes during celebrations. Marijuana has been used in the United States for quite some time for medicinal purposes and for recreational use, especially among poor whites, blacks, and Hispanics; it was only declared illegal by the federal government in 1937. Its popularity increased significantly among middle-class youth in the 1960s. Movements against the Vietnam War, the draft, and disenchantment with the policies of the federal government gave rise to rejection of parental values and confrontation with the establishment. Smoking dope/pot, long hair and beards, dingy clothing, and wire-rimmed glasses became symbols of antipatriotism. Marijuana became a drug of choice not only among college youth but gradually among high school youth. Fifty-one percent of American high school seniors graduating in the class of 1979 had used marijuana, and over half had used it in the previous month (Kandel, 1980, p. 241). Marijuana is not the social drug of choice, however, alcohol use in open parties is socially acceptable, and in one study of high school students, one third of the respondents reported getting drunk during the 2 weeks preceding the survey. Some experts consider alcohol "the drug of choice" among youth. Although American youth are more likely to have tried alcohol than marijuana, high school seniors in the 1970s were more likely to be marijuana smokers than drinkers (Beckman, Johnston, & O'Malley, 1981). Spiraling marijuana use has, over the years, affected a good deal of the population. Nationally, people who tried marijuana more than doubled between the early 1970s, 24 million in 1972 to 56 million in 1982, and 60 million in 1985. Nearly one in four people has tried marijuana and, at one time, over 20 million used it once or more in a month (President's Commission on Organized Crime, 1986, p. 48). During the past few years, however, marijuana use has been declining. Altogether, Americans spend over $25 billion per year on marijuana and consume about 130,000 pounds per day. Its current price ranges from $50 to $200 an ounce, quite a jump from $15 an ounce in 1960s. More potent marijuana is available now due to competition with other drugs; however, its use peaks among 18 to 21 year olds and tapers off among people in their thirties. Its use has stabilized and may decline due to the increasing number of older Americans (Gallagher, 1987, pp. 196–197).

What does pot do to the human mind and body? The psychoactive agent in marijuana is delta-9-tetrahydrocannibinol (THC). Its immediate impact is on the central nervous system; however, each user may have a combination of experiences, including dryness of mouth, increased heartbeat, red eyes, poor motor coordination, memory loss, feelings of exhilaration, distortion of identity, time, and distance, talkativeness, slow speech, hunger, and drowsiness.

Controversies regarding marijuana use center on its short-term behavioral and long-term health consequences; and experts and the public are sharply divided. Part of the concern also relates to the unknown adverse effects of marijuana and masking of mental problems and attributed to its use. Marijuana has been perceived as a drug that had no place in the Anglo-Saxon culture, and therefore it has been easier to accept alcohol than marijuana. Like any other drug, marijuana has its negative mental and physical effects and is suspected as a cause for lower motivation, poor judgment and productivity, short-term memory loss, chromosome, lung, heart, and brain damage, deterioration of the body's immunological and metabolic functions, and general impairment of mental abilities, including toxic psychosis. Yet we must not ignore that even if such adverse effects are found, they are determined by the amount and frequency of use and cross abuse (using a combination of substances) of drugs. Marijuana is not addictive and does not cause any withdrawal symptoms; however, long-term use may lead to higher tolerance levels and deterioration of lung functioning due to smoking. Unlike other drugs, marijuana use does not cause any personality disorders or antisocial activities, including crime. Critics charge that there is no significant evidence that marijuana is more dangerous than alcohol and that actually its effects are more manageable. Several studies have confirmed that marijuana does not cause any brain dysfunctions and has no effect on IQ and cognitive functioning, intellectual growth, or academic achievement. On the positive side, recent research on marijuana indicates that it has medicinal qualities and is useful in the treatment of glaucoma, nausea accompanying cancer chemotherapy, asthma, certain kinds of epileptic seizures, and nervous system disorders.

HEROIN

Heroin, named for its "heroic" qualities, was synthesized in the 1870s by a German pharmaceutical company. A derivative of opium (a powerful depressant substance found in the *Papaver somniferum* poppy plant) heroin is 3 times more potent than the parent drug morphine. Its addictive potential was soon established and it was stripped of medical respectability. Chinese immigrants, at the turn of the century, were blamed for the introduction of opiates in the United States, and prejudice against them brought tighter control of the commerce in narcotics of all kinds. By 1924, heroin manufacture was completely banned. It was designated as a "most dangerous drug" and associated with psychopathology, violence, organized crime, and later with the frightening AIDS epidemic, and it is the least widely used illicit drug. Pleasurable experiences reported by the heroin users have their darker side because of the ease with which a user can overdose. The President's Commission on Organized Crime (1986, p. 41) reported that in 1984 there were 1,046 deaths and 10,901 emergency room visits due to heroin overdose, the largest number of deaths of illicit drug users.

Other substances derived from opiates are morphine, codeine, and methadone. Known by its various slang names as "white stuff," "hard stuff," "junk," "smack," "scag," "horse," "M," "H," and "schoolboy," opium can be used in a variety of ways. It may be taken orally, smoked, sniffed (snorted), injected into the skin (skin-popping), and injected into the bloodstream (mainlining).

Most heroin is illegally imported from countries of southeast Asia, particularly Burma, Laos, Thailand (called the Golden Triangle), and Mexico. Of course, opiates are imported legally from countries of South and Southeast Asia by licensed pharmaceutical companies. Estimates are that there are between 500,000 and 1,000,000 heroin addicts in the United States and two to three times that number of occasional users, so-called chippers. The chippers are hard to identify because they use the drug to feel good or for "kicks" but they are not "hooked." Addiction results from frequent and regular use, developing a tolerance for higher doses. Many addicts use three to four injections a day; some switch to other drugs. Heroin users known to law enforcement agencies are those who are frequently involved in property crimes, such as stealing, robbery, burglary, and drug dealing to maintain a constant supply of the drug; such crimes cost society several billion dollars annually. The cost of supporting the drug habit for an addict may range from $5,000 to $50,000 a year. Addicts who cannot afford or find the drug suffer from withdrawal symptoms—chills, cramps, diarrhea, discomfort, excessive sweating, nausea, and weight loss. Hard-core addicts are a class in themselves; they are young, male, poor, uneducated, and residents of slums in large metropolitan areas (Clayton & Voss, 1981).

COCAINE, CRACK, AND "ICE"

Cocaine is a central nervous system stimulant drug, an alkaloid derived from the leaves of the coca plant. It is also known as "coke," "snow," "flake," "gold dust," "nose candy," "Peruvian," and "white girl," among others. When the mixture of cocaine, baking soda, and water is heated, the precipitated crystals are known as "crack." Although its purity is always suspect, crack is cheaper and quite potent. The major source of cocaine is the area around the Andes Mountains in South America and Bolivia, Colombia, Ecuador, and Peru, the countries where coca crops are raised and leaves are processed in the form of a paste. The paste can be swallowed or smoked with tobacco or marijuana. Further processing of the paste turns it into an odorless white powder that can be sniffed, injected into the veins, or smoked in "free-base" form (chemically purified by soaking it in ether). The light-weight powder can be smuggled easily; much of it is delivered by air, and shipments are broken down and delivered at major destinations in U.S. cities. Since 1980, the influx of smuggled cocaine has risen from about 25 tons to 125 tons a year and

> **BOX 7–1 • Cocaine Babies**
>
> Research has recently begun on babies born to cocaine users. Studies show that cocaine babies are premature, with a low birth weight. They have a high-pitched, frantic cry that may last for hours, and they spit more than healthy babies. Their arms and legs may tremble with the symptoms of withdrawal, and they are at greater risk for Sudden Infant Death Syndrome, or crib death. They suffer not only because of the cocaine but because cocaine-using mothers often use alcohol and other drugs as well. The Illinois Department of Children and Family Services, in January 1991, reported that the number of babies born with evidence of drug in their system (predominantly cocaine) jumped from 181 in 1985 to 2,404 in 1990. Black mothers used drugs most frequently during pregnancy—85.5% of the babies were black, 12.5% white, and 4.1% Hispanic.
>
> Although the impact of crack on the fetus is not fully identified, crack causes low birth weight and affects fetal brain cells leading to neurological damage along the pleasure pathways and other nearby parts of the brain. Damage to the brain impairs or alters a wide range of responses, including, the ability to respond to pleasure experiences, to communicate, to establish emotional attachments, or to make certain kinds of judgments. Crack babies appear to experience much greater anxiety and temperamental problems, such as low adaptability, low persistence, failure to sleep and awaken at normal, regular times, and difficulty in leaving their mothers when it is time for school. Initial experimental programs suggest that these children can benefit greatly from placement in highly structured, highly tailored educational day care settings beginning in early infancy.

See Hutchinson, J., 1991, pp. 31–32; and *Peoria Journal Star*, January 6, 1991, pp. D1–D2.

continues to increase (Morganthau, Greenberg, Murr, Miller, & Raine, 1986, p. 19).

Generally, recreational use of illegal drugs is on the decline; however, the use of cocaine and crack is on the rise. A survey conducted by the University of Michigan, Institute of Social Research, in 1987 found that 1 in 18 high school seniors admitted to trying crack; 14% said they had used cocaine in other forms. The survey did not include dropouts, who have a higher likelihood of using drugs. Among young adults, 6.7% had tried crack and 40% cocaine (Adler et al., 1988, pp. 64–75). In 1985, some 647,000 people used cocaine once a week or more according to the National Institute on Drug Abuse; by 1988, the number was 862,000; currently, the figure is estimated to be close to 3 million. About

246,000 people used cocaine daily in 1985; 292,000 in 1988; and chances are that the current figure is close to 300,000.

Why have cocaine and crack become drugs of choice? Their effects are rapid and their impact gives quick, temporary relief from life's demands, anxieties, and conflicts (see Box 7-1). Cocaine is a psychoactive drug. Taken intranasally, it takes 3 minutes to get high and its effects last about 30 minutes. When injected, it takes 15 to 20 seconds to experience orgasm-like pleasure. When it is smoked, either in free-base or crack, its effect is even faster (about 5 to 8 seconds); the rush lasts for a few minutes followed by an afterglow of about 20 minutes. The heightened pleasure experienced impels the user to use the drug over and over again and increases the likelihood of addiction.

The popularity of cocaine and crack are based on perceived experiences. First, they provide feelings of exhilaration, euphoria, elation, and well-being and create a voluptuous and joyous state of mind; second, they give the user confidence, a sensation of mastery and competence; and third, they provide increased energy and control over fatigue, a stimulating effect that allows the user to continue physical and mental activity more intensely and for a longer than normal period of time (Goode, 1990, p. 106). No wonder that cocaine has become the drug of junkies, cops, hookers, musicians, designers, stockbrokers, and corporate executives. In the 1980s, we reinvented cocaine. The first epidemic of cocaine abuse lasted from the 1890s to the 1920s, and the second began in the 1970s. Cocaine used to be a major ingredient in many patented and prescribed medicines in the United States as late as 1919, and in soft drinks, such as Coca-Cola, until 1903. At the turn of the century, it was suspected that cocaine was the drug of black people and was a cause of their involvement in crimes, especially violent crimes. Until the late 1960s, cocaine was known as the drug of the despised groups—blacks, poor whites, and criminals—but it gained popularity in the middle and upper classes by 1985. The new synthetic drug of the 1990s, even more potent and deadly than crack, is "ice," which may gain increasing popularity due to its more dramatic effects (see Box 7-2).

Psychological dependence on cocaine and crack has its negative effects, including anxiety, depression, short-temperedness, paranoia, impaired judgment and concentration, and loss of interest in work and family responsibilities. Often the drug takes hold of the person to the point that food, sex, and other means of entertainment are replaced by the cocaine high. In extreme cases, dependence leads to cocaine psychosis, marked by delusions, hallucinations, hearing voices, disconnected thoughts, imagined persecutors, and violent behavior. Testing for psychological dependence, Richard H. Swartz, Medical Director of

> **BOX 7-2 • The Fire of Ice**
>
> Tad Yamaguchi, age 20 and fresh out of college, saw a bright future when he found a job at an air freight company in Honolulu. His job was demanding. One of his superiors offered him a puff from a small glass pipe—a little something to help him get through the grueling 24-hour shift. He could not refuse and he said, "I felt alert, in control. It did not seem to have a downside." No wonder so many people in the office were using it. Yamaguchi had never done drugs before was now smoking every day and buying large quantities of the drug. Before kicking his habit a year ago, he had lost 35 pounds and was smoking for 4 days at a time and then crashing in a comatose sleep that lasted for 36 hours. Ice, *Methamphetamine*, is in a crystal form and is cooked in a laboratory using legally obtainable chemicals. The Japanese call it *shabu;* to Koreans it is *hiroppon*. It costs $50 a "paper," less than a gram. It is far more addictive and pernicious than crack or cocaine. It causes immediate, intense euphoria and increased alertness. The side-effects are aggressive behavior, hallucinations, paranoia, and fatal kidney failure (see Lerner, 1989, pp. 37–39).

Virginia Drug Rehabilitation Center, found that monkeys allowed unlimited supply of intravenous cocaine died of convulsions within 5 days (Morganthau et al., 1986, p. 22).

AMPHETAMINES

Amphetamines are synthetically derived stimulants. Phenylisopropylamine, or amphetamine proper, was first synthesized in the 1880s and first tested on human beings in the 1920s. Many such chemically related substances developed since the early twentieth century and as a group are known as amphetamines. While stimulants are available through physician's prescriptions (Benzedrine, Dexedrine, Methedrine, Desoxyn, and Ritalin), people who need them for nonmedical purposes or are addicted obtain them by faking symptoms of a disorder for which they are usually prescribed or seek them in the illicit drug market.

Amphetamines are also known as "speed," "fast," "pep pills," "bennies," "dexies," "footballs," "black beauties," "crystal," and "meth." Amphetamine congeners or sympathomimetic amines mimic or enhance the activity of the central nervous system and functions of the body by heightening arousal, increasing behavioral activity, and suppressing fatigue. As soon as they are swallowed, smoked, inhaled, or injected, the body's organic system reacts—the heartbeat speeds up, respiratory rate increases, pupils are enlarged, body temperature rises, blood pressure increases, and blood vessels are constricted (HMS-MHL, 1990, pp. 1–4). Amphetamines are similar to norepinephrine and dopamine neurotransmitters released in the body and brain; therefore, the introduction of the drug in the body directly affects the limbic system, which governs much of emotional life. Cocaine works in almost the same way, but amphetamines stay longer in the bloodstream and cause long-lasting intoxication, while cocaine's effects are more subtle and less dramatic. From the 1930s to the 1960s, the medical profession regarded amphetamines as a panacea for a variety of problems—opiate and nicotine addiction, seasickness, Parkinsonism, depression, fatigue, hyperkinesis (hyperactive disorder), controlling weight, and narcolepsy (a disorder with symptoms of sudden and irresistible daytime attacks of sleepiness), among other conditions. People have used them to stay awake, to perform better, to increase stamina, and to complete an uninteresting task. It is suspected that during the world wars, amphetamines were prescribed to soldiers to enhance their combat capability. In the 1970s, it became clear that amphetamines were ineffective for most medical purposes. However, they were used for the treatment of learning disabilities or conduct disorders in 3% of school-age children. But their effectiveness is limited. In about half the cases, the symptoms—hyperactivity, restlessness, impulsiveness, short temper, and difficulty in concentrating—persists in adolescence and adulthood, turning the children into drug abusers or antisocial personalities (HMS-MHL, 1990, p. 2).

"Speed freaks," who often inject amphetamines, experience an immediate rush of euphoria accompanied by dramatic hyperactivity, higher energy levels and vigor, incessant walking and talking, and daredevil physical endurance.

Amphetamines have serious side-effects. Acute intoxication may cause restlessness, tension, agitation, confusion, and irrational rage that leads to violence. High doses can produce delusional disorder, visual and auditory hallucinations, and some schizophrenia-like symptoms: hypersensitivity to sound, light, and touch; loss of interest in sex; and impotency.

BARBITURATES

Barbiturates, also known as "downers," are chemical compounds used by millions of people to slow down the action of the central nervous system. They have legitimate medical uses for certain conditions, including anxiety, insomnia, restlessness, high blood pressure, and epilepsy. Due to our rigid schedules and our high levels of concern about our health and perfection, we have little tolerance for variations in our sleeping habits.

Many young people experiment with barbiturates, but many middle-aged and older people use them as tranquilizers or sleeping pills without realizing that they are abusing the drug. Some people use barbiturates with amphetamines and alcohol to achieve a high, but this combination can be fatal. Women are more inclined to use these drugs. About 27,000 Americans die every year from barbiturate overdoses. Treatments are similar to other addictions but take longer than alcohol and opiate abuse.

HALLUCINOGENS

Hallucinogenic drugs, once called "psychedelics" (slang names—LSD, cubes, acid, STP, DMT, Mesc, PCP, or angel dust), act on the nervous system and produce significant distortions in consciousness and visual and perceptual imageries. LSD is one of the most potent synthesized drugs and can produce intoxication with minute amounts smaller than a grain of salt. *Mescaline* and *psilocybin* are natural substances derived from peyote and "magic mushroom," respectively. Dr. Albert Hofmann synthesized LSD (d-lysergic acid diethyomide) in Basel, Switzerland, in 1938, and in 1943 he accidentally inhaled a tiny amount of the drug. He experienced a "stream of fantastic images of extraordinary plasticity and vividness . . . accompanied by an intense kaleidoscopic-like play of colors." The drug (only 250 micrograms) caused him a feeling of timelessness, depersonalization, a loss of control, and extraordinary fear of going crazy or becoming psychotic (Goode, 1990, p. 103). Popular in the 1960s, LSD caused much hysteria in the public, and its use peaked in 1979. Hallucinogens today are used less frequently. Only 7% of all individuals who had taken LSD once or more in their lives took it during the past month (NIDA, 1986); however, its use is increasing steadily. There is no evidence that LSD enhances intellectual or creative ability, but it can cause acute psychosis, which requires hospitalization and psychotherapy to treat flashbacks, trauma, and dependence.

DELIRIANTS

Household cleaners, solvents, and consumer products, including glue, gasoline, lighter fluid, paint thinner, varnish, shellac, nail polish remover, and aerosol-packaged products, are used by people for "kicks" or to escape from problems and worries. Deliriants are also known as *inhalants* and are sniffed to achieve mild intoxication, followed by excitement and exhilaration. They produce a high sometimes accompanied by bizarre thoughts, aggressiveness, dizziness, loss of judgment, unconsciousness, and irreversible damage because their fumes or vapors replace the oxygen necessary for the brain and other vital organs.

NICOTINE

Concern about nicotine, the active ingredient in tobacco, has received much attention in recent years. However, it is one of the legal and most frequently used substances, in the form of cigarettes, cigars, snuff, and pipe and chewing tobacco. One out of three, or 60 million Americans, have smoked tobacco in the past 30 days (NIDA, 1986). Tobacco use accounts for 300,000 deaths per year in the United States, from lung and other kinds of cancer as well as heart disease and strokes. In 1988, the U.S. Surgeon General C. Everett Koop declared nicotine one of the most dangerous and addictive substances (Clark & Hager, 1988, p. 56). Nicotine is a mood-altering substance, a stimulant, and those who are hooked develop tolerance and the need to increase use. Its use is driven by strong, often irresistible urges and can persist despite repeated efforts to quit. Along with nicotine, tar, nitrogen dioxide, formaldehyde, and other chemicals pass into the bloodstream; the chemicals accumulate in the brain and seem to act on specific receptors in nerve cells. Cessation leads to withdrawal symptoms, including restlessness, irritability, poor concentration, headaches, sleep disturbances, increased appetite, weight gain, and depression.

On the hopeful side, 40 million Americans have already quit smoking in recent years on their own, and public awareness has promoted an increasingly smoke-free environment. Behavior modification, group therapy, and stress-reduction techniques have, to some extent, helped some people. Success rates are higher when lifestyle changes are accompanied by other wellness programs.

OTHER ADDICTIONS

Rarely do we think of food as being addictive, but overeating has the same behavioral manifestations as found in alcoholism or cigarette smoking. The consequence is obesity, which leads to further problems, such as functional difficulties, unattractiveness, poor self-image, anxiety, and conditions like high blood pressure, cardiovascular diseases, diabetes, and musculoskeletal problems. Estimates are that over 80 million Americans are overweight; among them 30 million are severely overweight; and about 10 million suffer from *hyperobesity*—extreme obesity in which a person is 100 pounds over the ideal body weight. Not all obese people have obsessions with food; they may have medical conditions. Obesity, however, may be a personality disorder, a product of underlying mental conditions involving loss of control over one's appetite and a preoccupation with eating. Stress, anxieties, and emotional neglect may characterize such compulsive behavior. Weight-loss programs, exercise gadgets, diet books, diet pills, diet aids, diet programs, and appetite-suppressing drugs are a $15 billion a year business.

Metabolic or endocrine anomalies can cause obesity, but these are rare. However, an excess of adipose cells (fat cells) in the body is a known cause. Overfeeding in childhood predisposes a person to excesses of these cells. Diet programs reduce the amount of fat in these cells but not the number of cells; consequently, as soon as the person returns to the original diet, weight increases again. Eating habits are part of a culture and are learned. In a consumer-oriented society, advertisements to sell food products reinforce food's pleasurable qualities for almost all occasions—dinners, parties, open houses, and celebrations.

EXPLANATIONS OF SUBSTANCE ABUSE

We know that drugs are used and abused for transforming mental states, but what causes such behavior? It is important for us to understand that one-time use or experimental use of a substance on a few occasions in one's lifetime does not make a person an addict. Often, such experiences are determined by numerous factors, including personalities and settings (Zinberg, 1984). Space limitations do not allow us go into detail; however, a brief discussion of biological, psychological, and sociological theories or explanations is in order.

Biological Explanations

The biological (physiological, genetic, neurological) model stresses that certain people, due to their biological makeup, are predisposed to substance abuse. They experience overpowering desire, compulsion, and craving dictated by forces beyond their control. They are hooked and helpless. Medical model studies on animals and humans have informed us, although inconsistently, that certain chemicals generate a strong physiological response, leading to the "disease theory of addiction"

(Abadinsky, 1989, p. 113). Drugs compensate for the deficiencies in the user's nervous system and restore the sense of well-being to stave off apathy and depression (Khantzian, 1985). This is why alcoholics and opiate addicts return to drinking or heroin use after periods of abstinence. For example, it is theorized that cocaine addiction may be due to dopamine depletion. Critics contend that biological explanations have medicalized a personal and social problem to the extent that instead of being deviant the victim is viewed as a patient with a medical problem. Many also suffer from the "self-fulfilling prophecy" of being a substance abuser. Social science studies show that drinking patterns of alcoholics do not conform to the "loss of control" theory. Success rates of alleviating problem drinking by nonmedical therapies, such as the 12-step program by Alcoholics Anonymous suggest that alcoholism is rooted in social and cultural systems rather than the biological makeup of the individuals. Class, race, ethnicity are associated with alcoholism and some groups are identified as "ethnic drinking subcultures" (Greeley, McCready, & Theisen, 1980; Marlatt, Demming, & Reid, 1973; Miller & Hester, 1980; Vaillant, 1983).

Psychological Explanations

From a psychological perspective, substance abuse is primarily a personality disorder (addictive personality) marked by highly temperamental, aggressive, demanding, paranoid, rebellious, irresponsible, withdrawn, impulsive, and histrionic characteristics. But many of these traits are also found among great intellectuals, artists, and inventors. Taking inventory of psychological variables to predict substance abuse has not been fruitful.

Sociological Explanations

Sociologists see substance abuse as an interactive phenomenon, a product of social settings and relationships. The National Institute on Drug Abuse (1989) reported several factors associated with adolescent substance abuse: a family history of substance abuse, poor and inconsistent parental supervision ranging from complete laxity to rigid controls, history of antisocial behavior or criminality, association with substance abusers, early aggressive behavior, lack of interest in school, and alienation. Merton's (1968) concept of anomie and modes of individual adaptation, especially retreatism and rebellion offer some insight. When individuals are confronted by the contradictions between goals and means, they are estranged from a society that promises them in principle what they are denied in reality. Substance abuse, ideally, allows them to attain a high and in that process reject conventional social norms. Substance abusers are also viewed as deviants, outlaws, and mentally disordered individuals, sometimes leading to a self-fulfilling prophecy. These labels assigned to substance abusers have changed through time, as have the substances abused. We pursue this argument further in Chapter 13.

CHAPTER REVIEW

1. What is substance abuse? How do we draw the line between use and abuse?
2. What factors influence the prohibition of a substance? Is it based on objective scientific tests or the philosophy of people in power?
3. Why do Americans seek, use, and abuse substances? What are some factors associated with substance abuse?
4. Alcohol is one of the most dangerous substances and is abused by more people than all other substances. Explain.
5. What are psychoactive drugs? Explain how depressants work on the human mind. Do they have any adverse side-effects?
6. The popularity of drugs changes over time. Why has crack/cocaine become the "drug of choice" in recent times?
7. Millions of Americans use substances every day, both legal and illegal. Why is substance abuse considered a mental health problem?
8. What distinguishes biological explanations of substance abuse from sociological explanations?
9. Distinguish between
   a. Hallucinogens and barbiturates
   b. Depressants and psychedelics
   c. Heroin and crack
   d. Tranquilizers and deliriants

FOR FURTHER STUDY

Abadinsky, H. (1989). *Drug abuse*. Chicago: Nelson-Hall.
Cahalan, D. (1987). *Understanding America's drinking problem*. San Francisco: Jossey-Bass.
Denzin, N. (1989). *The alcoholic self*. Beverly Hills, CA: Sage.
Goode, E. (1989). *Drugs in American society*. (3rd ed.). New York: Alfred Knopf.
Musto, D. F. (1988). *The American disease: Origins of narcotics control*. (rev. ed.). New York: Oxford University Press.

National Institute on Drug Abuse (NIDA). (1985). *Cocaine use in America: Epidemiologic and clinical perspectives*. Research Monograph 61. Rockville, MD: National Institute on Drug Abuse.

Peele, S. (1985). *The meaning of addiction*. Lexington, MA: Lexington Books.

Peluso, E., & Peluso, L. S. (Eds.). (1988). *Women and drugs: Getting hooked, getting clean*. Minneapolis: CompCare Publications.

Stephens, R. (1987). *Mood-altering drugs*. Beverly Hills, CA: Sage.

▶ 8
Sexuality and Mental Disorders

Throughout history, sexual expression has received a great deal of attention. One of the issues that has been difficult to address is what constitutes "normal" sexual behavior. What people do in their private sex lives may be significantly different from their public image. This reflects variations in people's beliefs about sex and sexual expressions. Human variations are so vast that what is acceptable in one culture or group may be considered deviant in another. Sexual relations are regulated in all known societies because of the belief that complete freedom in such relationships may lead to chaos.

CULTURE AND SEXUALITY

In Murdock's (1949, p. 268) first sample of 250 societies, he found that some societies recognize "privileged relationships" both before marriage and for married people that give the people legitimate sexual outlets with certain classes of kin. One of the most common privileged relationships is with cross cousins, who are also preferred marriage partners. Of 250 societies, 11 allowed sexual intercourse with a father's sister's daughter, and 14 with a mother's sister's daughter.

Murdock also found that most world societies do not see anything inconsistent between the regulation of sex in marriage and considerable freedom before marriage. Apparently, complete premarital chastity is a minority pattern around the world. Murdock reported premarital sexual relationships to be fully approved in 65 societies, conditionally approved in 43, mildly approved in 6, and forbidden in 44. In societies where premarital freedom is not permitted, premarital relations with cross cousins are permitted. Thus, about 70% of the societies for which data were available allowed premarital intercourse. However, this generalization should be considered with a word of caution. Many major nations and cultures, such as China, India, Japan, Egypt, and nations with predominantly Buddhist, Hindu, Islamic, and Catholic populations do not allow such premarital freedom, at least in theory.

In the United States and most of the Western world, sexuality has received much attention. Due to the impact of Anglo-Saxon tradition, it is considered a disruptive aspect of life and therefore has been the focus of regulation and, in many cases, a subject of controversy. Further, feelings of love and sex are so intermingled that sexual satisfaction is often equated with emotional satisfaction. Emotional intimacy thus has the underpinnings of sexual intimacy. When one goes wrong, probably the other would go wrong. Therefore, sex has turned into a big business. Are we obsessed by sex and so concerned about our sexual competency that we are always looking for reassurance or ways to improve it? Many popular magazines offer advice with no regard to people's emotions, values, or sexual appetites (see Box 8–1).

RECREATIONAL AND PROCREATIONAL SEXUALITY

The difference between the sexuality of other species and humankind is a remarkable one, especially when it comes to differentiating procreational sexuality (heterosexual relations for reproduction and continuity of family line) from recreational sexuality (a variety of sexual relationships for emotional satisfaction, release of physical tension, fun, and pleasure). At the human level, sexuality is no longer simply the expression of instinct but has become a matter of learned patterns of emotions (such as love and romance), attraction (intellectual as well as visual beauty or personal charm), activity (interpersonal gratifications through involvement in shared actions), and consummation (personal satisfaction or fulfillment derived from such relationships). We have romanticized sexuality in novels, poetry, art, and aesthetics and defined the limits of its manifestations through moral or cultural sanctions. Therefore, varieties of human sexuality encompass an enormous range from one culture to another, as do the concepts of "sexually attractive" and "sexually abnormal." How sex is viewed depends on the value placed on sexuality. Disentangling sexuality from procreation, many sexual variations are intended to add zest and richness to our lives, to enhance happiness,

BOX 8-1 • Are We Obsessed by Sex?

21 Hints for Outstanding Sex

1. *Put sex on the front burner*: Weekend mornings and afternoons are a good time for sex, when you have more energy for creativity and imagination.
2. *Pencil in sex on your calendar*: Consider sex a priority; consider it a date with your partner.
3. *Take sex out of the bedroom*: Variety is the spice of life. What about doffing the nightgown or checking into a motel?
4. *Change your position on sex*: Add variety; experiment a little.
5. *Take what comes*: Let sex take you wherever it goes. Sex is not only intercourse but a wide variety of experiences.
6. *Don't expect your partner to read your mind*: Talk about what satisfies you while taking a walk or over a cup of coffee.
7. *Show and tell*: One way of showing is to guide your partner's hand.
8. *Share the driving*: Men don't have to be the initiators all the time.
9. *Make lovemaking a special occasion*: Occasionally create some kind of romantic ambiance: candles and wine, or whatever makes you feel that it's special.
10. *Synchronize your watches*: Go to bed at the same time.
11. *Take the TV out of the bedroom*: Don't wait until you're drowsy for lovemaking.
12. *Make your own statistics*: Forget about terrorizing statistics. You don't need to keep up with the Joneses.
13. *Stay on your toes*: Avoid monotony; "If you are dead in the head you are dead in the bed."
14. *Let sex be human*: Don't expect it to be perfect every time.
15. *Take a good look at yourself*: Learn to appreciate your bodies.
16. *Give up your vices*: Alcohol, nicotine, and illegal drugs all affect your sexual appetite and hormone levels.
17. *Bring down the wall*: Tear down the "Berlin Wall" of unresolved hurt and anger.
18. *Enjoy sex in the slow lane*: A "beat the clock" attitude is rough on the total physical and emotional sexual experience.
19. *Find out other ways to relax*: Don't use sex for easing tension; it makes your partner think that he or she is a "service station."
20. *Whisper sweet nothings*: Say things such as, "I'm glad we are together" or "That feels good."
21. *Don't make lovemaking into a track meet*: If you are keeping a score board, you are setting yourself up for failure. Focus on sexual pleasure and satisfaction rather than performance.

Adapted from Zarrow, 1988, pp. 81–87.

to show love, and to derive satisfaction from physical as well as emotional intimacy. But as satisfying as it may be, sexuality at the human level is also more likely to go awry, endangering stability in human relationships, causing profound misery, pain, and frustration. It is worse for those who are viewed as extreme deviants—groups such as the Rene Guyon Society and the National Man–Boy Love League, who argue in favor of decriminalization of sex between children and adults and actively promote it. In cases where sexual expression becomes a means of victimization (such as incest or sexual assault), potential for mental problems for the victims and sometimes for perpetrators is not uncommon.

CHANGING SEXUAL VALUES

Our sexual values have been changing steadily. Compared to a generation ago, sexual problems have become an open subject of scientific investigation and people are less embarrassed about discussing the topic. Whereas in the 1940s only about 40% of male college students had premarital sexual experience, the figure increased to 65% in the mid-1960s and by 1980 had reached 77%. Among female teenage college students, while dating, premarital sexual experience rose from 19% in the 1940s, to 29% in the mid-1960s, and to 64% by 1980. By age 22, in 1978, 83% of college women already had premarital sexual experience (Robinson & Jedlicka, 1982, pp. 237–240). Traditional inhibitions about sexuality are declining among both sexes, and the change is especially pronounced among women. A 1980 study (Bell & Coughey, 1980, pp. 353–356) reported that 43% of college women experienced *cunnilingus* (stimulation of the female genitals by a partner's mouth or tongue) or *fellatio* (stimulation of male genitals by a partner's mouth or tongue) during casual dating, as did 63% while going steady and 74% while engaged. The growing awareness about sexuality has also increased concern over sexual satisfaction, sexual dysfunctions, and sexual disorders.

SEXUAL VARIATIONS OR DEVIATIONS: THE MORAL DEBATE

One of the issues (and a controversial one) is, who should decide what is morally right? What kind of behavior should be identified as sexual disorder? Again, we should look at the individual, situation, and audience. Sexual actions have personal and social consequences. An individual who enjoys masochism may allow his or her partner to be sadistic, while in other cases similar behavior may be considered abuse or cruelty. A pedophile (a person who has sexual interest in children) is not identified as a pedophile until his actions become known; otherwise he is viewed as someone who cares about children.

HOMOSEXUALITY

The American Psychiatric Association, on December 14, 1973, by a unanimous vote of its trustees, dropped homosexuality from the list of mental disorders (*DSM-II*). The APA stated that there is no evidence that homosexuals, because of their sexual preference, are more mentally disturbed than heterosexuals. Homosexuality itself is not known to cause any mental disorders, yet homosexuals may run the risk of mental problems because of the conflicts generated by their sexual orientation or due to society's reaction to their sexual preference. Although homosexuality is not a mental disorder, the public attitude toward it as deviant behavior continues to stigmatize those who practice it. Since the 1950s, the gay movement in the United States has gained significant ground, and gays are asking for their rights as equal partners in the social world.

Although sexuality is rooted in biology, sexual practices are socially constructed (Bell, Weinberg, & Hammersmith, 1981). What is erotic is conceptualized by society. What is taboo and what is sexually appropriate is also defined by society. Variations in sexual practices have been found throughout history. While heterosexuality (sexual relationships between opposite sexes) is the norm, and any deviation from it may be viewed as morally wrong, deviant, or pathological, sexual variations characterize humans. That is why Kinsey and his colleagues (1948, 1953) categorized individuals on a heterosexual–homosexual continuum. Homosexuality was practiced by ancient Babylonians and Egyptians and most of the world cultures. Hindu mythology taught that literature of sex was divine in origin. Vatsayayan's *Kamasutra* (sexology), recorded in the fifth century, probably the oldest surviving sex manual, describes almost all kinds of sexual practices and variations found today and more, including homosexuality. Many pieces of artwork in Japan and China and in Hindu temples in the Indian subcontinent illustrate a variety of sexual acts. In ancient Rome and Greece, male homosexuality was widely known. Many notable historical figures, including Plato, Sappho, Alexander the Great, Socrates, Virgil, Julius Caesar, Michelangelo, Oscar Wilde, Peter Tchaikovsky, Gertrude Stein, and Virginia Woolf, are known to have been homosexuals. Their sexual orientation probably did not adversely affect their intellectual and superior level of functioning (Crooks & Baur, 1987, p. 310). In many preliterate and non-Western cultures, homosexual relations are viewed as a part of life or growing up, although the majority of males in their adulthood lead heterosexual lives. The tolerance levels about variations in sexual preferences also vary from culture to culture. In fact, the terms *gay* and *lesbian* have probably been generally misunderstood and connote different meanings to different people. A gay person may take the role of a female, a male, or both.

In many cultures, such as Asia, Africa, and the Middle East, a person who takes the role of a male, or one who sodomizes, is not known as gay. The implication is that the person as a male is doing what males do. The term *gay* is reserved for the passive male sexual partners who take the female sexual role.

It was only a generation ago that the publication of the Kinsey reports, *Sexual Behavior of the Human Male* (Kinsey, Pomeroy, & Martin, 1948), and *Sexual Behavior of the Human Female* (Kinsey, Pomeroy, Martin, & Gebhard, 1953), shocked people and stirred up controversy by documenting the gap between puritan sexual values of the time and prevalent sexual practices (especially the hitherto unsuspected incidence of homosexuality). Based on interviews with 5,300 white males, the researchers found that 69% of those age 20 were exclusively heterosexual, while 5% were exclusively homosexual; by age 25, 79% were exclusively heterosexual and 3 to 4% were exclusively homosexual. More than 80% of males had premarital intercourse, 92% had masturbated, and nearly 60% of the sample said they had engaged in preadolescent sex play with another boy. A recent study by The Kinsey Institute for Sex Research, on a nationwide sample of 1,974 Americans, found that one man in three had a homosexual experience (Reinisch & Beasley, 1990). An analogous study of female sexuality revealed a parallel picture, but to a lesser extent. Thirteen percent of all American women had experienced at least one homosexual contact to orgasm, 7% had at least one experience but without orgasm, and 1 or 2% were identified as exclusively homosexual.

Evidence from various studies shows both negative and positive facets of the psychological functioning of homosexuals (Oldham, Farnill, & Ball, 1982, p. 45). The greater incidence of depression, drug and alcohol abuse, and attempted suicides is reported. The National Lesbian and Gay Health Foundation, based on a survey of 2,000 lesbians, reported that 21% had considered suicide often or sometimes, and 18% had actually attempted suicide (*Los Angeles Times*, 1988). Forming a gay identity leads to inner conflict and guilt, especially when laypeople as well as professional therapists view gay people as "sick." A study of 2,497 male homosexuals in Denmark, the Netherlands, and the United States found that those who were able to reject societal labels and commit themselves to gay life were able to resolve their emotional problems (Hammersmith & Weinberg, 1973).

SEXUALITY AND EMOTIONS

Often, factors associated with sexuality may vary from person to person. Some people are predisposed to sexual problems due to their upbringing, lack of information, learned incapacities, and experiences of sexual trauma. In fact, because sex has been given so much emotional importance in relationships, failure to have a satisfying sexual relationship creates a setting for conflict with partner, anxiety, and depression and sometimes threatens individual well-being. Fears, fantasies, disturbances, and a sense of frustration and deprivation are part of one's emotional world. Symptoms that are often common in other situations, such as stress, fatigue, anxiety, depression, agitation, insomnia, and excessive use of drugs and alcohol, are often involved in sexual disorders. A psychosomatic disorder may develop through mutual reinforcement of fears, excessive expectations, inadequate physical responses, and the partner's reaction (HMS-MHL, 1989, p. 2). For example, if a person finds out that his or her spouse is unfaithful (had an affair), it may lead to a variety of emotional consequences. It is not the sexual act in itself outside the marital bond, but the violation of the emotionality involved in the marital relationship. Moreover, having an affair may be either a cause or consequence of loss of love, emotional deprivation, frustration, strained relationships, or a means of satisfying certain needs. It could be a desperate act to save one's failing marriage.

SEXUAL DEVIANCE AND MENTAL DISORDERS

Generally, sexuality has a close association with mental disorders, as we discuss later in this chapter. However, the sexual activities that fall under the rubric *sexual deviance* are disapproved of by either the formal code of the society or by the normative judgments of a population, or both (Gagnon & Simon, 1967, p. 7). Such activities are far from comprising a homogeneous category. It would hardly be wrong to say that most humans experience, at some point in their lives, sexuality in ways that are viewed as deviant. Many private sexual activities may not be acceptable by prevailing normative standards but are not labeled as deviant simply because other people are unaware of them. Those who are vocal about their socially unacceptable sexuality or sexual practices are typically labeled as deviant (e.g., gays or lesbians, or those who prefer children as sexual partners).

In medical sciences, distinctions between sexual dysfunction and sexual disorder are blurred. These terms are often used synonymously because of the degree of overlap and the complex nature of human sexuality. In addition, there are no defined indices yet developed that can be used to measure any deviance or dysfunction. This leaves a lot of room for value judgments. Yet three elements are important to consider: (1) emotionality (e.g., satisfaction with one's sexuality, which varies from person to person); (2) distress (one's sexuality adversely affecting one's and one's partner's emotionality and interpersonal relationships); and (3) deviance (does one's sexuality have a potential for breaching society's norms and thereby threatening the well-being of society?).

SEXUAL DISORDERS

Sexual disorders refer to those sexual feelings, desires, and practices that are distressful and dysfunctional for the individuals involved and have a potential for adversely affecting their well-being and interpersonal relationships. Sexual disorders have a psychological component and are generally known as *psychosexual disorders*—such as gender identity disorders and paraphilias (e.g., exhibitionism, pedophilia, and voyeurism) —and often exist with a variety of sexual dysfunctions.

It is difficult to ascertain what is sexual disorder and what is not, because there is no agreement among professionals and the public on this issue and because of human variations and personal preferences. Pragmatists claim that in view of such vast variations, the term *sexual preference* explains better the sexual activities among humans.

We cannot rule out the impact of religion on the definition of sexual disorders, as we know that throughout history religion has significantly influenced the sexual morality of the time. For instance, homosexuality is viewed as an unnatural and sinful act in the Bible, and many Americans believe that it is unacceptable. Most societies find ways to circumvent or reject formal norms, and many consider such practices a private matter. This is why it is difficult to find comparable figures through survey techniques from various cultures on sexuality and sexual disorders. The unavailability of reliable data about sexual practices is probably the most significant single cause for the failure of family planning programs in the Third World nations.

Sexual disorders are divided into two groups: (1) the *paraphilias,* identified by sexual arousal and response to objects or situations that are not considered normal by society's standards; and (2) *sexual dysfunction,* which refers to inhibition in the sexual desire or psychophysiological inability to achieve sexual gratification (e.g., sustain an erection or achieve orgasm).

Paraphilias

Paraphilias are qualitatively different from physiological sexual dysfunctions. They may or may not involve physiological limitation or disability and are viewed as deviant behavior. However, paraphilias and sexual dysfunctions often share some common symptoms and are identified for clinical purposes. Paraphilias are a variety of disorders in which sexual arousal is primarily associated with certain objects, rituals, acts, situations, symbols, in the absence of which sexual satisfaction cannot be derived adequately. Due to their exclusive nature, paraphilias may interfere with reciprocal sexual activity with people who do not share the same paraphilic tendencies. While mild forms of this disorder may be found in many normal people and may not be dysfunctional, in many cases public manifestations lead to dangerous consequences. These sex-related disorders have many types of manifestations, ranging from exhibitionism to violent sexual assault, and their causes remain as elusive as the varieties they represent. There are intellectuals who believe that most paraphilias are harmless and so common that they should not be viewed as disorders. The *DSM-III-R* identifies nine paraphilias: exhibitionism, fetishism, transvestic fetishism, frotteurism, pedophilia, sexual masochism, sexual sadism, voyeurism, and a variety of other paraphilias.

Exhibitionism
Commonly known as indecent exposure, exhibitionism is a deliberate exposure of one's genitals to strangers under inappropriate circumstances. It is considered a disorder because the exhibitionist, usually a male, feels compelled to seek satisfaction of his sexual urges or sexual fantasies by exposing himself. Generally, exhibitionists are not dangerous. Common elements among exhibitionists include places and situations in which the behavior occurs, such as parks, department stores, theaters, elevators, and secluded areas of large buildings or other public places. Their victims are usually young women, and the exposure is generally limited to a one-time episode because the exposure is not intended to be person specific, though exhibitionists may prefer certain characteristics in their victims. For the victim, the act of an exhibitionist is emotionally upsetting and sometimes intimidating. Often, it is a cause of concern because many victims perceive it as prelude to a sexual assault. In rare cases, the exhibitionist makes suggestive overtures and masturbates before the victim. Many exhibitionists believe that exposing their genitals is pleasurable to their victims because many victims do not take official action. Some even believe that "so-called victims" may even like to approach them for sexual services. Among older men, in many cases, exhibitionism may be a product of senility, impaired judgment, and lost sense of decency.

Psychiatric etiology of this disorder is grounded in psychological explanations, and treatment is limited: (1) The exhibitionist seems to be seeking reassurance for underlying castration anxiety by exposing himself; (2) the exhibitionist suffers from sexual impotence, premature ejaculation, or sexual inadequacy and exposure is a mechanism for reassurance; and (3) the exhibitionist suffers from deep-seated feelings of masculine inadequacy. Interactionally, exhibitionism for the offender is a vicarious way of deriving sexual satisfaction, assuming that the victim is enjoying sex by looking at the exhibitionist.

Fetishism
Fetish refers to an inanimate object that arouses libidinal interest, often to the exclusion of genital impulses. In many historical and peasant societies, fetishes were employed to evoke supernatural powers to attract, protect, or destroy people, objects, and spirits and to control environmental situations, such as drought or an epidemic. Most fetishes in the Western world are objects associated with women, such as underclothing, cosmetics, hair, shoes, or jewelry. The person uses these articles for sexual excitement by holding, rubbing, kissing, fondling, tasting, or smelling the fetish object, often accompanied by masturbation. The fetish becomes a symbolic substitute for the female, and thus fetishism is a victimless sexual variant. Preoccupation with certain parts of the female body (e.g., cheeks, breasts, buttocks, legs, or hips) is known as *partialism*. The actual extent of this sexual variant is unknown, but it appears that males are more likely to be involved in fetishism.

Transvestic Fetishism
This is a victimless disorder, found among males, in which they derive sexual excitement and satisfaction by cross dressing. The male transvestite, although not necessarily a homosexual or transsexual, regards himself as a male and functions as a male (husband and father) but has tendencies and feelings of being a woman, and such urges arouse fantasies or cause distress. Research indicates that transvestites view themselves as "male" as well as "female," and cross dressing is a means to control the anxieties caused by such ambivalent identities. Contrary to popular belief, most transvestites do not cross dress in public places, and most are married, have children, are heterosexual, do not run into trouble with the law, and do not show significant signs of any kind of mental disorder (Buckner, 1970; Gosslin & Eysenck, 1980). It is not uncommon to find that transvestic fetishism may be accompanied by other tendencies, such as transsexualism, homosexuality, gender identity disorders, and a variety of sexual dysfunctions. Yet most transvestites are reluctant to alter their behavior. The people close to them may find the cross dressing a little uncomfortable, but it does not cause any serious problems for them. A male child who may have received more attention while dressed in female clothing may have strong cross-dressing tendencies. If these tendencies are distressing to the individual, they can be

treated through aversive behavior therapy; most other therapies have not been very effective.

Frotteurism

Frotteurism is probably least noticed because it is acted out in subtle and transient ways that have sexual overtones. Primarily a male deviation, it involves touching and rubbing one's genitals against a nonconsenting person, sometimes leading to ejaculation. The perpetrator seeks such opportunities in crowded places, such as department stores, escalators, subways and city buses, theaters, bars, restaurants, and in audiences at concerts and sports events, to name a few. The disorder is often ignored unless the perpetrator becomes persuasive and poses a danger to the victim. Explanations of this disorder are limited and have not been well researched. However, some believe the disorder reflects the person's inability to relate to the opposite sex and ingrained apprehensions about his ability to have a consummate relationship; others simply see it as situational deviance.

Pedophilia

One of the most complicated and probably least understood disorders is pedophilia, which involves a pathological interest in prepubescent children as sex objects. Most pedophiles are men, but occasionally women have been reported to be offenders. Pedophiles include those who have exclusive sexual interest in children of either sex but not in adults, and those whose interest is limited to young boys or girls only. They may expose themselves, caress or fondle the child's genitals, have the child manipulate their genitals, or engage in sexual intercourse. Although the perpetrator may be married or have been married and have children of his own, it does not deter him. Children (who are not psychologically and sexually mature) run the risk of considerable harm if sexually molested.

Sexual interest in children is thus viewed as pathological for several reasons: (1) Adults are not supposed to have sexual interest in children due to potential harm; (2) children cannot act as informed participants in sexual acts; (3) society is responsible for protecting the rights of those, including children, who cannot protect themselves; and (4) normative standards of society prohibit sex with children because such relationships are considered disruptive and morally wrong for the society as a whole. In some cases, when an offender is unable to find a victim on the outside, he may sexually victimize his own children. Such cases involve pedophilic incest, but not all cases of incest are pedophilic.

Most pedophiles are mild-mannered individuals who suffer from sexual inadequacy and inability to relate to mature members of the opposite sex and may suffer from sexual compulsion (see Box 8–2). Freud saw the plight and suffering of the pedophile as a product of castration, anxiety, with the expectation of rejection and failure in adult heterosexual relationships. He contended that pedophiles are "fixated" latently at the phallic stage and failed to resolve conflicts arising from faulty personality development. Some male pedophiles are masochistic and come from families in which the father was very controlling and dominant and did not allow opportunities for heterosexual relationships. Other pedophiles believe that their penises are small and they cannot adequately perform adult heterosexual acts; consequently they find children, who are less threatening and challenging, appropriate sexual partners. Though the size of the penis may be a concern for the pedophile, The Kinsey Institute New Report on Sex (Reinisch & Beasley, 1990, p. 94) purports that the average length of a man's erect penis ranges from 5 to 7 inches, and most women do not have a preference for a large penis.

Sexual Sadism

Sadism refers to a condition in which a person derives sexual pleasure from inflicting physical or psychological pain by controlling and humiliating sexual partners. The term *sadism* is derived from Marquis de Sade (1740–1814), a novelist who suffered from this disorder and listed 600 different varieties of sadistic acts. He was later committed as insane. Some observers question the relevance of the term itself because there are so many variations in sexual expressions. They believe it is wrong to blame sadists and ignore the intent of masochists. Furthermore, they argue, what is wrong if both parties involved prefer and enjoy such acts? Often, sadists derive erotic pleasure by slapping, whipping, shackling, suspending, biting, pinching, kicking, mutilating, and even killing their partners. Degrees of sadism vary, and many couples in the United States who do not seem to have this disorder utilize sadism in sexual foreplay, especially when they are under the influence of alcohol or drugs. More males are known to be sadistic, perhaps as a result of an emphasis on masculinity, domination, and a macho image. The extent of sadism is difficult to assess because participants often view it not as a disorder but as a sexual variant that intensifies erotic activity and makes it more enjoyable. But not all sadistic acts are benign.

In many cases involving serial killings, the offenders suffer from acute sexual sadism. The perpetrators not only commit sexual assaults but torture and eventually kill their victims, which is called *necrosadism*. Torturing and killing the victim provides them "sexual highs," as if they were experiencing a heightened orgasm. Edward Kemper, a serial killer, pointed out in an interview that torturing his victims was like having the most thrilling sexual experience; therefore, he

> **BOX 8-2 • The Making of a Pedophile**
>
> Jim, 22 years old, average looking, blond, slender, about 5 feet 11 inches, showed up at a psychiatrist's office. He was erratic, impatient and quite tense. Twenty minutes later he was called in. Jim began to explain, "I made this appointment, Doc, because I am having trouble, I thought you may have something ...or some advice!" I have had all kinds of girls, old and young, black and white...one oriental...pickups, townies, whores, and some real nice lays on campus. For some reason, I just didn't feel the thrill. I feel something is wrong. I have quit school, found a job, and rented a place. For some reason, I am attracted toward my neighbor's 9-year-old daughter; she is a nice little cute thing. She almost looks like my cousin, and I am very fond of her. But that is another story.... I have occasionally bought some candy for this girl, stare at her, and I sit out just to have a glimpse of her. I dream about her. One night I felt that somehow I should reach her in her bedroom, which is on the second floor of the house. I got out, but the neighbor's dog started barking and I had to cancel my plans. What should I do? I cannot control myself, it has been weeks that I haven't been able to sleep. I can't seem to get it out of my mind. I have even started to follow her and feel jealous if she talks to boys who take the same school bus. The thing that really gets me is that one of these days her parents might know all this and I will be in big trouble. What do you think?

Source: Author's files.

preferred killing the coed hitchhikers rather than having sexual intercourse with them. He attributed his sadistic acts to the extreme hatred toward women that resulted from his cold, dominant, and unloving mother. Some necrosadists mutilate the bodies of their victims, an act which is known as *necrostuprum*. The Hillside Strangler and his companion were known for various such practices. Lust killings (snuff films), sadism, and masochism in pornographic films and videotapes is a booming business in the Western world, which may allow people to relieve aggression through fantasizing about the sexual domination of others. Research does not indicate any relationship between watching such visual materials and actual behavior, although viewing is known as *moral sadism*. Sadism is used frequently in nonsexual contexts, where it simply means that a person derives pleasure from hurting someone.

Masochism
Austrian novelist Leopold V. Sacher–Masoch (1836–1895) described in his novels the phenomenon in which his characters derive sexual plea-

sure from experiencing pain, self-denial, and physical suffering. Sadism and masochism are known by the term *algolagnia* and represent the polar states of the subjugation–humiliation axis. Thus, *active algolagnia* is sadism, in which the offender inflicts pain to derive sexual pleasure; while *passive algolagnia* is masochism and refers to deriving sexual pleasure by receiving pain. A *moral masochist* is one who seeks pain, humiliation, and degradation. Some masochists achieve orgasmic experience when they are constrained by leather straps, ropes, chains, and handcuffs and are whipped, beaten, and tortured sometimes to the point of bodily harm or death.

Voyeurism

The term *voyeurism* was first used by a Frenchman, Coffignon. It refers to obtaining sexual pleasure through surreptitiously watching people undressing or naked or engaged in sexual acts. The terms *voyeurism* or *scotophilia* are not used in association with erotic films, burlesque shows, or pornographic magazines. Male voyeurs are known as "peeping Toms" who, while peeping, often masturbate. Although little research is available about voyeurism among females, voyeurism may not be limited to males. It is common among children due to curiosity; however, among adults, excessive moralism and social controls, puritan socialization, poor self-concept, emotional immaturity, and sexual inadequacy are responsible for voyeuristic tendencies. Instead of being involved in love making himself, the voyeur fantasizes about being a participant in a sexual act by watching the act and thus being in control of the situation. The mystery surrounding the sexual activities of other people offers the voyeur thrill and excitement. In severe cases, voyeuristic compulsion is so strong that a voyeur may cruise around at night, ferreting out places for peeping, and may risk arrest, being shot at as a burglar, falling off a roof, or being attacked by a dog. Most voyeurs have other sexual outlets (Oliven, 1974), and at least one fourth are married (Gebhard, 1965).

Other Sexual Disorders

A class of disorders that have a sexual component marked by distress and show symptoms of a variety of mental disorders are sex addiction, incest, and sexual assault.

Sex Addiction

It has long been known that those involved in sex-related offenses, whether intrafamilial or extrafamilial situations, have a high probability of repeating the offenses. Research by Groth, Longo and McFadin (1982) on Florida and Connecticut rapists and child molesters indicates that the offenders were involved in many undetected episodes and their recidivism rates are high. For example, they found that undetected sexual assaults reported by rapists ranged from 0 to 250. More than 67% had committed more than one offense, with an average of 5.2 offenses. Assaults by child molesters ranged from 0 to 30; 50% of them had committed more than one offense, with an average of 4.7 victims. In both cases, offenses were committed as early as 8 years of age, with the mean age for rapists being 18.8 and for child molesters 23.8 years. Recently, some researchers and therapists have begun to speculate that although sexual offenses are criminal acts, in light of the recidivism rates, it is possible that offenders do not have control over their behavior. If this is the case, sex offenders have a mental disorder and deserve treatment and rehabilitation rather than incarceration.

Patrick Carnes (1983) observed that frequent and repeat sexual abusers are *sexual addicts*. Sex addicts are those who are obsessed by excessive sexual thoughts and actions, to the point of adversely affecting their relationships. They seem to have no control over these thoughts. They are occupied by irrational and disordered thought processes that are supported by low opinions of themselves, distorted and unrealistic beliefs, and the inability to cope with stress and handle unpleasant emotions. The desire to capture euphoric feelings experienced at some crucial time in their lives is ever present, as are denial that they have a problem with sex and compulsion to satisfy unmet needs through sexual activity. Many cases of spouse abuse can be attributed to sex addiction. Through analysis of clinical case histories, Earle and Crow (1989, pp. 14–17) contended that due to these inadequacies the subject uses sex as an anesthetic and a drug. In other words, sex addiction is a mental problem and can be treated. Earle and Crow suggested that adaptation of 12 steps utilized by Alcoholics Anonymous has worked more effectively as a self-help approach than other kinds of therapies. Due to the limited research on this subject, it is premature for us to make any objective evaluation of the success rates.

Incest
Incest refers to sexual relations proscribed between members of a group by its cultural norms. Sexual relations between parents and children and siblings are incest. Such prohibitions, though they vary in content from culture to culture, are virtually universal. The consequences of inbreeding, such as low intelligence, severe mental retardation, and abnormal physical growth, as well as the moral, emotional, and interpersonal problems caused by incest are serious. For example, in the case of father–daughter incest, a father takes the role of a lover/husband and a

daughter takes the role of a wife/lover, which in turn leads to role confusion, role conflict, and mutual invalidation of values that govern parent–child relationships. Parents can be loving to their children, but not sexual. Incestuous fantasies or desires do exist, especially during the adolescent period, but they must not be acted out.

Stark (1984) estimated that there may be 15 million victims of incest in the United States today. Others indicate that as few as 10% of all cases of child molestation are reported (Kempe & Kempe, 1978). Herman (1981) found that 94% of incest cases involved father and daughter; biological fathers were the most frequent offenders, followed by step, foster, and adoptive fathers (Gordon & O'Keefe, 1984). In addition, another study found that at least 17% of boys are sexually abused by a family member (Finkelhor, 1979, p. 56). Mother–son incest accounted for only 4% of the cases (Maisch, 1972). Although numerous cases of toddler sexual abuse have been reported, incestuous relationships typically begin when the daughter is between 6 and 11 years of age and continue for at least 2 years.

Why does incest occur? Is there something wrong with the perpetrators, victims, and their families? The answer probably lies in the nature of interpersonal processes involved in the incestuous family. A variety of family situations, personality characteristics, and deprivations may be responsible for incestuous behavior. In most cases, victims are helpless. Gupta and Cox (1988) suggested that neither all incestuous relationships are alike, nor do they involve, as commonly believed, only one element of victimization. The incestuous relationships can best be described by the nature of relationships between the subjects involved. Gupta and Cox suggested that there are at least nine types of incest: masochistic, seductive, emotional, curative, situational, persuasive, sadistic, aggravated, and pedophilic. The incest perpetrators come from all classes, religions, and racial and ethnic groups. Justice and Justice (1979) classified incestuous fathers into three major categories:

1. The *symbiotic* personality, who is starved of closeness, a sense of belonging, and affection in childhood. The subtypes of this category include the *introvert*, who is totally isolated and derives pleasure from the child; the *rationalizer*, who uses lofty words and sentiments of morality but untenable reasoning for incestuous relations; the *tyrant*, who is overbearing and tyrannical; and the *alcoholic*, who loses his moral judgment and wants "to be taken care of."
2. The *psychopathic*, who is looking to "get even" for a deprived childhood, and sexual exploitation is an expression of hostility.
3. The *pedophiliac*, whose primary interest in sex, and incest is simply a symptom of his disturbance.

Mother–son incest usually involves an emotionally deprived woman looking for closeness with another man, which she finds in her son. Mother–daughter sexual acts symbolize the disturbed inner self of the mother and often have a masturbatory quality and lesbian tendencies (Forward & Buck, 1978; James & Nasjleti, 1983). Incest as a phenomenon thus represents various forms of mental problems, especially personality disorders, among the offenders. After-effects among the victims may include feelings of guilt, high levels of hostility toward the opposite sex, psychosomatic ailments, inability to handle conflict, feelings of unworthiness, depression, sexual difficulties, and mistrust of men.

Sexual Assault
The term rape is derived from a Latin word *rapere*, which means "to seize, steal, or carry away." The American Psychiatric Association does not include rape or sexual assault in its *DSM-III-R*. In most states, the term *sexual assault* is used to include a variety of behaviors involved in varieties of sexual aggression. For example, in cases where penile penetration may not have occurred, or evidence (such as traces of semen) may not be found, a person can still be charged with sexual assault. Often, sexual assault is not romantic or an act of love. It is an act of intimidation, coercion, force, or threat against the will of the victim (Jeffery, 1990, p. 379). Such an act may reflect a transient reaction to extraordinary stresses that may overwhelm the offender's coping resources, or it may be a result of an internal state of affairs in which the offender's resources and skills are developmentally defective or insufficient to cope with ordinary life demands in a mature and responsible fashion (Groth & Birnbaum, 1979, p. 73). The psychological turmoil leading to assault is often marked by an expression of power, anger, hostility, and violence and is commonly, but mistakenly, assumed to be prompted by sexual desire. Sexual assault is not primarily the aggressive expression of sexuality but the sexual expression of aggression, frustration, deprivation, revenge, and unmet nonsexual needs of the offender. Some convicted offenders described the experiences and rewards of rape as being similar to "riding the bull at Gilley's" (Scully & Marolla, 1985). Therefore, victims are not always determined by their looks, seductive dress, or behavior but by their availability and vulnerability. That is why victims can be of any age from infant to elderly, of both sexes, and of any class or looks. Groth, Burgess, & Holmstrom (1977) found that a large number of rapists suffered from sexual dysfunctions.

In legal terminology, the difference between *statutory rape* and *forcible rape* is that the former refers to a sexual act with a female under the legal age of consent. *Solo rape, gang rape,* and *date rape* are some other types in which motivations, group or peer pressure, and the urge to attain sexual conquests play a major part for the offenders. The victims are often accused of enticing the offender ("She asked for it"), and their character is placed on public trial. In many cases of acquaintance rape, especially on college campuses, male and female perceptions of sexual cues differ, leading to difficulties in distinguishing platonic friendliness from sexual invitation. Abbey (1987) found that 72% of women and 60% of men reported misperceived cues, implying friendliness with sexual attraction occurring most frequently at a party and with a casual friend. A review of several college campus studies using labels such as courtship violence, sexual aggression, sexual coercion, sexual victimization and rape, estimates a range from a low of 15% for rape to 78% for sexual aggression of some kind. Sexual intercourse or attempted intercourse incidence rates were found to be in the range of 15 to 25% (Ward, Chapman, Cohn, White, & Williams, 1991, pp. 65–71).

In most cases of violent sexual assault, the offender's view of sexual assault is significantly different from acquaintance sexual assault. Many experience the violent assault itself to obtain "sexual highs," as if they were on a roller-coaster ride. Many associate causing pain and suffering to the victim with sexual excitement, and torturing and killing with heightened sexual experience.

The developmental factors contributing to the personalities of sexual assaulters are not yet known. Some claim that they were sexually abused as children; others relate stories of an autocratic, unsympathetic, and cruel mother and an inadequate father. Abuse, neglect, maltreatment, abandonment, absence of affection and sense of belongingness, and perpetual crises in the family seem to be at the heart of the sexual assaults. The resentment and helplessness of victimization and the unresolved trauma remain in suspended animation and are reactivated whenever an opportunity arises (such as jealousy or a threat or challenge from a female). Three quarters of convicted rapists become repeat offenders, and psychological counseling has not been very successful in treating them. Recent research has used penile plethsmograph to measure penile erection (sexual arousal) as a response to a variety of sexual scenes, from child molesting to homosexuality, to determine the conditioning of the offender. Brain activity, endocrine and hormonal levels, and genetic endowment are being explored. Medroxyprogesterone acetate (MPA), known by its trade name *depo-provera*, has been very effective in helping offenders to control their sex drive; however, its effects last only as long as the drug is taken. The drug does not change offenders' hostility toward women and related psychopathic tendencies.

Gender Identity Disorders

One of the sexual disorders in both sexes is *ego-dystonic homosexuality*, which refers to an individual's mental state in which persistent unwanted homosexual orientation is present and is a source of personal distress, adversely affecting heterosexual desire. Another related disorder is *heterosexual* and *homosexual gender dysphoria*, which refers to discontent with one's biological sex (gender dysphoria) (see Box 8–3). Blanchard, Clemmensen, and Steiner (1987) investigated heterosexual and homosexual dysphoria among males and females and found that homosexual females reported that they first experienced cross-gender wishes at 5.99 years of age; the male homosexuals reported a mean age of 7.65 years; and heterosexual males reported a mean age of 9.82 years. The female gender dysphorics, almost without exception, are erotically attracted to members of their own sex, but this is not true of the males.

BOX 8–3 • Transsexualism: Is It a Mental Disorder?

Jamie was born James Bright 45 years ago, married, and had two children. At about age 32, he recognized that he had all the feelings women have and a strong compulsion to become a woman. He told his wife that he would like to live as a woman and maybe undergo sex change surgery and eventually marry a man. His parents were upset with his plans, and his wife decided to divorce him. She asked the court to allow her to have custody of the children with no visitation rights, because a transsexual father could be a bad influence on children. The court granted her divorce but maintained James Bright's visitation rights. Several psychiatrists and psychologists evaluated Bright and found no psychiatric problems. They advised, however, that sex change surgery would be recommended only after they were certain that Bright could not function adequately as a male.

Bright changed his name legally from James to Jamie and entered a university to major in psychology, where he met and married Debbie. Debbie, a mother of three children, claims that they have a lesbian relationship, and Jamie claims that Debbie is a "butch," the masculine role player, rather than the "fem," or female partner. They are cohabiting with a dilemma: If Jamie goes through the surgical sex change, she cannot be married legally to Debbie (in Illinois, same-sex marriages are illegal), and if they do without the benefit of the surgical sex change, Jamie's dream of being a complete woman will remain unfulfilled. Jamie is waiting to complete her degree and find a job so she can pay $10,000 to $15,000 for the sex change surgery.

Source: Author's files.

Males are differentially susceptible to one of the predisposing conditions—namely, fetishistic transvestism.

Attitudes toward sexuality have changed dramatically since 1960, ushering in the era of "sexual revolution." While the "new sexual morality" is viewed as a liberation from the rigid and archaic norms of the past, it has social and psychological consequences. Related interpersonal conflicts, anxieties, and frustrations take their toll and increase the chances of emotional instability. Researchers have been unable to identify conclusively any one set of variables to explain sexual preference. Cross-cultural evidence suggests that homosexuality and heterosexuality are variants of the same behavior, which is learned and originates in pleasure-seeking and role-taking potential that is present at birth.

From an interactionist perspective, homosexual relationships represent as many varieties of relationships as do heterosexual relationships. They are influenced by many motivational, interactive, social, and psychological factors, including learning, identity formation, and role taking. Except for episodic and situational homosexual behavior, same-sex sexuality is not simply sexual, however. On the contrary, like any heterosexual relationship, it is often affectionate, erotic, and romantic. Current research continues to support the contention that homosexual-heterosexual distinctions are an arbitrary means of categorizing and labeling people.

SEXUAL DYSFUNCTIONS

Human sexual relationships are mediated by psychological, physiological, and interpersonal factors and personal romantic and sensual beliefs. *Sexual dysfunction* refers to impairment in the desire and inability to achieve sexual gratification and is a source of personal distress. It is not the sexual dysfunction itself but its emotional and interpersonal consequences that become the cause of concern. With some exceptions, these dysfunctions may be associated with poor socialization, psychosexual development, and/or organic problems. Many of the dysfunctions we know now were not recognized only a few decades ago. Alfred C. Kinsey and his colleagues (1948, 1953), who pioneered studies of human sexuality, and recently Masters and Johnson (1966, 1970, 1975, 1986) demystified the problems of sexuality. Questions have been raised recently about the reliability of the findings in Kinsey reports because of the wide variety of data sources and methods used. But these remain the best studies available, in spite of their flaws, to examine changes in a historical context. Sexual deviance and sexual dysfunctions may or may not have any association. For example, a sexually deviant person may be

> **BOX 8–4 • Sexual Concerns and Facts**
>
> Men
>
> 1. More than 25% American men have had a sexual experience with another male during their teen or adult years. This experience does not necessarily lead to homosexual behavior.
> 2. The size of the male genitals has nothing to do with sexual competency or sexual satisfaction of a partner. This is more of a concern for men than for their female sexual partners.
> 3. It is usually difficult to tell whether people are or are not homosexual just by their appearance or gestures.
> 4. Between 30 and 40% of married men have had an extramarital affair (been sexually unfaithful to their wives).
> 5. Often, problems with erection begin with a physical problem, and most can be treated successfully. If a person has early-morning erections, impotence is a psychological rather than a physical problem.
> 6. Most men remain sexually competent after age 65; only 30% of them report chronic impotence, which is primarily due to a number of illnesses, drugs, and surgical procedures. More than 50% of men with diabetes become impotent, and one-fourth of men over 50 are diabetic.
> 7. A man can be sterile yet have a happy, satisfying sex life.
>
> Women
>
> 1. Between 30 and 40% of women have had anal (rectal) intercourse.
> 2. Sixty to eighty percent of women have masturbated, either as children or after they were grown. There is no evidence that masturbation is harmful.
> 3. Most women do not prefer a sexual partner with a larger than average penis (the length of an average man's erect penis is between 5 and 7 inches.
> 4. Menopause, or the "change of life," does not cause most women to lose interest in sex.
> 5. Women's external genitalia vary greatly in size, shape, and color and do not in any way affect their sexuality.
> 6. Many women worry about their breast size, but ideal breast shape or size has varied throughout time.
> 7. About 40% of women have orgasms during sleep; this becomes more common as women get older.

See Reinisch & Beasley, 1990; and Masters & Johnson, 1986.

sexually dysfunctional and might be involved in sexually deviant acts to seek gratification. Sexual dysfunctions, such as orgasmic disorder or erectile disorder, might cause personal distress, low self-esteem, and frustration and possibly psychosexual and other mental disorders.

Sexuality in general, until recently, received little scientific attention, and much of what was discussed in sex and marriage manuals was idealistic and often ill informed. Kinsey and his colleagues, and Masters and Johnson (1966, 1970, 1975, 1986), wrote ground-breaking works with optimistic therapeutic views indicating that most common human sexual dysfunctions can be treated. Dysfunctions affecting the male and the female are different due to physiological, cultural, and emotional differences. Often, sexual dysfunctions, though they may not appear to be the primary problem, can influence functioning in other areas of interpersonal relationships. Sexual myths continue to persist, often reinforced by commercialization of sex. Many of these myths are the sources of emotional concerns (see Box 8–4).

Male Sexual Dysfunctions

Generally, male sexual dysfunctions can be classified into three categories:

1. *Erectile dysfunction or impotence*: The most recent report of the Kinsey Institute for Sex Research (Reinisch & Beasley, 1990) points out that inability to achieve erection or hold erection prolonged enough for sexual intercourse is most often started by a physical problem. But even a physical problem might have psychosocial underpinnings. *Primary erectile dysfunction* means that the person has never been able to have an erection, while *secondary erectile dysfunction* refers to a person who earlier succeeded in having intercourse but is unable to have erection at least 25% of the time. Not having an erection on occasion is not an uncommon occurrence among men. One major factor is fear of sexual performance, which in turn dampens sexual arousal and becomes a self-fulfilling prophecy. About one-fourth of males suffer from this disorder by age 70, which may also be attributed to anxiety-induced cognitive interference. Healthy men and women are able to enjoy sexual activity in their 80s and 90s (Kaplan, 1975; Masters & Johnson, 1975, 1986).

2. *Premature ejaculation*: Also known as rapid ejaculation and often misconstrued as a form of impotence, premature ejaculation is associated with a belief that prolonged sexual intercourse with a greater control on ejaculation offers greater sexual satisfaction to the female partner and is a measure of a man's masculinity. Only half a century ago, men who were quick and intense in their sexual response were labeled as superior, influenced by the belief that sex was primarily for the male's pleasure, which is common among the least educated and lowest socioeconomic levels. With the rise of egalitarian values and increasing responsiveness among women, premature ejaculation is seen as a problem. Masters and Johnson (1986, p. 467) estimated that 15 to 20% of American men have at least a moderate degree of difficulty controlling rapid ejaculation.

3. *Inhibited male orgasm, retarded ejaculation, or primary ejaculatory incompetence*: This is the opposite of premature ejaculation. It provides prolonged coital activity, sometimes extending to an hour or two, much

to the delight of partners. It can be physically exhausting for both the partners, and for men it may turn into *dyspareunia,* characterized by pain in the penis, testes, and abdomen. Further adverse consequences may lead to perceptions that the female partner is not responsive, attractive, or is incapable of providing pleasure. Such incompetence might complicate reproductive goals and may be frustrating to the female partner, who might see it as intimidating, frustrating, and sometimes demeaning. This leads to accusations of "showing off" and placing unnecessary demands on the female. The extent of this disorder is unknown because many men who suffer from it are too embarrassed to seek treatment.

Female Sexual Dysfunctions

Until recently, female sexuality was not a major concern either of professionals or men in general, and a woman who discussed sexuality or sex in public was viewed as a deviant or suspected of being mentally disordered. However, the advent of the Pill in 1953 and other contraceptives allowed women to take charge of their own sexuality, especially reproduction. Publishing companies published how-to books, magazines articles focused on the subjects of sexual satisfaction and happiness and even offered recipes for attracting the opposite sex; radio and TV shows addressed issues opening up the unknown side of female emotions and sexuality. College courses, a variety of helping agencies, books, and magazines also disseminated knowledge about sex and sexuality. Sex-related surveys questioned one's adequacy as a sex partner. Even those who did not know that they had a sexual problem were now aware of their shortcomings and were willing to explore, experiment, and possibly seek help.

The following are some of the most common sexual dysfunctions found among women:

1. *Vaginismus*: Involuntary spasms at the entrance of the vagina prevent normal intercourse and are estimated to affect 2 to 3% of adult women (Masters and Johnson, 1986, p. 470). They are suspected to be caused by fear, possibly due to some earlier traumatic sexual experiences that might further contribute to mental problems associated with guilt, inability to meet one's sexual obligations, and poor self-worth.

2. *Anorgasmia*: Also known as *orgasmic dysfunction,* this refers to a condition of having difficulty reaching orgasm from any kind of stimulation. It is caused by a variety of factors such as lack of privacy, comfort, nd cooperation; poor timing; inappropriate style and mood; and fear. Masters and Johnson (1986, p. 472) estimated that 10% of women never experience coital orgasm, and another 10% experience it infrequently. This accounts for about 90% of sexual dysfunction cases among women. The stimulation of intercourse alone is not always sufficient for females to achieve orgasm. Many women require additional stimulation, such as manually stroking the clitoris to reach orgasm before, during, or after intercourse. Many men believe that penis–vagina contact is enough to achieve orgasm, which is not the case. The subjective quality of the orgasm varies widely among females and is governed by various conditions within the same female from time to time. Partners who lack skills and are not very communicative about the sexual satisfaction of their partners may become angry, resentful, frustrated, and withdrawn. This may eventually lead to other emotional problems, for both partners, associated with self-esteem, anxiety, failure, guilt, incompetency, rejection, and sexual frustration.

Sexual Desire Disorder

A common sexual dysfunction, which is associated with mental disorder and is found among both sexes, is *sexual desire disorder*. *Hyperactive sexual desire* relates to unusual, frequent, and persistent high sex drive. On the other hand, *hypoactive sexual desire* is an absence or deficiency of sexual desire or drive; *sexual aversion disorder* relates to avoidance of sexual activity, and *sexual arousal disorder* refers to a lack of a subjective sense of sexual excitement and pleasure. But who is to decide that there is a sexual problem? How much sex is enough and how many times a day, week, month, or year? Which partner is dysfunctional? In almost all cases, this judgment is left to the clinicians at the behest of one of the partners whose expectations are not met. In fact, there are no specific norms that ought to be followed. Some couples are happy with no or minimal sexual activity. Obviously, if there is a sexual problem its foundation is interactional. Because most of these disorders are reported along with other organic or mental problems, the extent of each of these disorders is difficult to ascertain.

AIDS AND MENTAL DISORDERS

AIDS (acquired immunodeficiency syndrome), a deadly infectious disease that is currently incurable, has become a serious threat to people involved in indiscriminate sexual relationships. The AIDS virus, known as human immunodeficiency virus (HIV), cripples the body's immune system, leaving victims open to a variety of infections and cancer, and weakens the immune system so it cannot fight pneumonia (pneumonia carinii) and a type of cancer (Kaposi's sarcoma). It is a fatal disease; 70% of the victims die within 2 years of its onset and about one-third of the victims develop a degenerative brain disorder. Most victims are gay males, and their suffering is compounded by the stigma associated with the disease. They are maligned, victimized, and ignored. The families and loved ones of the victims undergo traumatic experiences of impending death, stigma, loss of prestige, and inability to cope. Some feel helpless because they could not prevent the tragedy. AIDS is transmitted only by infected individuals through intimate sexual contact or exchange of body fluids, sharing of contaminated needles, and transfusion of blood. Homosexuals are not the only group affected by AIDS. Expectant mothers who have been infected can also transmit the disease to a child before or shortly after birth. AZT, a drug, is now being used to suppress or possibly reverse the infection. The psychological trauma of the sufferers may range from insomnia to suicidal tendencies.

The incidence of AIDS is reaching epidemic proportions. In 1981, only 266 cases were diagnosed in the United States. In early 1988, there were over 50,500 cases and about 29,000 deaths from AIDS. It is projected that by the year 2000 there will be 6,500,000 cases worldwide (Mann, 1989, p. 12). Although mental health research on people with AIDS is almost nonexistent considering the prognosis of their disease, many suffer from depression, anxiety disorders, and suicidal tendencies.

SEX THERAPY REVOLUTION

During the past two decades, sex therapy as a movement has gained some credibility. Masters and Johnson's (1986) sex therapy centers on understanding the physiology of sex acts, behavior, and interactive techniques, taking into account sexual partners' feelings, mood, inhibitions, sexual beliefs and anxieties, sexual defenses and avoidance, negative ideas, phobias, and panic attacks. Some believe that the success of their sex therapy is largely due to the focus on the couple rather than the individual, including the use of sex surrogates in dealing with the sexual problems of singles. Success rates have been reported to be near 100% in the area of premature ejaculation and vaginismus; however, success rates are lower for male erectile and female organismic dysfunctions. Studies suggest that marital and family therapy improves sexual relations more than sex therapy improves marriages (HMS-MHL, 1990, p. 3).

The most common source of sexual problems is the relationship between the partners. Masters and Johnson consider sexual disorders not disorders of individuals but of their relationships. Interaction is the core of most of our problems. On the positive side, a sexual disorder maintains the stability of a marriage or love affair by correcting the power imbalance. A woman who frequently fails to reach an orgasm may place the blame on her partner's inadequacy who often ejaculates prematurely or perceive it to be her own fault. Some may be satisfied with the way things are; some use defenses for their inadequacies; others place demands on sexual intimacy and satisfaction. Therefore, sexual disorders are shared and both partners are responsible for the solution of their problems.

Sex therapy has become a very lucrative business, and quacks as well as professionals have jumped on the bandwagon. Estimates are that in 1980 there were at least 1,200 "certified professionals" in the field and another 4,000 who claimed that they practiced innovative or new techniques (Clark, Gosnell, & Reese, 1980). The number is still growing.

Sexual deviance, sexual dysfunctions, and sexual disorders share some common elements but may or may not lead to mental disorders. Conceptualization of mental disorders may be determined by the individual's perception of the problem, a social situation that allows the individual to define it as a problem, and reactions of those involved in the situation.

Most sexual disorders have emotional underpinnings that often adversely affect personal adequacy, self-esteem, and personal competency. However, one must understand that there is no one yardstick by which to measure sexual adequacy. In sum, what most people do sexually is a personal matter, and as long as they feel adequate and satisfied, there is no cause for concern. In addition, most sexual problems are treatable (Reinisch & Beasley, 1990). We have no scientifically verifiable theory that can explain what causes sexual disorders, nor do we fully understand how various kinds of therapies actually work. Yet a competent therapist can help by offering appropriate insights and a course of action to reduce the symptoms of a sexual disorder.

In the next chapter, we discuss how social class, race, and ethnicity influence the nature and extent of mental disorders.

CHAPTER REVIEW

1. Cross-cultural studies inform us about varieties of sexual practices. Who decides the morality of sexual practices?

2. Explain the relationship between sexual deviance and mental disorders.

3. What is the relationship between sexuality and emotions?

4. Many sexual deviations are simply sexual variations. How do they relate to homosexual identities?

5. What are major paraphilias? What are the key characteristics of each?
6. What are the characteristics of pedophiles? Why is pedophilic behavior considered more dangerous than other paraphilias?
7. Sexual sadism and masochism are relative concepts. Is there any association between serial killings and sexual sadism?
8. Define sexual addiction. How does sexual addiction relate to sexual assault?
9. What is incest? In what ways are incestuous relationships associated with personality disorders and interpersonal processes in the family?
10. What are the differences between male and female sexual dysfunctions?
11. Identify and explain briefly the following:
    a. Gender dysphoria
    b. Transvestite fetishism
    c. Algolagnia
    d. Symbiotic personality
    e. Dyspareunia

FOR FURTHER STUDY

Goode, E. (1990). *Deviant behavior.* Englewood Cliffs, NJ: Prentice Hall.
Lester, D. (1975). *Unusual sexual behavior: The standard deviations.* Springfield, IL: Charles C. Thomas.
Masters, W. H., & Johnson, V. E. (1986). *Sex and human loving.* Boston: Little, Brown and Company.
Reinisch, J. M., & Beasley, R. (1990). *The Kinsey Institute New Report on Sex: What you must know to be sexually literate.* New York: St. Martin's Press.
Tower, C. C. (1989). *Understanding child abuse and neglect.* Boston: Allyn & Bacon.
Troiden, R. R. (1988). *Gay and lesbian identity: A sociological analysis.* Dix Hills, NY: General Hall.

▶ 9

Mental Disorders: Social Class, Race, Ethnicity, and Rural and Urban Living

As we discussed in Chapters 3 and 4, mental disorders are approached from a variety of perspectives. Sociologists focus on explaining the associations of mental disorders with structural elements of society, including class, ethnic or racial groups, institutional arrangements (such as political and occupational structures), and interactional patterns among groups (e.g., family, kin, and neighborhood). Sociologists whose research centers on sociodemographic factors, such as the distribution of a disease, injuries, drug addiction, suicides, and mental disorders, are known as social epidemiologists. *Social epidemiology* is the study of the incidence and prevalence of disease, impairment, and general health status across a population (Blazer, 1980; Wolinsky, 1980, p. 7). Mental health epidemiology draws on the works of a variety of scientists, among them physicians, psychiatrists, psychologists, biologists, neurologists, anthropologists, demographers, public health officials, and sociologists.

SOCIAL EPIDEMIOLOGY

Social epidemiologists' interests lie in the study of large aggregates of human populations, not individuals. They use a variety of sources relevant to their research. For example, to find the rates of substance abuse disorders, they might review admission rates in general and psychiatric hospitals, referrals to clinics, drug rehabilitation and community mental health centers, physicians' records, and police records.

In social epidemiology, two concepts are commonly employed: incidence and prevalence. *Incidence* refers to the number of new cases of a specific disorder occurring within a given population during a stated period, usually a year. For example, the incidence of schizophrenia in the United States in 1990 was 1% of the total population or 2,500,000 cases. In contrast, *prevalence* refers to the total number of cases of a specific disorder that exist at a particular time. It includes old as well as new cases. *Lifetime prevalence* refers to the number of people who have had a certain disorder at least once in their lifetimes. While *incidence* refers to the appearance of new cases, *prevalence* refers to the existence of all new and old cases. When incidence figures are based on the number of reports per 100,000 people, they represent the *rates* of a disease or disorder. For example, to compute state and county mental hospital admission rates for 1992, the admission figure is divided by the figure for U.S. population and multiplied by 100,000. Epidemiologists call these *crude rates* because they represent the number of cases within a given period. *Specific rates* relate to certain variables such as age, sex, race, education, or other characteristics. Some diseases or disorders result in higher death rates than others. The term *morbidity rate* refers to the incidence of death in a given population.

A *case* means an instance of disorder involving a person (e.g., a teenager with suicidal tendencies). Another term is *risk*, which refers to exposure to a disease or disorder. For example, children raised by depressed parents have a higher risk of becoming depressed. To find out the extent and rates of a variety of disorders (such as schizophrenia or bipolar disorder), the National Institute of Mental Health or other federal agencies conduct research in a set geographical area, known as an *epidemiological catchment area*, at intervals over an extended period. Such studies are useful in determining the rates of mental disorders, planning staff needs and funding, and guiding mental health policy.

ASSOCIATION AND CAUSATION

A controversy exists about the causal factors in mental disorders. Medical, psychological, and sociological explanations of mental disorders focus on different aspects. For example, are we sure that mental disorders are the cause of homelessness? Or is homelessness the cause of mental disorders? *Causal logic* involves the relationship between variables and a particular sequence where one event leads to another. These aspects or factors are known as variables. A *variable* is a measurable trait or characteristic that is subject to change under different conditions. If one variable is hypothesized to cause or influence another one, the first variable is the *independent variable* and the second is the *dependent variable*, because it is influenced by the independent variable. Such causal relationship may be influenced by yet another set of known and unknown variables, called *intervening variables*. Homelessness is not uniquely the result of mental disorders because two-thirds of homeless people are not mentally ill. Media reports are based on "street people" coming to shelters and psychiatric hospitals. Are these reports representative of the homeless? Researchers, instead of focusing solely on the homeless treated by psychiatrists, reviewed cases in the general population. They found that the proportion of homeless who had mental disorders was much less (Roth, Bean, Lust & Saveanu, 1985; Snow, Baker, Anderson, & Martin, 1986, pp. 407–408; Wright, 1989, p. 180). A large proportion of the homeless were those who lost jobs or lacked skills to find new jobs. Those who could not afford to pay high rents and those who ran into financial problems due to business foreclosures were included. Others were destitute or runaways or had no family or place to go. Contrary to common belief, mental disorders (independent variable) are not solely responsible for homelessness (dependent variable). Nor is homelessness (independent variable) the sole cause of mental disorders (dependent variable).

Association or *correlation* exists when a change in one variable coincides with a change in the other. Associations show that causality may be present; but they do not show cause-and-effect relationships. Mental disorder is not a typical or the only cause of homelessness; not all those who have mental problems become homeless. Nor do all those who are homeless become mentally impaired. Correlation among different variables, however, may offer plausible explanations and may guide research in the right direction. Some of these issues are addressed in the following pages.

SOCIAL CLASS

The *class system* is a social hierarchy primarily based on economic position, in which achieved characteristics can influence mobility. Social class membership or socioeconomic status is associated with crime rates, fertility and mortality rates, family size, age at marriage, sexual behavior, levels of education, nature of occupations, religious beliefs, political ideologies, and a variety of mental disorders. Income inequality, which is a characteristic of a class system, has significant differences in distribution from one country to another. One limitation of the income criterion is that it fails to consider sources of wealth besides income.

A member of the Dupont family (owners of Dupont Corporation), who was heir to millions of dollars, lived in a luxurious mansion but preferred to be a school teacher. His sanity was challenged by other family members. They argued that a person who is heir to such enormous wealth would not want to be a school teacher unless he or she were insane. Such inconsistencies in inherited wealth, occupation, and salary are not uncommon; however, sociologists rely on three techniques to determine one's social class position:

1. The *subjective method* assumes that people can identify their social class membership as they can their race, ethnic group, gender, or sex. This method has its shortcomings. For example, many people say that they are middle class when their income or savings are too meager to qualify them as members of this class. This is called *false class consciousness*.

2. The *reputational method* involves a group of people rating positions of various individuals in a group or community. It is limited in its application to small groups.

3. The *objective method* measures several variables, such as income, occupation, education, and prestige and so on to determine an individual's class position. *Prestige* refers to the respect with which an occupation is viewed by society. A supreme court judge has higher prestige than a police officer. *Esteem* is the reputation that a person has within an occupation. For example, Dr. Smith, a family physician, is a very pleasant person and popular with patients compared to Dr. Jones, a family physician, who is arrogant and indifferent. Since many families are now dual-career families, considering only the husband's income leads to inaccurate conclusions. Also, because more women are in lower paying occupations, such as secretaries and clerks, their work force participation leads to a general upgrading of the status of male-dominated occupations (Schaefer, 1992, p. 236). Such status change has extended mental health consequences.

Income distribution in the United States has been uneven, although it has not changed much in the past 100 years. The class stratification system in the United States is classified into five groups: the upper class, the upper middle class, the lower middle class, the working class, and the lower class. Rossides (1990, pp. 404–416) contended that these classes differ in ways other than income levels:

1. *Upper classes*, the very wealthy (about 1% of the U.S. population), include old guards, the old Yankee and upper level corporate businesspeople. They belong to exclusive clubs and social circles. The members of this class live in areas of the community considered the best and occupy positions of high prestige.

2. The *upper middle class* accounts for about 10% of the population and includes professionals, such as doctors, lawyers, and corporate managers, who wield considerable power and influence. They live in better and well-to-do areas of town.

3. The *lower middle class*, which represents about 30% of the population, includes lower level managers, nurses, and owners of small businesses. Many have college degrees but predominantly have high school diplomas and live in good residential areas.

4. The *working class*, about 40% of the U.S. population, includes manual and blue-collar workers, some of whom have gained economic security. Electricians, plumbers, and factory workers are included. Many have a high school education but largely have some vocational training. Their life centers in the family, neighborhood, labor union, the church, and other public places.

5. The *lower class* consists of the semiskilled, the elderly, single mothers with dependent children, and unemployed and unskilled individuals. They are conventional in their ideology, do not carry much weight politically, and their lives are restricted by scant resources (see Table 9-1).

According to a U.S. House of Representatives Committee on Ways and Means Report (1989, p. 986), for more than a decade, the purchasing power of the working and lower classes has been declining steadily. The share of U.S. wealth owned by the richest 1% of the population has increased from 21% in 1821 to 34.3% in 1983 (Batra, 1987).

TABLE 9-1 • Mean Income of Households by Race, 1987

Race	Number of Households	Mean Income	Percent Below the Poverty Line
White	77,284,000	33,526	10.1
Black	12,195,000	20,743	31.6
Hispanic	5,418,000	24,666	26.8

Adapted from *The Statistical Abstracts of the United States*, 1990, pp. 446, 448, and 480.

Sociologists hypothesize that the nature and extent of mental disorders are associated significantly with one's social position in the structure of society (that is, the class system). Early research on social class and mental disorders reported the highest rates of mental disorders among the lowest classes. While upper and middle classes showed higher rates of mood and anxiety disorders, lower classes have the highest rates of serious mental disorders, such as schizophrenia and personality disorders. However, this statement must be considered in view of several limitations of research (Dohrenwend & Dohrenwend, 1969, 1974a, 1975; Link, 1982; Link & Dohrenwend, 1989; Regier et al., 1988).

Epidemiological Studies

The Chicago Study
Robert E. Faris and H. Warren Dunham (1939), in the 1930s, conducted a study of the distribution of mental disorders in Chicago. Using the city map, they tried to locate 35,000 residents who had received psychiatric care from private and public mental hospitals. They found that the highest number of schizophrenics came from the slum areas of the city. The timing of their study coincided with the end of the Depression which may have indicated higher levels of schizophrenic symptoms among the poor. Not only Chicago, but the whole nation was ill fed, ill clothed, and ill housed. Faris and Dunham hypothesized that poverty was the major cause of social isolation. It was responsible for promoting symptoms of schizophrenia (such as hallucinations, delusions, disjointed thought processes, and extreme seclusiveness). Their finding that poor people have a higher likelihood of becoming schizophrenics was later questioned, because it can also be argued that schizophrenics have a higher likelihood of becoming poor. After realizing the validity of this argument, Dunham (1977, pp. 61–68), 40 years later, conceded that it is possible that schizophrenia can be the cause of poverty rather than poverty being the cause of schizophrenia. Nevertheless, the Chicago study has some merit. Based on the 1927 adult population of the city, rates of schizophrenia were the highest (700 per 100,000 population) in the central district of the city. The next highest rate (550 to 699 per 100,000 population) was in surrounding areas and south of the central district, where most poor people lived. The rates of schizophrenia clearly showed a positive relationship with poverty.

The study was replicated in 1960–1961 by Leo Levy and Louis Rowitz (1973) on 10,653 city residents admitted to mental hospitals. They largely confirmed the findings of the Faris and Dunham study. Although serious mental disorders such as schizophrenia and alcoholism were highly concentrated in lower class neighborhoods, schizophrenia was not as heavily concentrated among the poor as previously thought.

The New Haven Study

A study of mental disorders was undertaken in 1950 by August B. Hollingshead, a sociologist, and Fredrich C. Redlich, a psychiatrist, in the urban community of New Haven, Connecticut, to investigate the association between class and mental disorders. One of the objectives of this study was to test the validity of Faris and Dunham's (1939) Chicago study. The other objective was to reexamine the findings, on a wider scale, using inpatient as well as outpatient psychiatric populations. (The Faris and Dunham study was restricted to hospital admissions.)

Consistent with the five social classes of the United States, New Haven's class structure represented all five categories. Anxiety disorders were more common among the upper and upper middle classes. Schizophrenia was more prevalent among working and lower classes (see Table 9–2).

A 5% random sample across the five social classes from the nonpatient general population was selected. It was compared with people seeking psychiatric care in both public and private institutions, inpatients as well as outpatients. This study, in contrast to Faris and Dunham's study, specifically related socioeconomic status with chances of mental disorder using an index of social position correlates such as race, ethnicity, religion, location of residence, occupation, and education. This study also used *diagnosed* or *treated* cases rather than the *true* or *total*

TABLE 9–2 • Comparison by Social Class and General Population: The Distribution of Anxiety and Schizophrenic Disorders

Social Class	Normal Population (%)	Psychiatric Population		
		Total (%)	Anxiety Disorders (%)	Schizophrenia (%)
I	358 (3.1)	19 (1.0)	10 (52.6)	9 (47.4)
II	926 (8.1)	131 (6.7)	88 (67.2)	43 (32.8)
III	2,500 (22.0)	260 (13.2)	115 (44.2)	145 (55.8)
IV	5,256 (46.0)	758 (38.6)	175 (23.1)	583 (76.9)
V	2,037 (17.8)	723 (36.8)	61 (8.4)	662 (91.6)

Adapted from Hollingshead & Redlich (1953). "Social Stratification and Psychiatric Disorders," *American Sociological Review*, 18, 167.

prevalence of mental disorders. It did not include subjects who may have suffered from mental disorders but were not treated, or did not know if they had any mental disorder.

The New Haven study found the following:

1. A very significant relationship between social class and mental disorders existed. Five social classes representing a cross-section of the people in the area were identified—class I (upper), class II (upper middle), class III (lower middle), class IV (working class), and class V (lower). Class I contained only 3.1% of the population and only 1% of the psychiatric cases, while class V represented 17.8% of the population but reported 36.8% of the psychiatric cases.

2. Neuroses (anxiety disorders) were more concentrated at higher levels of the class structure and psychoses at the lower end of the class structure.

3. The psychiatric treatment received by the patients was associated with their position in the class structure. Of the broadly classified types of therapies—psychotherapy, organic therapy (use of drugs), and custodial care without treatment—psychotherapy was the primary mode of treatment in the higher classes. For example, psychoanalysis was restricted to classes I and II, the upper classes; patients in class V, the poor received psychotherapy by group methods in state hospitals.

The Hollingshead and Redlich research became the basis for many other studies and is one of the pioneering studies to show a relationship between kinds of mental disorders, treatment modes, and one's position in the class structure.

Some other generalizations that can be derived from this study are as follows:

1. Lower status individuals are more likely to come to the attention of psychiatric authorities and therefore are more often recorded as mentally ill.

2. Individuals in higher classes seek private professional help to deal with their problems early, whereas lower class individuals are more likely to be hesitant to seek psychiatric help, experience stigma in consulting a psychiatrist, and are not admitted to a mental hospital unless the problem becomes overwhelming.

3. Lower class individuals are more likely to come to the attention of psychiatric authorities as a result of a referral by the police or a social worker, while upper and middle class individuals are more likely to be referred by relatives and private physicians.

4. Certain behavior among lower class individuals may be perceived by middle and upper class members as antisocial behavior, especially among men. Psychiatrists find lower class behavior troublesome and are likely to label it as disordered due to their middle-class bias (Wilkinson, 1975).

5. Lower status individuals' mental problems are viewed as intrinsic to such individuals. They are not viewed as consequences of perpetual economic deprivation, poverty, job instability, and unemployment, which are directly related to psychological difficulties (Liem & Liem, 1978). The anxiety and stress caused by such conditions make lower status individuals highly vulnerable to a psychiatric breakdown (Kessler, 1979). However, one can argue that this cannot be the whole story, because often lower class individuals come to the attention of the psychiatric authorities following reports by other lower class individuals (Goode, 1990, p. 331). Although this argument may have some merit, other lower class individuals may report such behavior for reasons other than danger from the individual (including the intent to protect the neighborhood or to force the individual to seek help for mental problems). Nevertheless, this finding was important in that it influenced policy makers and government leaders to find ways to allow relatively easy and prompt access to mental health services for those who could least afford them yet needed them the most.

The Midtown Manhattan Study

The New Haven research was restricted to people diagnosed with and treated for mental disorders. Another study of the *true prevalence* of mental disorders among randomly selected households in midtown Manhattan was undertaken by Leo Srole and his colleagues (1962). It included 1,660 people between the ages of 20 and 59. Information about their background, history of mental disorders and treatments, and current mental health status was included. Once again, associations between one's position in the class structure and the probability of mental disorders were found. The least likelihood of mental disorder was found among higher socioeconomic groups, among people in the 20–29 age group, and among the upwardly mobile. The highest prevalence was reported among people of low socioeconomic classes, in the 50–59 age group, and among those with little chances of social mobility. The study was a step forward in the application of sociological methods in epidemiological studies of mental disorders. However, there were shortcomings: (1) During the study, the focus shifted from mental disorders to mental health (i.e., instead of looking for what should have been the indices of mental disorders, the study centered on indices of mental health); (2) the people who showed the absence of symptoms of mental disorders were viewed as mentally healthy (we know that symptoms alone are not enough for objective evaluation); and (3) many who do not show psychiatric symptoms of mental disorders often act in ways that might be identified as mentally disordered.

Srole (1975) compared the findings of socio-psychiatric epidemiology of midtown Manhattan between 1954 and 1974. This longitudinal research was an important step in epidemiology because it included treated as well as untreated cases of mental disorders. During the interim, sample size was reduced from 1,660 to 659 due to death of subjects, migration from the area, and difficulty in identifying the original respondents. In spite of these limitations, findings did not change the conclusions reached in the earlier study. Socioeconomic status was again found to be the major predictor of mental health status. Those who were in higher socioeconomic groups were less likely to be mentally disordered than those who were in lower levels of society. Such research, though fraught with certain limitations, allows researchers to evaluate change over time.

RACE

Does racial identity determine the nature and extent of mental disorders? It is difficult to dissociate race from other intervening variables, such as historical antecedents of immigration (e.g., slavery compared to voluntary migration), education, occupation, and class. The National Institute of Mental Health, although it reports periodically on aspects of mental health, does not report comparative figures on specific minorities. Specific groups, such as Southeast Asians in the United States, have received some attention recently. The latest and the fourth edition of *Mental Health, United States* (NIMH, 1990a) classifies mental patients into inpatient admissions, outpatient under care, and partial care under care. In all these categories, minorities show higher rates of mental disorders (Table 9–3). However, as far as mental health is concerned, all minorities are not alike, and research shows significant differences among them.

Black Americans

In 1990, more than 30 million or about 12.5% of the U.S. population was black or African American. The United States has the third largest black population in the world, after Brazil and Nigeria. In 1660, the British colonies had passed laws making blacks slaves for life. It was only in 1865 that the abolition of slavery became a fact throughout the United

TABLE 9-3 • Inpatient Admissions, Outpatient Care, and Partial Care under Care Psychiatric Services by Race,* United States, 1986

Race	Inpatient Admissions	Outpatient Care	Partial Care
White	1,204,876 (594)†	1,169,529 (576)†	101,092 (50)†
Nonwhite	391,187 (1,074)†	214,226 (589)†	32,102 (88)†

*All nonwhite racial groups.
†Rate per 100,000 civilian population.
Adapted from National Institute of Mental Health, *Mental Health, United States*, 1990a, pp. 156, 161, and 167.

States. Since then, blacks have advanced significantly, but disparities still exist between blacks and whites.

High rates of crime, family instability, unemployment, low educational levels and skills, and other symptoms of social disorganization among blacks lend some to believe that blacks suffer more from mental disorders than whites. Many early studies lacked methodological rigor, and some were even tainted to promote racism. Based on a review of these studies, Gallagher (1987, pp. 284–286) pointed out that, in the 1800s, several reports claimed that blacks were free of mental illness because of the special care they received as slaves. Higher rates of mental illness among the northern blacks were interpreted as a consequence of their freedom from slavery and entering the competitive world. Such reports did not advance our knowledge about the association of mental disorders with race but reflected the ethnocentrism of the time. A recent study in the United States found no differences in the prevalence of clinical symptoms of depression between 764 black and 773 white adult outpatients in a primary care setting (Zung, Macdonald, & Zung, 1988).

Employing more sophisticated research methodologies, researchers have consistently found that blacks have more mental disorders than whites. However, when class is held constant, the differences are not significant (Warheit, Holzer, & Avery, 1975). Black social scientists touched off a debate by arguing that life chances for blacks and their economic opportunities are far more determined by their social class than by their race (Wilson, 1980). Therefore, class may be a better determining factor in mental disorders than race. A study of the effects of a plant closing on General Motors auto workers found that less educated and uneducated workers, especially blacks, suffered high levels of anxiety, depression, and anguish (Hamilton, Broman, Hoffman, & Renner, 1990). Charles V. Willie (1979), a Harvard sociologist, maintained that economics is but one facet of the larger society. He argued that white racism permeates all social institutions, controlling entry to all desirable employment, earnings, housing, and social status. According to Willie, rampant institutional racism, racial tokenism, and racial injustice dominate the system and perpetuate the underclass. There is no question that blacks are overrepresented in the lower class and that the lower class shows an overrepresentation of the mentally impaired.

Studies of population characteristics and rates of admission to county and state hospitals show that blacks have higher rates of mental disorders than whites in all categories of age, sex, and marital status groups (NIMH, 1990a, pp. 140, 145) (see Box 9-1). Although higher rates of mental disorders among blacks can be explained by their disproportionately higher representation in the lower social class and their stressful economic and social conditions, other factors cannot be ignored:

1. Blacks, who are primarily poor, cannot afford costly psychiatric care compared to affluent whites, who can afford the services of private professionals. Most blacks seek help at county and state hospitals and clinics, the figures from which are commonly used for comparisons by federal agencies. This inflates the figures for blacks.
2. The level of mental health awareness among poor and racial minorities is lower due to less education and greater concern about stigma, so they do not seek help until problems become serious. This may be a key factor in the higher prevalence of schizophrenic symptoms among these populations.
3. Being a member of a lower class and being black negatively influences psychiatric assessment (Loring & Powell, 1988).
4. Using psychological well-being and quality of life measures (even when controlled for social class, age, and marital status), blacks show higher distress levels compared to whites (Thomas & Hughes, 1986).

The preceding explanation is limited because it ignores that many blacks are *lowest* in the lower class. The economic situation among lower class blacks is much worse than lower class whites because only 11% of black men 25 years old and over graduate from college compared to 25% of whites (Bureau of the Census, 1987), and unemployment rates for blacks aged 16 to 24 exceed 40% (Schaefer, 1990, p. 249). The federal government's Bureau of Labor Statistics regards as unemployed only those who are *actively* seeking employment. Many inner-city young blacks, frustrated with their failure to find a job, give up. This leaves out

> **BOX 9–1 • Is He Sane Enough to Die?**
> **The Case of "Double Bind"**
>
> The U.S. Supreme Court upheld the constitutionality of the death penalty in 1976. The Eighth Amendment bars cruel and unusual punishment and forbids the electrocution of insane people. Procedural permutations are still difficult to deal with. May a state execute a condemned killer who has gone insane while waiting on death row? Now the issue is not that capital punishment is morally wrong but to ensure that only sane people die.
>
> Alvin Ford, a black man, has been on Florida's death row since a 1975 conviction for murdering a police officer. His lawyers claim that he has become a paranoid schizophrenic. In 1983, three psychiatrists examined him. Only two of them diagnosed Ford as psychotic, but all three concluded that he understood the death penalty and could be sent to the electric chair. Did Ford commit the murder because of his mental problems? Or, are psychiatrists biased against Ford because he is young and black (black young men have the highest rates of schizophrenia, based on admission rates in county and state hospitals)? Can anyone figure out if he is faking?
>
> The ban on execution of the insane is ancient, based on the premise that an insane person could not make peace with God. Hence, execution would be a sentence to hell. Under English Common Law, that concept was adopted in part because an insane prisoner would be incapable of raising issues that could postpone punishment. Ford is in a "double bind." He must undergo psychiatric treatment, but if he wants to stay alive he must not recover.
>
> As long as Ford is found insane, he will be referred to a mental hospital for treatment. If he recovers, he will be executed.

Press & McDaniel, 1986, p. 63.

of official statistics millions of Americans who are effectively unemployed and have become an *underclass*, a segment of society that has fallen out of the class structure. People in this group have few chances of improving their life situation due to lack of skills and personal attributes; this effectively contributes to serious mental problems.

The constraints imposed by social class association might be more discouraging among blacks as they use the services of mental health professionals somewhat less than whites. Often, a mental health problem is precipitated by distressful economic conditions and inability to cope with poor physical health. Black women, like white women, are more likely to seek help than their male counterparts (Neighbors & Howard, 1987).

Hispanic Americans

The group identified as Hispanic Americans is the largest ethnic minority group in the United States, numbering over 12 million. It links a diverse population that shares a common language heritage and includes Chicanos (Americans of Mexican origin), Puerto Ricans, central and south Americans, and Cuban Americans. The Census Bureau estimates that by the year 2080, Hispanics will number 59.6 million—about 19.2% of the population—collectively outnumbering all other minorities in the United States (Bureau of the Census, 1986).

Mexican Americans, who make up 60% of the Hispanic population in the United States, have been represented in most mental health studies; however, research on other groups has not received much attention yet. Some have argued that low rates of mental disorders among Spanish-speaking people are due to the poor delivery of the psychiatric services. Other causes include language barriers, ignorance of cultural differences, prejudice, inaccessability, and diagnostic decisions based on middle-class values (Malgady, Rogler, & Constantino, 1988). Recent studies show either no difference or even less psychological distress than among non-Hispanics (Burnham, Timbers, & Hough, 1984; Ross, Mirowsky, & Cockerham, 1983; Ross, Mirowsky, & Ulbrich, 1983). Research on lifetime prevalence of suicide ideation and suicide attempts between Hispanics and non-Hispanic whites reported rates twice as high for whites. More women of each group reported higher rates than men. Disrupted marital bonds were typically associated with higher rates of suicide ideation and attempts. Research suggests that the higher the level of assimilation of Hispanics with the Anglo culture, the higher the chances of suicide ideation and attempts (Sorenson & Golding, 1988).

The new immigrants from Mexico are less likely to be mentally distressed. This is even true for Mexican American women who take jobs outside the home and also tend to domestic chores. Although most Mexican Americans are at the lower levels of the socioeconomic hierarchy, their mental health status is better than that of whites or blacks. This anomaly appears intriguing because it contradicts the view that lower class increases the chances of mental distress. However, there are some inherent characteristics in the Hispanic culture that contribute to better mental health.

Positive Mental Health among Hispanics

In the midst of poverty and higher levels of fatalism, another picture of Hispanic American life becomes visible. Hispanic Americans show better mental health despite discrimination, linguistic barriers, instability in employment, poor housing, limited educational opportunities, and sometimes questionable citizenship status. The elements that characterize positive mental health among Hispanics are as follows:

1. *Familism*: Hispanics are more familistic and take pride in meeting family obligations, which result in close bonds and in loyalty coming before individual needs. Many families are extended families of several generations, including cousins. Such relationships are emotionally and financially supportive, especially in times of crises (Moore & Pachon, 1985, p. 96).

2. *Strong kinship ties and friendships*: Active functional interdependence among kin, strong personal relationships, and supportive bonds among friends are common themes among Hispanic people. These provide protection against social isolation and allow individuals to handle personal crises at a group level, characteristics that are absent among Anglo and black cultures.

3. *Godparent–godchild relationships*: *Compadrazgo* is a tradition of knitting the community together by formalizing informal ties of friendship between a godparent and godchild. It symbolizes a sense of long-term security to the child should anything happen to the child's parents.

4. *Distinctive family roles*: The sense of virility, personal worth, dominance, and superiority among men, called *machismo*, is emphasized. *Marianismo* describes the qualities of femininity that are complementary to those of machismo in men. Feminists argue that these images are falsely glorified. Role complementarity minimizes power conflicts, competition between sexes, and enhances a greater degree of interdependence (Moore & Pachon, 1985).

5. *Strong religious orientation*: Highly spiritual in their religious beliefs, the Chicanos and Mexican Americans are able to cope better with frustration and crises. In 1986, 85% of Hispanics were Roman Catholics and 83% considered religion very important in their lives (Berger, 1986, p. 14).

American Indians

American Indian populations were decimated by various sicknesses that resulted from earlier contacts with settlers. American Indians are "the poorest of the poor." The 1980 census showed a 71.8% increase since 1970, from 792,730 to over 1.4 million. This is partly due to a high fertility rate, a 3% annual population increase (Parrillo, 1990, p. 239). More than half of the population lives on 267 Indian reservations. Relatively little research has been done on mental disorders among American Indians. Other pathologies, such as alcoholism, drug addiction, suicide, homicide, and juvenile delinquency, which are symptomatic of emotional problems, have received some attention.

Native Americans have a high mortality rate. Death from alcoholism is five times the national average, and people in the 25–34 age group have a terminal liver cirrhosis rate 15 times the national rate (Schinke, et al. 1985). Alcohol abuse is involved in 80% of their suicides. Drug and alcohol abuse is 20 times greater when compared to the whites in the same geographical area (May, 1982). Chronic unemployment, averaging 45 to 55%, and sometimes as high as 80%, is a serious problem. The education gap between whites and Native Americans has narrowed recently, yet the dropout rate among Indian youths is three times greater than that of whites and 50% higher than that of blacks and Hispanics. Many American Indian children never attend school.

Cultural marginality is a major obstacle in the lives of the Native Americans, which is also true for many other minorities. On the one hand, they seek to maintain a tribal identity and traditional cultural heritage, but on the other hand they want to succeed in the modern material world. The compartmentalization of these two worlds—one of individual competitiveness, personal recognition, and rewards and the other of group solidarity, tribal loyalty, and personal sacrifice—is a difficult act, leading to frustration.

Asian Americans

Americans of Asian descent are characterized by their racial and ethnic diversity. Successive waves of immigrations to the United States from Asia constitute a vast array of nationalities and cultures. Together, Asian Americans are the third largest minority after blacks and Hispanics. In 1990, they numbered 6.5 million, up from 1.4 million in 1970. In 1990, the largest groups of Asian Americans were Filipino (1,405,000), Chinese (1,259,000), Vietnamese (860,000), Korean (814,000), and Japanese (805,000), followed by Asian Indians (684,000), Laotians (260,000), Cambodians (185,000) and 261,000 from other countries of Asia (Schaefer, 1990, p. 347).

Asian Americans have the highest levels of income, education, and employment compared to other racial and ethnic groups, including whites. All Asian groups, except some recent refugees, show low rates of mental disorders and mental hospital admissions. This is intriguing, since Asian Americans are relatively alien to the dominant American culture. In fact, racial differences, language barriers, food habits, and religious practices and beliefs make them uniquely identifiable groups. In addition, observance of traditional sex roles, emphasis on the integrity of the family, and deference to and care of the elderly are important to

Asian cultures. Values center on concerns about what other people think, modesty, maintaining a low profile, respect for authority, and family's and friends' involvement in handling personal problems. Ironically, the same factors contributing to their minority status are, to a large measure, the strengths of these cultures and encourage Asian Americans to succeed. Former president Ronald Reagan praised them as "our exemplars of hope and inspiration." *Time, Newsweek,* and the *New York Times* have featured articles about Asian Americans with headlines like "A Formula for Success" and "Model Minority." Many Americans see Asian American groups as a "model," "ideal" or even "super" minority.

Recently, anti-Asian–American movement has gained strength and is particularly more visible in major inner-cities where small business ownerships have been replaced by the new immigrants from Asia. There have been cases of arson, robbery, and murder. Cultural differences, business success, and the new immigrants' inability to understand the frustration of the local people has played its part. Anti-Japanese sentiment is not new. It was noticed as early as the 1890s in the form of government and union restrictions when Japanese–Americans took jobs in the United States as laborers at low wages. Over the years Japanese products have gained respectability in the world, capturing a significant share of auto and electronics markets adversely affecting jobs in the United States. Trade surplus with Japan grows every year and Japanese are blamed for their unfair trade practices. The anti-Japanese sentiment makes the Japanese–Americans, as well as other Asian minorities, targets of discrimination and hostility and threatens their personal safety. Culturally, Asian people are not accustomed to show open hostility. Confronted with anti-Asian sentiment they discuss these issues in their own ethnic organizations, with sympathetic whites and political leaders. The mental health consequences of these reactions have been rarely assessed at the ethnic community level.

Filipino Americans
Not much has been written about Filipinos, though they were the second largest Asian group (775,000) in the United States in 1980 after the Chinese. They surpassed the Chinese in 1990, and now they are the largest group (1,405,000) among Asian Americans. Although Filipinos in social science research are considered Asians due to geographical and cultural reasons, they are unique Asians due to the impact of centuries of Spanish rule. American-born Filipinos have less formal education than other Asian immigrants and lower job status, and many of them are unskilled. Filipinos' strong loyalty to family and church help them handle crises. In the absence of fruitful mental health research on Filipinos, one may speculate that their situation is almost like Hispanic populations.

Chinese Americans

In 1990, there were 1,259,000 Chinese Americans, up from 435,000 in 1970. Early European settlers had little tolerance for the alien Chinese culture, although the Chinese were hard-working laborers. The anti-Chinese mood led to passage of the Exclusion Act in 1882, barring Chinese immigration, and the Act was not repealed until 1943. From the early immigrations, Chinese encountered blatant racism and discrimination, and their numbers threatened the dominant European culture of the United States. This fear of the *yellow peril*, the Chinese, has gradually given way to some positive images in the past few decades, primarily due to the success of the younger generation of Chinese Americans. At the same time, mental hospital admission rates are increasing for older Chinese Americans, who suffer from anxiety, paranoia, depression, and schizophrenia (Berk and Hirata, 1973). However, attributing these increasing rates to minority status alone is questionable. A recent study of 116 Chinese psychiatric outpatients in Shanghai, China, utilizing *DSM-III* diagnoses, found that affective disorders accounted for 26.7% of the sample. A full range of psychopathology was found, including schizophrenia, organic mental disorders, adjustment disorders, anxiety disorders, and paranoid disorders (Altshuler et al., 1988, pp. 872–875). Cockerham (1984) reported little difference in the prevalence of schizophrenia between Shanghai, where it was 0.7%, and the United States, where it was 1%. Rapidity of life, family strife, weakening of kinship bonds and friendship ties, and the stress of city life are responsible for some mental distress, irrespective of geographical location. Furthermore, the Chinese have their own psychiatric diagnostic manual that differs from *DSM-III-R* in many ways.

Chinese American families are undergoing remarkable changes. Strong networks of families, kin, friends, and fellow workers are weakening, as are the support systems that once played a considerable role in regulating behavior. Apathy, neglect, and loss of authority are the major factors affecting mental health among older Chinese Americans.

Indochinese Americans

Among the most recent immigrants to the United States are the people of Indochina—the Vietnamese (860,000), Cambodians (Kampucheans) (185,000), and Laotians (260,000). They were part of the former French Indochinese Union. They were given a reluctant welcome in the United States after the American withdrawal from South Vietnam in 1975. In April 1975, a Gallup poll reported that 54% of Americans were against sanctuary to these refugees, 36% in favor, and 12% undecided. The major concern was that these immigrants would further increase unemployment (Schaefer & Schaefer, 1975). Many Americans were concerned about the threat to American "national character" posed by the arrival of Indochinese. David Riesman called it the *gook syndrome*. *Gook* is a negative and derogatory term, at least partially created by the media, that derides Indochinese as the worst of a kind and not worth compassion (Luce, 1975, p. E19). Indochinese immigrant experiences have had mixed results. While many refugee children have done very well academically, families' adaptation to life in the United States has not been easy. Some groups, such as Cambodians, have undergone unusually severe traumatic experiences during the Pol Pot regime of 1975 to 1979 and many show signs of posttraumatic stress disorder.

Depression, guilt, regrets, and shame weigh heavily on the Indochinese, yet these are perceived as essentially private concerns. Talking

TABLE 9-4 • Value Conflicts between Indochinese/Asian Patients and American Psychotherapists

Indochinese/Asian Patients' Values	American Psychotherapists' Values
1. Interdependence and emphasis on family integrity and loyalty	Autonomy and independence
2. Preservation of tradition and values; "correct" social relationships	Relativity in values; situational ethics; rejection of authority
3. Holistic culture (i.e., people living in harmony with nature)	People versus nature; the need to master or control nature
4. View of mental illness as imbalance of cosmic forces or supernatural events	View of mental illness as a result of psychological and biological factors
5. No cultural analogy of extended psychological therapy	Belief that psychotherapy is valuable and promotes "growth"
6. Belief that cure should be rapid, healer active; little history of maintenance therapy	Awareness that a cure will be extended and time-consuming, and the therapist will often be passive
7. Fear of mental disorders	Comfortable attitude about mental disorders and their symptoms
8. Belief that individual's social and spiritual environment is a contributing factor in mental disorders	Belief that cosmic or spiritual forces have nothing to do with mental disorders
9. Immigrant status—insecure in language, vocation, and position in society	Secure status in society—language, vocation, and position

Adapted from Kinzie, 1985, p. 11.

about them to a stranger would be as discrete and commendable as parading nude in public. Suicide ideation among the Indochinese represents a personal decision based on normal motives and is not always considered pathological and reprehensible. The Indochinese have the same mental problems as are found among Americans. Their narrow definition of mental disorders covers only those conditions that are so disruptive that they derange the social order or endanger others in the community (Tung, 1985, pp. 10–15). Psychoses are viewed by the Indochinese as phenomena of a supernatural nature, effects of magical forces or demonic possession, a voodoo curse, or retribution for a sin or fault (Tung, 1980; Westermeyer & Winthrop, 1979). The role of willpower is considered essential in every facet of life (that is, to maintain constant control over one's behavior and emotions). Self-control is believed to work for prevention and for treatment. The differences we have discussed are important in devising a culturally sensitive mental health policy with some modifications for most Asian American populations (see Table 9–4).

Korean Americans

The fourth largest Asian American group is Korean Americans (814,000). The initial wave of Koreans came to the United States between 1903 and 1910, others in 1951 through 1964, and the third wave after 1965 with the passage of the 1965 Immigration Act. Most immigrated to the United States to improve the quality of life. They have encountered disenchantment, language difficulties, gender-role conflicts, stress, loneliness, alcoholism, family strife, and mental disorders. However, many are successful professionals. Korean Americans have particularly succeeded in small business operations in major cities. The riots in May 1992 following the acquittal of four white Los Angeles policeman in the beating of motorist Rodney King induced a convulsion of violence in Los Angeles that left 44 dead 2,000 injured, and over $1 billion in charred ruins. Many Korean-American businesses were looted and burned. Hurh and Kim (1987, 1990), based on research in Chicago and Los Angeles, where Korean Americans are concentrated, reported that compared to whites and other Asian Americans, Korean Americans show higher levels of depression. Married people, the elderly, the college educated and those employed in better occupations, and males have better mental well-being. One of the explanations is that Korean Americans are patriarchal and patrilineal people—they maintain an extended family system, strong kinship bonds, and ethnic ties. Women follow traditional roles; a substantial proportion of husbands do not perform household tasks, even when their wives are employed. Over half of Korean Americans are self-employed in small businesses. Many wives work long hours in these businesses, which is an added burden to their domestic responsibilities. Women who work outside family businesses with higher individual earnings complain of more somatic impairment due to higher levels of stress (Hurh & Kim, 1987). One common response of Korean females is not to marry males who expect them to behave in traditional female roles and to look for mates outside of the Korean community (Kitano & Daniels, 1988, pp. 115–116).

Contrary to the findings in the American population that the lower class has a greater prevalence of mental disorders, Korean Americans show low levels of mental health in the highest income category as well as mid-level occupations (Hurh & Kim, 1987). This shows that job stress and absence of acceptance and recognition by peers can be a frustrating experience. Churchgoers rate higher on mental well-being scores, and those who attend Buddhist temples rate low on mental health scores.

Japanese Americans
There were 148 Japanese in the United States in 1880; by 1990 they numbered 805,000. Japanese Americans show low rates of mental disorders (Kitano, 1969). The Japanese philosophy of life, stable family structure, acceptance of conventional sex roles, strong friendship support system, and ability to handle frustration in constructive ways has allowed them to show better mental health than other groups. Like other traditional societies, the Japanese do not identify many mental problems as problems but instead focus on the person's inability to follow the norms. To have better control in their lives, the Japanese either psychologically absorb their problems or insulate themselves, showing no external signs of mental instability. They believe that an individual's problem is his or her own; the individual should not bother others; and the individual should modify his or her behavior to resolve a problem. Some observers believe that the influence of Japanese culture buffers the effects of stress and that social support allows them to weather crises better than others (Kitano & Daniels, 1988). It is possible that mental disorders are underreported among Japanese Americans due to their affluence and ability to seek private mental health services. In any case, based on admission rates (which are used for comparisons), Japanese Americans exhibit low rates of mental disorders.

THE DOUBLE STANDARD IN MENTAL HEALTH: CLASS, RACE, AND ETHNICITY

Class, race, and ethnic variations affect perceptions and interrelationships among groups. The stereotypes are at work, and individual differences are ignored. For example, the poor are likely to be criminals; most homeless are black and most schizophrenics are black; Hispanics are lazy, illiterate, and least concerned about their emotional state; and the Japanese are smart and mentally healthy. But the *double standard* is at work. A double standard is a type of discrimination in which individuals or a category of people are judged by a different standard than used to judge one's own kind. As we discussed in Chapter 1, a person's location in the social order, situation, and audience defines his or her actions. The following is a case in point.

A black man in his thirties bought a pair of pants at a downtown clothing store in a small, Midwestern town. He came back the next day to return the pants because he thought they did not fit well. The clothing store clerk asked him to check another size, but there were not any in the same color and design. The customer asked the clerk to refund his money. The clerk hesitated and offered to give him credit, arguing that the store has a no-cash-refund policy. A heated argument developed, and the police were called. Assuming that most sales clerks and customers do not run into arguments and that the customer had not committed any crime, the police officer took the man to the psychiatric ward of the county hospital. The man was further enraged because he thought he did not deserve this treatment, and he threatened the hospital attendants to keep off. A psychiatrist was called in, who patiently approached the man and attempted to understand the episode. He found out that the man was a recently transferred electronics engineer with a major telephone company. After talking with the man, the psychiatrist could not find any reason to keep him in the psychiatric ward. The man was released promptly.

ETHNICITY, HEALING, AND MENTAL DISTRESS

There is a variety of ways in which cultures around the world handle emotional problems and distress. Their methods are different in many ways from Anglo or Western cultures. Many ethnic and racial groups in the United States, some to a lesser extent, observe their native cultural practices. Often, they are stigmatized and labeled as heathens or worse. Explaining this phenomena, Morris Rosenberg (1990) stated that people have "emotional logic" that they develop in the process of socialization. People visualize the connection between stimulus events (such as conflict, frustration, or stress) and emotional outcomes (such as depression, anxiety, or insomnia). Such outcomes are logically necessary when defining features of mental disorder (*DSM-III-R*, 1987).

Many ethnic groups view such natural outcomes or mental deviations in a holistic way. That is, the problems might be caused by unhappy ancestral or religious spirits, sorcery, witchcraft, family conflict, or failure to observe interpersonal norms. Many mental disorders, as well as physical illnesses, are viewed in relation to the total environment. The causal agents might be within the individual, natural, or unnatural. Abusing the natural system of the body through excessive eating and drinking or rejecting the normative system by immorality, excessive greed, or disrespect of authority or God can cause mental disorders. The goal is to ascertain the *cause* of the problem, to combat the problem in all possible ways, and physicians or psychiatrists are only among a few of the healing agents. If a mental problem is a product of divine punishment, it cannot be treated by medications or secular healing agents. It can only be treated by establishing contact with spiritual power, by prayers and sacrifices, and possibly through an intermediary (a shaman, priest, or faith healer).

RURAL AND URBAN LIVING

In 1790, 93% of the U.S. population worked on farms, compared to only 2% in 1990. The Bureau of the Census defines an incorporated area with fewer than 2,500 inhabitants as rural. About 23% of the U.S. population lives in such communities, but not all are farmers. Images of the beauty of rural settings are so popular that in 1986 a *New York Times* poll reported that 60% of Americans believe that farm life is more honest and moral than elsewhere, and 70% think that farmers have closer ties to their families than elsewhere. The images of urban life are reflected in positive as well as negative opinions. On the one hand, the city symbolizes opportunity, freedom, progress, excitement, variety, and change. On the other hand, it is rampant with artificial, stressful, lonely, and ugly experiences.

How "rural" is a rural area? Many rural inhabitants commute to work in the suburbs or small towns and spend more time in urban areas than in their home communities. Rural people are exposed to the same national news media and are connected to the urban areas through telephone, cable, and utility lines. Many of their children attend educational institutions in urban areas, and only some return to farming. Qualitatively, family ties and relationships with neighbors and friends, church members, and small local businesses are much closer in rural settings. Rural settings are a *gemeinschaft* (community) where most people know each other. Rural people are known to be fatalistic, puritanical, ascetic, conservative, uninformed, authoritarian, work oriented, family centered, and to have a distrust of the unknown (Hassinger, 1976). In contrast, *gesselschaft* (relationships in urban settings) tend to be impersonal, distant, and transitory.

Does urban living lead to high rates of mental disorders? Although there is a good deal of research on other indices, such as unemployment and income in rural areas, mental health research has received little attention. In a review of studies conducted in the 1970s, 8 out of 10 studies reported higher rates of mental disorders in urban areas, but the difference is small—only 1.1% (Dohrenwend & Dohrenwend, 1974b). In contrast, a 1984 ECA study of New Haven, Baltimore, and St. Louis reported higher rates of mental disorders among rural residents (Robins et al., 1984). This contradiction is relevant. There was an outward movement of rural populations to urban areas in the 1970s, but the trend reversed in the 1980s. This changed the rates of mental disorders in rural as well as urban areas.

There is overwhelming evidence that rural and urban living are both associated with certain kinds of mental disorders. However, a causal explanation of mental disorders and place of living would be oversimplification, partly due to the definition of the rural and urban settings. For instance, in many cases, people prefer to live in communities not far from an urban area so they can enjoy the semblance of rural life, privacy, a natural setting, and ample space, but at the same time they enjoy the amenities of urban living. The question is, should we call them rural or urban dwellers?

The most commonly cited figures in comparing mental disorders in rural and urban areas are hospital admission rates. These rates indicate that higher rates of affective disorders are found in rural settings, while anxiety disorders and personality disorders are higher in urban areas. Rates of schizophrenia are the same in both settings (Blazer, et al, 1985; Dohrenwend & Dohrenwend, 1975). Some explanations for these differences are as follows:

1. There is a higher tolerance level of mental impairments in rural settings, partly due to the relative simplicity of life and less concern about minor personal deviations.

2. Treatment facilities are generally located in towns and cities; people from rural settings do not seek help until they find that a disorder is disabling. Awareness of impairments is higher in the urban setting, with a few exceptions (poor sections of the city), and availability of treatment facilities allows more people to seek assistance (Eaton, 1974).

3. The stigma of mental disorder is likely to be felt more in the rural setting, due to ignorance or conventional thinking, compared to urban living, where anonymity, availability of treatment resources, and motivation to seek treatment are greater.

4. The conditions of urban life—transitory alliances, fragile relationships, crowding, loneliness, and other pathologies—may be responsible for higher rates of mental disorders.

5. Urban areas attract those who are job seekers, experimenters, adventurous, or may be "a little weird." This simply suggests that those who are not satisfied with rural life or those who are unstable move to the city (Srole, 1972). Frustrations of urban life further accentuate these people's problems. Many of the homeless or "street people" in the urban setting belong to this category. Gallagher (1987, p. 251) contended that this is because of the "self-selection" process whereby unstable people tend to settle in the cities rather than rural areas.

The financial crises of American farmers in the 1980s have led to hopelessness, poverty, alcoholism, drug addiction, domestic abuse, and a variety of mental health problems among farmers (Farmer, 1989).

The psychiatric treatment of mental disorders in the United States is a phenomenon influenced by the history and culture of the Western world. This is also true for racial and ethnic groups and rural and urban people in the United States, whose experiences are grounded in their own culture. We pursue this discussion further in Chapter 10.

CHAPTER REVIEW

1. What is social epidemiology? What is the role of social epidemiologists in mental health research?

2. What is the difference between association and causation? Explain with appropriate examples.

3. Social classes are known to be associated with mental disorders. How do class characteristics influence the nature of mental disorders in various groups?

4. Discuss and compare the findings of the Chicago Study and the New Haven Study. What were the limitations of these studies?

5. Leo Srole and his colleagues conducted research on the "true prevalence" of mental disorders in midtown Manhattan. How were the findings of this study different from previous studies?

6. William J. Wilson argued that problems of blacks are not determined by race but by class. How is race important in the prevalence of mental disorders?

7. In spite of the odds against Hispanic people in the United States, their mental health is better than many other groups. Explain.

8. Asian Americans come from lands and cultures very different from the United States. However, they have the lowest rates of mental disorders. Why? Explain.

9. In what ways are rural and urban living associated with the prevalence of mental disorders?
10. Explain the following terms:
    a. Epidemiological catchment area
    b. False class consciousness
    c. Familism
    d. Gook syndrome
    e. Emotional logic

FOR FURTHER STUDY

Dohrenwend, B. P. (1983). The epidemiology of mental disorder. In D. Mechanic (Ed.), *Handbook of health, health care, and the health professions* (pp. 157–194). New York: Free Press.

Kitano, H. H. L., & Daniels, R. (1988). *Asian Americans: Emergingminorities*. Englewood Cliffs, NJ: Prentice Hall.

Link, B. P. (1982). Mental patient status, work and income: An examination of the effects of a psychiatric label. *American Sociological Review, 47*, 202–215.

Link, B. P., & Dohrenwend, B. P. (1989). The epidemiology of mental disorders. In H. E. Freeman & S. Levine (Eds.) *Handbook of medical sociology* (pp. 102–127). Englewood Cliffs, NJ: Prentice Hall.

Moore, J. W., & Pachon, H. (1985). *Hispanics in the United States*. Englewood Cliffs, NJ: Prentice Hall.

Torrey, E. F. (1986). *Witchdoctors and psychiatrists*. New York: Harper and Row.

Wilson, W. J. (1980). *The declining significance of race: Blacks and changing American institutions* (2nd ed.). Chicago: University of Chicago Press.

▶ 10

Mental Disorders: Age, Gender, Marital Status, and Religion

One often wonders if there are certain characteristics that in some way describe people who are likely to suffer from mental disorders. *Ascribed* characteristics are those over which a person has little or no control, such as sex, age, race, and ethnicity. They remain the same regardless of effort or desire. In contrast, *achieved* characteristics are based on one's choice, merit, effort, or failure. For example, staying single is a matter of choice. Sociologists have found that certain kinds of mental disorders are more likely to be found among people who have certain ascribed or achieved characteristics. In some cases, a combination of these characteristics is at work.

Besides class, race, and ethnicity, there are other variables associated with mental disorders. Significant among them are gender, marital status, age, religion, education, occupation, family size, birth order, and rural versus urban living. Research indicates that each of these variables has an impact on an individual's well-being. Due to space limitations, we discuss only a few of them.

DATA SOURCES: THEIR STRENGTHS AND LIMITATIONS

There are at least three major sources of data concerning mental disorders:

1. National Institute of Mental Health (NIMH) data are collected by its Survey and Research Branch (SRB). This data does not include private office practices of psychiatrists, psychologists, and other providers, many psychiatric services operated by federal agencies other than the Department of Veterans Affairs, hospitals that do not have a psychiatric branch, psychiatric services of schools and colleges, halfway houses, community residential organizations, local and county jails, state prisons, and similar agencies.

2. Epidemiological catchment area (ECA) studies encompass a variety of community studies, especially those conducted after 1977 to determine the prevalence rates of mental disorders in the general population.

3. Topical or problem-specific studies (e.g., homelessness in New York City) are conducted by researchers and are often supported by federal, state, private, and charitable funding agencies.

It is obvious that although each of these data sources has its value, only epidemiological catchment area studies tell us about the actual prevalence of mental disorders.

Problems with Epidemiological Studies

The diversity of concepts and procedures used by different investigators to measure the extent of mental disorders has caused confusion, due to inconsistent methodological procedures and consequent findings. Some early studies relied on hospital admissions, while others have focused on general populations. Assuming that many individuals who have mental problems do not go for evaluations, we might expect to find differences in the rates of mental illness consistent with the research designs employed. Many who have mental problems, at least in the initial stages, consult their family physicians and are rarely classified as mental patients. Others believe that due to the complex nature of mental disorders, objective psychiatric diagnosis has not yet become possible, and they avoid seeking help.

Inpatient admissions, outpatient care, and partial care figures published by the National Institute of Mental Health (1990) about mental disorders do not tell us about the actual prevalence of mental disorders. Treatment in itself does not mean that a disorder has been present; furthermore, even if a disorder is known, many do not seek treatment. Treatment rates thus provide us only part of the whole picture. It may be that those who are treated were more aware, were more concerned about their mental health, were more aware of treatment facilities, or had problems so serious that they were forced to seek help. They may also have positive attitudes toward seeking treatment, or it may be that providers of psychiatric treatment were readily accessible to them.

A Presidential commission of experts in 1977 was asked to determine the amount of mental disorder in the United States and the extent to which those afflicted were underserved. Five research settings at five major universities in Baltimore, Durham, Los Angeles, New Haven, and St. Louis were established. All used the same *diagnostic interview schedule* (DIS), and the studies became known as the Epidemiological Catchment Area studies. They became the basis for ascertaining the actual prevalence of mental disorders, and they provide the best data available on the actual incidence of mental disorders.

AGE

In our society, age is a major issue in almost all domains of life, including mental health. From infancy to retirement, age plays a key role in defining social expectations and appropriate behavior. For example, when people are in their twenties, it is expected that they will marry. Similarly, retirement age is influenced by such expectations. Age is also a predictor of future marital status. Do we know at what age people are most vulnerable to mental disorders? Research to date is inconsistent in its findings. Over 20 years ago, in a review of 24 studies, Bruce P. and Barbara S. Dohrenwend (1969) reported the highest likelihood of mental disorders in middle age (12 studies), followed by old age (7 studies), and adolescence (5 studies).

To promote better understanding of the extent of mental disorders, NIMH (1990) recently began collecting figures about mental disorders in different treatment settings, including (1) inpatients, (2) outpatients, and (3) partial care clients. These three categories are further divided into people under care, those who are admitted, and those who are terminated. Further, principal psychiatric diagnosis and length of stay are also established. Some basic problems, however, are not resolved. These problems affect not only NIMH figures but community studies, too. Some of the problems relate to reporting, others to inconsistencies in gathering information, and yet others to basic diagnoses. The major problems are as follows:

1. NIMH admission figures relate to only those people who are treated for any one or a multiplicity of the mental disorders. These figures do not inform us of the true prevalence of mental disorders. For example, many who might have had mental problems may not have sought treatment and therefore are not included.

2. The lack of uniformity of studies is one of the major problems in portraying an accurate picture of the extent of mental disorders across all age groups.

3. Age is only one variable among many others, such as class, race, and education. It can be argued that it is not age but race or class association that may be responsible for certain kinds of mental disorders. There are few studies which have discussed the relationship of age at various states of the life cycle with mental disorders.

TABLE 10-1 • **Inpatient, Outpatient, and Partial Care Admission Populations in Psychiatric Treatment Programs, United States, 1986**

Age	Inpatient (%)	Outpatient (%)	Partial Care (%)
Total all ages	1,596,063 (100.0)	2,127,170 (100.0)	156,912 (100.0)
Under 18	112,215 (7.0)	552,141 (26.0)	18,400 (11.7)
18–24	216,419 (13.6)	296,335 (13.9)	26,671 (17.0)
25–44	838,488 (52.5)	956,337 (45.0)	76,339 (48.7)
45–64	298,498 (18.7)	255,375 (12.0)	27,990 (17.8)
65 and over	130,443 (8.2)	66,962 (3.1)	7,512 (4.8)

Adapted from National Institute of Mental Health, *Mental Health, United States,* 1990a, pp. 158, 164, 170.

At the moment, the best we can do is to understand the relationship of age to mental disorders based on NIMH figures, keeping these limitations in mind.

Mental Disorders and the Life Cycle

NIMH (1990a) figures suggest that in all kinds of inpatient psychiatric services (see Table 10–1), the largest group of patients in "under care" (48%) and "inpatient admissions" (52%) categories is from the 25–44 age group. Children and youth under age 18 represented only 7% of the *treatment* population. Only 8% were age 65 and older. Private psychiatric hospitals admitted a higher percentage (20%) of children and youth compared to only 9% in multiservice mental health organizations, 6% in nonfederal general hospitals, and only 5% in state and county hospitals.

A report submitted by the National Advisory Mental Health Council to the U.S. Congress estimated that between 17 and 22% or 11 to 14 million children suffer from some type of diagnosable mental disorder. About 12% of the 63 million young people in this country under age 18 suffer from some kind of maladjustment; another 7.5 million are presumed to be severely disabled by their mental disorder. The mental disorders seen in children and adolescents vary in their first appearance, levels of impairment, and long-term effects. The disorders include emotional disturbances, such as depression and crippling states of anxiety, behavioral problems characterized by disruptive and antisocial behavior, and developmental impairments. Often, these problems are accompanied by mental retardation, attention deficit hyperactivity, and sometimes depression and drug and alcohol abuse. One recent study estimated that the direct cost of treatment for mental illness in 1985 was $35 billion, with at least $1.5 billion being spent on children under age 15. This is a gross underestimation (NIMH, 1990, pp. 2–3).

The large number of children and youth obtaining treatment at private psychiatric hospitals suggests that children are at higher risk, even in those families that can afford expensive treatment. What about the children in poor families? Do they receive reasonable treatment? Higher tolerance levels in poor families, ignorance, fear of stigma, and concern over problems of scarcity and money discourage them. In many cases, other problems are so overwhelming that the possibility of a mental disorder of a family member is rarely explored. Only those whose problems become intolerable seek help at county and state clinics and institutions. Many of these children and youth never seek treatment. They show signs of neglect, sometimes abuse, and behavioral problems in school (Leerhsen, Lewis, Pomper, Davenport, & Nelson, 1985). Delinquent behavior might be one of the manifestations of deeper problems, as poor socialization and lack of a sense of responsibility may drive youth toward antisocial activities.

The period from age 25 to 44 is probably one of the most stable periods of one's life. However, people in this age group have the highest undercare, admission, and partial care rates. The rates in the 25-44 age group are 1,119 per 100,000, compared to 177 in the under 18 age group and 447 in the 65 and older group. The overall median age for inpatient admissions and inpatient undercare programs is 34 years, with the median age at veterans' medical centers somewhat higher (42 years), (NIMH, 1990a, p. 142–143).

The frequency of principal selected diagnosis of inpatients under care places schizophrenia as the most frequently reported disorder (44%), followed by affective disorders (22%), and alcohol-related disorders (12 to 19%). Of course, there are overlapping diagnoses—a person might be depressed as well as an alcoholic (NIMH, 1990).

Inpatient populations are distinctly different from people with milder forms of mental disorders. Their problems necessitate hospitalization. For example, certain kinds of depressive disorders can be treated without hospitalization, as can certain kinds of mild schizophrenia. It largely depends on the diagnosis and the level of functionality. It is not true that people are railroaded in psychiatric institutions indiscriminately. However, many clinicians look at the possible scenario in case such people are allowed to go without treatment. As we know, psychiatric diagnosis is not perfect, and even after extensive testing the objectivity of results is not certain. There is every likelihood that in spite of precautions and testing, clinicians cannot be sure about the actions of the subject examined. Wrong diagnosis may lead to dangerous consequences. Age is one of the major indices taken into account.

Aging and Mental Health

The average life expectancy in the United States has risen from 47 years in 1900 to approximately 75 years in 1991. In 1900, only 6.4% of the people in the United States were age 60 and older; by 1980 the number had increased to 16.1%. By the year 2050, those 60 and older are expected to account for 27.7% of the total U.S. population (U.S. Senate Committee on Aging, 1984). People are living longer and living healthier due to improvements in public health programs, better living conditions, increased medical technology, and greater health consciousness. However, as we noted in Chapter 1, the number of people suffering from mental disorders has increased rapidly.

A common stereotype based on folklore and myths is that as people age, senility is inevitable. This belief is so deeply ingrained in American society that the elderly are looked at with some degree of stigma. Some fear contact with or extended exposure to a senile person or one who has lost self-control. People often fear the aging process and worry about what it may do to them. Some are so frightened with the plight of older people that they develop a dislike and, in extreme cases, an irrational fear of the aged (*gerontophobia*).

As the number of elderly people increases (what demographers call the "graying of America"), the elderly have become more visible and so have their problems. All elderly are not alike. However, the negative stereotypes linger on. A majority of adults in the United States believe that older people think and move slowly and that, as they age, they become "set in their ways"—insecure, inflexible, uncreative, and increasingly conservative. It is commonly assumed that the elderly are dependent, childish and asexual, and "apt to complain" (Levin & Levin, 1980).

There is a built-in bias in diagnosing the problems of the elderly as problems of aging. The myths of intellectual decline and senility among the elderly are so prevalent in our culture that any cognitive confusion may be viewed as organic dysfunctionality. The same symptoms in a younger person are believed to be caused by discrete environmental factors and are therefore labeled as reactive rather than organic (Kermis, 1986, p. 104).

Aging women experience a double jeopardy arising from social, economic, and psychological conditions surrounding age and gender. Poverty, widowhood, and the dynamics of care giving translate into a vulnerability that is seen within the mental health system, particularly in diagnoses of Alzheimer's disease, alcohol and drug abuse and misuse, and depression (Bart, 1977; Rodeheaver & Datan, 1988).

GENDER

The terms *male* and *female* refer to a person's biological sex. But what is *feminine* or *masculine* is socially constructed, and the two together determine a person's gender identity. Sex identification does not vary across cultures but gender identity does, because gender identity is learned. There are people who believe that they are trapped in the wrong body. In such cases, their sexual (biological) identity is in conflict with their gender identity (sex-related appropriate behavior). Thus, *gender identity* refers to the self-concept of a person as being male or female. Although biological differences contribute to the development of gender, identity is largely determined by gender role socialization. Does sexual identity have any association with mental disorder? Edward Jarvis (1850, pp. 142–171) published a study of 250 hospitals in the United States and Europe in 1850 and reported that men experienced more stress and therefore were more subject to mental disorders. Pre-World War II studies, and other studies conducted prior to 1950, reported higher rates for males. Recently, the National Institute of Mental Health (1990a, p. 156) reported that white males have higher rates of mental disorder than white females. Males of other races have higher rates of mental disorders than females of their own race. Females of nonwhite races have the lowest rates of mental disorder (Chino & Funabiki, 1984).

Most studies of the true prevalence of mental disorders based on community surveys of nonhospitalized populations show significant gender differences. The following discussion is based on a review of studies reported by Link and Dohrenwend (1989). The findings are as follows:

1. No consistent gender differences were found in functional psychoses (based on reviews of 34 studies by Dohrenwend & Dohrenwend, 1974b, and 19 studies by Neugebauer, Dohrenwend, & Dohrenwend, 1980).
2. Women have higher lifetime rates of schizophrenia and schizophreniform disorder (Robins et al., 1984).
3. Rates of manic-depressive psychosis are generally higher for women.
4. Regardless of time or place, rates of neuroses (classified as anxiety disorders in *DSM-III-R*) are consistently higher for women.
5. Women have consistently higher rates of dysthymia, panic, obsessive-compulsive disorder, social phobia, simple phobia, and agoraphobia.
6. Women are more likely than men to have major depression.
7. Rates of nonspecific distress and demoralization are higher for women.
8. Men have consistently higher rates of personality disorders, regardless of time and place.
9. Men have higher rates of drug and alcohol abuse and dependence.

Let us examine how gender roles are associated with mental disorders.

Women

The impact of gender roles embraces the whole field of mental health. The stereotypes of men and women are so embedded in our culture that certain images are replete with biases: for example, women are emotional, finicky, weak, and talkative. Women are more likely than men to talk about their problems, especially emotional difficulties, and seek treatment for their suffering (Klerman & Weissman, 1980). In fact, figures from outpatient psychiatric clinics, hospitals, and therapists are consistent—women are more likely to be treated for mental disorders (Gove, 1979). The female role socialization allows women to express their feelings, their weaknesses, and problems. Brought up in a dependent role, women have the disadvantage of relatively low self-esteem and higher levels of helplessness. They play the demanding roles of a spouse, mother, and job occupant, along with a host of other roles (Lips, 1988, p. 208).

The move toward economic independence of women has added new roles and responsibilities. The two-paycheck family has increased the burden on the female role, making it more complex and stressful and time raising new expectations and new demands. Most women realize quickly that in the absence of someone sharing some of the responsibilities of their conventional roles, it is difficult to be effective in their new roles. This may lead to conflict, high levels of anxiety and frustration, and breakup of the family. Shedding of the dependent role in a largely male-dominated society has not been easy, and it has its costs. For solutions to these problems, women often seek the help of physicians and therapists, who often perceive medical problems rather than problems of changing roles and conflict in interpersonal relationships (Cox & Radlaff, 1984). Emotional reactions are often treated medically (i.e., psychotropic prescription drugs). Women use the majority of prescribed mood-altering drugs for a variety of anxiety disorders, insomnia, depression, and psychosomatic disorders. They are also the major abusers of these drugs (Verbrugge, 1982).

Men

Males are supposed to be autonomous, strong willed, tough, and in control. The masculine role, as it is culturally transmitted, does not encourage men to show emotions. Even in the face of crisis, they are expected to tough it out. This cultural expectation places men in a critical spot. When men suffer from emotional problems, they may attempt to conceal them, often by acting out in masculine ways (e.g., going to a bar and getting bombed, becoming alcoholic or addicted to drugs, or committing suicide), or they may let out aggression in violent ways (see Box 10–1).

Because most emotional problems are grounded in interpersonal relationships and are culturally transmitted, to effect any change in more than a

> **BOX 10–1 • Male Virgins and Their Self-Feeling**
>
> The number of people who are virgins at marriage has declined considerably. Among men, in the 1970s, premarital sexual experience was almost universal, 95%. In 1982, 66% of women had intercourse by age 19, and 82% by age 29 (Family Planning Perspectives, 1985). However, contrary to the image of the "imposing and adventurous" young male, many young men go through high levels of anxiety, shame, and guilt during these encounters. Some are left "hard and bitter" after the relationship is over and they experience rejection.
>
> On the other hand, for male virgins chastity is a disturbing personal problem because of the common myth that "it is bad because when a guy gets to college he is going to feel inadequate as a man if he does not have a certain amount of experience." Another virgin remarked, "I am not proud of my virginity, but the question of sex is really a very serious problem for a sensitive person. Since the atmosphere and girls are very permissive, it makes me even more tense."
>
> One striking characteristic about the virgins is the relative meagerness of their social contacts including dating. Some have anxiety in meeting girls; others have problems in coping with the threat of sexual relations. Virgins show higher levels of low self-esteem and self-confidence. They believe in traditional sex roles and a relatively high work ethic. But they pay higher costs in psychic terms, either do not marry or marry late. When they fall in love, they take it seriously, and breaking up for them leads to higher levels of dejection. The failure to live up to the expectations of the sexual role that their milieu regarded as the touchstone of masculinity has its emotional consequences.

For detailed case studies, see Komarovsky, *Dilemmas of Masculinity*, 1976, Chapter 4.

few people, it is necessary to alter the present cultural value structure. Coping skills work better when they are grounded in culture. Japanese and Hispanic Americans, for example, are better able to handle mental health problems than whites and blacks. This may be due, in part, to the culture in which these ethnic groups exist.

Gender Roles: Double Standard in Mental Health

Double standard means utilizing two different standards—one for men and one for women. These standards are part of public perceptions, and mental health professionals seem to be influenced by them, too. Irene Broverman and her colleagues (1970), in a study of male and female psychologists, found that women are subject to this double standard. Men are viewed with positive and socially desirable characteristics (such as aggressive, independent, competitive, less emotional, and in control) and their deviant behavior is tolerated more than that of women. This places women in a double bind. If they manifest characteristics associated with men, they lose their femininity; if they do not, they are faced with a variety of mental problems.

Gender roles predispose men and women to different stresses in different ways and determine help-seeking behavior in a variety of ways and frequencies. Because the gender stereotypes are already at work, they influence the symptoms and how they are diagnosed (Lips, 1988, p. 207).

MARITAL STATUS

By the end of January 1991, there were 2,445,000 marriages and 1,117,000 divorces in the United States (USDHHS, 1991). Does being married increase the chances of better mental health? Researchers report that married people have a lesser likelihood of suffering from mental disorders, and marriage has a positive and profound impact on recovery rates. Mental disorders are more common among singles. These associations are important; however, it is difficult to establish a clear causal relationship. Conversely, it can be said that those who have mental problems are more likely to stay single or those who are mentally stable are more likely to marry or stay married. A supportive, empathetic, and close family can have an insulating influence for its members and mitigate the onslaught of stressful factors in the family. Rigid and demanding sex roles and consequent conflict in a marital situation are often responsible for mental problems. Research findings are consistent in that (1) single individuals show higher rates of mental disorders compared to married individuals; (2) single people have longer stays in mental hospitals; (3) mental disorder rates are higher among separated, divorced, and widowed individuals; and (4) women generally show higher rates of mental disorders, and chances of developing a mental disorder are higher for formerly married people and widows, except that single, unmarried men have higher rates than their female counterparts (Gove, 1972; Kessler & Essex, 1982; Kessler & McCrae, 1981, 1984; Rodeheaver & Datan, 1988; von Zerssen & Weyerer, 1982). Thus, marital status is one of the major predictors of the mental health status of a person.

Gallagher (1987, pp. 228–229) pointed out that marital status is probably a better predictor of mental disorder for males than females. This is due to the differing cultural gender role expectations. Males are expected to be independent, aggressive, adventurous, and used to taking the initiative, characteristics that are inconsistent with a variety of mental disorders, including schizophrenia. Females may be able to mask their mental disorders by playing the conventional role—being passive, withdrawn, or aloof, qualities often expected by suitors in courtship situations. Therefore, males with mental disorders are discovered early, and this discovery may prevent them from marrying. The *social selection theory* suggests that mental disorder precedes marriage and in effect influences marital status (Turner & Gartrell, 1978). People with mental disorders are not likely to marry. But what if they could find their own kind? Like age, social status, religion, and other social and personal characteristics at work in homogamous marriages, the possibility of the presence of mental disorders in bonding cannot be ruled out. Research has not yet addressed this issue.

How about a situation in which marriage precedes mental disorder? While many people spend a large portion of their lives in marital bliss and more or less successfully raising families, the relationships that develop in the marriage are themselves often sources of stress and frustration. Nonetheless, another theory puts family in the center of the mental health field. It suggests that marriage is a mental health haven for the depressed, dependent, insecure, and the helpless. In addition to security, the new dyad in marriage as a team allows people to fend off problems they could not handle alone. Marriage may be the best thing that happens to them. If we reverse the sequence, marriage may not be the best cure for mental problems. People getting married to seek solutions to their mental problems have a higher likelihood of contributing to family problems. Meeting role expectations in marital life and handling conflicts places special demands on those who are emotionally vulnerable. Often, the impaired partner finds fault in the other partner's behavior, leading to mutual accusations and dissensions. Temper tantrums are, in many cases, manifestations of jealousy, hostility, insecurity, and inability to cope, and underlying such behavior may be higher levels of perpetual anxiety.

Married Men and Women

Marriage brings a change in the status and role of the newly married and adds responsibilities and restrictions. Marriage curtails the kind of freedom enjoyed in courtship. Higher rates of mental disorders among married women compared to unmarried women suggest that marriage is hazardous to the mental health of women. Gallagher (1987, p. 230) suggested that symptoms of female schizoid personality do not show until well after the wedding. It may not be the female's entering the marital role that causes problems, but the evolution of the mental disorder as interactions become more complex. When the honeymoon is over, reality sets in. The same characteristics viewed with admiration in courtship may now be seen as undesirable in a spouse. Women also find themselves under more strain in marriage because of "role overload." Not only are they expected to attend to household chores but also work to bolster family income. Further, research suggests that mental problems among women cannot be attributed to marriage (Warheit, Holzer, Bell, & Avery, 1976). NIMH figures on sex and marital status suggest that when compared with never-married women, married men have lower rates of mental disorders. Never-married men and women have the highest rates of mental disorders. These figures relate to only county and state mental hospital admissions, where generally lower classes seek treatment, and do not represent middle and upper classes.

Walter Gove and others (Busfield, 1982; Gove, 1972, 1979; Gove & Tudor, 1973) suggested that the role of married women is responsible for relatively higher rates of mental disorders among married women than married men. Married men seem to benefit more from marriage than women. The mitigating effect of marriage on men is due to the stabilizing effect of companionship and sharing of responsibilities by the spouse and children. Married men report fewer serious and chronic mental disorders and personality disorders that are otherwise common among men. In contrast, married women report more anxiety and depression compared to single women. The frustrations of the homemaker role, generally inferior and discriminatory situations in the job market, and an absence of clearly defined role expectations in middle age when children leave home may be related to the prevalence of anxiety and depression. Another explanation is that compared to married men, women play less gratifying roles and are constrained by the demands of motherhood, work, and domestic chores. Lower class women, with little education or skills, face more serious problems. Not only does money remain a problem, but the care of the children often overwhelms the mother who has few resources. The problem is compounded by lower class husbands who also have few resources. Desertion and divorce in the lower class further exacerbate the plight of single motherhood.

Two-Career Couples and Families

Families in which both spouses work are increasingly common, as are marriages with no children, called DINKS (dual income, no kids). Some put off parenthood until their careers mature. Many dual-career couples fight on two fronts:

1. They struggle to assume new roles and chores. Men may feel threatened and challenged by increasing economic independence of their wives. Wives may use their employment in a varieties of ways to gain more power.
2. They grapple with traditional societal expectations that women should be responsible for child rearing and care of the household. While a dual

income is to the advantage of the husband, who exchanges less power for a better living standard, for wives careers may cause inner guilt and disapproval of the spouse, which increase stress levels (Berg, 1987).

Inability to cope with stress and trying to be *superwoman* have harmful effects. Often, such pressures cause physical exhaustion, high levels of anxiety, and personal adjustment problems and affect intrafamily relationships and career goals. One study found that career women spend more time wishing that they were married to someone else and thinking about divorce than women who are homemakers (Staines, Pleck, Shepard, & O'Connor, 1978). The egalitarian values promoted by dual-career men and women lead to uncertainty in their relationships. Egalitarian women spend more time than egalitarian men on household duties and child care. Thus, women experience more stress than men (Vanyperen & Buunk, 1991). In addition, women value sociability and relationships more, while men stake their self-esteem in the social hierarchy. Research suggests that men and women try to bind themselves firmly to traditional identities (such as a great mother and a dedicated wife) as long as they believe that rejecting those identities will evoke negative reactions from others (Schwalbe & Staples, 1991).

The average U.S. marriage lasts only 9.4 years. It is not so much the dual-career situation, but the roles and demands of work and the necessary adjustments that tend to tear marriages apart. However, singlehood is no bliss either. High rates of mental disorders are found among never-married men and women. Marriage continues to be a popular institution and many continue to believe that although marriage is not without its problems, a good marriage is also a solution of our problems (see Box 10–2).

The Divorced and the Once Married

Among the most traumatic life events, divorce ranks second to death in the family (Holmes & Rahe, 1967). Divorce brings significant changes in the living situation, financial circumstances, and relations with others. But the most important change is in the emotional life of the people involved. Divorce speaks of personal failure and causes heartbreak, social stigma, and a sense of uncertainty. Termination of marriage is only symptomatic of much deeper problems in a relationship. It could also be the byproduct of emotional problems of one or both spouses. Marriage is the only institution that demands so much from the partners that is subject to disappointment. Considering the high rates of mental problems in the United States, it is likely that these problems affect marital life. The instability of family life in turn may affect emotional life.

> **BOX 10–2 • Divorce, Distress, and Attachment**
>
> Goode's (1956) study of divorced mothers reported that about two thirds experienced some level of trauma giving rise to distress. The trauma is as likely to be distressing for men as for women. Those who were left by a spouse and those who were leavers were distressed by the end of the marriage (Weiss, 1975). Marriages, happy or unhappy, contribute significantly to the well-being of the partners. There is no simple association between happiness attributed to marriage and the intensity of grief caused by separation and divorce. With minor variations, such grief is disabling for all.
>
> Many women are terrified by the idea of living alone after a divorce, although their marriage might have been burdensome. Others see marriage as a means of security to fend off anxiety. Further, some men and women, in spite of their separation, continue to be exasperated by the yearning for their spouse. Some have longing for the former spouse even after they have established new relationships. The marital bond appears to be unrelated to liking, respect, or admiration. Those who are separated reported they continue to like their spouses, but they would no longer live with them. The emotional tug resembles the *attachment bond* between children and parents. The loss of attachment is the primary cause of *separation distress* syndrome (Parkes, 1972), leading to anxiety, guilt, rage, hyperalertness, restlessness, and the feeling of fear and panic.

It is believed that divorce is much more difficult for women, probably because they are more expressive emotionally but also because most women are impoverished by divorce. Role overload (taking care of the home, children, learning new skills and work) becomes burdensome and stressful. Menaghan and Lieberman (1986) found that the impact of divorce may not be immediate. Those who were divorced, 4 years later, reported increases in depression and greater economic problems, the perception that one's standard of living had deteriorated, and less availability of close, confiding relationships. Admission rates to state and county mental hospitals suggest no significant difference between divorced and separated men and women. However, they rank second to the never married, who have the highest rates of mental disorders.

For the once married (separated, divorced, and widowed), their new marital status influences their total lifestyle. It is difficult to say how many people are thus affected. Admission rates in mental hospitals represent only a fraction of those who are affected by their personal or marital circumstances. Residence patterns in mental hospitals show that there are more married women than married men, and single men outnumber single

TABLE 10-2 • Admissions to County and State Hospitals, by Sex and Marital Status, 1980*

Marital Status	Male	Female	Both Sexes
Total	239,400	129,649	369,049
Never married	51.5%	34.2%	45.4%
Married	18.2	25.7	20.9
Divorced/separated	27.9	29.7	28.5
Widowed	2.3	10.4	5.2

*Includes individuals 14 years of age and over.
From National Institute of Mental Health, "Characteristics of Admissions to the Inpatient Services of State and County Mental Hospitals, United States, 1980." Mental Health Statistical Note No. 177. Washington, DC: Department of Health and Human Services, 1986.

women. Among the widowed, although they represent only a little over 5% of the resident population, the number of women is five times that of the men (see Table 10–2).

One-Parent Families

One-parent families have been on the increase in the United States for the past 3 decades. In 1984, 23% of U.S. households were headed by women. About 56% of black and 17% of white households were maintained by women, compared to only 3% by men without their wives. One of four children, or over 13 million children, under 18 lived in a single-parent household (Norton & Glick, 1986). Robert S. Weiss (1979) identified three sources of stress among single parents:

1. *Responsibility overload.* Single parents alone have to make decisions about family needs and well-being.
2. *Task overload.* Caring of home and children and bringing in money alone is physically and psychologically exhausting.
3. *Emotional overload.* Single parents must relentlessly cope alone with the stresses and strains of child rearing, work, and day-to-day life. Often, their emotional needs take second place after their children. Further, children raised in minority one-parent families have greater likelihood of emotional problems in turn causing greater stress to their mothers (Patterson, Kupersmidt & Vaden, 1990).

In a study of marital status, life strains, and depression, Pearlin and Johnson (1977) pointed out that the relationship between marital status and depression may be spurious and shaped not by marital status but its attendant characteristics. Sex, age, and race are particularly implicated. For example, women and blacks are markedly overrepresented in all categories of formerly married. After partialing out ascribed characteristics, Pearlin and Johnson found that there is an association between marital status and depression (see Table 10–3).

It is difficult to say that those who head one-parent families have more than their share of emotional problems and therefore cannot maintain the unity of the family, or that heading a one-parent family increases the likelihood of mental problems. A common belief is that women are naturally adept in raising children because they give birth to them. Also, they are accustomed to lower status and they have better control over their life events than men (Mulvey & Dohrenwend, 1984). But women who head one-parent families experience greater financial loss, are less likely to remarry, are more likely to carry the major burden of child care, and are less likely to learn skills to improve their life chances. The children in one-parent families are also affected adversely. A study of low-income mothers of young children, measured by the 20-item CES-D (Center for Epidemiologic Studies Depression Scale), reported a 48% prevalence rate of high depressive symptoms. Among unmarried women, everyday stressors were strongly associated with depressive symptoms compared to married women (Hall, Williams, & Greenberg, 1985).

TABLE 10–3 • Marital Status and Depression

				Types of Formerly Married		
Depression		Married	Never Married	Formerly Married	Widowed	Divorced	Separated
N		1589	288	415	172	141	102
High	1	12%	20%	27%	22%	27%	32%
	2	14	18	20	22	14	25
	3	18	23	17	15	16	23
	4	29	24	18	21	22	10
Low	5	27	16	18	20	21	10

Percent Distribution

Adapted from Pearlin & Johnson, 1977, pp. 704–715.

The Long Shadow of Parental Conflict

The level of parental conflict strongly affects the level of depression and withdrawal among children. It is higher among those children who live with one of the biological parents, especially single mothers (separated, divorced, or never married). Boys are more sensitive to marital disruption (Peterson & Zill, 1986, pp. 302–303).

The longitudinal research consistently finds that marital conflict impinges on parent–child relationships in ways that place children at greater risk for emotional and behavioral disorders (Amato, 1988). Marital distress precedes the development of problematic parent–child relationships. The link between dissonance in the marital relationship and poor parent–child relationships is stronger for girls than boys (Caspi & Elder, 1988). The influence of marital discord on child adjustment in intact families is similar to divorcing families (Tschann, Johnston, Kline, & Wallerstein, 1989). Aggression, conduct disorders, and delinquency (behaviors externalizing problems frequently exhibited by children) are among the behavior disorders most frequently associated with parental discord. Children observe and model the aggressive tactics of their parents. Disputing parents are also likely to have withdrawn and depressed children (Block, Block, & Morrison, 1981; Emery & O'Leary, 1984; Johnston, Gonzalez, & Campbell, 1987). Children model their avoidant strategies of conflict resolution after disputing parents, often withdrawing from angry situations and turning their anger inward.

Protracted marital conflict is a key factor in children's adjustment to divorce, when parents' energies are exhausted by preoccupation with their own emotional responses to the disruption of the family and numerous social and environmental changes (Cherlin, 1981; Weitzman, 1985). Wallerstein & Kelly (1980) pointed out that self-absorption of parents in their own problems, characterized by less consistent discipline, lower levels of affection, and rejection and depletion of the parental role can result in a temporary "diminished capacity to parent."

When a divorce occurs, it alters the quantity and quality of time parents spend with their children. The postdivorce situation is rarely congenial for the emotional growth of the children. The interaction between the custodial (usually mother) and noncustodial parent (usually father) remains strained and sometimes hostile due to past conflicts. Children are often caught in between and try not to show favor to a particular parent. In this process, parental authority tends to be undermined (McLanahan, 1989). Children whose parents were divorced are likely to develop "divorce syndrome" and are more likely to go through divorce. Often, they develop an antipathy to marriage. Divorce creates a sense of betrayal among the children. If they are young, they cannot understand why mom and dad cannot be part of the same family. Many children are so adversely affected emotionally that when they grow up they do not find themselves ready to marry. They delay their marriages as long as possible to handle their guilt and anger. This disinclination to marry is higher among white women than men (Amato, 1989; Peterson & Zill, 1986).

Reconstituted Families

Before 1900, 90% of marriages were first marriages. With the increasing incidence of divorce, remarriages have been steadily increasing, as have reconstituted families composed of stepparents and stepchildren. In 1980, remarriages accounted for 44% of the marriages in the United States, compared to only 31% in 1971 and about 17% in 1960. Men are more likely to remarry than women, but those who do not remarry suffer greater social isolation and ill health (Bumpass, Sweet, & Martin, 1990).

Remarriages bring the divorced person into a newly reconstituted family, and the remarriage is a new bond between one or both of the divorced parents. Children are expected to adapt to the new role of stepchildren. The roles of stepparents and stepchildren are not clearly defined in most Western societies. Many children have mixed feelings about parental divorce and often have a high level of resentment against one or both parents. Enforcing discipline by a stepparent becomes difficult. Children believe that natural parents are loving and caring and newcomer stepparents cannot love them in the same way. At best, a new stepparent is often perceived as an intruder in the family. Children often view the arrival of the new stepparent with latent suspicion, indifference, withdrawal, and sometimes with jealousy. Children believe they belong to their parents, and that they own their parents, and the entry of a stepparent implies that the ownership must be shared. Inherent in these relationships is the sense of competition between a stepparent and children.

The possibility of conflict between the stepparent and children can be a minefield of frustration and anger. "You may be my mother's new husband, but you are not my father, and I don't love you," or "Dad may love you, but you are not my mommy." Statements like these are disheartening for a stepparent. A stepmother reported, "relationships with my stepchildren have been a nightmare since I married him three years ago, and finally I was hospitalized for exhaustion and depression." A common opinion among stepparents is that stepchildren are spoiled. Biological parents typically make excuses for them because of their own guilt associated with the trauma of divorce (Burns, 1985, p. 100).

Studies on children's perception of family environment suggest that parental control is positively correlated with the competence of primary school children and negatively correlated with the competence of adolescents (Amato, 1989).

Although it is not always true that children in biological families are psychologically better off, reconstituted families pose a series of adjustment problems. In mother-headed families, male teens start taking some of the responsibilities of the male adult role. Female teens share the responsibilities of the mother, especially if she is working. But the emotional scars of divorce are probably never healed. When the single parent remarries, the family situation becomes more complicated. Children must adapt to a new set of roles and rules governing them due to the presence of a new authority figure. Often, stepparents assume that the reconstituted family is almost a biological family, but for children it is not. Children in their teens may seek emotional support from outside the family, particularly from peers, with limited success. The inconsistent role definition of adolescence puts a lot of pressure on them to seek the feeling of belonging. Some adolescents seek peer alliances to fill this emotional need and attempt to act like children from intact biological families. They may attempt to reduce the level of anxiety associated with the loss of belongingness by drinking, drug use, and acting out. Frequent auto accidents, juvenile delinquency, premarital pregnancies, drug addiction, and attempts to commit suicide are frequent manifestations and are often associated with emotional problems.

RELIGION

Gallup pollsters have interviewed Americans a dozen times from 1944 to 1981 about their belief in God. In 1944, 96% believed in God, compared to 95% in 1981 (Gallup, 1985). There are several hundred identifiable religious groups in the United States, of which at least 24 have a membership of over 1 million members. In 1984, there were about 53 million Roman Catholics, 15 million Southern Baptists, 9.3 million members of United Methodist Church, and 6 million members associated with Jewish congregations (Jacquet, 1987).

Religion has always played a significant role in defining sacred and profane, spiritual and secular, and the boundaries of cosmic phenomena. As a part of a culture, religion influences the concepts of mental disorders and their treatment. In many cultures, magical and religious practices are viewed as a part of the whole culture, thus becoming an integral part of the rehabilitative process. For example, in some cultures people possessed by the spirit of a god, deity, or pure and benevolent spirit of an ancestor are viewed as undergoing a religious experience that is considered prestige-enhancing for the subjects. Such assignment of meaning is relevant because it determines how a certain behavior is interpreted. Assignment of meaning to behavior, thoughts, fantasies, dreams, fears, delusions, and hallucinations is an essential part of the therapeutic process and is culturally determined. It is not surprising that cultures describe meaningful sequences of thoughts and acts by applying rules derived from religion to provide rational explanations for irrational behavior (Mendel, 1968, p. 400). Most religions, through their philosophical systems and ritual practices, provide interpretation of behavior and means of control. What may be called mental disorders in Western cultures may be viewed as spiritual experience in many non-Western cultures.

Whereas Durkheim saw the unifying force in religion as transcending diverse groups and individuals, Freud (1953) viewed it as "obsessional neurosis." Karl Marx described religion as an "opiate." He believed that religion often drugged the masses so they could not challenge the injustices caused by inequality but clung to the hope for salvation in an ideal afterlife. However, the relationship between religion and mental disorder is spurious at best, partly because simply believing in religion does not determine the degrees of religiosity. Religiosity itself is contingent on other variables such as age, sex, class, race, and education. Occasionally, psychotics in mental institutions describe religious imagery and delusions that are grounded in religion. Claims of being Jesus Christ or endowed with great spiritual powers or incarnations of God are not uncommon.

Research based on church attendance suggests that mental patients are less likely to be religiously committed than the general population (Stark, 1971). However, it is questionable whether church attendance alone is an objective measure of religiosity (Gallagher, 1987, p. 236). Antonovsky (1987) argued that those who enjoy a greater sense of coherence and order in their lives also have better physical and mental health, and this may result from religiosity whether or not church attendance is involved.

Peter Berger (1967) pointed out that religion offers a comprehensive framework for the ordering and interpretation of human events. Religious ideas provide meanings and means for adjusting to those "boundary experiences," major life events that call into question established understandings of reality.

Studies of psychological well-being and religious involvement offer the following insights:

1. Religious institutions nurture friendships and social ties that may eventually develop into secular ties. Group involvement thus protects the individual from social isolation (Witter, Stock, Okung, & Haring, 1985).

2. Members of religious communities enjoy informal support in moments of adversity and assistance in the problem-solving phases of coping with stress (Maton, 1989).

3. Interpersonal and familial relationships, work, and other dimensions of personal lifestyles are regulated by religious groups to promote fundamental norms regarding health behavior and bring deviants in line through sanctions (Umberson, 1987).

4. Collective participation in ritual events reinforces significant meaning to private beliefs and enhances the centrality of religious life experiences (Peterson & Roy, 1985).

5. Divine interaction, like other social relationships, tends to foster ability to resolve problematic situations relatively easily by defining them as God's will and absolves the individual from guilt feelings and their emotionally adverse consequences (Ellison, Gay, & Glass, 1989; Foley, 1988; Pollner, 1989).

At the microlevel, religion plays a significant role in providing solace in difficult times, mitigating the harmful effects of distressing situations in two ways: (1) stress suppression, and (2) stress buffering (Wheaton, 1985). Those who are engaged in religious pursuits are able to negate and compensate for distressing effects of stress. Stress-buffering effects occur at higher levels of stress and religiosity. Although they may vary across societal levels, they are effective in ameliorating the harmful effects of stress.

The frequency of devotional activity (e.g., prayer, Bible study) is particularly high among elderly adults (Guy, 1982). This is partly due to the availability of more time, limited mobility due to health problems, and utilization of intrapsychic strategies of coping to manage emotional problems, especially those perceived to be insoluble (Ellison, 1991). Pollner (1989) pointed out that for people with limited sophisticated cognitive resources or lower levels of formal education, religious faith offers a framework for interpreting daily life. However, it is difficult to say how much, if any, religious affiliation plays a role in psychiatric diagnosis. We will discuss this later.

Religion represents only a part of the value system by which individual behavior is governed, but the collective nature of religion has social consequences at the macrolevel. John Calvin (1509–1564), a leader of the Protestant Reformation, emphasized a disciplined work ethic, this-worldly concern, and rational orientation to life, which Max Weber later called the "Protestant Ethic." Calvin believed in the doctrine of *predestination*, which holds that one's predestined future will not be dependent on being righteous or sinful in the present life. Hard work at a vocation is an explicit hallmark of one's inner Christianity and an indication that a person will be rewarded in the afterlife. Ethics of hard work also served as a means of reducing anxiety but initiated a change favorable to capitalistic behavior. Max Weber (1958, original edition 1904) believed that religion helped shape the economic system. Although Weber did not argue that Protestant ethic was necessary for the development of capitalism, in a wider sense the values of hard work and success paved the way for rise of capitalism, not only in the Western world but in many nations of the world. The decline of religion with new rationality and belief in scientific ideas as an overriding force opened the way for individualism, weakening social bonds between the individual, family, and community, reflecting in high rates of divorce, alcoholism, drug abuse, and crime. Thus, decline of religion has emotional consequences for the society as a whole that gradually disintegrates the system of shared beliefs and values about the ultimate questions of life. In many ways Protestant ethic is not limited to any particular sect anymore but has become a cultural trait of the spirit of capitalism.

Research in the 1950s showed that Protestants were underrepresented in the psychiatric populations. Catholics were represented in proportion to their population size but showed very high levels of alcoholism. The Jewish people were overrepresented in the psychiatric population, with high rates of neurosis (Roberts & Myers, 1954).

Religious philosophies and affiliations have influenced the nature of mental problems and the ways in which people seek help. Srole and Langner (1969), in their midtown Manhattan study, found that attitudes toward seeking different kinds of treatment have a close association with religious affiliation. For example, in an answer to a hypothetical case of mental disorder, half of the Jewish respondents said that they would see a psychotherapist, compared to 23.8% of Catholics and 31.4% of Protestants. The highest treatment rate was found among Jewish people, twice as much as that of Protestants and 10 times higher than Catholics. However, religion alone cannot account for this discrepancy. Compared to Catholics and Protestants, a relatively larger proportion of the Jewish population is in high-paying professional jobs, is highly educated, and has greater concerns about health. On the other hand, Catholics mask their mental problems through inordinately high rates of alcoholism (Gallagher, 1987, pp. 236–238). As we can see, health-seeking behavior is a complex process. Religious affiliation might be one of the determinants of who suffers from what kind of disorder and who seeks help where. A new awareness among the clients has lead to the changes that often psychiatric treatment ignores their religious beliefs (Lund, 1990).

In a survey of the American Psychiatric Association's membership (1975), only 43% believed in God, contrasting sharply with more than 90% of the general public who professed belief. Religious affiliation determined where a person was treated. If the first contact was with a member of the clergy, the subject often ended up at religious-psychiatric clinic, while psychologists and psychiatrists referred more to the psychoanalytic and hospital outpatient clinic (Kudashin, 1969). The presence and absence of theistic beliefs not only influences subjects' choices of seeking treatment, it also influences therapists' choices about obtaining therapy. A survey of 3,000 mental health professionals, including psychiatrists, psychologists, and psychiatric social workers (Larson, Pattison, Blazer, Omran, & Kaplan, 1986), found that those with religious beliefs had received therapy much less often than did those with atheistic, agnostic, or no religious beliefs. This raises questions about the tracking of those who need treatment but do not obtain it and substitute religious practices for mental health treatment.

As we have discussed, age, gender, marital status, and religious variables have various degrees of impact on the likelihood of mental disorders. The interactive processes involved among these variables are influenced by interpersonal relationships, which can mitigate or accelerate the process. Ascribed characteristics cannot be changed, but achieved characteristics are subject to change. Those areas of human life that can be changed have the greatest potential for personal growth and happiness.

CHAPTER REVIEW

1. What is the difference between ascribed and achieved characteristics? How do they influence mental health outcomes?

2. Surveys on mental disorders are designed to learn the actual prevalence of mental disorders. What are their strengths and limitations?

3. How is age associated with mental disorders? Explain the discrepancies between the figures from National Institute of Mental Health and epidemiological catchment area studies.

4. Although the number of elderly is growing, NIMH figures suggest that they do not have higher rates of mental impairment. What are the biases that might lead to inappropriate treatment?

5. Studies of the true prevalence of mental disorders, in contrast to NIMH figures, suggest that women have higher rates of mental disorders than men. Explain.

6. Bruce G. Link and Bruce P. Dohrenwend in a review of epidemiological studies in 1989 reported gender differences in mental health. What are those differences?

7. Are women more vulnerable to mental disorders? If so, why?

8. What are the differences in the rates of mental impairment between married and single people? Are there any gender differences?

9. The two-career family is becoming the norm in the United States. In what ways do careers affect the mental health of women?

10. What strains do one-parent families face? How do these strains influence the mental health of parents and children?

11. Do parental conflict and divorce affect the mental health of children? Explain.

12. How is the reconstituted family associated with the likelihood of mental disorders?

13. Is there any association between religious affiliation and mental disorders? Evaluate the findings.

FOR FURTHER STUDY

Ashton–Jones, E., & Olson, G. A. (Eds.). (1991). *The gender reader*. Boston: Allyn and Bacon.

Cockerham, W. C. (1989). *Sociology of mental disorders*. Englewood Cliffs, NJ: Prentice Hall.

Dohrenwend, B. P., & Dohrenwend, B. S. (1976). Sex differences in psychiatric disorders. *American Journal of Sociology, 81,* 1447–1454.

Gupta, G. R., & Cox, S. M. (Eds.). (1987). *Deviance and disruption in the American family*. Lexington, MA: Ginn Press.

Leff, J., & Vaughn, C. (1985). *Expressed emotion in families*. New York: Guilford Press.

Link, B. G., & Dohrenwend, B. P. (1989). The epidemiology of mental disorders. In H. E. Freeman & S. Levine (Eds.), *Handbook of medical sociology*. Englewood Cliffs, NJ: Prentice Hall.

Motimer, J., & Borman, K. M. (Eds.). (1988). *Work experience and psychological development through the life span*. Boulder, CO: Westview Press.

▶ 11

Mental Disorders: Individual and Institutional Response

Ms. A, a 20-year-old, had suffered from serious depression, with acute insomnia and suicidal impulses. She complained that her depression started when her mother, an alcoholic, remarried and she could not get along with her stepfather.

"I received orders from the System," complained a young man. "There was no person, but the command was imperious and uttered in a loud gravel voice. I was doing some reading for my physics exam. Suddenly, without any warning, a voice commanded me to burn everything I had in my dorm. Surely I resisted the order but of no avail. I picked a bunch of matches from a drawer, ran out of my room, and started a fire in the trash can. The fire alarms went off."

A young woman said, "You know, my mother's hands bleed. She just can't resist washing them. I can't even keep count of how frequently she does that."

These statements show that mental impairments can take different forms. The impact of these disorders is experienced by those who suffer from them, as Lara Jefferson, a mental patient in a Midwestern state hospital in the 1940s, indicated succinctly: "I have learned through the grim lesson taught by my failure that my previous methods of trying to adjust to the problem of living were not the right ones. If my wrong way of thinking was the net my mind spun to entrap me, then it is certainly logic, that same sort of spinning cannot release me now that I am entangled. I do not know what is the trouble—only that something is wrong—terribly wrong. And I do not know how to right it" (Jefferson, 1964, p. 9).

Stories that receive public attention due to their bizarre theme or criminal acts, such as those committed by the Son of Sam (David Berkowitz), John Hinckley, or Jeffrey Dahmer, are rare. Nonetheless, such cases create public images of mentally disordered people as dangerous, even though the majority of people who have mental disorders are neither dangerous nor criminal. Millions of people suffer from frustrations, persistent anxieties, interpersonal conflicts, dysfunctionalities, and an inability to cope with routine demands in their lives. They do not make headlines, and many do not believe they have a mental disorder. Positive changes in personal situations, some good news, or pleasant encounters help put their emotional lives back on track. Many do not believe they need treatment, but some are so overpowered by their problems that someone else prods them to seek help. Still others believe they know what their problems are and that they can handle them. Of course, there are still others who are lost and do not even realize that their lives are in shambles or that their actions might be dangerous to themselves as well as others.

THE PERSON, SELF-FEELING, AND DEVIANCE

As we have indicated, the term mental disorder is both relative and complex. Some individuals feel that they are experiencing problems but cannot come to grips with the feeling. The feeling, which the person may believe to be wrong, bad, or unacceptable, causes inner conflict and when verbalized or translated into action influences relationships with others (Thoits, 1985). Some people, by their own initiative, are able to cope with the feeling in a positive way. Others are less fortunate; the feeling persists and is translated into actions, further complicating interpersonal relationships and leading the individual to be identified as deviant. The deviant label is conferred by those who also decide what can be done about it (Becker, 1963; Erikson, 1962). Thus it is the audience, which may be composed of family, kin, friends, co-workers, or people in the community, who eventually defines what the actions of the individual mean and how to respond. Once a deviant label is assigned to a person's behavior, it is likely to yield negative reactions from others that may hurt the person's feelings and accelerate the gravity of the problems. Anxiety, paranoia, and depression may be transferred into a range of manifestations, including overt hostility, senseless arguments, crying, insomnia, hypersensitivity, withdrawal, embitterment, and the blues.

Thomas Szasz insisted for over 30 years that it is often "deviant behavior" that attracts the attention of others to individuals, who are then viewed as experiencing mental disorders. The label results from the intolerance of people who believe that another's behavior is inappropriate and that the person needs to be treated. Thus, rather than seeking other ways to resolve the problem, we often push people to seek treatment, sometimes against their will. Szasz referred to this process as the *manufacture of madness*. In fact, he stated that this response to deviant acts is the basic cause of the proliferation in the numbers of the "so called mentally ill" and the unnecessary treatment of those who do not need it (Szasz, 1970b, 1987). The process of deciding whether or not treatment is appropriate occurs during what has been called the "prepatient phase" and involves diagnostic decisions made by others with whom the potential patient interacts, as well as by the individual in question.

PRINCIPAL DIAGNOSIS

Most people who are diagnosed as having mental disorders do not fit neatly into theoretical categories like pieces of a puzzle. Primary and secondary symptoms are evaluated on several axes. For example, NIMH (1990a) figures available for inpatient, outpatient, and partial care services indicate that schizophrenic disorders were found in almost 45% of inpatient and partial care populations, while outpatient cases exhibited similar symptoms about five times more frequently (300,000 cases). Affective disorders followed, ranging from 17 to 23%. Six other categories of disorders accounted for less than 5% of the diagnostic cases (see Table 11–1).

PREPATIENT EXPERIENCE

How people, at a personal level, conceptualize *where* to seek help is influenced by sociocultural factors, as is the issue of *whether* to seek help. As in cases of physical illness, those whose functioning is adversely affected due to the severity of the problem experienced are likely to seek professional help (Greenley, Mechanic, & Cleary, 1987; Mechanic, 1975; Tessler & Mechanic, 1978). The process of seeking help is like going through *rites of passage*, those step-by-step actions that may or may not identify a mental disorder. This process can be classified into two categories: (1) voluntary and (2) involuntary.

Voluntary Help Seeking

Voluntary help-seeking behavior involves the concern of the loved ones and exploration of therapeutic alternatives. The person is told, with some

TABLE 11-1 • Number and Percent of Total Persons by Selected Diagnoses, United States, April 1, 1986

Selected Principal Diagnoses	Total, All under Care					
	Inpatient Services		Outpatient Services		Partial Care Services	
	No.	(%)	No.	(%)	No.	(%)
Alcohol-related disorders	10,008	(6.2)	68,181	(4.9)	2356	(1.8)
Drug-related disorders	4,829	(3.0)	26,195	(1.9)	1510	(1.1)
Affective disorders	34,722	(21.6)	308,110	(22.3)	22,654	(17.0)
Schizophrenia	69,994	(43.5)	298,808	(21.6)	63,075	(47.4)
Personality disorders	3,893	(2.4)	81,731	(5.9)	6,479	(4.9)
Adjustment disorders	6,301	(3.9)	229,801	(16.6)	6,955	(5.2)
Organic disorders	9,001	(5.6)	—		—	
Social conditions	—		77,069	(5.6)	—	

Adapted from National Institute of Mental Health, Mental Health, United States, 1990a, pp. 159, 165, 171.

degree of concern, that alleviating the disturbed behavior is in everyone's interest.

Part of the problem in help seeking is knowing exactly what the problem is and who is supposed to treat it. For laypeople, a family member with a mental problem not only suffers himself or herself, but represents a threat to the normal functioning of the family. Some believe that the disorder is contagious. Therefore, the decision to seek help is influenced by those who are in close contact, such as members of the family, kin, and friends. The readiness to seek help varies among different groups, and this readiness, more than the number of symptoms, leads people into psychiatric treatment—a process of *self-labeling* occurs (Scheff, 1984, p. 114).

Once it is realized that a problem exists and a decision is reached that the problem requires professional attention, the help seeking involves six stages: (1) determining whether the problem is physical or emotional; (2) determining whether it is possible to alleviate the problem by personal effort, will, or changes in repertory of work and personal relationships; (3) ascertaining with whom the problem should or should not be discussed; (4) ascertaining who may be the most helpful or supportive people (relatives, friends, co-workers, etc.) in case hospitalization or extended care is needed; (5) determining which agency (clinic, hospital, community mental health center) will be helpful; and (6) if there is a choice, deciding who should be consulted for treatment—clergy, psychologist, family therapist, family physician, or psychiatrist (Kadushin, 1969).

The process of seeking help can be analyzed at three levels: (1) individual, (2) family, relatives, and friends, and (3) institutional.

The Individual Level

Feelings and emotions belong to individuals, but their roots are in social relationships. Thus mental disorder, although an individual phenomenon, adversely affects not only the individual but all those who are part of his or her social network. Bizarre behavior and personal suffering, at the individual level, evoke varying responses.

Family, Relatives, and Friends

Studies on the reaction of family members to a member who is later diagnosed as experiencing a mental disorder suggest that the families have an immense capacity to ignore, explain away, and tolerate abnormal behavior (Sampson, Messinger, & Towne, 1962). While some people and families are more conscious and concerned about their physical and mental health than others, as symptoms of mental disorder become more pronounced in the family member the tolerance level of other members gradually declines and is replaced by arguments, blame-placing, helplessness, and uncertainty. The process of figuring out—what should be done involves the following steps: (1) a feeling of discomfort that something is wrong; (2) placing blame on those who are suspected of causing strained relationships and being accessories in creating the problem; (3) denial and ambivalence, and exploring ways to ensure that the problem can be handled; (4) frustration, anger, and some degree of crisis, a feeling of "What did we do wrong?"; (5) fear of stigma, guilt, and shame and a concern that the problem may be mental; (6) identification of mental disorder(s) and readjustment of roles and ways of doing things in the family, isolating those who are involved in precipitating the problem; and (7) managing the stresses of taking care of a mental patient and acceptance of mental disorder as a social reality (see Raymond, Slaby, & Lieb, 1975).

A process of mediation occurs between a member who has symptoms of mental problems and other members of the family to find an agreeable way to deal with the problem. Class, education, religion, race, and ethnicity of those involved play a significant role in determining how soon and where people will seek help. Ignorance, beliefs, superstitions, and shame influence the decision making. As indicated in Chapter 9, lower class association, less education, superstitious attitudes, rural living, and ethnic membership tend to attenuate reaction to abnormal behavior and discourage help seeking. People with a college education, high socioeconomic status, egalitarian principles, and low religiosity tend to seek help from psychotherapists. People with high religious orientation and lower class association tend to seek religious counseling services. It appears that when seeking help, people look for their own kind (i.e., the orientation of help providers is consistent with the kind of help the clients are looking for).

Institutional Level

A variety of mental health service providers is available (Table 11-2). Accessibility alone does not determine help seeking; rather, it is influenced by socioeconomic status, rural/urban living, religiosity, ethnicity, and the costs involved in such services. For example, services of community health centers are largely utilized by indigent and poor clients. Those who are better off seek treatment at clinics and from private psychiatrists.

A nationwide survey by Joseph Veroff, Richard Kulka, and Elizabeth Douvan (1981) compared help-seeking behavior between 1957 and 1976. Although the sources of help were diverse, in 1957 those who sensed that they had a problem were likely to consult a physician who was not a psychiatrist. In 1976, compared to 20 years earlier, there was an increasing willingness to consult psychiatrists, specialists in treating emotional problems.

Residual Deviance: The Labeling Process

Some types of mental disorders are the result of organic causes, but most are not. There is also a broad area of symptomatic behavior that does not involve an assumption of illness. Thomas Scheff argued that most of what is labeled as mental illness might simply be rule breaking. Rule breaking refers to "a class of acts, violations of social norms, and deviance to particular acts which have been publicly and officially labeled as norm violations" (Scheff, 1984, p. 37). Becker (1963) suggested that "deviance is not the quality of the act a person commits but rather a consequence of the application by others of rules and sanctions to an 'offender.'"

Following this logic, Scheff argued that most psychiatric symptoms can be categorized as instances of *residual rule breaking* or *residual deviance*. The culture of a group provides terms for identifying norm violations, such as crime, sin, perversion, drunkenness, and bribery. After exhausting all such categories, there is always a residue of diverse kinds of violations for which the culture provides no explicit label or name (Scheff, 1963, p. 38). For example, expressions of respect or decency have great cultural variations. Major and minor violations are lumped together into a residual category, leading to the category of mental illness because there is no explicit label or name for many of such violations. A child who cannot sit still in a class, a teenager who is withdrawn and does not talk with his parents, a spouse who is overly concerned about cleanliness in the house are cases of residual deviance. At first glance they seem to be just common human variations.

TABLE 11-2 • Mental Health Organizations, United States, 1970-1986

Type of Organization	Number and Percent of Mental Health Organizations									
	1970 No. (%)		1976 No. (%)		1980 No. (%)		1984 No. (%)		1986 No. (%)	
All organizations	3005	(100)	3,480	(100)	3,727	(100)	4,438	(100)	4,747	(100)
State and county mental hospitals	310	(10.3)	303	(8.7)	280	(7.5)	277	(6.4)	285	(6.0)
Private psychiatric hospitals	150	(5.0)	182	(5.2)	184	(4.9)	220	(5.0)	314	(6.6)
Nonfederal general hospitals with separate psychiatric services	797	(26.5)	870	(25.0)	923	(24.8)	1,347	(30.4)	1,351	(28.5)
Veterans Administration medical centers	115	(3.8)	126	(3.6)	136	(3.6)	139	(3.1)	139	(2.9)
Federally funded community mental health centers	196	(6.5)	517	(14.9)	691	(18.5)	—		—	
Residential treatment centers for emotionally disturbed children	261	(8.7)	331	(9.5)	368	(9.9)	322	(7.3)	437	(9.2)
Freestanding psychiatric outpatient clinics	1,109	(36.9)	1,076	(30.9)	1,053	(28.3)	792	(17.8)	773	(16.3)
All other organizations	67	(2.3)	75	(2.2)	92	(2.5)	1,341	(30.2)	1,448	(30.5)

Adapted from National Institute of Mental Health, *Mental Health, United States*, 1990a, p. 27.

However, in psychiatric assessment these behaviors can be identified as mental disorders. In the prepatient phase, such behaviors are noticed by others and eventually identified as mental problems.

Madness as a Coping Strategy: The Paradox of Normalcy

Do people recover from mental disorders? Most do, unless they have suffered extensive neurological damage. In many cases, however, negative images of people with mental disorders linger, especially among those whose symptoms of mental disorders persist. Being a mental patient has become part of their identity. Their normal roles are disrupted, and the new identity includes elements of "craziness" or "madness." This new identity is a *master status* gained as a consequence of others' *social reaction* to their deviant behavior. That is, all other roles of the person become secondary to the *master role* of mental patient.

Most people are able to readjust to socially acceptable roles after transitory episodes of deviance (e.g., going through a period of depression due to job loss or divorce). Lemert (1951) referred to this as *primary deviance*. But some people have trouble dissociating from their deviant roles. For example, a regular heavy drinker may become an alcoholic. People may use the deviant role as a defense, attack, or adjustment against problems created by *social reaction* to their behavior (primary deviance). Acts that are consequences of such social reaction lead to *secondary deviance*, which often has a global impact on a person's behavior. It is at this stage that highly visible deviant behavior is seen by others as normal for people with mental disorders. In short, the person with a mental disorder thus achieves the new master status of mentally impaired. This process is called the paradox of normalcy. The paradox is that the individual's abnormal behavior is viewed as normal for that person.

When people suspect that their suffering may be due to something that needs attention, chances are that they may consult their physician. In fact, a significant number of people seek help from a general physician, and only in rare cases do they see a psychiatrist at the recommendation of a general physician. Some see clergymembers, psychologists, or family counselors. Those who are hospitalized are perceived as having problems serious enough to require extensive evaluation and treatment of their physical as well as mental conditions. Yet admission to a mental institution does not prove that a person is insane. It does, however, bring remarkable changes in status and role, from civilian to mental patient.

Involuntary Help Seeking

Involuntary help-seeking behavior is coercive; the person does not have a choice. Even in cases of voluntary help seeking, some degree of persuasion, or a sort of gentle coercion, is not uncommon. The major difference is that involuntary commitment is sought when the mental problem is serious and the behavior of the subject is unpredictable and dangerous. This may involve reasonable concern about the safety of the person, family, or public at large. Commitment to a hospital or mental institution may be court ordered or mandated by law due to prior or current pathological actions of the person. Any adult may ask for assistance to commit a person who may

BOX 11-1 • Should He Be Committed?: The Case of Don Dumby

Don Dumby (fictional name) is a man, age 38, 5 feet 11 inches tall, never married, and has spent most of his life as a farm hand in a small Midwestern community of 300. His parents knew there were some problems with Don but did not know what to do about them. Don's sister, single, age 40, who worked at a grain elevator, lived in a trailer with Don and had control over Don's meager earnings. She allowed Don boarding and lodging and some pocket money. Don had few friends, and his sister was a dominant mother figure for him. In his late teens, Don attempted dating with no success. He felt that girls did not like him, and he questioned to himself, "What do they want?" Often he bought small gifts to please girls in the area, only to be disappointed. In some cases, Don was threatened by the parents of the girls to keep his hands off. Other men teased Don that he didn't act like a man, and they told him, "Man, you have to be aggressive, gals are always looking for men." Don took chances during county fairs and was charged twice of fondling young girls, but he was released on probation due to his "mental conditions." Court-ordered testing showed that Don's reading and writing abilities, at age 34, were rated at a fifth-grade level.

Don's sister moved to a small university town to take a new job, and Don begged to tag along with a promise of finding a job. Finding no job in a new town, he began collecting aluminum cans all over the university campus. He used this as an opportunity to sexually assault coeds. Complaints led law enforcement authorities to release his profile, and Don was soon arrested. During his first hearing before the court, Don confessed that he committed the crimes even before the judge brought up the charges for his arrest. Given the situation, the judge ordered a psychiatric examination, and Don was reported to suffer from several mental disorders. He was placed in a minimum security prison to await hearing until he was found mentally fit to stand trial. Two years later, two psychiatrists testified that Don had recovered and understood his crimes. Due to his prior criminal record, Don was sentenced to 18 years in prison. A local reporter asked Don what he had to say about his sentence. The answer was crisp; "I found a place to live."

Source: Author's file notes.

pose a danger to himself or herself or to others. The term *danger* is subjective, and the laws are intended to protect those individuals who may be railroaded into asylums because of their odd looks, personal failure, or unfortunate circumstances. Varying degrees of proof are required to show that a person may be dangerous at a particular time or may have the potential for acting out dangerously. Of course, involuntary commitment can be requested by an individual facing serious mental difficulties as well.

Specific steps in involuntary commitment are as follows: (1) written statements three or more people that a certain person is dangerous to self or others; (2) an evaluation report by a psychiatrist supporting the alleged symptoms; (3) opinions of two other court-appointed psychiatrists; (4) appointment by the court of a lawyer (public defender) to represent the case, (5) a judicial hearing of the case, and possibly (6) another judicial hearing after the subject has undergone psychiatric treatment to determine if continued incarceration is warranted (see Box 11–1, based on a recent case).

Who Gets Committed?

There are two types of commitment: (1) voluntary and (2) involuntary. People can seek commitment in an institution for self-perceived mental conditions that they believe are serious, including the inability to control their violent behavior. Over the years, state laws have become more stringent in allowing people to seek voluntary commitment. In some cases, civil liberties groups have questioned the morality and legality of putting people in jails, shelters, and mental institutions, denying them their civil rights.

Involuntary commitment is court ordered. The court, on the advice of court-appointed psychiatrists, may order a person's commitment when the person has either acted or shows great potential intent for acting in ways injurious to himself or herself, society, or both.

CAREER OF A MENTAL PATIENT

People tend to tolerate behavior that may be a little odd or strange for various reasons, and those tolerated often continue to carry on with their lives with little or no intervention. Actions that have potential for leading to unmanageable crises are most likely to come to the attention of mental health professionals and law enforcement officials. Most people believe that mental illness is a condition for which a person is treated in a mental hospital, and many believe that those who are afflicted should go to a mental institution (Cummings & Cummings, 1957, pp. 101–102). Behavior that portends a crisis or potential of it puts a person on the path of formally becoming a mental patient. Erving Goffman (1961, pp. 125–130) called this process *the moral career of the mental patient*. He used the term *moral* for "the regular sequence of changes that *career* (any social strand in the person's course of life) entails in the person's self and in his framework of imagery for judging himself and others."

Most people do not come into the mental hospital willingly. When they find themselves being admitted, this is evidence to them that they are losing their minds or losing control of themselves. Perceptions of losing one's mind, such as high levels of anxiety due to stressful experiences or hearing voices, are based on culturally derived and socially ingrained stereotypes that determine *self-views* and *self-referral* (self-initiated help seeking). These are influenced by subcultures of class, race, and ethnicity and are not a product of abnormal psychology.

Apprehension and ambivalence during the prepatient stage in seeking help reaches its climax when people are faced with four classic alternatives: (1) imploring by their family and kin, threat of abrogation of family ties and withdrawal of emotional and material support unless cooperation is forthcoming; (2) use of legal resources to force help seeking in an institution; (3) use of a police escort on the way to an institution, often with a pretension that person's decision-making ability is diminished due to the mental problem; and (4) indifference, neglect, and abuse at the hands of those in the family, who are unable to cope with a person's problems. While most individuals with mental disorders never become patients in mental hospitals, some are institutionalized and begin patient careers.

In his classic work *Asylums*, Erving Goffman (1961) made insightful observations on the prepatient and inpatient experience. However, since Goffman's work, treatment of people with mental disorders has taken a new direction. Insurance companies need more business and more money, and they are willing to insure people for treatment of mental disorders. This gave rise to the influx of private mental hospitals. Such hospitals are available only to those who are affluent enough to pay rising insurance premiums, most of whom probably remain free from the stigma of mental disorders. The quality of treatment for those who are poor and resourceless and admitted to the state mental institutions remains largely the same as during the past decades. Following the initiation of the community mental health movement and introduction of psychoactive drugs, changes have occurred in length of time spent in institutions. At the time of Goffman's writing (1961), the career of the inpatient was characterized as follows:

1. A person who starts out with some rights, liberties, and satisfactions ends up on a psychiatric ward stripped of almost everything.
2. Passage from a person to a patient leads to betrayal by those such as spouse, parent, or kin leading the person toward hospitalization—a controlled setting. The labeled person may find that while everyone else's comfort was busily sustained his long-range welfare was compromised by putting him in an institution.
3. Whatever power, authority, or control over possessions the person held prior to becoming a patient was transferred to others—generally next-of-kin. Although they have the patient's personal interest at heart and consider it a moral duty to take care of the patient, their role changes from members of a family to guardians who are more in tune with the

institutional agents (mental hospital staff) due to their power, than the labeled person.
4. Although people are hospitalized for specific mental conditions, all past antecedents in the course of their lives become part of their patient records, some of those the patient would prefer not to talk about are used intentionally as part of the treatment process.
5. Most patients entering the institution strongly feel the desire not to be known to anyone as persons who are reduced to the controlled environment of the institution which is stigmatizing. To save their 'self respect,' they avoid talking to anyone or appear to be 'out of contact.' Such actions are often misconstrued by institutional staff as apparent symptoms of mental disorder, leading to further isolation of the person within the institution.
6. Regimentation of routines for inpatients becomes part of their daily existence in institutions such as jails, concentration camps, monasteries, and work camps. Actually, it is worse in a mental institution where the sanity of the patients has already been challenged and even attempts to act appropriately are viewed with a suspicious eye.
7. Assignment to a ward is an expression of the level of social functioning. This mirrors the status of the patient and attacks the inmate's view of himself. The psychiatric staff through verbal attacks remind him of his failures and require him to change through arranged confessional periods of private sessions or group psychotherapy. Most inmates experience some degradation.
8. In the subculture of the institution, most inmates tell sad tales indicating that they are not sick and that the trouble they got into was somebody else's fault. Their past lives had some honor and rectitude and the hospital has forced upon them the status of mental patient. Often there is some truth in such claims. These tales circulate as "gossip," and staff discredits such stories only to enhance patients' loss of faith. In short, the patient must accept the hospital staff's view of his self.
9. Case records do not indicate occasions when the patient showed the capacity to cope honorably and effectively with difficult situations, but only those which might have symptomatic significance for "sickness." Because the presence of "sickness" is already assumed, answers to embarrassing staff questions are treated as tainted. Moral neutrality claimed for medical statements and psychiatric diagnosis is sacrificed.
10. Finally, it is not uncommon for inpatients to experience feelings of abandonment by those who were formerly close. This may be especially true for *next-of-relation* upon whom a patient should be able to depend on most in times of trouble and who should be the last to doubt the patient's sanity. Goffman uses the term *complainant* for those who are not *next of relation* but play the role to start the person on the way to

hospitalization. Ironically, the patient returns to the same setting and people after recovery but is unable to erase, or suppress what has happened, since the mental disorder has become a social fact.

Undoubtedly, some aspects of Goffman's description remain accurate today, but since the career of the mental patient is typically much shorter and the institutional setting considerably more open, the inpatient experience has changed (as we discuss in Chapters 12 and 13).

The emotional price that mental patients pay is sometimes heartbreaking and often reinforces the symptoms of mental disorder. They are rejected, often in subtle ways, but sometimes openly, by the people in their own homes, neighborhoods, workplaces, and the community. It is difficult to say whether rejection is a cause or consequence of mental disorder. Most people have conceptions of mental disorders, although they may not always be accurate. They see a group of behavioral characteristics in people who appear odd, nonconforming, idiotic, or out of line and not simply "different". As we discussed in Chapters 1, 9, and 10, people who comprise the audience label the behavior as a mental disorder.

In an attempt to determine the extent to which people reject disturbed behavior, Lemkau and Crocetti (1962), in a study of an urban population, found that 91% of their sample identified the paranoid as mentally ill, 78% identified the simple schizophrenic, and 62% identified the alcoholic. Dohrenwend, Bernard, & Kolb (1962) found support for these findings, based on interviews of leaders in an urban area. They reported that all identified mental illness in the description of paranoid schizophrenia; 72% in simple schizophrenia; 63% in the alcoholic; about 50% in anxiety neurosis and in juvenile character disorder; and 40% in compulsive-phobic behavior.

The help sources that people with mental disorders utilize—namely, the clergy, physicians, psychiatrists, and the mental hospital staff—determine to some extent the degree of rejection. Lowest rejection occurs when a clergymember is consulted; it increases gradually when seeing a psychiatrist; and the highest rejection occurs when a person is a patient in a mental hospital. Ironically, help seeking in itself is not evidence of the presence of mental disorder; however, the sources of obtaining help influence the amount of rejection. Research by Derek L. Phillips (1963) suggests that description of a mental disorder plays a greater role in rejection than sources of help obtained.

THE MENTAL HOSPITAL: IS IT A TOTAL INSTITUTION?

The mental hospital as an institution evokes frightening imagery. Individuals whose mental problems are so severe that they cannot function adequately on their own and need extended care are placed in a mental hospital; this process is called *institutionalization*. Admission to an institution is a formal act intended to alleviate the mental problems a person is experiencing. In actuality, it transforms the person's life from a "civilian" to an "inmate." Goffman (1961) conceptualized mental hospitals as *total institutions* that share many common characteristics with jails, penitentiaries, POW camps, concentration camps, and monasteries. The characteristics of a mental hospital as a total institution are as follows:

1. The chief activity is not guidance but surveillance and constant compliance to the staff.
2. Inmates have restricted contact with the outside world.
3. There are unfriendly and antagonistic stereotypes of patients (bitter, secretive, untrustworthy, etc.) and staff (condescending, highhanded, and mean).
4. Patients' contact with treatment staff is limited, controlled, and mediated by attendants, and inmates are excluded from knowledge of the decisions regarding their fate.
5. Work, if it is performed by the patients, is controlled not by incentives but by the threat of punishment.
6. Patients are governed both by the official rules of the institution and by unofficial rules, those tacit understandings and uncodified activities that make their adjustment possible.
7. In every aspect, privacy of the patient and individual needs are sacrificed (e.g., conjugal relations are permitted as a reward for adapting to informal rules of the institution).
8. To survive in the world of the mental hospital, patients develop their own "subculture" and utilize "con tactics" of "working the system."
9. Attendance at therapy sessions is often taken as a sign that the participants have been treated (though participants often use their attendance to con the therapist to improve living conditions or obtain favors).
10. The inmates create their small "territories" (space near a corner, a bench, a radiator).
11. Although patients receive medication and therapy, emphasis is on adapting to institutional rules and acknowledging the authority of the staff.
12. The institution, which is supposed to treat the mental condition of the patient, contributes to the maintenance of the mental symptoms that brought the person there in the first place.
13. The likelihood of patient recovery is reduced the longer the patients stay in the institution, as their ability to meet challenges in the outside world is marred.

TABLE 11-3 • Prepatient, Patient and Postpatient Characteristics

Patient Status	Symptoms	Social Reaction and Treatment Strategies
Prepatient	Constant uneasiness, feelings of discomfort, actions over which the person seems to have no control, symptoms of high levels of anxiety or depression, inability to sleep, some signs of paranoia and hostility, too quick or too slow social responses, eventually interactional difficulties, irrational logic, hyperactivity	Members of the family, close friends, and co-workers observe symptoms. Family members attempt to explore the causes of the problem and consult someone they can trust (clergy, physician, and possibly a psychiatrist).
	Disturbance of thought and affect, perplexed identity, frightening "cosmic" or "oceanic" feelings, bizarre delusions, hallucinations, social isolation, loosening of associations, and a clear deterioration in functioning	The person may be hospitalized and if symptoms persist may be admitted to a psychiatric ward. Family cautiously protects itself by referring to the situation as a medical problem. Also, everyone does his or her part of fence mending to avoid, guilt, shame, and stigma. Subject's stay in the hospital is of short duration.
Patient	Symptoms of the disorder become crystallized and chronic, serious difficulties in functioning and uncertainty prevail.	Family, friends and co-workers seek possible explanations, and their apprehensions of the presence of mental disorder are confirmed; the prepatient undergoes hospital admission formalities and takes a "new role" of mental patient; former network of relationships is replaced by new relationships of patients, staff, and attendants.
Postpatient	Symptoms of disorder, although present, are controlled; side-effects of drugs, apprehension, difficulty in taking responsibility, withdrawal from group activities; uncomfortable in the presence of others	Stigma shows in subtle ways, and observers are skeptical about complete recovery; various kinds of rejection are experienced by the former patient; treatment continues.
	Indications of partial recovery	Supportive actions of family, friends, and possibly co-workers
	Complete recovery	Gradual reintegration

Again, Goffman accurately described the circumstances surrounding long-term institutionalization, and his description remains useful in analyzing the lives of patients who are committed for long periods of time. The average length of institutionalization today, however, is quite short, and it is unlikely that patients suffer the degradations described by Goffman to the same extent (see Table 11-3).

Types of Mental Health Institutions

Mental health organizations provide inpatient, outpatient, and partial care services to the public. Such organizations include, among others, (1) state and county mental hospitals, (2) private psychiatric hospitals, (3) nonfederal general hospitals with separate psychiatric services, (4) veterans' administration medical centers, (5) federally funded community mental health services, (6) residential treatment centers for emotionally disturbed children, (7) free standing psychiatric outpatient clinics, and (8) other organizations, including freestanding psychiatric partial care and multiservice mental health organizations (see Table 11-2).

The quality and kinds of services and costs vary from one agency to another. In addition, outpatient services are offered incidental to other bodily diseases at private clinics by physicians. Community mental health centers offer basic mental health services for the needy and charge for services based on one's income. Private psychiatric services are the most expensive and can be afforded only by those who are relatively affluent or covered by health insurance.

In the early 1980s insurance companies started offering generous psychiatric benefits in an attempt to increase their profits. Some saw in this change a big pot of money, and went after it. The number of private, for-profit psychiatric hospitals shot from 220 in 1984 to 444 in 1988. There is every likelihood that the number will be increasing. The new hospitals made fabulous profits and did much good by offering sound treatment in comfortable settings. But the market changed when employers believed the sting of rising health costs. Also the stay in these hospitals were extended from weeks to months to make more profits forcing the insurance companies to change their reimbursement rules, which, in turn, forced the hospitals to play games of survival. In some cases, in a desperate attempt to keep the hospital beds filled and insurance benefits continued, private psychiatric hospitals used tactics of forcing their clients to return to the hospital involuntarily (see Cowley et al., 1991).

The total number of mental health organizations in the United States rose steadily between 1970 and 1986, from 3,005 organizations in 1970 to 4,747 in 1986. The number of organizations with inpatient services rose from 1,734 in 1970 to 3,039 in 1986. Also, the number providing outpatient services rose from 2,156 in 1970 to 2,946 in 1986. The partial care growth rate was phenomenal between 1970 and 1986, from 778 programs in 1970 to 1,947 in 1986 (NIMH, 1990a).

A discussion of the sources of revenue and expenditure in mental health services is enlightening. Figures from NIMH (1990a, pp. 6–9) suggest that $19 billion was generated by mental health organizations in 1986: 36% from state mental health agencies; 26% from Medicare, Medicaid (includes federal and state share), and other federal sources; 21% from client fees; 8% from local sources; and 10% from all other sources. Total expenditures by mental health organizations increased from $3.3 billion in 1969 to $18.5 billion in 1986. Per capita (per person) expenditures ranged from $16.53 in 1969, at the current dollar value, to $77.10 in 1986.

However, these expenditures do not show *hidden costs* stemming from the painful personal and social experience of mental disorders. The hidden costs are those direct and indirect personal and social consequences for which no figures or values are known. They relate to the value of lost jobs, loss of life due to neglect and abuse, murders, sexual assaults, juvenile delinquency, drug abuse and alcoholism, auto accidents, and a host of other social maladies.

A major reason for the rapid growth in the number of mental health institutions and related expenditures is the number of people seeking help, which has been increasing steadily. There is certainly a class bias in favor of better treatment for those who have the ability to pay and seek help early. It has been argued that with the development of community mental health programs and introduction of new psychotropic drugs, it is safer for the mentally impaired to lead relatively independent lives in their own communities. Psychoactive drugs have been in extensive use since 1955. However, there is a controversy over whether these drugs actually affected the drop in the inpatient population in state and county hospitals. Instead, the decline may have resulted from policy changes for economic as well as humanitarian reasons that hastened the mass release of patients in the middle 1960s that became known as *deinstitutionalization;* (see Chapter 12 for details).

Figures from NIMH (1990a, p. 32) suggest that while there was a decline in inpatient populations between 1969 and 1986 in state and county mental hospitals, there was also a dramatic increase nationwide in all other help-providing programs and institutions. One of the explanations is that most of the residents in state and county hospitals come from lower classes, ethnic minorities, and urban ghettos and are social outcasts whose long-term residence in a mental health facility involves more custodial care than psychiatric treatment. Furthermore, to protect the civil rights of citizens, many states initiated legislation to make it more difficult for patients to be admitted to state mental hospitals. The logic is that if patients have to stay on psychoactive drugs for extended periods inside an institution, they can do the same outside, where family and community can be involved in their recovery. This could lead to an enormous saving for taxpayers.

Who Gets the Attention in Mental Hospitals?

The generic term *mental hospital* has a negative image. Most were built during the later part of nineteenth and early part of the twentieth century. Many were developed or constructed in response to the crusade of Dorothea Dix, who led the first crusade in the United States to attend to the needs of people of limited resources with mental disorders. The unflattering image of the mental hospital emerged from a long history of inhumane treatment of residents. This image became the subject of popular novels; even today, some are known as "snake pits," while others are viewed as havens for the wealthy. Most rank somewhere in between. The quality of care depends on several factors, such as staff qualifications, maintenance of facilities, currency of equipment, financial resources, public support, and the mission of the institution. Appleby and colleagues (1967) classified mental health facilities in two polar categories: (1) institution centered, and (2) patient centered. Some of the relevant characteristics each type are discussed in Table 11-4.

Length of Stay

During 1986, on an average, patients stayed for treatment 10 and 11 days, respectively, in inpatient nonfederal general hospitals and multiservice mental health organizations. On the average, stays in private psychiatric hospital were 24 days, Veterans' Administration medical centers 23 days, and 28 days in state and county hospitals. Minorities had the longest median stay—30 days. The under 18 and 65 and over age groups had much longer stays, 43 days; while the age group between 18 and 64 stayed only 26 days. Among children and youth, type of hospital was not related to length of stay. In private psychiatric hospitals, white males stay longer (26 days) than black males (17 days). For women, race did not make any significant difference. Their average stay was 22 days. White males' longer stays can be partially attributed to health insurance payments, which many black males cannot afford (NIMH, 1990a, p. 144).

Staff

Most mental health institutions have a status hierarchy in their organizations, and some degree of bureaucracy prevails. Psychiatrists (physicians specializing in the treatment of mental disorders) receive the highest

TABLE 11-4 • Characteristics of Institution-Centered and Patient-Centered Mental Hospitals

Institution-Centered	Patient-Centered
1. Traditional, custodial-type hospitals where the treatment approach is to segregate residents from the rest of the society.	Innovative, open, and largely resident-oriented structure with an emphasis on freedom to communicate and eventually return to society.
2. Residents' lives are regimented and controlled.	Residents' schedules are adapted to their needs, and residents are encouraged to be involved in activities that help in their rehabilitation.
3. Residents are destined to stay for a long time, with no recovery in sight.	Resident stay is generally short term, and recovery is anticipated.
4. Staff attitudes toward residents is one of neglect and occasional abuse, and the quality of care leaves much to be desired.	Staff is trained to be empathetic and treat residents with care and compassion. Focus is on the individual and defined therapeutic goals.
5. Authoritarian routines govern residents' lives, and they conform to hospital rules out of fear of physical sanction.	The residents are treated with some degree of respect as clients who expect professional services, sanctions are rarely used.
6. Extensive and sometimes indiscriminate use of psychoactive drugs, including ECT.	Administration of drugs and other therapeutic procedures is closely monitored.
7. Residents are frequently reminded of their craziness and of languid existence.	Demeaning references to the client's status or behavior by the staff are viewed as unethical and unprofessional and not tolerated.
8. Residents remain far removed from the upper levels of the psychiatric staff hierarchy; the most frequent staff contact is with ancillary personnel.	Personal contact with psychiatrists and other therapeutic staff is a priority.
9. Residents are considered qualitatively different and inferior due to their socioeconomic, racial, and ethnic characteristics.	Residents are viewed not as inmates but as those who failed to cope with relatively minor problems and whose characteristics help assure recovery
10. Primary mission of these hospitals is to offer basic services with some focus on rehabilitation.	Centers tend to function in businesslike atmosphere utilizing a variety of therapeutic techniques with greater emphasis on rehabilitation.
11. Most are supported by federal, state, and local taxes and grants or subsidized. Cost of care is low.	Most are run by corporations or are privately owned. Costs are high and are partially paid by health insurance.

salaries and the most prestige. At the other end of the pay/prestige scale are administrative, clerical, and maintenance staff. Irrespective of the affiliation of the mental hospital (federal, state, church, county, etc.), in regard to funding, the hierarchical structure is essentially the same. Based on qualifications, salaries, authority, responsibility, and prestige, the hierarchy of staff is as follows, with numbers in parentheses showing employment status in August 1986 (NIMH, 1990a, p. 47):

A. Professional Patient Care Staff
1. Psychiatrists (26,199); 2. other physicians (5,855); 3. psychologists (25,272); 4. social workers (47,491); 5. registered nurses (75,876); 6. other mental health professionals (BA and above) (63,182); and 7. physical health professionals and assistants (29,948).

B. Other Patient Care Staff
Other mental health workers (less than BA) (121,673).

C. All Other Staff
Administrative, clerical, and maintenance staff (160,200). In the preceding hierarchy, we cannot ignore the presence of other patients, with whom an inpatient shares most time and activities. While the nursing staff is the largest employee segment in state and county mental hospitals (30 to 35%), the administrative, clerical, and maintenance is the largest (30 to 35%) in private psychiatric hospitals (NIMH, 1990a, pp. 11, 15). The latter also obtain more services from other mental health professionals (psychologists, social workers, and a variety of counselors) compared to state and county hospitals.

Typically, in a large mental hospital, the chief psychiatrist, who may also be the administrative head, plays the crucial role in setting the tone of operation of the institution.

The Patient Role

As indicated earlier, when people become inpatients, their interactions with the rest of society change dramatically. A new set of relationships evolves within the mental hospital, and those who were close prior to admission become gradually distant. The individual assumes the *sick role*. Sobel and Ingalls (1964) explained, "by sick role we mean the behavior and attitudes expected of the patient to which he tacitly and explicitly agrees when he becomes a patient." Thus, for patients, it does not seem to matter what kind of treatment they are going to receive, whether they are going to be administered psychoactive drugs or ECT. They are expected to behave in a predictable fashion congruous with the behavior and actions of their doctor, in this case the psychiatrist. If they do not cooperate, not only will the healing process be impeded but tension between them and the doctor may emerge.

Initiation into the successful practice of a role is begun in the socialization process. Just as one learns to become a law-abiding citizen or a good spouse, one learns to become a patient. Parsons (1951, pp. 436–437) stated that as medical patients, people are expected to be passive and dependent and be helpless to a great extent, although they are not held responsible for their illness. They are expected to seek competent professional help, the choice of which is best determined by others (relatives and friends), and they are expected to be incompetent or unable to judge their doctor's expertness. Moreover, they are not expected to make judgments about their own recovery; these are left to the doctor and relatives. They are viewed as being in no position to make major decisions when ill. Medical patients, whose problems are not mental, when they take the "sick role" are expected to be compliant, passive, and dependent as if their medical problems have disabled them not only physically but mentally, too.

Medical problems are qualitatively different from mental problems. In the sick role of a mental patient, the doctor–patient relationship is not always clear due to emotional qualities and incompetencies inherent in the status of "mental patient." The situation presents "an assumption of mental illness," which may involve consequent patient perceptions of incompetencies on the part of the therapist ("She's not doing me any good") and uncertainty and helplessness on the part of the patient.

Social class is clearly related to the patient's conception of the "sick role" (Dohrenwend & Dohrenwend, 1975; Hollingshead & Redlich, 1958; Imber, Nash, & Stone, 1955; Mechanic & Volkart, 1960). Social science research during the last 40 years has consistently suggested that social class is significantly related not only to the recovery rates but also the type of treatment selected and the choice of the therapist. Patients from the lower socioeconomic stratum often prove uncooperative to the physician's regimen. Not only do many believe that physicians are snobs and look down on lower class patients, but physicians shun them because they want something other than talking (psychotherapy). Many believe that unless a physician has performed some procedures and possibly prescribed some medications, he or she has done nothing. In other words, they do not seem to differentiate between mental and medical problems. Therefore, many treatment endeavors initiated by physicians and therapists turn out to be self-fulfilled failures. Therapists may believe that their client does not believe in them or their procedures and that their therapeutic efforts are sure to fail, increasing the likelihood that this will be the case.

The labeling approach points out that stereotypes often carry negative images. When applied by people in power, they can have very negative consequences for subordinate people or groups, whether accurately or falsely identified. William I. Thomas (1923, pp. 41–44) saw that the "definition of the situation" can mold the behavior of the individuals. He contended that not only do people respond to the "objective features of a situation" or "person" but also to the meaning the situation entails. The physician–patient relationship is a "situation" often governed by stereotypes of class, race, ethnicity, age, and gender, with the result that false definitions become accurate. This is known as the *self-fulfilling prophecy*. Individuals or groups begin to display the same characteristics that were said to characterize them. Thus, a young teenager who is praised for being emotional, shy, and withdrawn may focus on learning to be reticent and compliant to gain approval and attention.

The Social World of the Ward

A ward is a residential unit in a mental institution. Wards are classified based on their patients' psychiatric traits. The chronic patients, whose stay is longer, and the acute, severely disturbed patients are separated from those whose symptoms are mild and whose stay is short. Many whose symptoms were acute at admission but later subsided are allowed more freedom than those whose behavior is unpredictable and could possibly be irresponsible or violent. Life in a ward is programmed, and activities are scheduled. There are often significant differences in the modes of operation, use of authority, quality of life, freedom enjoyed by the inpatients, and staff attitudes toward patients between private and public psychiatric hospitals.

The most frequent patient contact with staff is with orderlies, attendants, custodial staff, practical nurses, and nurses aids, who are supervised by licensed registered nurses. In some institutions, activity and occupational therapists are employed to help prepare patients to adjust in the community after they have been released.

The head nurse is a powerful position and has a great impact on patients' lives. Not only are head nurses responsible for organizing therapy sessions and administering of drugs, but they also influence administration decision making. They keep in touch with patients through the informal reports they obtain from other staff. They are not only a link between the administration, staff, and patients, but they are more likely to be the mouthpiece of the administration due to their participation in policy-making meetings. Being in the middle of the flow of information, the head nurse occupies a unique position of influence. The principal character in Ken Kesey's popular novel *One Flew Over the Cuckoo's Nest*, Miss Ratched (or Big Nurse) may not be representative of head nurses in the United States, but she illustrates how a cold, calculating, and bitter person in this position can destroy the sanctity of an institution.

Most importantly, the most frequent contact a patient has is with other patients, especially those who are willing to talk, share their stories and past experiences, and empathize. Many assign nicknames to their friends and foes, including the staff, and communication is sometimes in code.

Quality of life in state institutions is relatively monotonous and rigidly regulated by a few staff members. Periodically, there are chaotic or violent episodes. Collective disturbances are symptomatic of the high alienation from the place among patients due to the restrictive conditions in which they live and the rigid and negative attitudes of staff (Meyer, 1968).

In its intrinsic sense, *place* describes a person's role and status in the framework of a social occasion, situation, and organization. Situations of social interactions define roles and expectations governed by the structure of norms that are routinely accepted as the correct ways of doing things. Individual and collective deviations from these norms are handled in a variety of ways (e.g., not greeting a person, showing indifference, avoiding social contact, expressing subtle and sometimes open but guarded criticism of the behavior in question). People with mental disorders, due to their psychological and social disabilities (not by preference but because of their mental state), are likely to violate, challenge, or reject what Goffman referred to as "place." Their natural actions and responses are viewed as deviance. If sane people acted in the same way, their actions would be viewed as logical, relevant, and worthwhile. Patients' failure to meet expectations of "place," due to their mental conditions, has enormous consequences; it leads to further alienation (Goffman, 1971, pp. 385–390).

Degradation Ceremonies: The Process of Depersonalization

Harold Garfinkel (1956), utilizing ethnomethodology, examined the process whereby the public identity of an individual is transformed into something looked on as lower in the scheme of social types. A case in point here is the new identity of a mental patient. Garfinkel contended that "communicative work directed to transforming an individual's total identity into an identity lower in the group's scheme of social types is called a *status degradation ceremony*." The new identity refers to a *motivational* rather than a *behavioral* type (i.e., not what the individual could have done to sustain his or her status/identity but what the group holds to be the ultimate grounds or reasons for the new identity). Thus, people who are labeled by their fellows as mentally impaired undergo *degradation ceremonies* that change their total identity—they become a mental patient. Shame, guilt, boredom, and morose existence are indicators of the moral indignation surrounding this change. This transformation does not involve the substitution of one identity for another, as Garfinkel (1956, p. 3) put it, "like the overlooked parts of a fresh assembly, any more than the woman we see in the department-store window that turns out to be a dummy carries with it possibilities of a woman. It is not that the old object has been overhauled; rather it is replaced by another. One declares, *Now*, it was otherwise in the first place."

In addition to going through the degradation ceremonies, the person's dehumanizing process continues, especially in state mental institutions. Reducing a person to an "object" or "number" is an inherent feature of the "work" situation in an institution where only a few people (staff and orderlies) are considered sane. They simply work, and no one speaks with one's work. The mental patient is looked at as if he where a piece of machine in an assembly line. Attendants, during the person's admission, look on him or her with suspicion, do not speak to the subject, but give orders (take your clothes off, take a shower, dry yourself, etc.) and search everything. Personal belongings are put aside only to be replaced by the uniform of a patient. Daily, weekly, or monthly routines such as mass bathing and therapy sessions focusing on personal and private matters further deteriorate the morale of inpatients (Goffman, 1961). In the subculture of a mental institution, the psychiatric staff's custodial orientation is high and reinforced by the fact that the highest ratings go to the more restrictive staff. Personal accounts of former patients are in many ways heartrending. Treating patients as inferior, out of their minds, and guilty of failure lends itself to the "loss of identity," a dehumanizing process often reflected in withdrawn, indifferent, and mute behavior and *depersonalization*. Some of these former mental patients, who lost everything, including their identity and dignity, end up on the streets, homeless.

THE EX-MENTAL PATIENT EXPERIENCE

Release from the institution is based on the behavior of the individuals within the institution. However, psychiatric evaluation of mental disorders is not as accurate as determining the level of blood sugar or as certain as surgical removal of an unwanted growth. A person who may appear "healed" in the closed setting of an institution may turn out to be something else in the outside world. Often, release is not based solely on a person's mental condition but on the availability of a support system—family members who are willing to take care of the person, a place to live, and a job waiting.

One of the ironies of the patient's release from a mental institution is his or her return to the same social environment in which the mental disorder had been fostered. Release from the institution brings about a new label, "mental patient—now recovered," which puts the former patient in a difficult situation even when he or she is on the path of recovery. Not only does the former patient have to deal with the problems of readjustment, but also with stigma.

The Family Reaction

Getting a family member admitted as a mental patient may provide some immediate relief to the family, but it has numerous consequences. Instead of being a productive family member, the patient becomes a dependent. At the same time, however, as soon as a mental disorder is defined as a "disease" by the specialists, other family members may feel relief not just because most diseases can be cured, but because none of them is now held responsible for the mental disorder. Of course, the disease model of mental disorder, as it is popularized in most institutions, raises hope in the family that some medication will eventually work, and therefore no change is needed in the existing relationships in the family. The family's reaction to the ex-mental patient member can be classified in four categories: (1) empathetic cooperation to assist the person; (2) stay indifferent and provide minimal help; (3) neglect the person, and let the person recover with little or no contact; and (4) reject or disown the person. Many mental disorders are qualitatively different from organic disorders in that the behavioral aspects of mental disorders typically jeopardize existing relationships. For example, the presence of chronic schizophrenic tendencies in a family member may evoke hostility, violence, discord, fear, humiliation, and high levels of stress in the family. Even affective disorders can produce intolerable situations in which understanding, patience, and compassion do not work. Often, the family finds itself in a double bind.

Research suggests that the longer a person stays in an institution, the greater are the chances that family bonds will be weakened (Grusky, Tierney, Manderscheid, & Grusky, 1985). But short-term hospitalization might have an opposite effect; it may strengthen the family to face the trauma collectively and delay some disruptive actions, such as a separation or divorce (Kreisman & Joy, 1974). Hospitalization itself brings about changes by removing from the family scene the perpetrator (or in some cases, the victim) of family discord. Also, hospitalization puts the burden of changing on the patient, who should in turn mend his or her ways to adjust to reality. Research has shown that upper- and middle-class families are more tolerant of having a former mental patient in the family and are more optimistic about recovery (Freeman & Simmons, 1961, 1963).

The Community Response

Communities' responses are determined by three factors: (1) overt symptoms and actions of ex-mental patients, (2) communities' own attitudes about people with mental disorders, and (3) perceived and felt negative impact of people with mental disorders in the neighborhood and the community.

Those who have anxiety, affective disorders, and personality disorders often do not exhibit observable symptoms or odd and "crazy" characteristics in public. Public attitudes seem to be influenced by dangerous cases sensationalized by the media and by encounters with people who are retarded or are physically deformed. For many, even the presence of such individuals is intolerated. For example, a middle-aged man with mild symptoms of schizophrenia used to stand outside a downtown clothing store in a small Midwestern town. He would stand there for hours, often talking to himself and occasionally making funny noises, but he did not bother passersby or customers. The clothing store owner thought he was unsightly and probably discouraged customers. Once he tried to persuade the man to go somewhere else. He notified the police. The police took no action because the man was on public property and had done no harm. Finally, the store owner decided to talk with the man and found that the man was bored at home, so he came to watch the people on the city square. The store owner bought the man a bicycle so he could ride around and see people. Now the man shows up only occasionally at the store to thank the owner for the bike.

Studies of community reactions toward ex-mental patients began in the early 1950s and show consistently negative public attitudes (Cummings & Cummings, 1957; Rabkin, 1974; Townsend, 1976). A study of New York City residents by Bruce Link (1982) reports that ex-mental patients are employed in less-well-paying jobs. Further, if people know that individuals are ex-mental patients, they shy away from them, especially if they perceive them to be dangerous. Perception, in other words, influences the degree of social distance. Link and his colleagues thus maintained that negative labels continue to influence the social interaction patterns of former mental patients, often isolating them from potential fulfilling relationships, long after their recovery (Link, Cullen, Frank, & Wozniak, 1987).

How do ex-mental patients fare in the face of these discouraging facts? Kreisman and Joy (1974) reported that 30% of patients released from mental hospitals return to the hospital during the first year following discharge. Over an extended period, the figures are even more bleak. They found that, in New York state, 60% of all admissions to state hospitals were readmissions. Readmissions for many occur more than once and for some become a way of life. Using Goffman's (1961) term, they referred to these series of hospitalizations as the "career" of the mental patient. New social policies of integrating the ex-patient sooner with the family and community, with the intent of helping recovery, have resulted in a series of hospitalizations as opposed to the old pattern of chronic and prolonged hospitalization. There are two basic issues involved here:

1. In the minds of the community members, "Once a mental patient, always a mental patient." Once the label of mental patient has been assigned to a person, it is very difficult to cast off that label. In Scheff's view, the deviance as mental disorder becomes part of person's permanent identity (Scheff, 1974, 1984).

2. The social situation into which the ex-mental patient enters and resumes his or her life after release from the institution is of vital importance. Sensitivity, understanding, and emotional support on the part of the spouse, family, and co-workers can play a positive role in regaining the status of a normal person. Huffine and Clausen (1979) studied, over a 20-year period, a group of 36 married men, most of whom were under the age of 40 and who suffered from schizophrenia. They attempted to find out if their mental condition affected their family life and their occupational careers. Twenty years later, at the end of the study, when only 29 of the subjects could be contacted, Huffine and Clausen found that about one third were symptom free. Another one third showed mild symptoms off and on; and about one third continued to experience severe symptoms and were hospitalized at least four times during the period of the study. Obviously, results were mixed but they also direct us toward some degree of optimism. However, we should remember that schizophrenia is a clinical diagnosis, the extent and severity of the disorder can make a lot of difference in recovery. Not all schizophrenics share the same characteristics to the same extent because schizophrenia is a group of disorders, and these variations can make a difference in postpatient experience.

In light of the aforementioned results, some researchers have questioned the validity of the "labeling" theory, which indicates that being a mental patient accords a permanent deviant status (Gove, 1979). However, Huffine and Clausen (1979) suggested that getting a person to treatment often reduces the symptoms and provides respite from intense interpersonal turmoil, which is common due to the presence of the disorder. But they also pointed out that the functional level of the ex-patient and attitude of the spouse and support of the family, friends, and co-workers may be positive contributing factors in the recovery.

In this chapter, we have discussed three significant phases and the issues associated with prepatient, patient/inpatient, and ex-patient. These theoretical categories provide us with some understanding of the lives of those who experience mental disorders—how their lives are affected, and how they affect the lives of others. The issues are complex, and there are no easy or quick answers. The emotional costs some patients pay cannot be estimated easily.

CHAPTER REVIEW

1. Although the number of resident patients has declined during the past decades, the number of people with mental disorders has increased. Thomas Szasz has attempted to analyze this phenomenon What are his explanations?

2. What steps are taken when people seek help? What do we mean by levels of help seeking? Explain.

3. What are the differences between voluntary and involuntary help seeking? Answer your question with appropriate examples.

4. Goffman used the term *career of a mental patient*. What implications does this concept have in understanding the future of a person with mental disorders?

5. What do we mean by "a total institution"? How does a mental patient care center become a total institution? Explain.

6. Are there any differences in the quality of treatment in various types of mental health institutions? What are the differences between patient- and institution-centered institutions?

7. There is a well-structured hierarchy in a mental hospital. Who has the most power? In your view, who has control over the life of the patients in Ken Kesey's popular novel (and movie) *One Flew Over the Cuckoo's Nest*?

8. How do families respond to members who are ex-patients? Explain the differences in family reactions and their association with the recovery outlook.

9. Does the community response play a significant role in the adjustment of people who are ex-patients? What factors hinder this adjustment?

10. Labeling theory suggests that once labeled a "mental patient," the person begins a long-term career as a mental patient. What are the grounds on which this theory has been questioned?

11. Explain briefly the following:
    a. Steps in involuntary help seeking
    b. Paradox of normalcy
    c. Hidden costs
    d. Sick role
    e. Alienation from the place

FOR FURTHER STUDY

Goffman, E. (1961). *Asylums*. Garden City, NY: Doubleday.
Goffman, E. (1971). *Relations in public*. New York: Basic Books.
Grusky, O., & Pollner, M. (Eds.). (1981). *The sociology of mental illness*. New York: Holt, Rinehart and Winston.

Link, B. G., Cullen, F. T., Frank, J., & Wozniak, J. F. (1987). The social rejection of former mental patients: Understanding why labels matter. *American Journal of Sociology, 92,* pp. 242–258.

National Institute of Mental Health. (1990a). *Mental health, United States, 1990.* R. W. Manderscheid & M. A. Sonnnenschein (Eds.). DHHS Pub. No. (ADM) 90-1708. Washington, DC: U.S. Government Printing Office.

Scheff, T. J. (1984) *Being mentally ill: A sociological theory.* (2nd ed). New York: Aldine.

Spitzer, S. P., & Denzin, N. K. (Eds.). (1968). *The mental patient: Studies in the sociology of deviance.* New York: McGraw-Hill.

▶ 12
Public Policy, Homelessness, and the Law

The care and treatment of people with mental disorders has undergone dramatic changes, especially during the later half of this century. These changes, following World War II, included a new focus on and understanding of environmental factors as contributors to mental disorders. Since 1955, these changes have not only reflected new treatment methods but have largely defined the new role of the federal government in mental health policy. This policy is important because it reflects the national goals and objectives with respect to people suffering from mental disorders. Contrary to popular opinion, that most people visit psychiatrists when faced with mental problems, the National Center for Health Statistics found in 1985 that only 2.8% or 17,989,000 visits out of a total of 636,386,000 visits to all physicians in the United States were made to psychiatrists. People visiting neurologists accounted for only 0.8%, or 4,992,000 visits. These figures suggest that, initially, most mental problems are treated by general and family practice and internal medicine specialists, which account for 30.5 and 11.6 visits per 1,000 persons per year, respectively (NCHS, 1988, p. 1).

PUBLIC POLICY AND MENTAL HEALTH

Experiences during World War I suggested that mental health services were essential for military personnel, especially those in combat and under stress. At the beginning of World War II, there were shortages of mental health personnel. There were only 3,000 psychiatrists, and other ancillary staff were in acute shortage. In 1990, there were approximately 36,000 psychiatrists in the United States and even more impressive increases in the fields of clinical psychology, social work, and psychiatric nursing. The factors responsible for this phenomenal increase included the findings of selective service screening. An estimated 1,875,000 men of 15 million examined between January 1942 and June 1945 were rejected because of psychiatric disabilities (Mechanic, 1989, p. 86). Many who were discharged for disability allegedly had neuropsychiatric problems (Felix, 1967, pp. 28–29). Obviously, there was a need for preventive and treatment programs in the area of mental health at a broader level.

Critics charge that selective service screening was a failure, in part because psychiatric evaluation criteria were not adequately developed. Due to time pressures, one psychiatrist examined as many as 200 Army recruits per day, spending an average of 2 minutes on each recruit. No attempt was made to ascertain the personal history of psychotic episodes among the recruits, and the evaluation process was marred by numerous flaws (Deutsch, 1949, p. 463). Nonetheless, on the positive side, greater attention to public policy concerning mental health programs resulted, leading to the passage of the Mental Health Act by congress in 1946 and creation of the National Institute of Mental Health (NIMH).

David Mechanic (1989, p. 81), a sociologist, summarized the factors associated with the community mental health movement in the following way: (1) Early prevention was deemed necessary since it was assumed that mental illness was a simple continuum from mild to severe dysfunction, in contrast to a collection of heterogeneous disorders; (2) the population at risk and population dynamics were unchanging; and (3) mental health resources for outpatient psychiatric care were perceived as more cost effective than hospital care.

COMMUNITY MENTAL HEALTH

The concept of community mental health (CMH) care has a long history dating back to medieval times. In the late 1800s, the work of Dorothea Dix, Phillipe Pinel, and later of Jane Addams led to an increased concern for the well-being of the poor and disadvantaged. Interest in these groups waxed and waned for the next half century. Federal aid to states for mental health programs declined during the Korean War (June 1950 to July 1953). The Hoover Commission (1955, p. 72) found that aid to states had been significantly reduced while research had been increasing. However, there was some optimism emerging in the mental health field. Simultaneously, research in France during the early 1950s showed promise that some drugs that were used to calm patients during and after surgical procedures could be used to alleviate symptoms of certain mental disorders. The introduction of psychoactive drugs in treating mental disorders was dubbed the *second revolution in mental health*, following the introduction of psychoanalysis by Sigmund Freud. Pharmaceutical companies initiated extensive research and came up with a variety of drugs for the treatment of schizophrenia, manic depression, and a host of other disorders. At the same time, states were increasingly concerned that they could no longer afford the ever-increasing costs of institutionalization, and large custodial institutions could not deal effectively with increasing numbers of people seeking help. With the passage of the Community Mental Health Services Act in 1954, New York state was the first to create mental health boards to offer at subsidized rates a range of mental health services, including outpatient care. The American Medical Association and American Psychiatric Association joined hands to establish a Joint Commission on Mental Health and Illness, and Congress passed community mental health legislation in 1955. The organizational structure of community mental health centers, although intended to be consistent nationwide, was largely dictated by funding sources, program need, and availability of trained personnel (see Table 12–1).

The rhetoric of community mental health in the United States gained momentum in the 1960s, influenced by the thinking of intellectual elites, politicians and public policy makers, concerned citizens, and the general public (Grob, 1987). Epidemiological studies, from Faris and Dunham (1939) to Link and Dohrenwend (1989), over 6 decades revealed that certain classes of people are more vulnerable to mental disorders. The findings confirmed the view that certain sections or classes, who had been impaired but neglected for quite some time, needed attention. The caregiving settings varied based on one's socioeconomic background, ranging from the conventional medical model to modern person-oriented therapeutic techniques (Cox, 1971).

Political and social activism in the 1960s brought to light the dehumanizing conditions of mental institutions on one hand and limited access of the poor to treatment facilities on the other. President John F. Kennedy (1961–1963) was committed to the idea of community care, especially because it served the needs of lower and lower-middle classes, which his administration believed were long ignored.

Primary prevention and *immediate attention/treatment* were the core objectives of the CMH program, and its foundation was a public health approach to mental health. Thus, mental health programs were extended to public schools, social service agencies, nursery and day-care

TABLE 12-1 • Organizational Structure of Community Mental Health Centers

Program Director	Board of Directors Executive Director Psychiatric Consultants Clinical Director	Financial Director
Planning Fiscal development Grant management Educational programs Data processing Fiscal development Grant management Educational programs Data processing Vocational programs specialist (vocational evaluation, sheltered workshop, transitional employment, job club) Expediter Rehabilitation assistants Residential supervisors	Clinical/case supervision Clinical assistants' work supervision Mandated follow-up services Supportive and outreach counselors' guidance Mental health counselor Substance abuse guidance services School consultant Rehabilitation therapists	Fiscal planning Budgeting Patient accounts/billing Purchasing Facility/utilities

Note: Responsibility to coordinate the services lies with the executive director. In many cases, psychiatric services are obtained on a referral basis. The variants of these organizations are commonly determined by funding rather than program needs; therefore, the quality of services varies.

programs, church programs, law enforcement agencies, youth organizations, and special target groups like children and the poor. In some cases, what Cockerham termed *boundary busting* was involved, wherein community health workers went beyond the boundaries of traditional psychiatry (1989, p. 281). As it turned out, many of these programs remained superfluous, but they allowed the psychiatric enterprise to revise and modernize concepts of the psychiatric profession, to broaden its mandate and functions, and to reach and treat people in the community (Manning and Zucker, 1976). President Lyndon Johnson's idea of the "Great Society" was hindered by disenchantment with the Vietnam War and its social and economic costs, which placed CMH programs in jeopardy. The political climate and social policies changed with the Nixon administration, which decided to phase out the CMH program and even impounded money already appropriated by Congress for the program. Severe budget cuts were made during the Reagan administration, with the argument that to maximize the effectiveness of the programs states should fund and administer them. In spite of changing administrations at the federal level, the objectives of the program remain the same (although cutbacks have always influenced their effectiveness):

1. To ensure that a person in need of mental health care can obtain it promptly at a local community mental health center before the problem becomes too complicated or severe
2. To improve the odds that such help, with no hospitalization, would be less stigmatizing than being in a hospital for an extended length of time
3. To improve the chances that a person may be able to stay on the job and remain productive while under treatment
4. To hasten recovery based on the notion that the support of the family and kin and the person's involvement in the community are better for a person's mental health
5. To reduce the burden on the medical system
6. To improve chances that a variety of mental health treatment approaches could be followed for the best results
7. To create a policy to provide basic mental health services to the community in the interest of the citizens
8. To improve chances that services would be more effective, as they would be monitored more closely by a board of local citizens and specialists
9. To reduce the operational costs of inpatient/resident mental health services
10. To allow communities to devise preventive/educational mental health programs for the well-being of community members
11. To encourage those who are less likely to seek help to visit a local center at a modest cost based on the ability to pay
12. Through the use of psychoactive drugs, to treat the symptoms of mental disorders on an outpatient basis to enable those seeking help to recover sooner

All these factors gave rise to community psychiatry and an outpatient community mental health care system.

Public Policy and Deinstitutionalization

Changes in mental health policy in the 1950s and 1960s led to a transfer of care for the mentally ill to local communities through community mental health programs. This led to the release of a large number of mental patients from hospitals for the mentally disordered into communities, where they could continue to seek help when needed without being institutionalized. The underlying assumptions were (1) that long-term institutionalization was not beneficial to the recovery of mental patients; (2) that community life, where support from family and friends is readily available, would be more conducive to recovery; (3) that the new psychoactive drugs would alleviate the symptoms of mental impairment and increase the chances of mental patients to lead relatively productive lives; (4) that the new policy would reduce the costs of care of the mental patients in mental institutions significantly, thereby reducing the burden of tax on the states and the federal government; and (5) that the social climate of the time encouraged experimenting with more innovative programs and policies to seek alternative methods of treating mental disorders.

Transfer of care of mental patients from mental institutions to community mental health agencies is known as *deinstitutionalization*. The net result of this process, in sheer numbers, was that the inpatient/resident population in mental health institutions declined from 512,501 in 1955 to 160,862 in 1986 (NIMH, 1990a, p. 154). But deinstitutionalization was not as great a success as it was anticipated to be. Many mentally impaired people could not survive on the outside, partly because of inadequate personal resources and support systems. Monitoring of care has been ineffective and inadequate. Poor staffing and funding, local politics, bureaucracy, and public apathy and absence of workable job training programs all placed the well-intended program in a predicament. Many severely impaired people became homeless or were placed in jails.

THE HOMELESS

The term *homeless* refers to those who do not have a place to live or, in E. Fuller Torrey's (1988a) words, people who have "nowhere to go." The beggar who stretched a suppliant palm toward passersby in ancient Rome and medieval Paris can be found today in American towns and cities.

In addition to problems of semantics, there are problems of conceptualizing homelessness due to the images created by the media over the years. There are fewer of the hobo-like characters described by Anderson (1923); now there are men, women, children, teenagers, elderly, and families of every description. It is hard to imagine that an affluent country like the United States, which provides billions of dollars in foreign and military aid to other nations for strategic reasons, would fail to devise a reasonably humane policy toward its own homeless citizens.

The Stewart B. McKinney Homeless Assistance Act (P.L. 100-77) attempted to identify the homeless for purposes of providing government services. A homeless person is "an individual who lacks a fixed, regular, and adequate nighttime residence; or an individual who has a primary nighttime residence that is a supervised or publicly operated shelter designed to provide temporary living accommodations (including welfare hotels, congregate shelters, and transitional housing for the mentally ill); an institution that provides a temporary residence for individuals intended to be institutionalized; or a public or private place not designed for, or ordinarily used as, a regular sleeping accommodation for human beings" (U.S. General Accounting Office, 1987). The Ohio Department of Mental Health (Hope & Young, 1986, p. 19) defined a homeless person as someone who sleeps or lives in (1) limited or no shelter for any length of time (e.g., vehicles, condemned or abandoned buildings); (2) shelters or missions run by religious organizations or public agencies for any length of time; (3) cheap hotels or motels, when the length of stay or intent to stay is 45 days or less; and (4) other unique situations that do not fall into categories 1 through 3, and the length of stay is 45 days or less (e.g., the tent cities set up in California, or living with relatives and friends).

There is no question that the homeless population is highly differentiated. Rossi and associates (1987, p. 1336) suggested that the homeless can be classified into at least two categories: (1) the literal homeless (people who clearly do not have access to a conventional dwelling and who would be homeless by any conceivable definition of the term), and (2) precariously (or marginally) housed (people with tenuous or very temporary claims to a conventional dwelling of more or less marginal adequacy). The problem of homelessness is thus perceived as a problem of shelter, a home, and nothing more. It fails to take into account why homeless people *are* homeless, such as lack of skills, loss of job or income, and absence of a support system or family. But is there something more than not having a home? Why did these people become homeless in the first place? Are we talking about the cause or the consequence? Should we say that providing shelter alone will solve the problems of the homeless? Do we address the issue of the factors associated with a stable personal, family, and social life? Why do policies in regard to the homeless simply address the question of mere shelters and soup kitchens? Partly at least, the public and the policy makers believe that many, if not all, homeless are mentally impaired or social failures. There are others who believe that homelessness is a lifestyle of choice. This belief absolves everyone including the government to take responsibility for the predicament of the homeless.

Based on various estimates, the number of homeless in the United States ranges from 300,000 to over 3,000,000 (CBS, "48 Hours," 1989; Ford Foundation, 1989; Johnson, 1990, p. 46). Exacting the number of homeless is a difficult task. A 1988 report by the U.S. Department of Housing and Urban Development (HUD) estimated that there were between 250,000 and 300,000 homeless in the United States on a given day. The National Coalition for the Homeless (1988) estimated in 1986 that there were at least 60,000 homeless in New York City; 20,000 in Baltimore; 15,000 in Philadelphia; 25,000 in Houston; 14,000 in Dallas; 4,500 in Phoenix; 10,000 in San Francisco; and 50,000 in Los Angeles.

On March 22, 1990, the U.S. Bureau of the Census announced that it was attempting to count the homeless. This represented the government's effort to quell the rising dissatisfaction among people who see the government as representing rich, insensitive people, as unconcerned about the plight of the homeless—a group of people who do not count politically because they do not vote. The Census Bureau, for the 1990 census, sent thousands of census takers into the streets, alleys, and parks to count the homeless. Yet, probably it failed to count all the homeless because no one was certain where to find them (Dunn, 1991).

Who Are the Homeless?

The term *homeless* has been used by laypeople, media, politicians, and social scientists in a variety of ways. They are individuals and families usually categorized as social failures, rejects, and drifters. Either as a result of their personal problems or failed marriages, they are identified with deviance, crime, alcoholism, drug addiction, mental disorders, with unsightly looks, and with living in sloppy and unsanitary conditions. In addition, many of their basic needs are unmet. Their situation implies the absence of resources, family and community ties, and adequate shelter (U.S. Department of Health and Human Services, 1988, p. 1). Only those who are found on the sidewalks, entryways to hotels, phone booths, city streets and parks, and those who are wandering around are generally noticed by the public. There are numerous others who live in abandoned buildings, automobiles, enclaves under railroad bridges, and cardboard makeshift enclosures. They are forced to lead a marginal life on the fringes of society, taking meals only when they can find them, cleaning themselves whenever they can sneak into a washroom somewhere, and finding shelter where they can. Their torn, shabby, and unclean clothing, which they may have picked up on the streets, constitutes their only garments. Often penniless, their only

TABLE 12-2 • Ten Most Frequently Cited Reasons for Last Emergency Room Visit by 754 Homeless People in New York City Shelters

Reason	No.	%
1. Traumatic injury	297	39.4
2. Respiratory ailment	75	10.0
3. Stomach problem	37	4.9
4. Pneumonia	34	4.5
5. Orthopedic problem	30	4.0
6. Oral health problem	24	3.2
7. Epilepsy or seizure	22	2.9
8. Heart problem	20	2.6
9. Mental illness	19	2.5
10. Pain of unspecified origin	16	2.1
11. Other physical condition	180	23.9

Adapted from Padgett & Struening, 1991, p. 835.

belongings are the rags that they carry in bags or carts. They have drifted too far, well past the limits of decency and respectability. They have nowhere to go, are lost in the midst of plenty. They have no one to relate to or to seek help from and are often deep into the callous world of anonymity. Some have problems of alcoholism and mental derangement. Public apathy is not uncommon. We are not prepared to appreciate the consequences of social failure. The homeless do not make success stories. The public views their very existence as a shame, a distasteful fact of life, and perhaps a tragedy.

Traditional means of counting the homeless have been ineffective and unsuccessful because (1) the homeless do not have a fixed address or residence; (2) they drift in and out of homelessness, in and out of shelters and communities; (3) they have no identification, such as a driver's license; (4) most of them do not know where to go to seek any assistance, if any is available; and (5) due to their misery and frustration, many of them are so distressed and disoriented that if they did not have any emotional problems in the first place, they seem to have some now. Clearly, a portion of the homeless do have mental problems, some short term and others chronic. A 1987 survey (Padgett & Strueing, 1991) of 1,152 homeless adults in New York City shelters shows that two-thirds

(767) of the sample reported using an emergency room at least once in their lives and about 27% (313) reported use within the previous 6 months. Although traumatic injury was the most cited reason, psychotic ideation or depressive symptoms precipitated the need to seek emergency assistance (see Table 12-2).

Composition of the Homeless Population

Historical evidence showing compassion for the homeless has been mixed at best, for various reasons, and the care received by the homeless has also varied depending on how they are viewed—as those who experienced bad times or as those who experienced a mental disorder. It is often perceived as surprising if a person who has lived on the street for quite some time can talk sense, and the public may not perceive him or her as a "normal" person. Most people shy away from the homeless and the negative images in people's minds are reinforced by the media. Media's efforts to educate the public about public issues has its negative as well as positive consequences. Selective reporting of the most tragic cases not only stigmatizes them, but it also shuts doors to the opportunities they can seek. During the early decades of this century, most homeless were men. Single, never-married men, with little education and few skills, who were unemployed or who worked at unstable jobs, represented the vast majority of the homeless. Since the awakening of public concern about the homeless in the last 2 decades, the structure of the homeless population has also changed drastically. Recent reports indicate that there is a substantial number of families in the homeless population and that their number is increasing, as is the number of children and older individuals in this population. It appears that homeless families are the fastest growing segment of the homeless population (ABC, "20/20," 1989; McCheney, 1987, p. 4). Over 30% of the homeless are families (National Coalition for the Homeless, 1988, p. 1). Most of these families are headed by single women (McCheney, 1987, p. 4).

Homelessness is still predominantly a male condition. A Chicago study found that three of four (76%) homeless people were men. Blacks and American Indians were overrepresented, while whites and Hispanics were underrepresented. The average age of the homeless in Chicago was 40 years, although there were some under the age of 25 and a few over the age of 65. The homeless were not very different in education from the general population, and the typical homeless person was a high school graduate (Rossi et al., 1987, p. 1337).

The U.S. Department of Education estimated the number of homeless children in the United States at 220,000 (Coles, 1989, p. 188). About 30%, or 65,000, of them are not regularly attending school. Another source suggests that at least 100,000 children are homeless in the United States on any given night, not counting the runaways. The National Coalition for the Homeless estimated in 1988 that about 750,000 children were homeless and that 57%, or 427,500, did not attend school regularly (Coles, 1989, p. 188). There is no way of knowing at this time how many children may be living temporarily with friends, relatives, foster parents, and other individuals or families.

Is Homelessness a Lifestyle of Choice?

Every winter, the media reports and tests the nation's conscience as subfreezing temperatures settle in and the homeless look for refuge. At many places, they are turned away. Deaths and frozen bodies and scattered anecdotes give way to chilly facts. Although employment may be low (often it does not appear to matter), cities and voluntary groups across the nation are swamped with thousands more requests for shelter. In Philadelphia alone, 15,000 received emergency family housing in 1983—five times the number sheltered in 1981. Although auto sales were stronger in Detroit in 1983, the city estimated that homelessness had increased by 50%. The Salvation Army alone, in St. Louis, received over 4,155 requests for shelter, up by 47% over the previous year (Alter et al., 1984, p. 20).

No part of the nation has been spared. Homelessness is everywhere. In Atlanta the first overnight shelter was opened in 1979; in 1984 the city had 27. The public has often questioned how many are enough. Sometimes the public and politicians have reacted to the homeless with hostility. The mayor of Tucson, Arizona, who was elected to his 13th year in office on a platform that included a vow to get "the transients the hell out of town," beefed up patrols of police to look for suspicious transient behavior. Phoenix even went a step further and in 1981 adopted an Anti-Skid Row Ordinance that discourages blood banks, bars, soup kitchens, and flophouses; even the Salvation Army was forced to close its doors to the homeless. These steps were deemed necessary to protect Arizona's image as a sunny paradise. The unwanted sight of the homeless is bad for business and bad for the state. Though a relationship has not been proved, increasing crime rates in certain areas are also blamed on the homeless.

Although the number of homeless in Arizona and Massachusetts is estimated to be roughly the same (between 5,000 and 10,000), the latter created 13 shelters on a 75–25 basis with community groups, assigned more state case workers, opened a 24-hour hotline for referrals, and changed welfare rules to accommodate people without permanent addresses so they could receive benefits. In addition, the Massachusetts legislature approved close to $200 million for low-income housing (Alter et al., 1984, p. 26). Federal attempts to address these problems have been inconsistent, and in view of the budget deficit, any program that simply costs money but does not pay immediate dividends is viewed with a great degree of skepticism. As is the case with the budget deficit, no one is looking at the problem of homelessness and its long-term impact on the nation as a whole. A new class of people is emerging, which is not only homeless but has less of everything, and the social consequences are alarming. Having a mass of 3 million homeless people at a given time is not simply a moral question anymore but also an economic question that must be addressed. If there is no reasonable policy to put these people to work, shelters alone will not solve the problem. The same taxpayers who would like to have ordinances to keep the homeless out of sight will pay not only in terms of economic costs but other costs too, such as high crime rates, drug addiction, and other social pathologies.

Mental Health and Homelessness: A Controversy

How many homeless have mental disorders? It depends on where the figures are obtained and who obtains them. There are three sources of information: (1) federal and state government agencies, (2) the media (popular news magazines, television, etc.), and (3) academic research. The inconsistent figures have jeopardized policies addressing the problem of homelessness.

David Snow and his colleagues (1986, pp. 407–408) attempted to find the actual rates of mental impairment among the homeless. They first reviewed popular magazines such as *Time*, *Newsweek*, and *People* found a consistent portrayal of the homeless who had spent time in mental hospitals. They examined studies done in Boston, New York, and Philadelphia that indicated that homeless people who sought help at emergency shelters and psychiatric hospitals often had a diagnosable mental disorder. Media reports indicated that one third to three fourths of the homeless were mentally ill. Further review showed that media reports used the figures not from the general population of the homeless but from the shelters and psychiatric hospitals. The findings of these reports are questionable, as they suggest that most homeless are mentally ill. The media has offered no rationale to explain how anyone can maintain "sanity" by living on the streets in the major cities of the United States. Although the media brought the problem of homelessness to the forefront, the reliability of figures about the homeless mentally ill remain questionable (Arce, Tadlock, Vergare & Shapiro, 1983; Bassuk, Rubin and Lauriat, 1984). But media alone is not in this quandary; federal and state agencies also remain uninformed. In November 1986, the director of the National

Institute of Mental Health testified before Senator Lowell P. Weicker's Subcommittee on Appropriations regarding neglect of the seriously mentally ill, especially people with schizophrenia. The chart presented in testimony showed that 58% of all individuals with schizophrenia had been officially lost (unknown). In 1986, NIMH had a budget of over $250 million, but seemingly no one was embarrassed (Torrey, 1988b, pp. 34–35).

In studies that focused on the homeless in the general population, rather than solely on the homeless treated by psychiatrically based agencies under emergency conditions, the proportion of homeless found to be mentally ill was only 16.2%, including 10.8% who had a history of institutionalization (Ohio Department of Mental Health, 1984; Roth et al., 1985; Snow et al., 1986, pp. 407–408).

Not all homeless are alike; nor are their mental problems alike. A large-scale study throughout Ohio, based on a sample of 979 homeless people, revealed that 31% of the homeless had only one symptom of mental disorder, 13% showed two or more symptoms, and less than 5% were found to be candidates for a structured, protective environment (Snow & Anderson, 1987). These conflicting reports show that the "popular image" of the homeless is questionable.

The images of the homeless have been changing through time. What is rarely addressed is that the homeless are products of changing personal circumstances and relationships and of society's values. An increase in narcissism, the breakup of the family, impersonalization, an increasingly technical job market, rising rents and cost of living, loss of jobs in those sectors where people with limited skills can be employed, and disenchantment and frustration all have influenced the emotional life of people. There is evidence that work has its own therapeutical value (Gupta, 1990). Many of those who fail to cope become homeless. Of course, traditional factors, such as divorce, alcoholism and drug addiction, mental problems, absence of affordable housing, and lack of reasonable financial resources with which to maintain oneself have contributed as well. The new homeless are children, divorced, elderly and the families (Thorman, 1988).

It is commonly believed that in the 1940s most of the homeless were skid-row bums; the 1960s was a period of turmoil and political dissent, and drug addicts were added to the ranks of the homeless. The introduction of psychotropic drugs in the treatment of mental disorders gave a false hope that those who had mental problems could survive outside institutions, and the innovation of community health programs was expected to take care of follow-up. More than 560,000 individuals released from mental institutions from 1955 to 1984 were on their own to deal with their lives, and many were left with no shelter (Russell, 1984,

p. 20A). This process of deinstitutionalization in itself does not offer us an adequate explanation of the rising flux of the homeless. From 1965 to 1980, more than 60,000 former mental patients were released from New York State institutions alone; the national figure is estimated at 366,000 between 1955 and 1975. Interviews with the users of New York City shelters conducted by the New York State Psychiatric Institute found that 14% had some history of hospitalization for emotional problems, 14% for drinking troubles, and another 14% for drug problems. The majority of homeless single individuals did not spend time in mental institutions. Even among the 22% of men in emergency shelters who once were institutionalized, almost half had been discharged at least 5 years before they became homeless. Two thirds of the homeless in families were children (of the 16,640 family homeless who were officially "temporarily housed by New York City" in 1985, 10,912 were children) who had no history of institutionalization (Marcuse, 1987, pp. 426, 428–429). Clearly, it is unwise to think that all homeless are mentally impaired. Except for the care-giving institutions, no one really wants to know who these people are. Overall, an estimated 44% are from racial and ethnic minorities (Burt & Cohen, 1989; Ford Foundation, 1989, p. 20). Lumping all kinds of people in the category of homeless has created an underclass of people who are clearly discriminated against.

Stereotypes of the homeless as alcoholic bums, drug abusers, and mentally ill prevail because they are the most visible segment of the homeless population and possibly the most neglected one. People commonly believe that homelessness is a lifestyle of choice, and no one but the homeless themselves is responsible for the kind of life they lead. This unsympathetic attitude is also based on the belief that these homeless are deviants who have rejected the acceptable lifestyle of the majority. Their looks and limited possessions and willingness to while away their time in public places often suggest that they are either insane or antisocial.

The homeless include the perpetually unemployed and underemployed, seasonally employed, and in some cases the fully employed. They include Vietnam veterans who still have difficulty coping with the memories of war; farmers whose farms, machinery, and homes were foreclosed; middle-aged widows who could not afford to pay the high cost of housing; teenagers who preferred running away from home to parental abuse; deserted or abused women who do not have the skills to find a job; and older men and women who lost the battle to problems of old age. Unlike previous generations of homeless, today's homeless are younger, better educated, and have more stable employment histories (Ropers, 1988, p. 16).

In 1988, a survey of 27 major cities was sponsored by the U.S. Conference of Mayors in an effort to determine the degree of hunger and homelessness, especially in the major cities of the United States. Requests for emergency shelter compared to the previous year had increased by 13%, and an average of 19% of such requests could not be met. The need for shelter among homeless families increased by an average of 18%. The homeless were turned away due to lack of space in shelters in three fourths of these cities.

The composition of the cities' homeless population represented 49% single men, 13% single women, 34% families, and 5% unaccompanied youth. Many of them are a "new breed" of homeless, significantly different from the homeless of the past 5 decades. They are much younger, usually in their thirties. In the past, most homeless were white, but the new homeless are overrepresented by racial and ethnic minorities. They are more destitute and desperate and share about the same levels of mental problems, alcoholism, drug abuse, and physical disabilities as the general population. Social isolation among the homeless is rampant; they have few friends and little or no contact with relatives. The "social disaffiliation" found among the homeless, without enduring and supporting ties to family, friends, or kin, in itself might be a factor in homelessness (Rossi, 1989, p. 26). The homeless have been pushed out of the social structures that might help them and often resist any effort to be brought in. Becoming homeless further compounds their problems, and they end up in places they should not be and with people they should not be with.

A survey of homeless adults living in beach areas near Los Angeles reports a high rate of prior psychiatric hospitalization. Lillian Gelberg and her associates (1988, pp. 191–196) contacted 529 people who had spent the previous night outdoors, in a shelter, in a hotel, or in the home of a relative with whom they did not expect to stay for too long. All were homeless for an average of 2 years; 73% were men; 64% were white; 44% had been in hospitals for psychiatric reasons, including alcoholism and drug dependence; 21% had made an outpatient visit for a mental or emotional problem within the past year; and 41% had never used mental health services. Those who were hospitalized seemed to have serious symptoms of mental disorders and other problems, such as psychosis, suicide attempts, felonies, daily drinking, and delirium tremens. The surprise was that they all scored at the same level as the general population on a questionnaire estimating human well-being. Of course, beach areas of Los Angeles do not represent the homeless population elsewhere in the nation, but public policy makers might use such findings when discussing the homeless. It is difficult to say whether mental problems experienced were consequences or causes of homelessness. Either way we look at it, the problems need attention.

Jobs, Shelter, and the Homeless

Although recent concern about the plight of the homeless has generated a lot of celebrity and media interest, the issue that must receive attention is not the homeless person who needs an overnight shelter but his or her situation. That situation requires not just short-term attention and assistance but something that would sustain the person for a long period of time. The band-aid approach has not worked, and the number of homeless is ballooning. In some communities that cannot afford to provide assistance, the homeless have been offered one-way bus tickets to some distant community in another state. This policy of "passing the buck" to other communities and states has been termed *Greyhound therapy.* This indicates that past and current policies to handle the problems of the homeless have not worked. Assigning blame to the homeless for their miseries and misfortunes and benign neglect of federal and state government and often of the local or city administration have compounded the problem further. Most cities have failed repeatedly to attend to the needs of the homeless and every winter are reminded of their failures. Why have no serious steps been taken to tackle the problem? Obviously, the homeless do not count. They are not an organized lobbying or "political action group" or a vote pool that might benefit politicians, like the American Association of Retired Persons (with 27 million members and growing by 8,000 every day). The AARP is the nation's largest special-interest organization, nearly twice the size of the AFL-CIO (Hornblower, 1988). It has a good deal of political clout. As many as 73% of the elderly participated in the last presidential election. The scattered homeless individuals and groups probably will never have the political power to influence social policy.

The failure of programs for the homeless can be attributed to the fact that most policy makers are unaware that homelessness is a "total phenomena"—once you are in it, it is not easy to break the cycle. The Senate Committee on the Homelessness, on May 10, 1990, listened to the success story of a California mother with six children in an attempt to find out how she was able to succeed when so many others failed. Her answer was that she was able to find a job—one of the voluntary organizations helping the homeless assisted her in getting training and finding a job. She insisted that there is no way she could have escaped from her plight if the agency had not realized that a job was the most important part of her rehabilitative process.

Homelessness is not in itself a disease—it is a byproduct of individuals' and families' experiences. In this era of technological revolution and challenging job skills, those who cannot retrain and retool might lose their jobs. And those whose job skills are out of time are going to be laid off. The business climate of the nation is also changing rapidly; there is no certainty that what happens in Japan, Brazil, or the Middle East is not going to influence one's own job. Industries cannot keep people on the job if they are not able to sell their products. Many of the homeless thus cannot be blamed for what they did not do.

There are, of course, other issues that relate directly to the problems of homelessness and associated causes. Let us examine them to determine their impact.

1. *Housing.* One of the explanations, and probably the most relevant, is that there has been a housing shortage in general. The construction boom of the 1970s has ended because the incentives (such as deductions for those investors whose taxable income is over 100,000), to construct new buildings and apartment houses have disappeared and home loans carry high interest rates. This affected the poorest and those with limited income the most. Most homeless come from the poorest areas of the central city, where there is the greatest number of abandoned apartment buildings (30,000 units per year in the 1970s in New York City). Public housing is no longer built to replace other buildings. The New York City Housing Authority had a waiting list of 200,000 households for 190,000 units; the turnover rate is 3.3% per year (Marcuse, 1987, p. 426). The situation applies to almost all major cities, including smaller cities where construction in the 1980s was at a standstill. Redevelopment projects in downtown areas of major cities have replaced housing for the poor with housing for the rich.

2. *Higher rent.* One characteristic of the homeless is that they are poor. If they have friends and relatives who are better off, they often cannot help or do not want to help. In the past, people who are now homeless lived in flophouses or occupied single rooms or the cheapest of apartments. In New York City alone, new housing and condominiums have replaced over 109,000 single-room occupancy units since 1971 (Marcuse, 1987), and the city pays up to $36,500 per family to house people in welfare hotels. The welfare hotel owners are happy; their syndicate has donated $104,800 to city politicians since 1980.

3. *Jobs.* Most homeless are those who are pushed out of the job market. The unemployment rate went up from 5% in 1970 to 10% in 1982, and has been going up further in the 1990s. One problem is finding a job that pays enough to make ends meet, because real wages have been shrinking. Once a person has been out of circulation from the job market, chances of getting a decent job diminish year by year. These people fill the ranks of the unemployed. Even those who are marginally employed are always at risk of being laid off, and they eventually fill the ranks of the homeless.

The Policy Issues

There is no disagreement that the homeless need attention and past and current policies to handle the problem have not been successful. Generally, public indifference and government insensitivity are to blame. While military and other international aid programs continue to flourish, the people who need the most help at home are neglected. Opportunism prevails, and even those programs that are supposed to help the poor are not only poorly managed but help the rich politicians and real estate developers. The scandals in the Reagan administration, at HUD, are a case in point, as is the mismanagement of the savings and loan industry, estimated to cost the American public over $500 billion. Homelessness is shocking and distressing, not because it looks bad but because of what it says about the society we are part of. If this issue is not addressed now, it will become an intergenerational problem, like the "poverty syndrome," which has become a national liability with no clear solutions in sight. What ought to be done is quite clear, but how it can be accomplished is debatable. In any case, some of these policy issues are worth considering:

1. Currently, there are three kinds of housing for the homeless—emergency shelters, transitional housing, and permanent housing. These should be retained; however, better coordination of these housing efforts is needed badly. If these are to be run by private organizations, tax or other incentives should be provided to realtors, builders, and owners. There should be a law that no homeless person will be without a shelter; this is as much in the interest of the nation as it is in the interest of the homeless person. Zoning laws should take into account that inexpensive housing is not replaced by high-priced complexes. In other words, cities and communities should be encouraged to maintain low-cost housing for the benefit of all, especially the poor.

2. The agency that is responsible for handling the cases of the homeless should evaluate job-related skills of the homeless and make efforts for job placement. Those who are willing to retool themselves should be encouraged to do so at the cost of the state, possibly with an extended low-cost loan to meet the start-up costs of a new business. Through careful evaluation, it should be determined if each person is able to handle such a responsibility, with rules regulating and safeguarding the investment. Public control should be exercised over economic development grants so the jobs created and benefits received are widely shared. The public should be educated that the policy is in the community interest.

3. There should be a clear understanding of the responsibilities among community mental health agencies, law enforcement personnel, hospitals, and voluntary organizations. These organizations should see

to it that the homeless person receives needed attention, and transfer of care should be determined by competent professionals. Those who need extended care at an institution should be so directed. Federal law should prohibit the involuntary transfer of the homeless (so-called "dumping" from one city or state to another), and there should be penalties assigned when such practices occur.

Public education about the homeless is very important. These programs for the homeless will bring them back into the mainstream of work and productivity.

As their numbers have been increasing, the homeless themselves have been organizing, and a few concerned citizens, celebrities, and supporters have staged some militant actions (sit-ins and public demonstrations). However, the homeless are an exceptionally difficult constituency to organize. Without popular support, public concern, and vocal and influential allies they will continue to play an essentially symbolic role in the broader political context.

Erving Goffman (1959, 1963a, 1963b, 1967) used several appropriate concepts to explain the sociology of interaction and the consequences of such interactions. He discussed the "rules of irrelevance" in encounters and pointed out that "definition of the situation" is largely determined by what shall be attended and not attended. He stated that while participating in encounters, those feelings that militate against interaction, especially positive interaction (which enhances sociability), are encouraged to sustain interaction. Further, Goffman discussed social involvement, suggesting that it is our expectation that people be involved because those who are involved are actively contributing to society and those who are uninvolved are a liability and are perceived as indifferent to society's needs. This leads to *disaffiliation*. Their disaffiliation has no positive use for society because they do not work toward realizable goals. Through time, their roles become diffused and irrelevant, leading to role confusion and loss of "acceptable social identity." Their disaffiliation, as observed by others who are affiliated, becomes a cause of concern not only because they see disaffiliation as something unacceptable but because they are afraid to associate with such people for fear of their own failure. Goffman also discussed "personal resources," which influence the anatomy of encounters. Adequate personal resources lead to positive encounters, while lack of them lead to disdain or indifference. The plight of the homeless in the United States can be explained appropriately in light of Goffman's concepts.

Among the homeless, as well as among other individuals with mental disorders, there are some who are dangerous to themselves or others. In response to these individuals, legislation has been passed and court decisions handed down. Let us now turn our attention to the relationship between mental disorders and the law.

MENTAL DISORDERS AND THE LAW

American law derives its tradition and rationale from the British legal system. Under British common law, a person could not be convicted of a crime if he or she did not understand the consequences of the act or know that the act was a crime. Those who lack these abilities and have committed criminal acts are not held responsible for their actions and can claim insanity as a defense. Sometimes such claims, made by culprits who have committed the most heinous crimes and do not seem to have mental problems, lead to public outcry and complaints about the travesty of the U.S. legal system. In essence, the culprit is not saying that the crime has not been committed but is contending that if he or she had been sane, the crime would not have been committed. In effect, one's mental problems are the cause of the crime committed. Mental disorders are not punishable under criminal law, and people who have no control over their behavior due to the presence of mental disorders are to be treated so that criminal acts may not be repeated. Thus, the insane are relieved of criminal responsibility.

The Insanity Defense

Recent changes in U.S. law, especially with respect to the insanity defense, are viewed by many as illogical and unprogressive. One of the reasons for public outcry against the insanity defense is that people can be jailed for a minor crime, such as shoplifting, if they are normal or sane. On the other hand, people who have committed acts injurious to others, such as murder or mass murder, may escape punishment as criminals by using insanity as a defense. They may be committed to a mental institution, which is a sort of punishment in itself. The new verdict pretends to deal with mental disorders of those who commit crimes, but all it does is put a new label on convicts (Franklin, 1987, p. 94). They may also be released after a relatively short period of time. Thus, from one perspective, the punishment does not fit the crime.

The assassination of President John F. Kennedy in 1963, by Lee Oswald, is now a part of our history. However, Jack Ruby, who murdered Lee Oswald before millions of television witnesses and entered a plea of not guilty by reason of insanity, reminds many of us of the purported abuse of the insanity defense. On March 3, 1981, in Washington, DC, John Hinckley, Jr., attempted to assassinate President Reagan. President Reagan was shot and wounded. Hinckley was tried and on June 21, 1982 was acquitted by reason of insanity, igniting a swift and vociferous public outrage. As soon as Hinckley's verdict was announced, the state of Delaware passed a bill allowing juries to find a defendant in a criminal trial guilty and at the same time mentally ill. Thirty other states followed, including Georgia, Illinois, Indiana, Kansas, Kentucky, Michigan, New Hampshire, New Mexico, Pennsylvania, and Tennessee.

Contrary to the popular belief that many career criminals get away with little or no punishment, the insanity plea is rarely invoked (about once in a thousand cases). Hinckley's case brought to the forefront the fear that thousands of insane are being acquitted and are being released to the communities with no reasonable safeguards.

Can an insane person stand trial? If the person is found to be insane, legally he or she is unable to understand the consequences of the criminal act. The defendant, in such a case, will be committed to a mental hospital. However, one most significant element in determining the competency to stand trial is to ascertain if the defendant understands the nature of the criminal act and its consequences. Whether a person is competent to stand trial is determined by a judge in consultation with one or more psychiatrists, and this decision is not necessarily influenced by the nature and severity of the crime in question. The defense attorney becomes the spokesperson for the defendant and makes legal moves based on his or her own judgment and the judgments of psychiatric professionals about the defendant's ability to stand trial.

Whether or not people with mental disorders are more likely to commit serious crimes, the public outcry against insanity as a defense has dictated that legislators change the statutes to provide less protection for those claiming insanity. For example, on September 17, 1981, in the state of Illinois, the statutory provision providing for a plea or verdict of "guilty but mentally ill" became a law. In effect, this meant that a person who committed a crime, even though he or she was insane or insane at the time of committing the crime, could be held responsible and be sentenced to undergo punishment as well as treatment (Cunningham, 1985).

Historically, tests of competency have focused on "capacity to understand" the consequences of acts committed and "passionate state of mind."

Who is and who is not mentally competent remains open to debate. Can psychiatrists objectively determine if a person is mentally incompetent due to mental disorder? No one is sure, including the psychiatrists themselves. The answer to this question has wider legal implications, because psychiatrists are the expert witnesses who are called on by the courts to ascertain the sanity of people on trial. Their testimony determines the destiny of those people.

Lee Coleman, a California psychiatrist who has testified in over 100 trial cases ranging from competency to predictions of violent behavior, stated that "there is no way of accurately assessing someone's state of mind in the past, no way to determine criminal intent scientifically, and no reliable way of predicting future dangerousness, a point granted by the American Psychiatric Association" (Coleman, 1984). Given the state of matters at this time, the best we can say is that in the absence of better alternatives, the U.S. judicial system seeks advice from the psychiatric experts, and unfortunately their opinions are taken as objective facts, which they are not. Similarly, *guilty but mentally ill* is a "contradiction in terms" that defies legal as well as psychiatric principles. A person cannot be guilty if declared insane according to Anglo-American law. This verdict's introduction is obviously a compromise with groups who would not tolerate leaving the insane, if they committed crimes, unpunished (Page, 1985). In essence, the new law is clear in its intent that whatever mental disorder or illness is, it is no defense. Also, it implies that if mental disorders are present, the state is not obligated to offer treatment. Courts can make arbitrary judgments to mandate psychiatric treatment only in cases in which a court is convinced that treatment is warranted. In a way, the new law takes away the rights of those who have mental disorders and takes us back to the ages when people with mental disorders were treated as criminals.

M'Naghten Rule

American law assumes free will, moral responsibility, and *mens rea* (intent, mind, or mental state harmful to society). If a person does not possess free will and *mens rea*, there can be no moral or legal responsibility. During the reign of Edward I (1272–1307) in England, the use of mental disorder as an excuse for criminal actions was established. In 1843, Edward Drummond (who was private secretary to the British Prime Minister) was shot and killed by Daniel M'Naghten, who mistook Drummond for Sir Robert Peel, the prime minister of Great Britain. M'Naghten was found to be suffering from psychotic delusions (a symptom of paranoid schizophrenia) and believed that he was persecuted by Peel and his men. M'Naghten was found not guilty by reason of insanity and sent to a mental institution. This decision of the court is known as the *M'Naghten rule* (Cockerham, 1989, pp. 314–318; Jeffery, 1990, pp. 426–429).

The M'Naghten rule states that the defendant is not guilty if "the accused was laboring under such defect of reason, from a disease of the mind, as not to know the nature and quality of his act, and if he did know it, that he did not know that what he was doing was wrong" (Jeffery, 1990, p. 428; Moore, 1980, pp. 28–29). It is known as the *test of rationality* or the *right and wrong test*. In other words, by legal definition and *not* medical definition, was the defendant rational at the time of the crime? Insanity is not a medical term but a legal term. Therefore, evaluating psychiatrists must translate the legal term into medical terms, such as psychosis, schizophrenia, or personality disorder. Jeffery (1990, p. 428) pointed out that in this translation there is room for misinterpretation and disagreement. Three major criticisms are leveled against the M'Naghten rule:

1. It only takes into account the intellectual awareness of the person and not the emotional state, such as charged with passion or an irresistible impulse or overstimulation of emotions (Cockerham, 1989, p. 316). For example, a woman might threaten and kill her husband with a gun or knife when she is emotionally upset and convinced that she cannot take the abuse anymore.

2. It does not allow the psychiatrist to testify in medical terms, only in legal terms (Jeffery, 1990, p. 428).

3. It allowed the inclusion of only those cases with serious mental disorders with observable symptoms and was not a comprehensive measure of insanity.

In spite of the criticism, the M'Naghten rule remained on the law books for many years.

The Durham Rule

The Durham rule superseded the M'Naghten Rule in 1954, led by Judge David Bazelon of the District of Columbia Court of Appeals (*United States v. Durham*, 214 F.2d 862, 1954), and it addressed the aforementioned criticism. A new criterion was set. According to the Durham rule, "an accused is not criminally responsible if his unlawful act is a product of mental disease or of mental defect." Incidentally, the Durham rule did not define the terms *mental disease* or *mental defect;* however, it included alcoholism, drug addiction, neuroses, and psychopathy. This rule equates legal insanity with mental disorder. While it is possible that mental disorder may be one of the elements in legal insanity, the presence of mental disorder does not necessarily lead to legal insanity. The Durham rule received much impetus from the popularity of psychoanalytical theories, beginning in the 1920s, which discussed instinctual drives, sexual repression, energies, and ego stages. All these added to the idea that people with mental disorders are in a fundamental sense compelled to act as they do and are thus not responsible for their actions (Moore, 1980, p. 32). However, the issue here has been *causation.* The Durham rule received lukewarm support from the law makers but not from the courts. They did not see much improvement over the M'Naghten rule with the introduction of the Durham rule, except to "pass the buck to the jury."

The *substantial capacity* standard was introduced in the *Model Penal Code* as a solution in 1955. The rule included the core elements of the Durham rule and maintained that the terms *mental disease* and *mental defect* do not include abnormalities manifested only by repeated criminal or otherwise antisocial conduct (Perkins, 1969, p. 877).

For many of us, what is called *insanity* poses some serious questions. Often, those who claim insanity do not apparently show any intellectual impairment; rather, many are articulate, intelligent, and socially competent. We must remember that the defense of insanity is invoked only in serious criminal cases to escape punishment, and many who commit such crimes escape detection in a good number of cases because of ingenious planning of their crimes. Most convicted serial killers used clever tactics to trap their victims. They did not show any signs of mental impairment, clinically or otherwise, and most were caught by accident, not because of intensive patrolling or smart police strategies. Only a few claimed insanity as a defense. Is it possible that people may have diminished capacity or *partial insanity*?

It is believed that the mind is not composed of independent compartments, but it is a unit in itself. Its parts are so interrelated and interdependent that unsoundness at any point disturbs the soundness of the whole (Perkins, 1969, p. 879). This idea remains controversial because although research has identified the regions of the brain, the mind still remains a mystery. For example, how can we explain that *savants* (as in the movie Rainman) have extraordinary ability to handle complex mathematical calculations, do exceptional art work, and remember musical compositions after hearing them only once, to the point that they are able to perform them without practice? At the same time, they are unable to do third-grade arithmetic or to read and write at a fourth-grade level (CBS, "60 Minutes," 1989). Another example is *Tourette's syndrome,* which involves *tics*—uncontrollable multiple motor movements such as blinking the eye, twitching the mouth, licking the lips, shrugging the shoulders, twisting the neck, clearing the throat, blowing through the nostrils, and grimacing. These are accompanied by sounds such as grunts, clicks, yelps, sniffs, or words (Carson et al., 1988, p. 514; ABC, 20/20, 1992). Of course, these are neurological problems, but exactly how the mind relates to many neurological conditions is yet to be known. Therefore, insanity is a legal label, yet its identification is determined by behavioral symptoms and actions, not necessarily by the state of mind. Can insanity be faked? Yes, because there is no instrument yet available by which we can truthfully and objectively assess state of mind. David Berkowitz, (Son of Sam), although declared psychotic by psychiatrists who examined him, later recanted most of his early statements, including commands of the neighbor's dog asking him to kill. The Hillside Strangler, Kenneth Bianchi, tricked several psychologists and psychiatrists by presenting himself as a case of multiple personalities. He claimed that he did not know if he strangled and killed more than 20 women over a period of five years. Under hypnosis, he contended that his other personalities committed the crimes, for which he should not be held responsible (the existence of multiple personalities was used as a symptom of insanity). Later, he confessed that his act of multiple personalities, as well as hypnosis, was a hoax.

The fact is that though the insanity plea is rarely invoked, due to the absence of appropriate instruments, its truthfulness or validity cannot be ascertained easily. This does not mean that insanity does not exist. Because of the suspicions associated with insanity, sometimes those who are actually insane do not receive fair treatment from the authorities or those who are not insane are taken for insane. For example, many street people or homeless are automatically labeled as insane. There are stories of the homeless that they had to act insane or violent to get attention or police protection from the dangers posed by their homeless life on the streets (Alter et al., 1984). Insanity has a host of manifestations, ranging from weakness of intellect to incorrigible criminality. Based on its extent or degree, insanity can be divided into two categories: (1) total or global insanity, which entails alienation of the mind with total deprivation of memory and understanding or one's incapacity to relate with one's environment; and (2) partial or selective insanity, which involves incompetent use of certain situations, things, objects, or the incapacity to be effective, possibly with some degree of dementia.

The Durham rule thus not only broadened the area of symptoms associated with mental disorders but also enlarged the scope and domain of psychiatry. Actions previously defined as deviant behavior, such as alcoholism, are now diagnosed as mental disorders. As Jellinek (1960, pp. 58–59) pointed out, "Alcoholism is an illness if the medical profession recognizes it as such." In the same vein, if alcoholism is a disease, the alcoholic is a patient and therefore deserves the attention of a physician. And if alcoholism is a mental disorder, it raises the therapeutic concerns of psychiatrists. In the process of protecting the rights of the insane, we have legitimized the power of psychiatry to rule their lives.

Criminality and Mental Disorders

The United States Court of Appeals for the Second Circuit, in 1966, in an opinion by Judge Irving R. Kaufman, replaced the prior rule for the circuit with a new test of criminal responsibility recommended by the American Law Institute. The new ruling states that "a person is not responsible for criminal conduct if at the time of such conduct as a result of mental disease or defect he lacks substantial capacity either to appreciate the wrongfulness of his conduct or to conform his conduct to the requirements of law" (*United States v. Freeman*, 357 F.2d, 606, 2d Cir., 1966). Judge Kaufman showed dissatisfaction with the M'Naghten rule, suggesting that it is old fashioned and unscientific. In his view, the rule has not been consistent with modern medical science. He asserted that he was opposed to any concept that divides the intellect, the emotions, and the will. What we see here are the underpinnings and the revival of the medical model that mental disorder is a disease and that "mental conditions," if present in people, cause them to commit criminal acts. There is also an assumption that normal people do not commit criminal acts. Research has yet to prove conclusively a direct relationship between mental disorders and criminal acts. Further, we search for intent, gain, motive, or objective in a criminal act and often interpret them as cause(s), when they are not actually causes but elements involved in a criminal act and possibly consequences. For example, the discovery of the killing of 17 young men and subsequent dismemberment by Jeffrey Dahmer, over a period of 13 years, speaks of deeper personality problems of Dahmer that may have been caused or influenced by more than one factor. Killing and dismembering of bodies by Dahmer is simply a consequence (see Box 12–1). When faced by bizarre actions of people, we readily declare (often after the fact) that the person must have some kind of mental disorder. It seems that we have abused the term *mental disorder*, time and time again. We find an easy escape in using insanity as an explanation as well as a defense, possibly the only defense that many defense attorneys can use to protect their clients from execution (see Boxes 12–1 and 12–2). In many cases, ghastly crimes become sources of big money deals for the criminals as well as their attorneys. The more bizarre a crime story, the more it pays in royalties from books, movies, and public appearances; and agents and attorneys work hard to benefit from the crime.

Criminal law is based on the existence of free will, intent, and moral responsibility. In the Western world, including the United States, the legal position with respect to human behavior is based on rationalism and mind–body dualism—the body is physical and therefore subject to the scientific laws of determinism, whereas the mind is nonphysical and is not subject to the scientific laws of determinism (Jeffery, 1990, p. 67).

> **BOX 12–1 • Is Jeffrey Dahmer Insane?**
>
> On May 27, 1991, in Milwaukee, two neighbors of Jeffrey Dahmer called 911 operators and police and told them that there was a young boy, naked, bleeding, and incoherent, on the street near Dahmer's apartment. Police investigated and questioned Dahmer and dismissed the incident as a domestic dispute between adult homosexuals. The 14-year-old Laotian boy, Konerak Sinthasomphone, became Dahmer's 13th victim.
>
> Dahmer, 31, a former chocolate factory worker and Army veteran, was arrested after a partially handcuffed man flagged down police on July 22, 1991, and took them to Dahmer's apartment, where they found 11 dismembered bodies. During the last 13 years, Dahmer lured his victims to his apartment by offering them money to pose for pictures and watch videos. He would then drug them, strangle them, and dismember their bodies while taking photos of the various stages of dismemberment.
>
> Dahmer, as a teenager, lived in Bath township (population 9,015), Ohio. After his arrest, he confessed that when he was a teenager he killed Steven Hicks and dismembered his body, smashed it, and twirled around the pieces from a cliff. He confessed to killing 17 young males since 1978; in most cases he dismembered their bodies. He often refrigerated body parts, boiled them, and there was evidence that he consumed them. It was not only a case of a serial killer but also of cannibalism.
>
> On September 10, 1991, Dahmer pleaded innocent to 15 murder charges and said if convicted he would claim insanity. Defense attorney Gerald Boyle said, "This is not an evil man, this is a sick man." He offered more grisly stories about Dahmer, including that while in eighth grade Dahmer developed sexual fantasies about young men, at 14 he daydreamed of sex with corpses, he read newspaper obituaries of dead young men, and cruised a cemetery to unearth bodies. He was looking for partners over whom he can have "total control." Prosecutors argued that Dahmer "knew at all times that what he was doing was wrong," describing details of his planned killings. Dahmer was later found guilty of murder by a jury of 14 people and has begun serving Wisconsin's mandatory life-in-prison consecutive terms with no chances of parole.

For details see *Chicago Tribune*, 1991, September 11, Sec. 1, p. 3; Mathews & Springen, 1992, p. 31; and Miller, Rogers, & Haessley, 1991, pp. 28–29.

However, in the classical tradition, the purpose of criminal law is to seek retribution and revenge against a person involved in a criminal act. The principle is to right a moral wrong and to establish a moral principle. Implied in this principle is the intent of criminal law to punish at least some so others will be deterred from criminal conduct. The

> **BOX 12-2 • The Unabashing Adventures of a Serial-Rapist: Was He Addicted to Pornography?**
>
> On July 20, 1989, Randall Joseph Wedding, 34, an architect, a well-dressed and well-groomed Tempe, Arizona man, was found guilty of 32 criminal acts against female leasing agents. Police dubbed him the "Rental Agent Rapist," and he faced a total of 952 years in prison. Wedding sexually assaulted rental agents as they showed apartments or offices. He was indicted on 13 counts of sexual assault, 6 counts of aggravated sexual assault, 6 counts of kidnapping, and 6 counts of burglary. The attacks began in March 1986 and continued until June 1988; they occurred in Phoenix, Mesa, Tempe, and Chandler.
>
> Key evidence against Wedding included positive identifications from the victims, fingerprints, and rope and weapons found at his home that matched items during the assaults. Wedding's defense attorney, Stephen Rempe, described Wedding as a "pornography addict" who began reading *Playboy* magazine when he was only 8 and advanced to hard-core movies by the time he was 16. He was spending $300 a month on porno films. He knew the names of porno stars, and his victims resembled some of them. Wedding asked for the insanity defense due to his pornography addiction.
>
> Frank Osanka, a Chicago-based sociologist and a noted pornography expert, failed to confirm Wedding's proposed defense that he was a "pornography addict" or insane when female leasing agents were attacked.

Adapted from Whiting, 1989, p. C-1.

retributive school of thought thus posits the principle of intentional wrongdoing and intentional punishment.

Are People with Mental Disorders Dangerous?

Dangerousness is a vague term. It relates to the potential for harming self or others. That potential is not necessarily an objective fact, because many who appear dangerous may not be dangerous; it may simply be their lifestyle. What may be perceived as dangerous by one person or group may be viewed as normal by another person or group. Often, prejudices and biases against certain individuals and groups based on their looks, dress, color, actions, or general appearance play a significant role in defining dangerousness. For example, many street people in major cities are generally perceived as dangerous. But this is not the case; many simply failed to survive in the competitive world of social existence. Most crimes are not committed by people with mental disorders. It can be safely said that among those who have mental disorders, some may be dangerous while others are not.

Public policy with respect to metal health demands the will, support, and commitment of the people. Governments at state and federal levels must take responsibility to intensify efforts in the area of prevention of mental disorders. The phenomenon of mental disorder cannot be isolated from other aspects of life, such as job, housing, or family life. Simply changing the laws such as "guilty but insane" would not discourage people from committing serious crimes.

Chapter 13 focuses on current trends in the treatment of mental disorders. We have come a long way. Currently, there is a trend among people in the United States to explore alternative ways to remain physically and mentally healthy.

CHAPTER REVIEW

1. How did public policy influence the creation of community mental health programs in the United States?
2. What are the objectives of community mental health programs in the United States?
3. What is deinstitutionalization? What are its successes and failures?
4. Who are the homeless? Is homelessness a lifestyle of choice? What kinds of problems do the homeless face?
5. In what ways is homelessness associated with mental disorders?
6. How can the increasing number of homeless be explained? Why is homelessness called a "total phenomenon"?
7. What steps do you think are necessary to alleviate the problem of homelessness?
8. What are the problems associated with the insanity defense? Is it possible to evaluate objectively the state of mind of a person?
9. What are the differences between the M'Naghten rule and the Durham rule?
10. Is there any relationship between criminality and mental disorders? How can we reconcile with the law "guilty but insane"?
11. Briefly explain the following:
    a. Second revolution in mental health
    b. Greyhound therapy
    c. Disaffiliation
    d. Substantial capacity
    e. Dangerousness

FOR FURTHER STUDY

Brown, P. (1985). *The transfer of care: Psychiatric deinstitutionalization and its aftermath*. New York: Routledge.
Hope, M., & Young, J. (1986). *The face of homelessness*. Lexington, MA: D. C. Heath.
Institute of Medicine. (1988). *Homelessness, health, and human needs*. Washington, DC: National Academy Press.
Kozal, J. (1988). *Rachel and her children*. New York: Crown Publishers.
Mechanic, D. (1989). *Mental health and social policy*. Englewood Cliffs, NJ: Prentice Hall.
National Coalition for the Homeless. (1988). *Over the edge: Homeless families and the welfare system*. Washington, DC: National Coalition for the Homeless.
Redburn, F. S., & Buss, T. F. (1986). *Responding to America's homeless: Public policy alternatives*. New York: Praeger.
Ropers, R. H. (1988). *The invisible homeless: A new urban ecology*. New York: Human Sciences Press.
Rossi, P. H. (1989). *Without shelter: Homeless in the 1980s*. New York: Priority Press Publications.
Thorman, G. (1988). *Homeless families*. Springfield, Illinois: Charles C. Thomas.
U.S. Department of Health and Human Services. (1988). *The homeless mentally ill: Service needs of the population*. Rockville, MD: National Institute of Mental Health.
Wright, J. D. (1989). *Address unknown: The homeless in America*. New York: Aldine de Gruyter.

▶ 13

Treatment of Mental Disorders: Current Trends

Heather, a 20-year-old white female and a junior in college, complained that her middle-class parents were too harsh on her, especially during her early college years. Her father seemed indifferent and overly occupied by his insurance business, while her mother, a homemaker, rarely appreciated anything she did. She felt she had been "put down" for reasons she did not know. When she started dating, her parents did not like the young man. They were rude to him several times, she insists. One of the major complaints of her parents was that she was naive and indiscreet because she preferred to date boys who, although they were handsome, had no future. To get attention from her parents, she cried, argued, threw temper tantrums, and threatened to commit suicide. On the recommendation of the family physician, Heather was examined by a psychiatrist. She admitted that the men she dated criticized her in public and dictated her life. She felt she did not like their behavior, but at the same time she was attracted to them. They were easygoing, funny, and good company. But something would go wrong, and in a few months they would drop her. She began to realize that there was something wrong with her. The psychiatrist suggested that she suffered from low self-esteem and depression and prescribed antidepressants. During the seventh and most recent romantic breakup, while living in the dorm, she attempted suicide by cutting her wrists. During her recovery in the hospital, she expressed guilt to her parents. Her parents, in turn, assured her of their love and understanding, subtly suggesting to her that she was a beautiful woman and deserved better in life. Heather says she had never heard such words from her parents, and she believes their words helped her to recover sooner than she thought possible.

Cases like Heather's are not uncommon, and they show that the answers to many of our mental problems lie in our interpersonal relationships. Such unresolved problems become mental disorders and sometimes can lead to serious consequences for the person and the family.

Mental disorders are qualitatively different from medical problems. It is often relatively easy to diagnose problems in the heart, stomach, or liver, but it is not yet possible to diagnose and treat mental disorders with the same degree of accuracy. As we all know, attorneys often try to press charges against the incompetency or misjudgment of psychiatrists in releasing mental patients who had fine records of behavior in the institution but committed the most heinous crimes as soon as they were released. This is a controversy that cannot be resolved easily because we have not yet reached the level of scientific objectivity to predict human behavior at the individual level. Technological advances have revolutionized the diagnosis and treatment of many neurological problems, but only a small fraction of mental disorders are neurological problems. We are at the threshold of understanding the brain, but we are still far from understanding the mysteries of the mind.

THE INDIVIDUAL VERSUS SOCIAL ENVIRONMENT

As we have discussed in chapters 3 and 4, when a person suffers from a mental disorder, the focus of the treatment is the person. Various therapeutic means, such as drug therapy and psychotherapy, are used to modify his or her behavior. Apparently, the behavior of the individual is seen as intolerable by those who make up the person's environment and who also directly influence and define the person's behavior. The assumptions that govern the psychiatric approach, and to a great extent psychotherapy, are that mental disorders exist within people, either organically or psychologically or both. The role of social environment is either ignored or given little significance. Once the diagnosis of mental disorder is made, the individual is expected to undergo treatment, with the presumption that the problem is with the individual, not in the social environment. At the same time, the therapeutic effort is to encourage and subtly persuade individuals to understand and adapt to their social environment—those interactions and relationships that may be the causes as well as the consequences of their mental disorders. These approaches provide at least partial answers to the questions (1) Why are there high rates of mental disorders in the United States? and (2) Why do they keep increasing? Even though significant strides have been made in understanding the brain and diseases of the body and in using psychoactive drugs, we are confronted with the problem of treating mental disorders. Surely, we are treating or controlling them, but not curing them.

The factors involved in focusing on the individual and not on the social environment are as follows:

1. It is easier to blame or stigmatize an individual for one's behavior rather than one's family, kin, friends, or co-workers.

2. Although mental disorder may be a reaction to the behavior of others, it is easier to modify or control the behavior of the individual compared to a whole group; this is why the objective of therapy is to modify the thought process and behavior of the affected individual.

3. Most current treatment strategies are strongly entrenched in our history and culture, in which the medical model or health model has remained influential for a long time, leading to the belief that mental disorder is a disease and therefore the individual needs to be treated.

4. Individualism in Western societies, including the United States, is a venerable ideal, and an individual with mental disorder is perceived as one who failed to cope or survive and consequently deserves rehabilitation.

5. Societies that embody organic solidarity and complexity (Durkheim, 1938), such as the United States, display a low level of tolerance for deviance or dissimilarities in behavior because they are considered threatening to the social order.

6. The unappealing reality is that pharmaceutical companies and psychotherapists, among others, derive economic gain and livelihood from the treatment of mental disorders that is conducted on an individual basis; they will not benefit from preventive programs even though such programs may benefit everyone else.

7. The exploitative orientation of the media (popular magazines, TV and radio programs), the publishing industry, and other lobbying groups has brought scientific breakthroughs to the public's attention, assuring that biological rather than social explanations receive attention, sometimes in defiance of the scientific truth. There is no effective lobby for social research and sociotherapies to counteract the powerful lobby for biological research and treatments (Kleinman, 1988, p. 73). Often, even the legitimate criticisms by social scientists that many mental disorders have their origins in social situations rather than individual human biology are taken as affronts.

8. The cultural system, the political economy, and the socialization process emphasize that the individual should take responsibility for his or her actions and emotions. Therefore, whenever the individual is faced with an

emotional problem, it is perceived as the personal problem of the individual.

As we discussed in Chapter 1, most people who believe they have mental disorders seek help within the general health system. Professionals who treat mental disorders are a diverse group. There is a need of culturally sensitive mental health research (Rogler, 1989). Seeking help is a personal and private matter for many. Even the professionals who treat people for mental disorders are not supposed to divulge such personal information about clients to anyone. We prefer to focus on the individual in sorting out the origins of mental problems, not the social environment. One of the major problems in identifying a mental disorder is *somatization* (see Chapter 5).

THERAPIES

Goals of Therapies

Assessing the mental condition of emotionally disturbed individuals is a difficult task. The thoroughness and accuracy of evaluation determines what kind of therapy is appropriate in a particular case. It depends on the professional and perceptive qualities of the therapists and the cooperation of the subjects, who often hesitate to reveal all the facts surrounding their mental disorders.

The goals of therapy are as follows:

1. To identify and understand the individual's symptoms of distress and their severity within the context of the overall level of functioning and the environment
2. To assess the individual's major strengths, resources, and limitations, including ability to understand the nature of mental disorder, motivation level, capacity for change, attitude toward treatment programs and therapists, and status of the support systems
3. To evaluate specific conditions that may have been responsible for maintaining and exacerbating the current distressful emotional condition of the individual
4. To assess modifications in the self and interpersonal relationships to alleviate conflicts and to promote the individual's well-being through a planned course of action

The core of therapy is to change the individual's modes of thinking, feeling, interpreting, and experiencing in positive ways, thereby encouraging the individual to adapt to the environment. The goal of therapy is not necessarily to change the environment, the interactive processes, which is a very

> **BOX 13-1 • Advice Givers Strike Gold**
>
> Advice giving is a multimillion-dollar business. Selling advice to men and women by self-appointed experts is not new. In 1808, Samuel Jennings authored *The Married Lady's Companion*, offering advice to women—"it is in your interest to adapt yourself to your husband, whatever may be his irrationalities or peculiarities." During the past decade, men have been the target and are accused of their wives' or lovers' problems. Some are even reproached that they hate women. Are the men listening? In any case, for the authors and publishers it is a gold mine. Do these books solve any problems or precipitate them? We are not sure. If number of copies sold is any indicator, awareness about sorting out relationships is increasing. However, the payoff may not be for the readers but for the authors and the publishers. Just look at this list:
>
> | | | Hard | Soft |
> |------|--|---------|-----------|
> | 1987 | C. Cowan and M. Kinder
Women Men Love, Women Men Leave | 165,000 | NA |
> | 1986 | S. Forward and J. Torres
Men Who Hate Women & The Women Who Love Them | 400,000 | 1,000,000 |
> | 1985 | C. Cowan and M. Kinder
Smart Women, Foolish Choices: Finding the Right Men and Avoiding the Wrong Ones | 500,000 | 1,500,000 |
> | 1985 | Robin Norwood
Women Who Love Too Much: When You Keep Wishing and Hoping He Will Change | 270,000 | 2,229,000 |
> | 1983 | Dan Kiley
The Peter Pan Syndrome: Men Who Have Never Grown Up | 180,000 | 910,000 |
> | 1981 | Colette Dowling
The Cinderella Complex: Women's Hidden Fear of Independence | 200,000 | 1,423,000 |

Adapted from Shapiro, 1987, pp. 64–65.

difficult or an impossible task to accomplish, but to anticipate changes due to the change in the behavior of the suffering individual. A good deal of therapy centers on the individual, and there is only so much individuals can do to modify their own behavior if the environment they are part of is basically dysfunctional or pathological. A variety of therapies address this question and attempt not only to treat individuals but their environments, too.

Although the goal of therapy is to bring the person back to normal levels of emotional and social functioning, it is advisable for a competent therapist to integrate the knowledge of the individual's physical and medical problems for a coherent overall picture of the individual's mental condition. If the individual's mental disorder has coexisting biomedical maladies, it may be appropriate to treat the latter first or concurrently. In any case, as we discussed in Chapter 4, with few exceptions, the psychiatric approach views most mental disorders as organic problems, and therefore medical examination of the individual is a prerequisite for further treatment.

Therapists

Advice giving is not a new phenomenon. Elderly, grandparents, wise people, priests, ministers, community and educational leaders, philosophers, astrologers, palm readers, witch doctors, and a variety of magic and religious practitioners have played the role of counselors for a long time. During past decades, advice giving has been professionalized through education, certifications, and training programs. However, most states do not require any specified qualifications for a person to be a therapist.

Advice giving has become a lucrative business in recent years. The media, publishing industry, counseling agencies and a variety of individual author-counselors have gained considerable attention. One of the most rewarding is to offer advice through a book addressing most personal issues (see Box 13–1).

We come across people with little or no education in human relations claiming to be expert counselors or therapists. Chances are they may do more harm to their clients than the clients may be aware of. Most counseling clients, due to their own apprehensions and sense of decency, do not ask therapists questions about their qualifications. Those who are qualified to help include the following:

1. *Psychiatrists*: Primarily trained in internal medicine with an MD (Doctor of Medicine), psychiatrists specialize in the treatment of mental disorders with varying orientations in psychotherapy, including psychoanalysis, and further specializations, such as child, adolescent, or geriatric psychiatry. Most psychiatrists use contributions of social sciences, especially psychology, to complement medical treatment of mental disorders through the use of psychotropic drugs and ECT. They are responsible for the treatment of mental patients in institutions and are often called on to testify in courts about the mental status of the accused.

2. *Psychologists*: Trained in psychological theory and research (PhD, DEd, or DPsy) and sometimes with a Master's degree and supervised training, psychologists are licensed by the state to conduct psychological testing. Clinical psychologists diagnose and treat mental disorders. Psychologists are currently asking that they be licensed on a limited basis, to prescribe psychotropic drugs for the treatment of mental disorders. Arguments in favor of this request are that it will reduce costs, make drug therapy more accessible to those who need it the most, provide prompt attention in those areas where psychiatric services are not readily available, and lessen the burden on the services of psychiatrists (Purvis, 1990, p. 95).

3. *Social Workers*: Social workers (MSW) primarily offer mental health and marriage and family counseling. They work with psychiatrists in hospitals, mental institutions, community mental health centers, and other human services agencies.

4. *Counselors*: Counselors (MS, PhD, or DEd) are a diverse group with varied educational training, with emphasis on the individual, marriage and family, addictions, and other areas of mental health counseling. However, some agencies employ counselors who do not have adequate training or education and are not able to offer quality services. This has occasionally brought disrepute to the counseling profession.

5. *Applied Clinical Sociologists*: These sociologists (PhD) specialize in the application of sociological knowledge in a variety of areas of personal and social problems. Their focus is on interpersonal relationships. Some of them, depending on the application of their knowledge in the area of mental health, are also known as psychiatric sociologists.

BOX 13–2 • The Quick-Fix Revolution

Art therapy	Paradigmatic therapy
Beach therapy	Paraverbal therapy
Bioscream therapy	Past lives therapy
Breathing therapy	Pet therapy
Creative-aggression therapy	Phenomeno-structural therapy
Dance therapy	Plant therapy
Drama therapy	Primal therapy
Eidetic (intuition) therapy	Seaside therapy
Future-oriented psychotherapy	Self-therapy
Hypnosymbolic therapy	Soap opera therapy
Logotherapy	Street therapy
Mirror image therapy	Reality therapy
Money therapy	Telephone therapy
Mud bath therapy	Travel therapy
Music therapy	Water therapy

Theories used by therapists are modified to suit their personal style as well as the practical needs of the people under treatment. Expertise is a body of knowledge most trained therapists have, but it is not synonymous with expertness, and the effectiveness of therapy is influenced by therapists' own human qualities. Therapists learn to extemporize their techniques to apply them skillfully in a way appropriate to each case.

THE THERAPY REVOLUTION

Over 250 brands of psychotherapies were listed in the *Psychotherapy Handbook* in 1980. Many of them are called *short-term* or *brief therapies*. Creative, imaginative people as well as con artists are in the field catering to the needs of a diverse clientele. The numbers keep on increasing, but their success rates are largely unknown (see Box 13–2). Not only has the question of who qualifies as a therapist become confusing in the last 2 decades, but the "psychotherapy field has been invaded by mail order ministers, encyclopedia salesmen, assorted misfits and odd opportunists who have claimed equal standing" (Torrey, 1988a, pp. ix–x).

Why has there been such a proliferation of therapies and therapists in the United States in recent times? As we discussed in chapter 1, this growth is related to some factors that have been an intrinsic part of our culture and lifestyle:

1. It is in response to our increasing inability to effectively manage our personal lives and lives' problems by ourselves.
2. The elements of personal privacy and independence, individualism, and narcissistic values have restricted our openness even to those who have been generally concerned about our emotional welfare, such as parents, siblings, close kin, and friends.
3. We believe that there is someone—a psychiatrist, a psychologist, a counselor—who can "fix" our problems. Often, we equate our emotional problems with other problems, such as breaking down of a car or a home heating system, parts of which can be replaced to bring them into working order.
4. We have no time or patience to resolve conflicts in our personal lives; our intent to seek help is not associated with combating the problems, but with escaping from them. We look for "quick fixes." And therapists do "what we ask them to do," *not* "what they are supposed to do"; thus their efforts often lead to mixed results.

5. The institutional structures such as family and church, which have in the past been havens for those who needed help, are marred by pathologies, abuse, scandals, and greed, encouraging therapists to fill the void.
6. Affluence and comforts have their price; our low tolerance for differences or deviances or intrinsic human variations and incapacities has allowed us to discover new maladies with new "labels" and to seek treatment for them.
7. Adoption of the disease model to diagnose and treat mental disorders has further exempted us from the responsibility to mend our ways to alleviate our mental disorders, freeing others close to us from guilt. In this process, we have transferred the responsibility of treating our mental disorders to third parties (therapists). When such treatment fails to do what we expected, we switch, look for alternative or experimental therapies, sometimes in vain.
8. Our approach to therapy is almost like buying a "product"—use it, consume it, and discard it; buy it again when needed. The consumer-oriented sale of therapy has encouraged con artist therapists with few or no credentials to enter the field. For some, being a therapist means only doing a "good business," and this approach has brought disrepute to the whole profession.

SELF-HELP, MUTUAL HELP, AND SUPPORT GROUPS

Alcoholic Anonymous, Overeaters Anonymous, Recovery Inc., National Alliance for the Mentally Ill, Depressive Anonymous, Trichotillomania Support Network (for people who pull their hair out strand by strand), Children of Alcoholic Parents, and Gamblers Anonymous are eight of 500,000 self-help, mutual help, and support groups in which over 15 million Americans participate. These groups are voluntary organizations to aid participants who face a common concern or problem through self-reports, discussion, practical tips, emotional support, and positive attitude (Brown, 1988). The participants, many of whom retain their anonymity, are known for their near religious fervor and commitment to the cause of improving their own lives through peer support. They have discovered that talking and listening to their fellow sufferers has a soothing effect on their mental state, and they can relate to those stories. Most communities have local chapters of national organizations. In addition, there are 3,000 mental health organizations throughout the United States with local affiliates designed to meet the needs of those suffering from mental disorders such as anxiety, depression, schizophrenia, and phobias.

Alcoholic Anonymous (AA), one of the oldest, most effective, and well-known self-help groups, was founded in 1935 in Akron, Ohio, by Dr. Robert Smith and a New York stockbroker named Bill Wilson, both heavy drinkers. They made no breakthroughs about the causes or cure of alcoholism, which are still awaited. They discovered that the only way to deal with their problems was to share feelings and experiences with other heavy drinkers. This had a more powerful therapeutic value and was a better aid to recovery.

AA is estimated to have a diverse worldwide membership of over 2 million, representing a variety of ethnic, religious, class, race, age, and sexual preference groups. In the 1980s, it doubled its membership, when more women joined in large numbers. As a voluntary organization, it has few rules, almost no hierarchy, no restriction to membership, but a shared goal of recovery. Its 12-step recovery program features taking responsibility for oneself and one's addiction, personal honesty, willingness to change, mutual support, and acknowledgment of a higher power in the universe. Many of these self-help groups have helped people recover from disorders that are commonly perceived as diseases.

Norman K. Denzin explained the workings of self-help groups through the symbolic interactionist approach (see also chapter 7). He contended that alcoholism is the cultural phenomenon and the alcoholic is a divided self—one part is the sober self and the other is the divided self. The divided self magnifies deep-seated negative emotions—resentment, anger, fear, self-loathing, self-pity, self-hatred, despair, anguish, remorse, guilt, and shame (Denzin, 1987, p. 135). Those who become active in AA are socialized into the group's new way of thinking, norms, values, a distinctive argot, emotional involvement, group support, self-revelation, and reinterpretation of one's life story. The alcoholic thus reassesses life events, guided by the group, and finds ways to improve his or her life.

The success of AA has led to similar groups nationwide, and these groups have probably done much good for people with emotional problems. What these consciousness-raising groups did is to remove the disease label from personal problems and throw it out the window. These groups set the tone for the self-help revolution by giving people a chance to come out and see others who—despite having some very recognizable flaws and problems—were surviving, thriving, and even smiling (Leerhsen, Lewis, Pomper, Davenport, & Nelson, 1990, p. 54).

SCIENTIFIC FOUNDATIONS OF THE TREATMENT OF MENTAL DISORDERS

Questions about the treatment of mental disorders are as intriguing as they were in medieval times. With the increase in public awareness about mental disorders, many questions need to be answered. These answers depend on who is answering—a psychiatrist, a psychologist, or a sociologist (who, because their domains overlap, are looking at the problem of mental disorder from different perspectives). A psychiatrist looks at depression as an illness that can be treated with drugs and possibly some psychotherapy; a psychologist might see depression as a result of childhood experiences; and a sociologist might see it as a deviant act due to one's personal and social circumstances. There is some evidence that certain individuals may be vulnerable to depression. Psychiatric research has yet to validate the claim that it is a disease of the body. The question is, then, what are we treating?

Until the early 1950s, the treatment of severe mental disorders was still in its rudimentary phase. In many mental institutions in the United States, with thousands of patients, psychosurgeries or lobotomies (surgically operating on the lobes of the brain) were performed on select cases to control violent or intolerable behavior. Lobotomies were crude at best but may be called the "forerunners of modern neurosurgery." The pharmacological revolution (discovery of psychotropic drugs) replaced psychosurgery and influenced the widespread use of Freudian psychoanalysis.

In most cases, drugs have instant effects, and their monitored use encouraged therapists to avoid time-consuming and costly therapeutic practices, such as psychoanalysis, which sometimes could go on for years. This is not to say that in certain cases people with complicated mental disorders may not require treatment for an extended period. For a long time, it has been difficult for psychiatrists to reconcile the two diametrically opposite philosophies of treatment—the organic and the psychoanalytical. But there has been a blessing in this contradiction. Psychoanalysis is highly subjective, speculative, and subject to interpretation. For example, Freud's explanation of suppression of instincts and the Oedipus complex as causal factors in mental disorders is still questioned by those who believe that although such phenomena may exist, there is no proof that they are the cause of mental disorders. Therefore, what could not be explained about a mental disorder organically or medically was possible to explain psychoanalytically. On the other hand, both organic and psychoanalytical models are *person-centered* approaches to mental disorders, suggesting that the causes of one's mental disorder are *within* the person. The major weakness of these approaches is that they blame the victim for their mental problems and rule out the impact of the person's interactions in the social environment. Consequently, the circumstances responsible for the manufacture of mental illness are ignored; further, a label of mentally ill is assigned to the victim (Scheff, 1984; Szasz, 1970a). A situation of double jeopardy occurs for the victims. First, they are labeled and held responsible for owning their mental disorders. Second, all those who were part of the process of precipitating the emotional trauma, which may be the cause of mental disorder for the victim, are exempted because in the therapist's view the mental disorder dwells in the person. The stronghold of this therapeutic tradition continues. Estimates are that roughly three quarters of psychiatrists utilize psychoanalysis in various ways in treating mental disorders. Still, psychotropic drugs are seen as a boon in managing mental disorders.

While claims are made that most mental disorders are treatable (Sargent, 1989, p. iii), we continue to see increased rates of mental disorders in spite of better treatments. Many of the so-called mental disorders are in fact not mental disorders but reactions to difficult and disheartening situations (e.g., financial problems, going through a divorce, and loss of a job). Many others that should not be considered mental disorders are (such as conflicts emerging from the two-career family, changing gender role expectations, and issue-related opinions). We ignore that many of our problems originate from our rapidly changing society, straining our relationships, causing significant amounts of affliction and grief. Sociologists contend that most of our mental problems are products of social interactions with individuals and groups. If anything is to be done to alleviate a mental problem, it is to evaluate interactions and modify them to eliminate unhealthy conflict and replace them with positive and adaptive relationships. Thus, sociologists hold the *system of relationships* responsible for most mental disorders, which is conceptualized as blaming the system. One can argue that sociologists are by their intellectual tradition apt to blame the system as opposed to the individual. Research suggests (as we discussed in chapters 9 and 10) that sociological variables are at work and show a close association with our socialization, gender roles, class, race, and religion.

While the psychiatric enterprise continues to expand its list of mental disorders (*DSM-III-R*, 1987), the public is becoming more sensitive to its needs and exploring new ways to solve personal problems (see Box 13–2). Popular books and magazines, workshops, seminars, and training programs have mushroomed during the last 30 years. The quick-fix therapy revolution has brought so many brands of new therapies that it is difficult to keep track of them, and many are of questionable worth. The marketing strategies of quick-fix therapists and their organizations, to solve all kinds of problems, have attracted an enormous clientele. But what about their scientific value? Professionals in the academic and practicing field reject many of the claims as nonsense because of their ballyhoo gimmicks with little substance. In the absence of rigorous evaluations of these new therapies, only ephemeral reports are available, and the public not only loses faith in therapists, but sometimes the problems are worsened.

New Trends in Psychiatric Assessment

Over the last 25 years, attempts have been made to improve on the quality and objectivity of psychiatric assessment. The most recent changes are reflected in the *DSM-III-R*. Compared to the previous areas of assessment, current psychiatric enterprise is relatively open and willing to utilize contributions of social sciences (i.e., to consider the role of social environmental factors in mental disorders and their treatment). The recent trend in assessment includes the following:

1. Diagnosis of the subject's personality and mental problems and a program of intervention are offered.
2. Emphasis is not limited to psychopathology but includes areas of competency.
3. More attention is paid to the characteristics of the environment and their influence on the psychopathology of the individual.
4. Individuals are allowed to play a more active role in their own treatment management.
5. Alternative treatment strategies are explored.
6. The multiaxial classification in *DSM-III-R* is intended to assess not only the symptoms (Axis I), but personality (Axis II), physical disorders (Axis III), stress caused by situational and experiential factors (Axis IV), and the individual's functional competency (Axis V).
7. A variety of adjunctive therapies, such as art therapy, music therapy, and occupational therapy, are now utilized to assess the effectiveness of the rehabilitative process.
8. Success of programs and institutions is evaluated in the context of the effectiveness of the services to patients.

MODERN MEDICINE AND THERAPEUTIC PRACTICES

Modern advances in the medical field have facilitated a variety of new treatments due to technological breakthroughs in diagnostic techniques and pharmacology. Teamwork among scientists has revolutionized our knowledge about many diseases and their treatments.

The key concept for the followers and practitioners of the medical or biological model is the *endogenous* psychiatric condition, because problems are believed to stem from the psychobiology of the person. Thus, *endogenicity* rules out any other factor that might be associated with any mental condition or mental disorder.

Therapies: Neurological, Biochemical, and Psychiatric

Neuroscience is the scientific study of the nervous system, including its structure, functions, and abnormalities. Neuroscientists attempt to explain behavioral phenomena in neural terms, including abnormalities in the brain. The question is, which class of mental disorders is caused by brain dysfunctions? Although claims about brain dysfunction as a cause have been advanced for many mental disorders, the clearest findings relate to only certain kinds of schizophrenia. With respect to schizophrenia, found in about 1% of the U.S. population, it is not yet clearly known what else is involved besides brain damage or abnormalities. Also suspected are the contaminating interference of psychosis, poor motivation, or limited effort.

Since 1978, neurodiagnostic technologies, especially computerized tomography (CT), have revolutionized knowledge about chronic schizophrenia. Three sites of the brain are tested for prefrontal cortical dysfunction, temporolimbic dysfunction, and left hemisphere dysfunction. These abnormalities can be traced by linking neuropsychological paradigms with neurophysiological and neuroradiological imaging measures, including regional cerebral blood flow (RCBF), positron emission tomography (PET), single photon emission computed tomography (SPECT), brain electric activity mapping (BEAM), magnetic resonance imaging (MRI), and CT (Seidman, 1990, pp. 29–31). These technologies are only useful diagnostic tools. However, treatment is a different matter, especially in chronic schizophrenia, where damage to the brain may be present or far advanced and drug therapy may no longer be effective. Such damage may be a one-time episode or a progressive disease. The variations in dysfunctions in various regions of the brain are attributed to the behavioral distinctions among schizophrenics. One third of schizophrenic cases belong to the unresponsive or untreatable category. Among other treatment alternatives that have received attention is *neurosurgery*, but it is viable only in cases of identifiable and localized lesion in the brain. No one has yet succeeded in human brain transplant. In addition, there are problems in conceptualizing schizophrenia, because the term represents a group of disorders, many of which may not have biological roots.

Biologically oriented or medical model therapists assume that brain dysfunction is present in most mental disorders, including anxiety disorders, bipolar, phobic, and obsessive-compulsive disorders. In actuality, we have just begun to understand the brain, and the presence of mental disorder is possible without the presence of brain damage in cases other than schizophrenia.

For example, by studying a pedigree of Old Order Amish, a genetically isolated religious group in rural Pennsylvania who came to the United States in the 18th century, Janice A. Ege and John R. Kelsoe of the National Institute of Mental Health (NIMH) concluded that, as of now, there is no one genetic marker allegedly suspected to be the cause of bipolar disorder (*Psychiatric News*, 1990, p. 2). The rates of depression among the Amish are equal to the rest of the population. Here the focus is on the genes, and gene therapy in humans is advancing rapidly. It has its consequences. Identifying a group of people with a defective gene is stigmatizing for the whole group, determining for them that they are depressed because of this lacuna in their genetic heritage and possibly they are genetically inferior. Holden (1986) pointed out that the leading researchers in the field now agree that there is no evidence that depression occurs solely from biological causes, and longitudinal studies offer evidence that environmental factors are more to be blamed for recurrent episodes of depression.

But what about the brain? A group of researchers from the National Institute of Mental Health, at the end of a 5-year study of major depression, concluded that interpersonal and cognitive therapies were not significantly inferior to the drug imipramine (Tofranil) treatment. Actually, most subjects were close to full recovery at the end of the 20-week study regardless of the type of treatment received (*Psychiatric Times*, 1990, p. 32). Another study suggested that cognitive behavior therapy is effective in the treatment of anxiety disorders (Goldfried, 1990, pp. 54–55).

If success rates of drugless psychotherapies are as effective as psychoactive drug therapy in a variety of mental disorders, why then are drugs used in treatment? The drugs help in stabilizing and often calming the subjects, who are often desperate. Long-range outcome, however, is better if the individual's interactions are modified in treating a mental disorder. While drug therapy is useful in managing the disorder, it is not a cure. For example, some depressed subjects do not respond to psychotropic drugs as expected, and although some of the reasons for nonresponse may be "biological," others are not. Depending on the definition of nonresponse, reports vary from 8 to 40%. This may be due to noncompliance, treatment intolerance or sensitivity, or serious side-effects. While nonresponse to psychotropic drugs can be handled easily by alternative drugs, other variables are equally important. The success of the treatment is determined by other variables, such as subjects' attitudes or patterns of thinking, rejection of a drug, a general negative approach to pharmacological treatment, fear of addiction, feelings of self-reproach and being unworthy of help, and excessive concern about side-effects. Family and close friends, who are usually the subject's immediate interpersonal circle, not only influence the response to treatment but also the probability of relapse and readmission to a hospital (Halbreich, 1990, pp. 18–19).

Psychotropic Drugs and Drug Dependency

There is always a possibility that in the process of alleviating the mental disorder, drugs may cause side-effects and some degree of dependency. In the process of weaning subjects from their mental disorders, sometimes a dependence on prescribed medications is created. This is especially true in the case of illicit drug dependence and addictions, where prescribed drugs replace the illicit drugs. While we consider one morally right and the other wrong, such a scenario is not uncommon if the actual social environmental conditions and patterns of interaction where the mental problem was created do not change.

Culturally, long-term treatment through prescription drugs is ethically acceptable even if turns into dependence, although the function of both drugs may be almost the same (such as to relieve anxiety, fear, or some environmental stress).

There may be more than one ailment, but specific drugs are directed to treat specific disorders. Obviously, we cannot ignore the business aspect of the treatment of mental disorders. As we discussed in chapters 1 and 4, mental health is a big business. All those involved benefit from it. One classic argument from the practitioners of the medical model is that it is not necessary to know the cause of a mental disorder to treat a mental disorder; the most important goal is to alleviate the symptoms of disorder. Arthur Kleinman, MD, a professor of Anthropology and Psychiatry at Harvard Medical School, stated, "There is a systematic resistance to dealing with social sources of depression and other psychiatric conditions. Perhaps the idea strikes clinicians as simply too difficult to operationalize in practical programs. Perhaps it is too threatening, since it suggests that expensive social programs may be more availing in the long run as prevention than the use of drugs and psychotherapy to treat individual episodes of disease" (1988, p. 73).

Many mental disorders are not as clearly identifiable or neatly categorized as we would like. In that sense, each person with mental disorders is a unique case. For the most part, manifestations of mental disorders are shaped by people's own experiences.

PSYCHOTHERAPY

Psychotherapy is essentially a technique employed by therapists, including psychiatrists, to mitigate emotional problems and mental disorders. Unlike drug therapy, which is commonly utilized by medical practitioners and psychiatrists, psychotherapy (known as "talk therapy") is the main instrument of healing and treating among nonmedical therapists.

The objectives of psychotherapy are (1) to modify patients' modes of thinking, (2) to encourage them to develop better understanding of their social environment that influences their thinking, and (3) to alter those interactions and relationships that are believed to be the causes of distress. However, the philosophy of psychotherapy is not necessarily aimed exclusively at those who are or believe to be suffering from mental disorders to "cure" their "sickness"; it can be also utilized by people who are psychologically healthy and want to gain better insight into their perceived or potential interpersonal problems. Although the objectives of psychotherapy remain the same, scholars differ in their approaches. These variations largely reflect intellectual orientations, suggesting strengths and limitations of certain kinds of psychotherapies and their preferential use.

Most psychotherapies have been influenced by Freud's psychoanalytical model of personality development. Freud called attention to psychodynamic factors that motivate behavior, focusing on the role of the unconscious in understanding the conscious (i.e., the behavior of the individual). He developed therapeutic procedures for understanding the character of one's personality. No approach is without its shortcomings; this is true of Freud's, too.

The following section evaluates some of the most common psychotherapies and their role in therapeutic practice.

Types of Psychotherapy

Psychoanalytical Therapy

Freudian psychotherapy has three primary objectives: to modify the individual's thought process by uncovering the unconscious to the conscious level; to strengthen the ego so the individual can understand his or her personal situation based on reality and dissociate from instinctual cravings and actions; and to modify behavior to adapt with real-life situations. Gerald Corey (1986, p. 14) observed the following:

> *For Freud consciousness is a thin slice of the total mind. Like the greater part of the iceberg that lies below the surface of the water, the larger part of the mind exists below the surface of awareness. The unconscious, which is out of awareness, stores up all experiences, memories, and repressed material. Needs and motivations that are inaccessible—that is, out of awareness—are also outside the sphere of conscious control. Freud believed that most psychological functioning exists in the out-of-awareness realm.*

At the heart of psychoanalytical therapy is the attempt to bring about a resolution to the conflict emerging from the clash between id, ego, and superego over psychic energy—leading to anxiety. Such anxieties may be real or imagined and may cause a set of moral dilemmas affecting a person's emotional state that are identified as mental disorder.

The basic components of psychoanalytical therapy are as follows:

1. *Free association:* The subject is asked to lie on the proverbial couch, free his or her mind from routine preoccupations, and express verbally whatever comes to mind freely regardless of how trivial or bizarre the thought may be. The therapist's attempt is to identify "repressed emotions" in the unconscious and relate them to current events in the subject's life.

2. *Interpretation:* The therapist makes appropriate interpretations of the subject's unconscious.

3. *Dream analysis:* Symbolic meanings are derived from the analysis of the dreams reported by the subject.

4. *Analysis of resistance:* This is an attempt to figure out what prevents a subject from expressing unconscious materials, which may include any feeling, idea, belief, superstition, or attitude.

5. *Transference:* Psychoanalysts typically play the role of anonymous people during therapy and expect the subjects to make projections onto them—reacting to the therapists as they did to their mother, father, or significant other. Freud believed that transference is the key to allowing a person to achieve insight into the influence of past conflicts (especially the first 5 years of life), working through a similar emotional conflict, or *transference relationship*, with the therapist.

Within the field of psychoanalytical therapy, there are others who do not agree with Freud's position, including Karen Horney, Erich Fromm, Harry Sullivan, and Alfred Adler. Adler (1870–1937), in particular, rejected Freud's contentions and stressed that (1) human behavior is purposeful and goal oriented and motivated by social urges rather than by sexual urges; (2) the conscious, not the unconscious, state is the nucleus of human personality; and (3) humans strive for self-realization, security, mastery, superiority, and perfection. Even the feelings of inferiority may be the wellspring of creativity. Alderians go beyond merely accepting the role of heredity and environment and see great potential in human abilities. The emphasis is on reeducating people and reshaping society by focusing on attitudes, beliefs, values, and goals. In this sense, Adler and his followers are more realistic, humanistic, and sociological than their compatriots (Corey, 1986, p. 47).

Some of those who have undergone psychoanalytical treatment and training insist that psychoanalysis and psychiatry, the booming business of mind therapy, are like guild structures. In many cases, money, power, and prestige become synonymous with arbitrary abuse of power, and it can be termed a malignant professionalism (see Cowley et al., 1991, pp. 50–52; Masson, 1990).

Cognitive Behavior Therapy

The intent of *cognitive behavior therapy* is to get subjects to see their mental disorders as stemming from a negative, distorted view of the self and the environment. The treatment process involves (1) relaxation training, as a skill for coping with anxiety; (2) breathing training, involving diaphragmatic as opposed to thoracic breathing; (3) cognitive restructuring, whereby the "dangerous" nature of environmental events is reappraised as are the internal sensations during the consultation sessions associated with anxiety; (4) simulation of panic sessions during the therapy sessions by means of hyperventilation, exercise, or a controlled setting in which coping can take place; (5) graduated exposure to situations that are the cause of anxiety; and (6) and involvement of the significant members of the family in the treatment process.

Interpersonal Therapy

Eric Fromm criticized psychoanalytical theory for its neglect of crucial social factors. By focusing on orientations, he suggested that people adapt in their social interactions with others. He contended that these basic orientations to others or to the social environment contain the roots of much psychopathology.

Interpersonal therapy aims at getting the subject to understand internal, unconscious, and conscious conflicts, underlying mental distress, and to learn to resolve conflicts and work out more adaptive ways of relating to others. The underlying assumption is that the subject's attitude, feelings, and ways of relating to others produce a significant amount of *negative surplus*, contributing to unpleasant feelings. Here the causal factors are not so important as the *interactive processes* that require a positive direction and outcome between the subjects and their environment.

Another interpretation of interpersonal therapy is rooted in *social exchange* (Homans, 1961), which emphasizes that people form relationships for the purpose of satisfying their needs or obtaining their goals. An interactive process thus becomes an *exchange process* in which each person is bargaining or trading. When we experience a bad bargain such that the rewards are not worth the cost, either we reach an accommodation or a compromise or terminate our role in the exchange process. We run into the risks of bad bargains in everyday life, leading to aggravation, frustration, anxiety, and disenchantment, which become the foundation of our psychopathologies.

Eric Berne (1964) examined the games people play. He hypothesized that the games we play involve some sort of role playing of which we are not quite aware and often not prepared for. In some cases, we are blamed for actions we did not intend, and the actions we contemplated did not result in what we actually aimed for. For example, a teenager complains that she could not do well in college because her mother harangued her to do well in school. People play games by using defenses to compensate for their inadequacies, failures, and idiosyncrasies that adversely affect their relationships. These games destroy the honesty and empathy in relationships, furthering the alienation of the individuals and creating an environment of distrust and distress.

Behavior Therapy

The objectives of behavior therapy are to map the cognitive dimension of the subjects and offer various action-oriented methods to assist them in embarking on a course to change their behavior. *Behavior therapy* and *behavior modification* are often used synonymously, and their foundations are grounded in experimental psychological research. The basic principles of the behavioral approach, such as *classical conditioning,* were formulated by J. B. Watson, B. F. Skinner, and, in the 1950s, by Joseph Wolpe, Arnold Lazarus, and Hans Eysenck and are a radical departure from the psychoanalytical approach. *Operant conditioning* relates to many of our everyday actions, such as eating, reading, and talking. B. F. Skinner (1974) advanced this approach by suggesting that learning cannot occur in the absence of some kind of negative or positive reinforcement. Positive reinforcement, such as reward, praise, or money, yields positive behavior change that tends to be repeated. Negative reinforcement involves withdrawal, avoidance, and removal from the unpleasant stimuli. Mental disorders are thus viewed as products of negative reinforcement. Current diversities and practices in behavior therapy have raised many questions about its appropriate use, efficacy, and relevance.

Existential Therapy

Existentialism is a school of intellectual thought, not exactly a therapy, propounded by Dostoevski, Kierkegaard, Nietzsche, Sartre, and Buber, and lately by Frankl, May, and Yalom. In therapeutic practice the emphasis is on what makes us *human* and on understanding deep human experiences. It grew out of a concern about humanness and human existence in the face of an increasingly technological world. On the one hand we see meaninglessness, alienation, indifference, boredom, and isolation, and on the other we encounter alarming episodes of drunkenness, drug addiction, suicides, divorces, and homicides.

The goal of existential therapy is to enable individuals to accept the burden of freedom, autonomy, and personal responsibility and venture down new pathways. The role of the therapist is to free individuals who are inwardly enslaved by their anxieties and uncertainties caused by everyday challenges and entrapped in past disheartening and victimizing experiences (see Box 13–3).

Person-Centered Therapy

The *person-centered* approach derives its meaning from the humanistic aspect of existential perspective. From this perspective, individuals are viewed as competent, trustworthy, and masters of their own destiny. They have a vast potential to change their lives, resolve conflicts, and to give new direction to their thought processes without direct intervention by

> **BOX 13-3** • **Better Consult a Philosopher**
>
> Anxiety can come in different shapes and forms, from a teenage rebellion to mid-life crisis. In an age of fierce competition and frenzied pace of life, it is no wonder one can lose sense of direction. Some imagine retiring at age 40, being a millionaire at 30, or doing something no one has done ever before. As the varieties of our anxieties increase, so do the number of therapies and therapists. "Well, those things which used to mean so much to me a few years ago don't mean much anymore," said one stockbroker in his late thirties. "You know all the scandals on Wall Street make my job the job of a pimp. I don't know what this country is coming to. Maybe I should change careers. Right now, I don't know where I'm going, what I want to do."
>
> Rather than seeking advice from psychiatrists or psychologists, some people in Europe go to philosophers (doctors of philosophy), who treat anxieties of the present with the wisdom of the ages. There is even an Institute for Philosophical Practice and Counseling near Cologne, Germany. Some of these philosophers contend that people are used to thinking about themselves in psychological terms but maintain that "that is not the only truth." Help seekers are called "clients," not patients, and an hour-long session costs about $50. Typically, the clients are those who are going through a disorienting experience—divorce, retirement, or a career change. The philosophers offer the framework in which people can discover new ways to look at problems, to think them through differently, and to reflect on them. The traditional therapists do not like philosophers' "rationalizing." But the philosophers say that they do not do therapy. But they can offer questions—and isn't the goal of psychotherapy "rationalizing"?

See *Newsweek*, 1990, p. 45.

therapists. Carl Rogers espoused *nondirective counseling* against the directive, well-established, and traditional psychoanalytical and behaviorist approaches. It was later renamed *client-centered therapy* (Rogers, 1951). The emphasis in this therapy is on the positive aspects of human nature and its concomitant frailties. It is free from the Freudian view of seeing people as helpless and crippled creatures trapped in their early childhood experiences. Rogers questioned the role of experts (therapists) with their superior and patronizing position, who direct, instruct, punish, control, and manage the lives of those who seek help. Most effective therapists, according to Rogers, have the following attitudinal attributes: (1) genuineness—they do not mask their behavior with superfluous interest and actions; (2) caring—they promote acceptance by their concern for the subject; and (3) insight—they attempt to gain deeper understanding of the subject's problems.

Rogers's approach evokes optimism and allows people to take charge of their affairs to build an emotionally healthy life.

Gestalt Therapy

Gestalt is a variant of existential therapy. The basic aim of the therapy is to encourage people to take responsibility, find their way in life, and gain maturity through life experiences. Frederick S. Perls (1893–1970), who served in the German Army as a psychiatrist, worked with brain-damaged soldiers during World War I and came to see humans as a whole rather than a sum of discretely functioning parts. He emigrated to the United States in 1946 and founded The New York Institute of Gestalt Therapy. He believed in increasing the awareness of subjects by allowing them to feel, sense, interpret, and evaluate the outcome of their actions by themselves. To him, the therapist's role is to guide the subject to come to grips with his or her emotions, conflicts, failures, and frustrations, which cannot be separated from the subject's other experiences. Often, subjects with mental disorders are believed to avoid problems in a variety of ways rather than facing them head on, thus creating an impasse in personal growth. Perls (1969) contended that anxiety is the "gap between the now and the later." The objective of therapy is to integrate the personality of the individual "here" and "now" and allow it to have the capacity to confront the problems and resolve them.

Reality Therapy

The goal of reality therapy is to hold individuals responsible for their behavior (Glasser, 1965, 1981). Disenchanted by the inadequacies of psychoanalytical therapy, William Glasser (1925–) developed reality therapy. A consulting psychiatrist at Ventura School for Girls, a facility for the treatment of juvenile girls, in California, Glasser found that to bring any change in the behavior of subjects under his treatment, the first step was to develop psychological strength to evaluate their own behavior.

Reality therapy derives from phenomenology, or the view that the world is not perceived the way it *is*, but the way it is *perceived*. We control our perceptions of the world to fit our individualized world. Reality therapy thus presents a contrasting view from other therapies. It suggests that people gear all their behavior to fulfill their needs, such as sense of self-worth, belonging, being free, and being in control of their destiny. Many mental problems are consequences of thwarted efforts, leading to pain and frustration with life. The major weakness of Glasser's reality therapy is that he placed secondary importance on environmental and external forces, suggesting that behavior is not caused by these forces but rather by our inner world and needs. He said that the brain works as a control system that deals with the real world and thereby attempts to control our personal world. The objective of the therapy is to recognize *actions* in the reality that our anxieties, fears, and inadequacies are the results of our choices.

Family Therapy

One of the major problems with most therapies, except interpersonal therapy, is that they center on the person rather the whole realm of the person's social environment. The focus of family therapy is the family, not the individual. The underlying assumption is that the family is the primordial group and the most influential in a person's life; therefore, to achieve any positive change it is necessary to treat all members of the family or the dysfunctional family. Although family therapy derives its principles and techniques from a variety of therapies, the primary objective is to realign relationships to achieve better adjustment of all individuals in the family, including the so-called identified patient (Foley, 1989, p. 455).

The three essential elements considered in family therapy are as follows: (1) The family, as an open *system*, is made up of interdependent parts maintaining the family's wholeness and perpetuality: (2) relationships in the family are *interlocking triangles*, which are basic building blocks maintaining the family's emotional network and equilibrium; and (3) relationships are transformed by means of positive and negative *feedback*, by which equilibrium is destroyed and restored.

Alfred Adler, Harry S. Sullivan, and R. D. Laing moved the therapies from biological and intrapsychic mode to the interpersonal. Gregory Bateson, Don Jackson, Jay Haley, and John Weakland (1956) discovered that in schizophrenic families, double bind occurs regularly. For example, the victim is placed in a situation that whatever choice he or she makes is unacceptable. Frequent episodes of double bind not only confuse a person but put him or her at a constant disadvantage, leading to deviant behavior that is eventually termed mental disorder. A variety of processes of fusion of identities, schism and skew, pseudomutuality, confusion, obfuscation, and mystification in the family are known to have associations with mental disorders for family members.

ASIAN THERAPIES

Ideally, therapies are supposed to be secular, apolitical, and free from other biases. Since most mental disorders are not really like medical problems, their nature and expression is often shaped by culture. This is why the effectiveness of therapy is largely determined by a shared worldview of therapists and their clients. Another issue is the locus of the mental problem: Is it the individual or the social environment or both? In many ways, prevention and treatment of mental disorders in non-Western cultures is different from Western cultures. The physicians, priests, spiritualists, indigenous faith healers, herbalists, witch doctors, and quacks offer a variety of therapies (Kakar, 1982; Torrey, 1986). In a way, we have come full circle. What we call quick-fix therapies in the Western world may have been invented by non-Western societies long ago.

The Asian therapies have their origins in various nations and cultures of Asia. The term *Asia* represents a geographical region rather than a particular culture. Thus use of the term *Asian therapies* undermines subtle and relevant differences in various cultures of Asia. Experimental studies in the United States have demonstrated that certain Asian therapies can induce psychological, physiological, and psychotherapeutic effects. Roger Walsh, professor of psychiatry, social sciences, and philosophy at the University of California at Irvine, called Asian therapies *transpersonal* (extending beyond the person and his or her immediate desires) because they do not focus much on pathology (Walsh, 1989, p. 547). Studying how other cultures tackle their mental problems enriches our knowledge and, to some extent, frees us from our ethnocentric mold of thinking. It allows us to appreciate human variations and alternative ways to conceptualize a broader view of human nature and its maladies. Scholars have come to believe that technological changes have dramatically transformed the lives of the people in the Western world, and people are confronted with many existential issues, such as freedom, rationality, isolation, meaninglessness, and narcissism. Some believe that Asian therapies might have some answers.

The Asian therapies, as they are known in the West, are largely derived from certain aspects of Hinduism and Buddhism, the origins of which can be traced back almost 3,000 years. Considering the amorphous, all-encompassing, rather global nature of these religions (they are viewed as a way of life), concepts like meditation and yoga can be conceived as much secular as religious. There may be at least 100 million people in the world, particularly in Asia, who routinely meditate or do yogic exercises. It was not until the 1960s that some things called "Asian" or "Eastern" received much attention in the West. Generally, they were misunderstood and dismissed.

The underlying themes in Asian therapies are as follows:

1. A person's sense of identity and consciousness can reach levels of enlightenment.
2. Personal pathologies can be countered by regular yogic, meditational, and other similar exercises, and possibly by cultivating a greater sense of respect for oneself and others.
3. The mind is the core of one's existence, while the body is simply an organic shell. The body is seen simply as a means for the mind to experience sorrow or joy; therefore, fostering peace and harmony in the

mind is the ultimate goal, which in turn is refreshing and healthy for the body.
4. The human psyche can be conceived only holistically because it influences and is influenced by spiritual, social, and cultural forces and relationships; consequently, preventive steps against pathological forces are essential by maintaining a heightened sense of well-being and empathy for others.
5. Some self-directed exercises or therapies can be done alone, some foster transference, and some require group participation or the guidance of a mentor or guru. Even in those therapies that appear to be solitary, the goal is to benefit the self so it can relate better to others or can enhance spirituality.

Meditation and Yoga

Meditation and yoga are two Asian psychotherapies that probably have received the most scientific attention in the West. *Meditation* refers to a family of practices that cultivate specific mental qualities, such as awareness, concentration, joy, love, empathy, and compassion. The ultimate aim is to train attention in order to bring mental processes under voluntary control; to gain deep insight into the nature of mind, consciousness, and identity; and to develop optimal states of psychological well-being (Walsh, 1989, p. 548). *Yoga* refers to a family of disciplines encompassing moral principles, lifestyle, spirituality, intellectual veracity, meditation, and physical exercises. For followers of yoga, it is a lifestyle that may include physical discipline (*hatha*), meditation (*raja*), spiritual knowledge (*jnana*), devotion to supreme being (*bhakti*), and dispassionate action (*karma*). In the West, *hath yoga*, which is only one aspect of yoga that refers primarily to physical exercises such as breath control, relaxation, and conditioning, has come to mean yoga.

Findings based on several hundred experimental studies of meditation and yoga suggest that these therapies are effective in the treatment of a variety of mental disorders. Their role is preventive as well as curative. Traditional benefits in stress management include gaining a heightened sense of well-being or managing psychological or psychophysiological disorders. Research indicates that meditation reduces generalized anxiety and specific phobias and can help reduce the symptoms of many somatic disorders. Psychiatric patients in hospital settings have also benefited from meditation. Drug and alcohol use can be reduced or eliminated by daily meditation (Shapiro, 1980, 1982; Walsh and Shapiro, 1983; Wilber, Engler, and Brown, 1986). The most startling finding in the nonclinical populations is that meditators change more than nonmeditators (the control group) in the direction of enhanced confidence, self-esteem, sense of self-control, empathy, and self-actualization. Further, meditation may enhance longevity (Langer, 1988; Walsh, 1989). Meditation and yoga bring a deep and healthy self-transformation, encompassing shifts in attitudes, thoughts, awareness, lifestyle, and relationships.

Morita and Naikan

Conceptualization of therapies in Japan, is influenced by the philosophy of Buddhism rather than advances in brain research. The Japanese are clear about the origins of most mental disorders. Stigma associated with mental disorder is high in Japan. Families make special efforts to conceal any signs of mental distress to avoid tarnishing the family name. The presence of mental disorder not only shows that a person has a flaw, but it also reflects adversely on the family. The disease model of mental disorders has little effect on the treatment of mental disorders, except when evidence of organic dysfunction is overwhelming.

One of the Japanese therapies is *morita*. It is designed to treat affective, anxiety, obsessive-compulsive, and phobic disorders. The therapy is guided by the following principles:

1. Symptoms of mental disorders are accepted and reinterpreted for the subject not as inadequacy of personality but rather as a reflection of perfection. Rigidity in thought is intended to be replaced by flexibility. This process of reattribution has a significant place in most Eastern therapies.
2. A fuller participation in life's activity is encouraged to dissipate undesirable thoughts. Most mental disorders are viewed as products of isolation of the self, loneliness, and troubling thoughts.
3. The self is directed away from undesirable thoughts through active engagement in other activities. People who are highly involved are considered emotionally healthy. There is some evidence that *morita* is effective (Ishiyama, 1986).

Another therapy, *naikan*, is derived from Buddhism, which evokes active concern for other human beings and a recognition of human interdependence. The aim of this therapy is to encourage self-reflection and self-assessment of what other people have contributed to the person's life and what the person in turn has done for others. The process is to remind people how their mental condition might be causing difficulties to others as well as to themselves. Expression and realization of a sense of gratitude toward others, especially the people who are close to the subject, is an essential part of therapy. It is intended to remind distressed people that imperfections are part of life and that weaknesses, inadequacies, and failings in them do not reduce other people's love and appreciation for them.

At the core of this therapy is the Buddhist wisdom that confrontation and blaming others is not the solution to any problem. *Morita* and *naikan* therapies focus on individuals, their relationships, and mind and thought processes, rather than the brain.

Generally, the Chinese do not believe in the dualism of mind and body, and healing practices are influenced by Taoist philosophy. The practice of *tai chi chuan* includes meditation and relaxation exercises that are known to have a therapeutic effect. Acupuncture, massage, and medicinal herb treatment are also used to alleviate psychological distress by restoring the balance between life forces within the body and between the body and the universe. The social world of the Chinese is fairly regulated according to Confucian philosophy; therefore, psychological or social deviance is probably less common in China compared to other cultures (Porkert, 1979).

Asian psychotherapies offer several advantages over other clinical interventions. They are preventive, do not require professional help or drug therapy and hospitalization, and are inexpensive. There are no side-effects. Further, they allow individuals freedom to be in charge of their own lives, enhancing psychological and physiological well-being and growth. In essence, Eastern wisdom says, "If you feel good about yourself, it will be radiated on others."

There are many more therapies, but space limitations do not allow us to discuss them all. The aforementioned therapies are used in a variety of combinations. Of course, their success depends on the nature of the mental disorder, the effectiveness of the therapists, and the cooperation of the help seekers.

CONCLUSION

As we come to the end of this text, a number of observations seem in order. The history of mental disorders is long and complex, and we have more issues than we have resolved. Old issues, such as the brain–mind controversy, continue to plague us, and new issues, such as the rapid proliferation of therapeutic strategies, have arisen. Still, some conclusions appear to be warranted.

Most mental disorders are not organic in nature. This is not to imply that organic causes should not be considered initially (they must be) but suggests that once such causes have been ruled out, continuing to treat mental disorders as if they had organic causes is likely to be fruitless. Most such disorders rest in the mind, not the brain, and causes and treatments must take this into consideration. Even when organic causes are present, there are likely to be nonorganic manifestations and consequences. The mind exists in interactions with others and is dependent on those interactions. Thus, focusing exclusively on either the brain or the individual in treating mental disorders is likely to be useless. The NIMH figures suggest that the incidence of mental disorders has been consistently increasing. Projections are that in the 1990s, 50 to 60 million people in the United States will experience mental disorders. However, there is no panic anywhere, although NIMH considers mental disorders a number-one health problem. Added to this are the problems of homelessness, drug abuse and alcoholism, suicide, juvenile delinquency, the ever-increasing spectrum of crime, abuse of our loved ones, and many emotionally disabled people. It does not seem possible that a quarter of the U.S. population could be mentally ill. A society or a civilization would have a difficult time surviving if such a phenomenal number of its people were mentally ill. No epidemic would parallel its enormity.

Issues such as class, family structure, race, age, and gender cannot be neglected if we intend to alleviate problems associated with mental disorders. Individual therapies may help in this regard by enabling the individual to recognize the importance of these other factors and the need to consider relationships in working through mental disorders. Drug therapy may calm the individual enough to make such insights possible, but except in relatively infrequent organic cases will not solve the problem, and the drugs' side-effects may exacerbate and prolong the difficulties.

Understanding that deviance is a normal, necessary component of human behavior is essential, as is awareness that what is labeled deviant differs with time, place, and audience. These three factors must be considered in our attempts to modify deviant behavior. Increased deviance is part and parcel of rapid social, economic, and industrial changes, which affect all of us. Attempting to encourage deviance that has positive consequences while limiting the damage of "negative deviance" (mental disorders) is indeed a difficult task. The task is unlikely to be accomplished by "fly-by-night" schemes and quick-fix artists. Continued scientific research and open communication among all those interested in dealing with the origins, nature, and consequences of mental disorders hold the most promise for eventual success.

CHAPTER REVIEW

1. To transform the individual is the goal in the treatment of mental disorders, to transform not the individual's social situations. Discuss factors leading to blaming the victim.

2. Who are the professionals who treat mental disorders? Does their treatment affirm the dominance of the medical model and the failure of the mental health delivery system?

3. What are the goals of therapy? Is it possible to achieve these goals in spite of enormous variations in therapies, their assumptions, and techniques?

4. Why has there been a "therapy revolution"? What factors have fostered a quick-fix therapy revolution in the United States?

5. To what extent does scientific evidence support the biological basis of mental disorders, including depression and bipolar disorders?

6. The psychiatric assessment based on *DSM-III-R* claims to be comprehensive. What does it and what does it not include in treating a person with mental disorders?

7. What are the essentials of psychotherapy? How has psychotherapy been influenced by Freud's psychoanalytical theory? What are the major criticisms directed against Freud's psychoanalytical approach to mental disorders?

8. Psychotherapy has its grounding in a variety of theories. Discuss the differences among cognitive, interpersonal, and existential therapies.

9. In what ways are Asian therapies different from Western therapies?

10. Asian therapies are termed "transpersonal therapies." What are the essential goals of yoga and meditation?

11. Explain the conceptual differences between the following:
    a. Morita and naikan therapy
    b. Person-centered and reality therapy
    c. Yoga and meditation
    d. Neurological and psychiatric
    e. Somatization and transference

12. Identify the following:
    a. Endogenous psychiatric condition
    b. Computerized tomography
    c. Free association
    d. Negative surplus
    e. Interlocking triangles
    f. Double bind

FOR FURTHER STUDY

Corsini, R. J., & Wedding, D. (1989). *Current psychotherapies*. Itasca, IL: F. E. Peacock.
Kleinman, A. (1988). *Rethinking psychiatry*. New York: Free Press.
Walsh, R., & Shapiro, D. H. (Eds.). (1983). *Beyond health and normality: Explorations of exceptional psychological well-being*. New York: Van Nostrand Reinhold.
Szasz, T. S. (1987). *Insanity: The idea and its consequences*. New York: John Wiley & Sons.
Torrey, E. F. (1986). *Witchdoctors and psychiatrists*. New York: Harper & Row.

References

Abadinsky, H. (1989). *Drug abuse: An introduction.* Chicago: Nelson-Hall.
Abbey, A. (1987). Misperceptions of friendly behavior as sexual interest: A survey of naturally occurring incidents. *Psychology of Women Quarterly, 11,* 173–194.
Adler, J., Carroll, G., Washington, F., Gonzalez, D., Emerson, T., Drew, L., Namuth, T., Witherspoon, D., Abbott, N., Murr, A., Lerner, M. A., Clifton, T., & Miller, M. (1988). Hour by hour crack. *Newsweek,* November 28, 64–75.
Alexander, F. G., & Selesnick, S. T. (1966). *The history of psychiatry.* New York: Harper & Row.
Alter, J., Stille, A., Doherty, S., Greenberg, N. F., Agrest, S., Smith, V. E., Raine, G., & Junkin, D. (1984). Homelessness in America. *Newsweek,* January 2, 20–29.
Altshuler, L. L., Xida, W., Haiqing, Q., Qiang, H., Weiqi, W., & Meilan, X. (1988). Who seeks mental health care in China?: Diagnosis of Chinese outpatients according to DSM criteria and the Chinese classification system. *American Journal of Psychiatry, 145,* 872–875.
Amato, P. R. (1988). Long-term implications of parental divorce for adult self-concept. *Journal of Family Issues, 9,* 201–213.
Amato, P. R. (1989). Family processes and the competence of adolescents and primary school children. *Journal of Youth and Adolescence, 18,* 39–53.
American Broadcasting System. (1989). Homeless kids. February 9.
American Broadcasting System. (1992). Tourette's syndrome. 20/20, July 3.
American Psychiatric Association. (1975). *Psychiatrists' viewpoints on religion and their services to religious institutions and ministry: Task force report 10.* Washington, DC: American Psychiatric Association.
American Psychiatric Association. (1987). *Diagnostic and statistical manual of mental disorders* (Third edition, revised). Washington, DC: APA.
Anderson, N. (1923). *The hobo: The sociology of homeless men.* Chicago: University of Chicago Press.

Andreasen, N. C. (1984). *The broken brain*. New York: Harper & Row.

Antonovsky, A. (1987). *Unravelling the mysteries of health*. San Francisco: Jossey-Bass.

Appleby, L., Smith, R. J., Ellis, N. C., & Henry, J. (1967). Institution-centered and patient-centered mental hospitals: A comparative analysis of polar types. In S. K. Weinberg (Ed.), *The sociology of mental disorders* (pp. 212–218). Chicago: Aldine.

Arce, A. A., Tadlock, M., Vergare, M. J., & Shapiro, S. H. (1983). A psychiatric profile of street people admitted to an emergency shelter. *Hospital and Community Psychiatry, 34*, 812–816.

Arenberg, J. K., Countryman, L. F., Bernstein, L. H., & Shambaugh, G. E. (1990). Van Gogh had Meniere's disease and not epilepsy. *Journal of American Medical Association, 264*, 491–493.

Arthur, R. J. (1971). *An introduction to social psychiatry*. Baltimore, MD: Penguin Books.

Ashton-Jones, E., & Olson, G. A. (Eds.). (1991). *The gender reader*. Boston: Allyn & Bacon.

Barnes, D. M. (1987). Biological issues in schizophrenia. *Science, 235*, 430–433.

Bart, P. (1977). Depression in middle aged women. In V. Gornick & B. Moran (Eds.), *Women in sexist society* (pp. 233–242). New York: Basic Books.

Basham, A. L. (1959). *The wonder that was India*. London: Sedgewick and Jackson.

Bassuk, E. L., Schoonover, S. C., & Gelenberg, A. J. (1983). *The practitioner's guide to psychiatric drugs* (2nd ed.). New York: Plenum.

Bassuk, E. L., Rubin, L., & Lauriat, A. (1984). Is homelessness a mental health problem? *American Journal of Psychiatry 141*, 1546–1550.

Bateson, G. (1978). The birth of a matrix of double-bind and epistemology. In M. M. Berger (Ed.), *Beyond the double bind* (pp. 39–64). New York: Brunner/Mazel.

Bateson, G., Jackson, D. D., Haley, J., & Weakland, J. (1956). Toward a theory of schizophrenia. *Behavior Science, 1*, 251–264.

Batra, R. (1987). An ominous trend to greater inequality. *New York Times*, May 3, F2.

Becker, H. S. (1963). *Outsiders*. New York: Free Press.

Beckman, J. G., Johnston, L. T., & O'Malley, P. (1981). Smoking, drinking, and drug use among American high school students. *American Journal of Public Health, 71*, 59–69.

Bell, A. P., Weinberg, M. S., & Hammersmith, S. K. (1981). *Sexual preference: Its development in men and women*. Bloomington: Indiana University Press.

Bell, R. R., & Coughey, K. (1980). Premarital sexual experience among college females, 1958, 1968, and 1978. *Family Relations, 29*, 353–356.

Benjamin, L. S. (1976). A reconsideration of the Kety and associate study of genetic factors in the transmission of schizophrenia. *American Journal of Psychiatry, 133*, 1129–1133.

Berg, B. (1987). The guilt that drives working mothers crazy. *Ms.*, May, 56–59, 67–68.

Berger, J. (1986). Hispanic Catholics found to hew to tradition. *New York Times*, February 9, 14.

Berger, P. (1967). *The sacred canopy.* Garden City, NY: Doubleday.
Berger, P., Berger, B., & Kellner, H. (1973). *The homeless mind: Modernization and consciousness.* New York: Random House.
Berger, P. & Luckmann, T. (1967). *Social construction of reality.* New York: Doubleday Anchor.
Bergman, R. (1973). A school for medicine men. *American Journal of Psychiatry, 130,* 663–666.
Berk, B. B., & Hirata, L. C. (1973). Mental illness among the Chinese: Myth or reality. *Journal of Social Issues, 29,* 149–166.
Berne, E. (1964). *Games people play: The psychology of human relationships.* New York: Grove Press.
Biederman, J., Faraone, S. V., Keenan, K., Knee, D., & Tsuang, M. T. (1990). Family-genetic and psychosocial risk factors in DSM-III attention deficit disorder. *Journal of the American Academy of Child and Adolescent Psychiatry, 29,* 526–528.
Black, J. L., & Bruce, B. K. (1989). Behavior therapy: A clinical update. *Hospital and Community Psychiatry, 40,* 1152–1158
Blanchard, R., Clemmensen, L. H., & Steiner, B. W. (1987). Heterosexual and homosexual gender dysphoria. *Archives of Sexual Behavior, 16,* 139–151.
Bland, R. C. (1981). Schizophrenia: Sociocultural factors. *Canadian Journal of Psychiatry, 26,* 186–188.
Blau, P. M. (1964). *Exchange and power in social life.* New York: John Wiley & Sons.
Blazer, D. (1980). The epidemiology of mental illness in later life. In E. Busse & D. Blazer (Eds.), *Handbook of geriatric psychiatry* (pp. 249–272). New York: Van Nostrand Reinhold.
Blazer, D., George, L. K., Landerman, R., Pennybacker, M., Melville, M. L., Woodbury, M., Manton, K. G., Jordan, K., & Locke, B. (1985). Psychiatric disorders: A rural/urban comparison. *Archives of General Psychiatry, 42,* 651–655.
Block, J. H., Block, J., & Morrison, A. (1981). Parental disagreement on child-rearing orientations and gender-related personality correlates in children. *Child Development, 52,* 965–974.
Blumer, H. (1969). *Symbolic interactionism.* Englewood Cliffs, NJ: Prentice Hall.
Bowen, M. (1960). A family concept of schizophrenia. In D. Jackson (Ed.) *The etiology of schizophrenia* (pp. 346–388). New York: Basic Books.
Brent, D. A., Perper, J. A., Goldstein, C. E., Kolko, D., Allan, M. J., Allman, C. J., & Zelenak, J. P. (1988). Risk factors for adolescent suicide. *Archives of General Psychiatry, 45,* 581–588
Bridges, K.W., & Goldberg, D. P. (1985). Somatic presentation of DSM-III psychiatric disorders in primary care. *Journal of Psychosomatic Research, 29,* 563–569.
Brim, O. G. (1976). Theories of the male midlife crises. *Counseling Psychologist, 6,* 2–9.
Brody, B. A., & Englehardt, H. T., Jr. (1980). *Mental illness: Law and public policy.* Dordrecht, Holland: D. Reidel.
Broverman, I. K., Broverman, D. M., Clarkson, F. E., Rosenkrants, P. S., & Vogel, S. R. (1970). Sex role stereotypes and clinical judgments of mental health. *Journal of Consulting and Clinical Psychology, 34,* 1–7.

Brown, P. (1985). *The transfer of care: Psychiatric deinstitutionalization and its aftermath.* New York: Routledge.
Brown, P. L. (1988). Troubled millions heed call of self-help groups. *New York Times.* September 16: 1, 7.
Buckner, H.T. (1970). The transvestic career path. *Psychiatry, 33,* 381–389.
Bumpass, L., Sweet, J., & Martin, T. C. (1990). Changing patterns of remarriage. *Journal of Marriage and Family, 52,* 747–756.
Bureau of the Census (1986). *Projections of the Hispanic population of the United States: 1983 to 2080.* Series P-25, No. 995. Washington, DC: U.S. Government Printing Office.
Bureau of the Census (1987). *Statistical Abstracts.* Washington, DC: U.S. Government Printing Office.
Bureau of the Census (1990). *Statistical Abstracts of the United States,* (110th ed.). Washington, DC: U.S. Government Printing Office.
Burgess, A. W. (1985). *The sexual victimization of adolescents.* (DHHS Pub. No. ADM 85-1382). Rockville, MD: National Institute of Mental Health.
Burnham, M. A., Timbers, D. N., & Hough, R. L. (1984). Two measures of psychological distress among Mexican Americans, Mexicans and Anglos. *Journal of Health and Social Behavior, 25,* 24–33.
Burns, C. (1985). *Stepmotherhood.* New York: Harper & Row.
Burt, M. R., & Cohen, B. E. (1989). Differences among homeless single women, women with children, and single men. *Social Problems, 36,* 508–524.
Busfield, J. (1982). Gender and mental illness. *International Journal of Mental Health, 11,* 46–66.
Busfield, J. (1986). *Managing madness: Changing ideas and practice.* London: Hutchinson.
Cable News Network (CNN). (1990). August 12.
Cahalan, D. (1987). *Understanding America's drinking problem.* San Francisco: Jossey-Bass.
Camara, K., & Resnick, G. (1988). Interparental conflict and cooperation: Factors moderating children's post-divorce adjustment. In E. M. Hetherington & J. D. Arasteh (Eds.) *Impact of divorce, single parenting, and stepparenting on children* (pp. 169–195). Hillsdale, N.J.: Erlbaum.
Campbell, A. (1987). Self definition by rejection: The case of gang girls. *Social Problems, 34,* 451–466.
Cameron, N. (1943). The paranoid pseudo-community. *American Journal of Sociology, 49,* 32–38.
Cantor, N., & Genero, N. (1986). Psychiatric diagnosis and natural categorization: A close analogy. In T. Millon & G. Klerman (Eds.), *Contemporary directions in psychopathology: Toward the DSM-IV* (pp. 233–256). New York: Guilford Press.
Carnes, P. (1983). *Out of the shadows: Understanding sexual addiction.* Minneapolis: CompCare.
Carpenter, W. T. (1987). Approaches to knowledge and understanding of schizophrenia. *Schizophrenia Bulletin, 13,* 1–8.
Carson, R. C., Butcher, J. N., & Coleman, J. C. (1988). *Abnormal psychology and modern life.* Glenview, IL: Scott, Foresman.

Carstairs, G. M., & Kapur, R. L. (1976). *The great universe of Kota.* Berkeley: University of California Press.
Caspi, A., & Elder, G. H. (1988). Emergent family patterns: The intergenerational construction of problem behavior and relationships. In R. Hinde & J. Stevenson-Hinde (Eds.), *Understanding family dynamics* (pp. 191–224). New York: Oxford University Press.
Cherlin, A. J. (1981). *Marriage, divorce, remarriage.* Cambridge, MA: Harvard University Press.
Chesler, P. (1973). *Women and madness.* New York: Avon Books.
Chicago Tribune. (1991). Dahmer claims insanity in plea. September 11, section 1, p. 3.
Chiles, J. A., Strosahl, K. D., Ping, Z. Y., Michael, M. C., Hall, K., Jemelka, R., Senn, B., & Reto, C. (1989). Depression, hopelessness, and suicidal behavior in Chinese and American psychiatric patients. *American Journal of Psychiatry, 146,* 339–344.
Chino, A. F., & Funabiki, D. (1984). A cross validation of sex differences in the expression of depression. *Sex Roles, 11,* 175–187.
Clark, M., Gosnell, M., & Reese, M. (1980). The sex therapy revolution. *Newsweek.* November 17, 97–100.
Clark, M., & Hager, M. (1988). Getting hooked on tobacco. *Newsweek.* May 30, 56.
Clausen, J. A. (1976). Mental disorders. In R. K. Merton & R. A. Nisbet (Eds.), *Contemporary social problems* (pp. 103–139, 4th ed.). New York: Harcourt Brace Jovanovich.
Clayton, R. R., & Voss, H. L. (1981). *Young men and drugs in Manhattan: A causal analysis.* Rockville, MD: National Institute on Drug Abuse.
Cockerham, W. C. (1979). Labeling theory and mental disorder: A synthesis of psychiatric and social perspectives. In N. Denzin (Ed.), *Studies in symbolic interaction* (pp. 257–280, vol. 2). Greenwich, CT: JAI Press.
Cockerham, W. C. (1984). Mental disorder in Peoples' Republic of China. *Journal of International and Comparative Social Welfare, 1,* 40–51.
Cockerham, W. C. (1989). *Sociology of mental disorder.* Englewood Cliffs, NJ: Prentice Hall.
Cockerham, W. C. (1990). Becoming mentally ill. In N. Denzin (Ed.), *Studies in symbolic interaction* (pp. 339–350, vol. 11). Greenwich, CT: JAI Press.
Cohen, A. K. (1959). The study of social disorganization and deviant behavior. In R. K. Merton, L. Broom, & L. Cottrell, Jr. (Eds.), *Sociology today* (pp. 478–481). New York: Basic Books.
Coleman, L. (1984). *The reign of error: Psychiatry, authority and law.* Boston: Beacon Press.
Coles, R. (1989). Lost youth. *Vogue.* July, 186–189.
Columbia Broadcasting System (CBS). (1989). "48 Hours." February 6.
Columbia Broadcasting System (CBS). (1989). "Sixty Minutes—Savants." May 14.
Conrad, P., & Schneider, J. W. (1980). *Deviance and medicalization: From badness to sickness.* St. Louis: Mosby-Year Book.
Cooley, C. H. (1902). *Human nature and the social order.* New York: Scribners.
Cooley, C. H. (1966). *Social process.* Carbondale: Southern Illinois University Press.

Corey, G. (1986). *Theory and practice of counseling and psychotherapy* (3rd ed.). Belmont, CA: Brooks/Cole.
Corsini, R. J., & Wedding, D. (1989). *Current psychotherapies*. Itasca, IL: F. E. Peacock.
Cowley, G., Springen, K., Leonard, E. A., Robins, K., & Gordon, J. (1990). The promise of prozac. *Newsweek*, March 26, 36–41.
Cowley, G., Carrol, G., Katel, P., Gordon, J., Edelson, J., Springen, K., & Hager, M. (1991). Money madness. *Newsweek*. November 4, 50–52.
Cox, S., & Radloff, L. S. (1984). Depression in relation to sex roles: Differences in learned susceptibility and precipitating factors. In C. Wisdom (Ed.), *Sex roles and psychopathology* (pp. 123–144). New York: Plenum.
Cox, S. M. (1971). *Ideology, negotiation, and emergent organization: A comparative analysis*. PhD dissertation. Urbana: University of Illinois.
Cox, S. M., & Conrad, J. J. (1991). *Juvenile justice* (3rd ed.). Dubuque, IA: Wm. C. Brown.
Criminal Justice Newsletter. (1986). Advances found in specialized treatment of sex offenders. *17*, 5–6.
Crooks, R., & Baur, K. (1987). *Our sexuality* (3rd ed.). Menlo Park, CA: Benjamin Cummings.
Cummings, E., & Cummings, J. (1957). *Closed ranks*. Cambridge, MA: Harvard University Press.
Cunningham, S. C. (1985, October). Guilty but mentally ill: A growing panacea. Paper presented at the annual meeting of the Midwestern Criminal Justice Association, Chicago, IL.
Davidson, L. L., Rosenberg, H. L., Mercy, J. A., Franklin, J., & Simmons, J. T. (1989) An epidemiologic study of risk factors in two teenage suicide clusters. *The Journal of the American Medical Association, 262,* 2687–2692.
Degler, C. N. (1974). What ought to be and what was: Women's sexuality in the nineteenth century. *American Historical Review, 79,* 1467–1490.
DeLong, R. (1990). Lithium clinically useful in range of childhood behavior disorders. *The Pyschiatric Times, 7,* 13–16.
Dentler, R. A., & Erikson, K. T. (1959). The functions of deviance in groups. *Social Problems, 7,* 98–107.
Denzin, N. K. (1968). The self-fulfilling prophecy and patient therapist interaction. In S. Spitzer & N. K. Denzin (Eds.), *The mental patient: Studies in the sociology of deviance* (pp. 349–358). New York: McGraw-Hill.
Denzin, N. K. (1983). A note on emotionality, self and interaction. *American Journal of Sociology, 89,* 402–409.
Denzin, N. K. (1984). *On understanding emotion*. San Francisco: Jossey-Bass.
Denzin, N. K. (1987). *The alcoholic self*. Newbury Park, CA: Sage Publications.
Deutsch, A. (1949). *The mentally ill in America: A history of their care and treatment from colonial times* (2nd ed.). New York: Columbia University Press.
Deutscher, I. (1973). *What we say, what we do*. Glenview, IL: Scott, Foresman.
Dobkin, M. (1968). Folk curing with a psychedelic cactus in the north coast of Peru. *International Journal of Social Psychiatry, 15,* 23–32.

Dohrenwend, B. P. (1983). The epidemiology of mental disorder. In D. Mechanic (Ed.) *Handbook of health, health care, and the health professions* (pp. 157–194). New York: Free Press.
Dohrenwend, B. P., Bernard, V. W., & Kolb, L. C. (1962). The orientation of leaders in an urban area toward problems of mental illness. *American Journal of Psychiatry, 118*, 683–691.
Dohrenwend, B. S., & Dohrenwend, B. P. (1969). *Social staus and psychological disorder: A causal inquiry.* New York: Wiley Interscience.
Dohrenwend, B. S., & Dohrenwend, B. P. (1974a). *Stressful life events: Their nature and effects.* New York: John Wiley & Sons.
Dohrenwend, B. P., & Dohrenwend, B. S. (1974b). Social and cultural influences on psychopathology. *Annual Review of Psychology, 25*, 434–435.
Dohrenwend, B. P., & Dohrenwend, B. S. (1975). Sociocultural and social factors in the genesis of mental disorders. *Journal of Health and Social Behavior, 16*, 365–392.
Dohrenwend, B. P., & Dohrenwend, B. S. (1976). Sex differences in psychiatric disorders. *American Journal of Sociology, 81*, 1447–1454.
Dunham, H. W. (1977). Schizophrenia: Sociocultural factors. *Hospital Practice, 12*, 61–68.
Dunn, W. (1991). Census tactic on homeless missed mark. *USA Today*, April 12, 3A.
Durkheim, E. (1938). *The rules of sociological method.* Chicago: University of Chicago Press.
Durkheim, E. (1947). *Elementary forms of religious life.* (J. W. Swain, Trans.). New York: Macmillan. (Original work published 1912)
Durkheim, E. (1951). *Suicide.* New York: Free Press. (Original work published 1897)
Earle, R., & Crow, G. (1989). *Lonely all the time: Recognizing, understanding and overcoming sex addiction for addicts and co-dependents.* New York: Pocket Books.
Eaton, W. W. (1974). Residence, social class, and schizophrenia. *Journal of Health and Social Behavior, 15*, 289–299.
Eaton, W. W. (1980). A formal theory of selection for schizophrenia. *American Journal of Sociology, 86*, 149–158.
Ehrenwald, J. (1956). *From medicine man to friend.* New York: Dell.
Eisenberg, L. (1987). Preventing mental, neurological and psychosocial disorders. *World Health Forum, 8*, 245–253.
Eitzen, D. S. & Zinn, M. B. (1992). *Social problems* (5th ed.). Boston: Allyn & Bacon.
Elkin, I., Shea, M. T., Watkins, J. T., Imber, S. D., Sotsky, S. M., Collins, J. F., Glass, D. R., Pilkonis, P. A., Leber, W. R., Docherty, J. P., Fiester, S. J., & Parloff, M. B. (1989). National Institute of Mental Health Treatment of Depression Collaborative Research Program: General effectiveness of treatments. *Archives of General Psychiatry, 46*, 971–982.
Ellis, A. (1967). Rational-emotive psychotherapy. In D. Arbuckle (Ed.), *Counseling and psychotherapy* (pp. 78–99). New York: McGraw-Hill.
Ellis, A. (1984). Rational-emotive therapy. In R. Corsini (Ed.), *Current psychotherapies* (pp. 167–206, 3rd ed.). Itasca, IL: F. E. Peacock.

Ellison, C. G. (1991). Religious involvement and subjective well-being. *Journal of Health and Social Behavior, 32,* 80–99.
Ellison, C. G., Gay, D. A., & Glass, T. A. (1989). Does religious commitment contribute to individual life satisfaction. *Social Forces, 68,* 100–123.
Emery, R. E., & O'Leary, K. D. (1984). Marital discord and child behavior problems in non-clinic sample. *Journal of Abnormal Child Psychology, 12,* 411–420.
Erikson, K. T. (1962). Notes on the sociology of deviance. *Social Problems, 9,* 307–314.
Evans, R. (1989). Consigned to the shadows. *Geographical Magazine, 61,* 23–25.
Eysenck, H. J. (1970). The effects of psychotherapy. In G. P. Stone & H. A. Faberman (Eds.), *Social psychology through symbolic interaction* (pp. 718–770). Waltham, MA: Ginn-Blaisdell.
Fabrega, H., Jr. (1982). Culture and psychiatric illness: Biomedical and ethnomedical aspects. In A. J. Marsella & G. M. White (Eds.), *Cultural conceptions of mental health and therapy* (pp. 39–68). Dordrecht, Holland: D. Reidel Publishing.
Family Planning Perspectives. (1985). Recently wed women more likely to have had premarital sex. *17,* 142.
Farber, S. (1981). *Identical twins reared apart: A reanalysis.* New York: Basic Books.
Faris, R. E., & Dunham, H. W. (1939). *Mental disorders in the urban areas.* Chicago: University of Chicago Press.
Farmer, V. (1989). Ten major problems face rural families today. *Illinois Agri-News,* August 2.
Felix, R. H. (1967). *Mental illness: Progress and prospects.* New York: Columbia University Press.
Festinger, L. (1957). *A theory of cognitive dissonance.* Stanford, CA: Stanford University Press.
Finkelhor, D. (1979). *Sexually victimized children.* New York: Free Press.
Flaherty, J. A., Channon, R. A., & Davis, J. M. (Eds.). (1988). *Psychiatry: Diagnosis and therapy, '88/'89.* Norwalk, CT: Appleton & Lange.
Foley, D. P. (1988). Eleven interpretations of personal suffering. *Journal of Religion and Health, 27,* 321–328.
Foley, V. D. (1989). Family therapy. In R. J. Corsini & D. Wedding (Eds.), *Current psychotherapies* (pp. 455–502). Itasca, IL: F. E. Peacock.
Ford Foundation. (1989). *Affordable housing: The years ahead.* New York: Ford Foundation.
Forward, S., & Buck, C. (1978). *Betrayal of innocence: Incest and its devastations.* New York: J. P. Tarcher.
Foucault, M. (1967). *Madness and civilization.* New York: Mentor.
Foucault, M. (1973). *The birth of the clinic.* New York: Pantheon Books.
Foucault, M. (1979). *The history of sexuality. Vol. 1: An introduction.* London: Allen Lane.
Franklin, D. (1987). Mind. *Hippocrates,* September–October, 94–96.
Freeman, H. E., & Simmons, O. G. (1961). Feelings of stigma among relatives of former patients. *Social Problems, 8,* 312–321.
Freeman, H. E., & Simmons, O. G. (1963). *The mental patient comes home.* New York: John Wiley & Sons.

Freud, S. (1953). *The future of an illusion*. New York: Liveright.
Freud, S. (1961). *Civilization and its discontents* (J. Strachey, Trans.). New York: W. W. Norton.
Freud, S. (1965a). *Group psychology and the analysis of the ego* (J. Strachey, Trans.). New York: Bantam.
Freud, S. (1965b). *The interpretation of dreams*. New York: Avon Books.
Fromm-Reichman, F. (1948). Notes on the development of treatment of schizophrenia by psycoanalytic psychotherapy. *Psychiatry, 11*, 263–273.
Gagnon, J. H., & Simon, W. (Eds.). (1967). *Sexual deviance*. New York: Harper & Row.
Gallagher, B. J., III (1987). *The sociology of mental illness* (2nd ed.). Englewood Cliffs, NJ: Prentice Hall.
Gallup, G. (1985). *Religion in America—50 years: 1935–1985*. Princeton, NJ: Religion Research Center.
Gallup, G. G., Jr., & Maser, J. D. (1977). Tomic immobility: Evolutionary underpinnings of human catalepsy and catatonia. In J. D. Maser & M. E. P. Seligman (Eds.) *Psychopathology: Experimental Models* (pp. 335–357). San Fransisco: W. H. Freeman.
Garfinkel, H. (1956). Conditions of successful degradation ceremonies. *American Journal of Sociology, 61*, 420–424.
Gebhard, P. H. (1965). Situational factors affecting human sexual behavior. In F. Beach (Ed.), *Sex and behavior* (pp. 483–495). New York: John Wiley & Sons.
Gebhard, P. H, Gagnon, J., Pomeroy, W., & Christenson, C. (1965). *Sex offenders: An analysis of types*. New York: Harper & Row.
Gelberg, L., Lin, L. S., & Leake, B. D. (1988). Mental health, alcohol and drug use, and criminal history among homeless adults. *American Journal of Psychiatry, 145*, 191–196.
Gelman, D., Kasindorf, M., King, P., & Miller, M. (1986). Quick fix therapy. *Newsweek*. May 26, 74–76.
Gelman, D., King, P., Hager, M., Raine, G., & Pratt, J. (1985). The food-mood link. *Newsweek*. October 14, 93–94.
Gerhart, U. C. (1990). *Caring for the chronically mentally ill*. Itasca, IL: F. E. Peacock.
Glasser, W. (1965). *Reality therapy: A new approach to psychiatry*. New York: Harper & Row.
Glasser, W. (1981). *Stations of the mind*. New York: Harper & Row.
Goffman, E. (1959). *The presentation of self in everyday life*. Garden City, NY: Anchor Books.
Goffman, E. (1961). *Asylums*. Garden City, NY: Anchor Books.
Goffman, E. (1963a). *Behavior in public places*. New York: The Free Press.
Goffman, E. (1963b). *Encounters*. Indianapolis: Bobbs-Merrill.
Goffman, E. (1967). *Interaction ritual*. Garden City, NY: Anchor Books.
Goffman, E. (1971). *Relations in public*. New York: Basic Books.
Gold, H. R. (1957). *Psychiatry and the Talmud*. Vol. 1, No. 1. New York: Jewish Heritage.
Goldfried, M. R. (1990). Cognitive-behavior therapy effective in treatment of anxiety disorders. *The Psychiatric Times, 7* (May), 54–55.

Goldman, N., & Ravid, R. (1980). Community surveys: Sex differences in mental illness. In M. Guttentag, S. Salasin, & D. Belle (Eds.), *The mental health of women* (pp. 31–55). New York: Academic Press.

Goldstein, M. J. (1987). Psychosocial issues. In D. Shore (Ed.), *Schizophrenia* (pp. 171–185). Rockville, MD: National Institute of Mental Health.

Goode, E. (1989). *Drugs in American society* (3rd ed.). New York: Alfred Knopf.

Goode, E. (1990). *Deviant behavior* (3rd ed.). Englewood Cliffs, NJ: Prentice Hall.

Goode, W. J. (1956). *After divorce.* New York: Free Press.

Goodman, A. G., Goodman, L. S., Rall, T. W., & Murad, F. (1985). *Goodman and Gliman's the pharmacological basis of therapeutics* (7th ed.). New York: Macmillan.

Gordon, B. L. (1949). *Medicine throughout antiquity.* Philadelphia: F. A. Davis.

Gordon, L., & O'Keefe, P. (1984). Incest as a form of family violence: Evidence from historical case records. *Journal of Marriage and Family, 46,* 27–34.

Gosslin, C. C., & Eysenck, S. B. G. (1980). The transvestite "double image": A preliminary report. *Personality and Individual Differences, 1,* 172–173.

Gottesman, I. I., McGuffin, P., & Farmer, A. E. (1987). *Clinical genetics as clues to the "real" genetics of schizophrenia.* Schizophrenia (Special Report). Rockville, MD: National Institute of Mental Health.

Gough, H. G. (1948). A sociological theory of psychopathy. *American Journal of Sociology, 53,* 359–366.

Gove, W. R. (1972). The relationship between sex roles, marital status and mental illness. *Social Forces, 51,* 34–44.

Gove, W. R. (1979). Sex, marital status, and psychiatric treatment: A research note. *Social Forces, 58,* 89–93.

Gove, W. R., & Tudor, J. (1973). Adult sex roles and mental illness. *American Journal of Sociology, 77,* 812–835.

Gratteau, H. (1985). Little help for "guilty but mentally ill." *Chicago Tribune,* section 1, April 30, 1.

Greeley, A. M., McCready, W. C., & Theisen, G. (1980). *Ethnic drinking subcultures.* New York: Praeger.

Greenley, J. R., Mechanic, D., & Cleary, P. D. (1987). Seeking help for psychological problems: A replication and extension. *Medical Care, 25,* 1113–1128.

Greer, S. (1964). Study of parental loss in neurotics and sociopaths. *Archives of General Psychiatry, 11,* 177–180.

Grinker, R. R., & Harrow, H. (1987). *Clinical research in schizophrenia: A multidimensional approach.* Springfield, IL: Charles C. Thomas.

Grob, G. N. (1987). The forging of mental health policy in America: World War II to new frontier. *Journal of History of Medicine and Allied Sciences, 42,* 410–446.

Groth, A. N., Burgess, A.W., & Holmstrom, L. L. (1977). Rape, power, anger, and sexuality. *American Journal of Psychiatry, 134,* 1239–1243.

Groth, A. N., & Birnbaum, H. J. (1979). *Men who rape: The psychology of the offender.* New York: Plenum.

Groth, A. N., Longo, R. E., & McFadin, J. B. (1982). Undetected recidivism among rapists and child molesters. *Crime and Delinquency,* July, 450–458.

Grusky, O., & Pollner, M. (Eds.). (1981). *The sociology of mental illness.* New York: Holt, Rinehart & Winston.

Grusky, O., Tierney, K., Manderscheid, R. W., & Grusky, D. B. (1985). Social bonding and community adjustment of chronically mentally ill patients. *Journal of Health and Social Behavior, 26*, 49–63.

Gupta, G. R. (1990, July). Work, mental health and the homeless. Paper presented at the XII World Congress of Sociology, International Sociological Association, Madrid, Spain.

Gupta, G. R., & Cox, S. M. (1988). A typology of incest and possible intervention strategies. *Journal of Family Violence, 3*, 299–312.

Guy, R. F. (1982). Religion, physical disabilities and life satisfaction in older age cohorts. *International Journal of Aging and Human Development, 15*, 225–232.

Halbreich, U. (1990). Psychosocial aspects influence response to antidepressants. *The Psychiatric Times, 7* (June), 18–19.

Hall, L. A., Williams, C. A., & Greenberg, R. S. (1985). Supports, stressors, and depressive symptoms in low income mothers of young children. *American Journal of Public Health, 75*, 518–522.

Hamilton, V. L., Broman, C. L., Hoffman, W. S., & Renner, D. S. (1990). Hard times and vulnerable people: Initial effects of plant closing on autoworkers' mental health. *Journal of Health and Social Behavior, 31*, 123–140.

Hammersmith, S. K., & Weinberg, M. S. (1973). Homosexual identity: Commitment, adjustment, and significant others. *Sociometry, 36*, 56–79.

Harding, C., Brooks, G. W., Ashikaga, T., et al. (1987). The Vermont Longitudinal Study of persons with severe mental illness—I: Methodology, study sample and overall status. *American Journal of Psychiatry, 144*, 718–726.

Harvard Medical School Mental Health Letter (HMS-MHL). (1989a). Families in the treatment of schizophrenia—Part I, 5 (June), 1–4.

Harvard Medical School Mental Health Letter. (1989b). Sexual disorders—Part I, 6 (December), 1–3.

Harvard Medical School Mental Health Letter. (1990). Sexual disorders—Part II, 6 (January), 1–4.

Hassinger, E. W. (1976). Pathways of rural people to health services. In E. W. Hassinger & L. Whiting (Eds.), *Rural health services: Organization, delivery and use* (pp. 164–187). Ames, IA: Iowa State University Press.

Herman, J. (1981). *Father-daughter incest.* Cambridge, MA: Harvard University Press.

Heston, L. (1966). Psychiatric disorders in foster home reared children of schizophrenic mothers. *British Journal of Psychiatry, 112*, 819–825.

Hewitt, J. P. (1984). *Self and society* (3rd Ed.). Boston: Allyn & Bacon.

Hoeper, E. W., Nyczi, G. R., & Cleary, P. D. (1979). Estimated prevalence of RDC mental disorder in primary care. *International Journal of Mental Health, 8*, 6–15.

Holden, C. (1986). Depression research advances, treatment lags. *Science, 233*, 723–726.

Hollingshead, A. B., & Redlich, F. C. (1953). Social stratification and psychiatric disorders. *American Sociological Review, 18*, 163–169.

Hollingshead, A. B., & Redlich, F. C. (1958). *Social class and mental illness: A community study.* New York: John Wiley & Sons.

Hollister, L. D. (1980). A look at the issues: Use of minor tranquilizers. *Psychosomatics, 21*, 4–6.

Holmes, T., & Rahe, R. (1967). The social readjustment scale. *Journal of Psychosomatic Research, 11,* 213–218.
Homans, G. C. (1961). *Social behavior: Its elementary forms* (rev. ed.). New York: Harcourt Brace Jovanovich.
Hoover Commission. (1955). *Task force report on federal medical services.* Washington, DC: U.S. Government Printing Office.
Hope, M., & Young, J. (1986). *The face of homelessness.* Lexington, MA: D. C. Heath.
Hornblower, M. (1988). Gray power. *Time,* January 4, 36–37.
Huffine, C. L., & Clausen, J. A. (1979). Madness and work: Short- and long-term effects of mental illness on occupational careers. *Social Forces, 57,* 1049–1062.
Hurh, W. M., & Kim, K. C. (1987). *Korean immigrants in the Chicago area: A sociological study of migration and mental health.* Interim Report to NIMH. Macomb: Western Illinois University.
Hurh, W. M., & Kim, K. C. (1990). Adaptation stages and mental health of Korean male immigrants in the United States. *International Migration Review, 24,* 456–479.
Hutchison, J. (1991). What crack does to babies. *American Educator,* (Spring), 31–32.
Imber, S. E., Nash, E. H., Jr., & Stone, A. R. (1955). Social class and duration of treatment. *Journal of Clinical Psychology, 11,* 281–286.
Institute of Medicine. (1988). *Homelessness, health and human needs.* Washington, DC: National Academy Press.
Ishiyama, F. (1986). Morita therapy. *Psychotherapy, 23,* 375–380.
Jacquet, C. H., Jr. (1987). *Yearbook of American and Canadian churches.* Nashville: Abingdon.
James, B., & Nasjleti, M. (1983). *Treating sexually abused children and their families.* Berkeley, CA: Consulting Psychologists Press.
Jarvis, E. (1850). On the comparative liability of males and females to insanity, and their comparative curability and mortality when insane. *American Journal of Insanity, 7,* 142–171.
Jefferson, L. (1964). I am crazy wild this minute: How can I learn to think straight. In B. Kaplan (Ed.), *The inner world of mental illness* (pp. 3–42). New York: Harper & Row.
Jeffery, C. R. (1990). *Criminology.* Englewood Cliffs, NJ: Prentice Hall.
Jellinek, E. M. (1960). *The disease of alcoholism.* Highland Park, NJ: Hillhouse Press.
Johnson, A. B. (1990). *Out of bedlam: The truth about deinstitutionalization.* New York: Basic Books.
Johnston, J. R., Gonzalez, R., & Campbell, L. E. G. (1987). Ongoing post-divorce conflict and child disturbance. *Journal of Abnormal Child Psychology, 15,* 493–509.
Jones, E. E., & Davis, K. E. (1965). From acts to dispositions: The attributional process in person perception. In L. Berkowitz (Ed.), *Advances in experimental social psychology* (pp. 220–266, vol. 2). New York: Academic Press.
Julian, R. M. (1985). *A primer of drug action.* New York: W. H. Freeman.
Justice, B., & Justice, R. (1979). *The broken taboo: Sex in the family.* New York: Human Sciences Press.

Kadushin, C. (1969). *Why people go to psychiatrists*. New York: Atherton Press.
Kakar, S. (1982). *Shamans, mystics and doctors*. Boston: Beacon Press.
Kandel, D. (1980). Drug and drinking behavior among youth. *Annual Review of Sociology, 6,* 235–285.
Kaplan, H. I., & Sadock, B. J. (1988). *Synopsis of psychiatry: Behavioral sciences, clinical psychiatry* (5th Ed.). Baltimore: Williams and Wilkins.
Kaplan, H. S. (1975). *The illustrated manual of sex therapy*. New York: Quadrangle/New York Times Book Co.
Katon, W., Ries, R. K., & Kleinman, A. (1984). The prevalance of somatization in primary care. *Comprehensive Psychiatry, 25,* 208–215.
Katon, W., Vitaliano, P. P., Russo, J., Jones, M., & Anderson, K. (1987). Panic disorder: Spectrum of severity and somatization. *Journal of Nervous and Mental Disease, 175,* 12–19.
Keilitz, I. (1989). Legal issues in mental health care: Current perspectives. In D. A. Rochefort (Ed.), *Handbook on mental health policy in the United States* (pp. 363–384). New York: Greenwood Press.
Kelly, H. H. (1983). The process of causal attribution. *American Psychologist, 28,* 107–128.
Kempe, R., & Kempe, C. (1978). *Child abuse*. London: Fontana.
Kemper, T. (1981). Social constructionist and positivist approaches to sociology of emotions. *American Journal of Sociology, 87,* 336–362.
Kephart, W. M., & Jedlicka, D. (1991). *The family, society, and the individual* (7th ed.). New York: HarperCollins.
Kermis, M. D. (1986). *Mental health in later life*. Boston: James and Bartlett Publishers.
Kessler, R. C. (1979). Stress, social status, and psychological distress. *Journal of Health and Social Behavior, 20,* 259–272.
Kessler, R. C., & Essex, M. (1982). Marital status and depression: The importance of coping resources. *Social Forces, 61,* 484–507.
Kessler, R. C., & McRae, J. A. (1981). Trends in the relationship between sex and psychological distress—1957–1976. *American Sociological Review, 46,* 443–452.
Kessler, R. C., & McRae, J. A. (1984). A note on the relationship of sex and marital status to psychological distress. *Research in Community and Mental Health, 4,* 109–130.
Kety, S. S. (1974). From rationalization to reason. *American Journal of Psychiatry, 131,* 957–963.
Kety, S. S. (1976). Studies designed to disentangle genetic and environmental variables in schizophrenia: Some epistemological questions and answers. *American Journal of Psychiatry, 133,* 1134–1137.
Kety, S. S. (1983). Mental illness in the biological and adoptive relatives of schizophrenic adoptees: Findings relevant to genetic and environmental factors in etiology. *American Journal of Psychiatry, 140,* 720–727.
Khantzian, E. J. (1985). The self-medication hypothesis of addictive disorders: Focus on heroin and cocaine dependence. *American Journal of Pyschiatry, 142,* 1259–1264.
Kiesler, C. A., & Sibulkin, A. E. (1987). *Mental hospitalization: Myths and facts about a national crisis*. Newbury Park, CA: Sage.

Kiev, A. (Ed.). (1964). *Magic, faith, and healing.* New York: Free Press.
Kiev, A. (1972). *Transcultural psychiatry.* New York: Free Press.
Kinsey, A. C., Pomeroy, W. B., & Martin, C. E. (1948). *Sexual behavior in the human male.* Philadelphia: Saunders.
Kinsey, A. C., Pomeroy, W. B., Martin, C. E., & Gebhard, P. H. (1953). *Sexual behavior in the human female.* Philadelphia: Saunders.
Kinzie, J. D. (1985). Overview of clinical issues in the treatment of Southeast Asian refugees. In T. C. Owan (Ed.), *Southeast Asian mental health* (pp. 113–136). DHHS Pub. No. (ADM) 85-1399. Rockville, MD: National Institute of Mental Health.
Kitano, H. H. L. (1969). Japanese American mental illness. In S. C. Plog & R. B. Edgerton (Eds.), *Changing perspectives in mental illness* (pp. 256–284). New York: Holt, Rinehart and Winston.
Kitano, H. H. L., & Daniels, R. (1988). *Asian Americans.* Englewood Cliffs, NJ: Prentice Hall.
Kleinman, A. (1988). *Rethinking psychiatry: From cultural category to personal experience.* New York: Free Press.
Kleinman, A., & Good, B. (Eds.). (1985). *Culture and depression.* Berkeley: University of California Press.
Klerman, G. L., & Weissman, M. M. (1980). Depressions among women: Their nature and causes. In M. Guttentag, S. Salasin, & D. Belle (Eds.), *The mental health of women* (pp. 160–186). New York: Academic Press.
Kline, M., Johnston, J. R., & Tschann, J. M. (1991). The long shadow of marital conflict: A model of children's postdivorce adjustment. *Journal of Marriage and Family, 53,* 297–309.
Kline, N. S. (1954). Use of *Rauwolfia* serpentina in neuropsychiatric conditions. *Annals of New York Academy of Science, 54,* 107–132.
Komarovsky, M. (1976). *Dilemmas of masculinity: A study of college youth.* New York: W. W. Norton.
Kotulak, R. (1989). Inside the brain. *Chicago Tribune* (special series, May 8–15), 1–20.
Kreisman, D. E., & Joy, V. D. (1974). Family response to the mental illness of a relative: A review of the literature. *Schizophrenia Bulletin, 10,* 34–57.
Krech, D. R. C., & Ballachey, R. (1962). *Individual in society: A textbook of social psychology.* New York: McGraw-Hill.
Langer, E. (1989). Minding matters: The consequences of mindlessness/mindfulness. In L. Berkowitz (Ed.), *Advances in experimental social psychology* (pp. 137–168). New York: Academic Press.
Larson, D. B., Pattison, E. M., Blazer, D. G., Omran, A. R., & Kaplan, B. H. (1986). Systematic analysis of religious variables in four major psychiatric journals, 1978–1982. *American Journal of Psychiatry, 143,* 329–334.
Lebra, W. (Ed.). (1976). Culture-bound syndromes, ethnopsychiatry and alternate therapies. *Mental Health Research in Asia and the Pacific—4.* Honolulu: University Press of Hawaii.
Leerhsen, C., Lewis, S. D., Pomper, S., Davenport, L., & Nelson, M. (1985). Reading, writing and divorce. *Newsweek,* May 13, 74.

Leerhsen, C., Lewis, S. D., Pomper, S., Davenport, L., & Nelson, M. (1990). Unite and conquer. *Newsweek*, February 5, 50–55.

Lehman, A. C., & Myers, J. E. (1989). *Magic, witchcraft, and religion.* Mountain View, CA: Mayfield Publishing Co.

Leff, J., & Vaughn, C. (1985). *Expressed emotion in families.* New York: Guilford Press.

Lemert, E. M. (1951). *Social pathology.* New York: McGraw-Hill.

Lemert, E. M. (1967). *Human deviance: Social problems and social control.* Englewood Cliffs, NJ: Prentice Hall.

Lemkau, P. V., & Crocetti, G. M. (1962). An urban population's opinion and knowledge about mental illness. *American Journal of Psychiatry, 118,* 692–700.

Lerner, M. (1989). The fire of "Ice." *Newsweek,* November 6, 37–39.

Levin, J., & Levin, W. C. (1980). *Ageism: Prejudice and discrimination against the elderly.* Belmont, CA: Wadsworth.

Levine, D. N., Carter, E. B., & Gorman, E. M. (1976). Simmel's influence on sociology—I. *American Journal of Sociology, 81,* 813–845.

Levine, E. M. (1981). Middle class family decline. *Society,* January, 78.

Levy, L., & Rowitz, L. (1973). *The ecology of mental disorders.* New York: Behavioral Publications.

Lidz, T. (1972). The influence of family studies on the treatment of schizophrenia. In C. J. Sager & H. S. Kaplan (Eds.), *Progress in group and family therapy* (pp. 616–635). New York: Brunner/Mazel.

Lidz, T., & Fleck, S. (1985). *Schizophrenia and the family* (2nd ed.). New York: International University Press.

Liem, R., & Liem, J. (1978). Social class and mental illness reconsidered: The role of economic stress and social support. *Journal of Health and Social Behavior, 19,* 139–156.

Link, B. G. (1982). Mental patient status, work, and income: An examination of psychiatric label. *American Sociological Review, 47,* 202–215.

Link, B. G., & Cullen, F. T. (1986). Contact with the mentally ill and perceptions of how dangerous they are. *Journal of Health and Social Behavior, 27,* 289–303.

Link, B. G., Cullen, F. T., Frank, J., & Wozniak, J. F. (1987). The social rejection of former mental patients: Understanding why labels matter. *American Journal of Sociology, 92* (May), 1461–1500.

Link, B. G., & Dohrenwend, B. P. (1989). The epidemiology of mental disorders. In H. E. Freeman & S. Levine (Eds.), *Handbook of medical sociology* (pp. 102–127). Englewood Cliffs, NJ: Prentice Hall.

Lips, H. M. (1988). *Sex and gender.* Mountain View, CA: Mayfield Publishing Co.

Lombroso, C. (1968). *Crime: Its causes and remedies.* Montclair, NJ: Patterson Smith. (Original work published 1911)

Loring, B., & Powell, B. (1988). Gender, race, and DSM-III: A study of the objectivity of psychiatric diagnostic behavior. *Journal of Health and Social Behavior, 29,* 1–22.

Los Angeles Times. (1988). Suicide rates are higher among gays and lesbians. August 23, 11A.

Luce, C. B. (1975). Refugees and guilt. *New York Times,* May 11, E19.

Lund, D. S. (1990). Psychiatry charged with ignoring patient's religious beliefs. *The Psychiatric Times, 7,* 24–25.
Maisch, H. (1972). *Incest.* New York: Stein & Day.
Malgady, R. G., Rogler, L. H., Costantino, G. (1988). Ethnocultural and linguistic bias in mental health evaluation of Hispanics. *American Psychologist, 42,* 228–234.
Mann, J. M. (1989). Global AIDS in the 1990s. *Chicago Medicine, 92,* 12–17.
Manning, P. K., & Zucker, M. (1976). *Sociology of mental health and illness.* Indianapolis: Bobbs-Merrill.
Marcuse, P. (1987). Why are they homeless? *The Nation,* April 4, 426–429.
Marlatt, G. A., Demming, B., & Reid, J. B. (1973). Loss of control drinking in alcoholics: An experimental analogue. *Journal of Abnormal Psychology, 81,* 223–241.
Maretzki, T. W. (1981). Culture and psychopathology in Indonesia. *Transcultural Psychiatric Research Review, 18,* 237–256.
Masson, J. M. (1990). *Final analysis: The making and unmaking of a psychoanalyst.* New York: Addison-Wesley.
Masters, W. H., & Johnson, V. E. (1966). *Human sexual response.* Boston: Little, Brown.
Masters, W. H., & Johnson, V. E. (1970). *Human sexual inadequacy.* Boston: Little, Brown.
Masters, W. H., & Johnson, V. E. (1975). *The pleasure bond: A new look at sexuality and commitment.* Boston: Little, Brown.
Masters, W. H., Johnson, V. E., & Kolodny, R. C. (1986). *Sex and human loving.* Boston: Little, Brown.
Mathews, T., & Springen, K. (1992). Secrets of a serial killer. *Newsweek,* February 3, 43–49.
Maton, K. I. (1989). Community settings as buffers of life stress? Highly supportive churches, mutual help groups, and senior centers. *American Journal of Community Psychology, 17,* 203–232.
Matza, D. (1969). *Becoming deviant.* New York: Prentice Hall.
May, P. A. (1982). Contemporary crimes and the American Indian: A Survey and analysis of literature. *Plains Anthropologist, 27,* 225–238.
McCall, G. J., & Simmons, J. L. (1978). *Identities and interactions.* New York: Free Press.
McCheney, K. Y. (1987). Homeless families: How they got that way. *Society, 36,* 4.
McLanahan, S. (1989, August). The two faces of divorce: Women's and children's interests. Paper presented at the Annual Meeting of the American Sociological Association. San Francisco.
Mechanic, D. (1975). Sociocultural and psychological factors affecting personal responses to psychological disorder. *Journal of Health and Social Behavior, 16,* 393–404.
Mechanic, D. (1989). *Mental health and social policy.* Englewood Cliffs, NJ: Prentice Hall.
Mechanic, D., & Volkart, E. H. (1960). Illness behavior and medical diagnosis. *Journal of Health and Human Behavior, 1,* 86–92.

Mednick, S. A. (1978). Berkson's fallacy and high-risk research. In L. C. Wynne, R. L. Cromwell, & S. Matthysse (Eds.), *The nature of schizophrenia: New approaches to research and treatment* (pp. 442–452). New York: John Wiley & Sons.
Melekian, B. (1990). Police and the homeless. *Law Enforcement Bulletin, 59*, 1–7.
Menaghan, E. G., & Lieberman, M. A. (1986). Changes in depression following divorce. *Journal of Marriage and Family, 48*, 319–328.
Mendel, W. M. (1968). The non-specifics of psychotherapy. *International Journal of Psychiatry, 5*, 400–402.
Menninger, K. (1963). *The vital balance: The life process in mental health and illness.* New York: Viking.
Merton, R. K. (1968). *Social theory and social structure.* New York: Free Press.
Meyer, J. M. (1968). Collective disturbances and staff organization on psychiatric wards: A formalization. *Sociometry, 31*, 180–199.
Miller, A., Rogers, P., & Haessly, L. (1991). Serial-murder aftershocks. *Newsweek*, August 12, 28–29.
Miller, W. R., & Hester, R. K. (1980). Treating the problem drinker: Modern approaches. In W. R. Miller (Ed.), *The addictive behaviors* (pp. 204–221). New York: Pergamon.
Mills, J. (1987). *The underground empire: Where crime and governments embrace.* New York: Dell.
Money, J., & Tucker, P. (1975). *Sexual signatures: On being man or woman.* Boston: Little, Brown.
Moore, J., & Pachon, H. (1985). *Hispanics in the United States.* Englewood Cliffs, NJ: Prentice Hall.
Moore, M. S. (1980). Legal conceptions of mental illness. In B. A. Brody & H. T. Engelhardt (Eds.), *Mental illness: Law and public policy* (pp. 25–69). Boston: D. Reidel Publishing Co.
Morganthau, T., Greenberg, N. F., Murr, A., Miller, M., & Raine, G. (1986). Crack and crime. *Newsweek*, June 16, 16–22.
Morganthau, T., Mabry, M., Genao, L., & Washington, F. (1991). Race on campus: Failing the test. *Newsweek*, May 6, 26–27.
Mortimer, J., & Borman, K. M. (Eds.). (1988). *Work experience and psychological development through the life span.* Boulder, CO: Westview Press.
Mulvey, A., & Dohrenwend, B. S. (1984). The relation of stressful life events to gender. In A. U. Rickel, M. Gerrard, & I. Iscoe (Eds.) *Social and psychological problems of women.* Washington, DC: Hemisphere.
Munakata, T. (1989). The socio-cultural significance of the diagnostic label "nuerasthenia" in Japan's mental health care system. *Culture, Medicine and Psychiatry, 13*, 203–213.
Murdock, G. P. (1949). *Social structure.* New York: Macmillan.
Murphy, J. M. (1976). Psychiatric labeling in cross-cultural perspective. *Science, 191*, 1019–1028.
Musto, D. F., (1988). *The American disease: Origins of narcotics control* (rev. ed.). New York: Oxford University Press.

Myers, J. K., Weissman, M. M., Tischler, G. L., Holzer, C. E., Leaf, P. J., & Stoltzman, R. (1984). Six-month prevalence of psychiatric disorders in three communities: 1980 to 1982. *Archives of General Psychiatry, 41*, 959–967.

National Center for Health Statistics, C. Nelson. (1988). *Office visits to neurologists—1985: Advanced data from vital and health statistics.* No. 158. DHHS Pub. No. (PHS) 88-1250. Hyattsville, MD: Public Health Service.

National Coalition for the Homeless. (1988). *Over the edge: Homeless families and the welfare system.* Washington, DC: National Coalition for the Homeless.

National Institute on Alcohol Abuse and Alcoholism. (1985). *Report.* Washington, DC: U.S. Government Printing Office.

National Institute on Drug Abuse (NIDA). (1985). *Cocaine use in America: Epidemiological and clinical perspectives.* Research monograph 61. Rockville, MD: National Institute on Drug Abuse.

National Institute on Drug Abuse (NIDA). (1986). *Highlights of the 1985 National Household Survey on Drug Abuse.* Rockville, MD: National Institute on Drug Abuse.

National Institute on Drug Abuse. (1989). *American current illicit drug use drops 37 percent.* NIDA, Notes 4.

National Institute of Mental Health. (1985a). *The 14 worst myths about recovered mental patients.* Rockville, MD: Department of Health and Human Services.

National Institute of Mental Health. (1985b). *Obsessive-compulsive disorders.* Washington, DC: U.S. Government Printing Office.

National Institute of Mental Health. (1986). Characteristics of admissions to the inpatient services of state and county mental hospitals, United States, 1980. *Mental Health Statistical Note.* No. 177. Washington, DC: Department of Health and Human Services.

National Institute of Mental Health. (1987). *Special report: Schizophrenia.* Rockville, MD: U.S. Department of Health and Human Services, Public Health Services.

National Institute of Mental Health. (1988). *Mood disorders: Pharmacological prevention of recurrences.* (Consensus Development Conference, Vol. 5, No. 4), Washington, DC: U.S. Government Printing Office.

National Institute of Mental Health. (1989). *Panic disorder in the medical setting.* By W. Katon. DHHS Pub. No. (ADM) 89-1629. Washington, DC: Superintendent of Documents, U.S. Government Printing Office.

National Institute of Mental Health. (1990a). *Mental Health, United States, 1990.* R. W. Manderscheid & M. A. Sonnenschein (Eds.), DHHS Pub. No. (ADM) 90-1708. Washington, DC: U.S. Government Printing Office.

National Institute of Mental Health. (1990b). *National Plan for Research on Child and Adolescent Mental Disorders* (A Report to the U.S. Congress). DHHS Pub. No. (ADM) 90-1683. Rockville, MD: National Institute of Mental Health.

Neighbors, H. W., & Howard, C. S. (1987). Sex differences in professional health seeking among adult black Americans. *American Journal of Community Psychology, 15*, 403–416.

Neki, J. S. (1973). Psychiatry in Southeast Asia. *British Journal of Psychiatry, 123*, 257–269.

Nelson, C. (1988). *Office visits to neurologists—1985: Advance data from vital and health statistics*. No. 158. Hyattsville, MD: U.S. Department of Health and Human Services, Public Health Service.
Neugebauer, R., Dohrenwend, B. P., & Dohrenwend, B. (1980). Formulation of hypotheses about the true prevalence of functional psychiatric disorders among adults in the United States. In B. P. Dohrenwend, B. S. Dohrenwend, M. S. Gould, B. G. Link, R. Neugebauer, & R. Wunsch–Hitzig (Eds.), *Mental health in the United States: Epidemiological estimates* (pp. 45–94). New York: Praeger.
Newmann, J. P. (1984). Sex differences in symptoms of depression: Clinical disorder or normal distress? *Journal of Health and Social Behavior, 25*, 136–159.
Newsweek. (1990). Doctors of philosophy. January 15, 45.
Nielson, A. C., & Williams, T. A. (1980). Depression in ambulatory medical patients. *Archives of General Psychiatry, 37*, 999–1004.
Norton, A. J., & Glick, P. C. (1986). One parent families: A social and economic profile. *Family Relations, 35*, 9–17.
Ohio Department of Mental Health. (1984). *Homeless in Ohio: A study of people in need*. Columbus: Ohio Department of Mental Health.
Oldham, S., Farnill, D., & Ball, I. (1982). Sex role identity of female homosexuals. *Journal of Homosexuality, 8*, 41–46.
Oliven, J. (1974). *Clinical sexuality* (3rd ed.). Philadelphia: Lippincott.
Orleans, C. T., George, L. K., & Houpt, J. L. (1985). How primary physicians treat psychiatric disorders: A national survey of family practitioners. *Archives of General Psychiatry, 42*, 52–57.
Owan, T. C. (1985). *Southeast Asian mental health*. Rockville, MD: National Institute of Mental Health.
Oyebola, D. D. D. (1980). Traditional medicine and its practitioners among the Yoruba of Nigeria. *Social Science and Medicine, 14A*, 23–29.
Padgett, D. K., & Struening, E. L. (1991). Influence of substance use and mental disorders on emergency room use by homeless adults. *Hospital and Community Psychiatry, 42*, 834–837.
Page, L. (1985). Mental illness defense called baseless. *Peoria Journal Star*, section A, November 23, 16.
Papolos, D. F., & Papolos, J. (1988). *Overcoming depression*. New York: Harper & Row.
Parkes, C. M., (1972). *Bereavement*. New York: International University Press.
Parrillo, V. N. (1990). *Strangers to these shores* (3rd ed.). New York: Macmillan.
Parsons, T. (1951). *The social system*. New York: Free Press.
Patterson, C. J., Kupersmidt, J. B., & Vaden, N. A. (1990). Income level, gender, ethnicity and household composition as predictors of children's school-based competence. *Child Development, 61*, 485–494.
Pearlin, L. I., & Johnson, J. S. (1977). Marital status, life strains and depression. *American Sociological Review, 42*, 704–715.
Peele, S. (1985). *The meaning of addiction*. Lexington, MA: Lexington Books.
Peluso, E., & Peluso, L. S. (Eds.). (1988). *Women and drugs: Getting hooked, getting clean*. Minneapolis: CompCare Publications.

Peoria Journal Star. (1991). Cocaine babies. January 6, D1–D2.
Perkins, R. M. (1969). *Perkins on criminal law.* Mineola, NY: The Foundation Press.
Perls, F. (1969). *Gestalt therapy verbatim.* Moab, UT: Real People Press.
Peterson, J. L., & Zill, N. (1986). Marital disruption, parent–child relationships, and behavior problems in children. *Journal of Marriage and Family, 48,* 295–307.
Peterson, K. C., Prout, M. F., & Schwarz, R. A. (1990). *Post traumatic stress disorder—a clinical guide.* New York: Plenum.
Peterson, L. A., & Roy, A. (1985). Religiosity, anxiety, and meaning and purpose: Religion's consequences on psychological well-being. *Review of Religious Research, 27,* 49–62.
Peterson, W. P. (1946). *The Hippocratic wisdom.* Springfield, IL: Charles C. Thomas.
Phillips, D. L. (1963). Rejection: A possible consequence of seeking help for mental disorders. *American Sociological Review, 28,* 963–972.
Pidano, A. E., & Tennen, H. (1985). Transient depressive experiences and their relationship to gender and sex-role orientation. *Sex Roles, 12,* 97–110.
Piers, G., & Singer, M. B. (1971). *Shame and guilt.* New York: W. W. Norton.
Pigache, P. (1973). The witch doctor as a psychotherapist—science or suggestion? *World Medicine,* May 16, 45–47.
Pollner, M. (1989). Devine relations, social relations, and well being. *Journal of Health and Social Behavior, 30,* 92–104.
Pope, H. G., (1983). Distinguishing bipolar disorders from schizophrenia in clinical practice. *Hospital and Community Psychiatry, 34,* 322–328.
Pope, H. G., Janas, J. M., & Lipinski, J. F. (1983). Heretibility of schizophrenia. *American Journal of Psychiatry, 140,* 132–133.
Porkert, M. (1979). Chinese medicine: A traditional healing science. In D. S. Sobel (Ed.), *Ways of health: holistic approaches to ancient and contemporary medicine* (pp. 147–177). New York: Harcourt Brace Jovanovich.
President's Commission on Organized Crime. (1986). *America's habit: Drug abuse, drug trafficking, and organized crime.* Washington, DC: U.S. Government Printing Office.
Press, A., & McDaniel, A. (1986). Is he sane enough to die. *Newsweek,* July 7, 63.
Price, S. J. (1990). Divorce. In D. H. Olson & M. K. Hansen (Eds.), *Report to the National Council on Family Relations* (pp. 221–232). Minneapolis: National Council on Family Relations.
Psychiatric News. (1990). Expanded Amish study weakens claim for genetic marker for bipolar disorder. 25 (March), 2.
Psychiatric Times. (1990). NIMH researchers contend psychotherapy effectiveness measurable by clinical trials. 7 (January), 32–33.
Purvis, A. (1990). Unlocking the pill bottles: Psychologists vie for the right to prescribe drugs. *Time,* December 17, 95.
Rabkin, J. G. (1974). Public attitudes toward mental illness: A review of literature. *Schizophrenia Bulletin, 10,* 9–33.
Rappaport, H. (1977). The tenacity of folk psychiatry: A functional interpretation. *Social Psychiatry, 12,* 127–132.
Raymond, M. E., Slaby, A. E., & Lieb, J. (1975). Familial responses to mental illness. *Social Casework, 56,* 492–498.

Regier, D., Goldberg, I. D, & Taube, C. H. (1978). The de facto U.S. mental health service system. *Archives of General Psychiatry, 35,* 685–693.

Regier, D. A., Boyd, J. H., Rae, D. S., Myers, J. K., Kramer, M., Robbins, L. N., George, L. K., Karno, M., & Locke, B. Z. (1988). One-month prevalence of mental disorders in the United States: Based on five epidemiologic catchment area sites. *Archives of General Psychiatry, 45,* 685–693.

Reinisch, J. M., & Beasley, R. (1990). *What you must know to be sexually literate.* New York: St. Martin's Press.

Reynolds, B. (1989). This illness is so common but so misunderstood. *USA Today.* October 5, 9A.

Reynolds, D. (1981). Naikan psychotherapy. In R. J. Corsini (Ed.), *Handbook of innovative psychotherapies* (pp. 544–553). New York: John Wiley & Sons.

Right, J. W. (1989). *The universal almanac 1990.* Kansas City: Universal Press Syndicate.

Roberts, B. H., & Myers, J. K. (1954). Religion, national origin, immigration, and mental illness. *American Journal of Psychiatry, 110,* 758–762.

Robbins, L. N. (1966). *Deviant children grown up.* Baltimore, MD: Williams & Wilkins.

Robbins, L. N., Helzer, J. E, Weissman, M. M., Orvaschel, H., Gruenberg, E., Burke, J., & Regier, D. A. (1984). Lifetime prevalence of specific psychiatric disorders in three sites. *Archives of General Psychiatry, 41,* 949–958.

Robinson, I. E., & Jedlicka, D. (1982). Change in sexual attitudes and behavior of college students from 1965 to 1980: A research note. *Journal of Marriage and Family, 44,* 237–240.

Rodeheaver, D., & Datan, N. (1988). The challenge of double jeopardy: Toward a mental health agenda for aging women. *American Psychologist, 43,* 648–656.

Roff, J. D., & Knight, R. (1981). Family characteristics, childhood symptoms, and adult outcome in schizophrenia. *Journal of Abnormal Psychology, 90,* 510–520.

Rogers, C. (1951). *Client-centered therapy.* Boston: Houghton Mifflin.

Rogler, L. H. (1989). The meaning of culturally sensitive research in mental health. *American Journal of Psychiatry, 146,* 296–303.

Ronson, G. (1986). Alienation of ethnic minority students at a predominantly white university. *Journal of Higher Education, 57,* 58–77.

Ropers, R. H. (1988). *The invisible homeless: A new urban ecology.* New York: Human Sciences Press.

Rosen, G. (1963). Social attitudes to irrationality and madness in 17th and 18th century Europe. *Journal of History of Medicine and Allied Sciences, 18,* 220–240.

Rosenberg, M. (1990). Reflexivity and emotions. *Social Psychology Quarterly, 53,* 3–12.

Rosenhan, D. (1973). On being insane places. *Science, 179,* 250–258.

Rosenthal, D. (1970). *Genetic theory and abnormal behavior.* New York: McGraw-Hill.

Rosenthal, D., Wender, P. H., Kety, S. S., Weiner, J., & Schulsinger, F. (1971). The adopted-away offspring of schizophrenics. *American Journal of Psychiatry, 128,* 307–311.

Ross, C., Mirowsky, J., & Cockerham, W. C. (1983). Social class, Mexican culture, and fatalism: Their effects on psychological distress. *American Journal of Community Psychology, 11,* 383–399.

Ross, C., Mirowsky, J., & Ulbrich, P. (1983). Distress and the traditional female role: A comparison of Mexicans and Anglos. *American Journal of Sociology, 89,* 670–682.

Rossi, P. H. (1989). *Without shelter: Homeless in the 1980s.* New York: Priority Press Publications.

Rossi, P. H., Wright, J., Fisher, G., & Willis, G. (1987). The urban homeless: Estimating composition and size. *Science, 235,* 1336–1341.

Rossides, D. W. (1990). *Social stratification: The American class system in comparative perspective.* Englewood Cliffs, NJ: Prentice Hall.

Roth, D., Bean, J., Lust, N., Traian, S. (1985). *Homeless in Ohio: A study of people in need.* Columbus: Ohio Department of Mental Health.

Rowe, C. J. (1989). *An outline of psychiatry.* Dubuque, IA: Wm. C. Brown.

Runyan, W. K. (1981). Why did Van Gogh cut off his ear: The problem of alternative explanations in psychobiography. *Journal of Personality and Social Psychology, 40,* 1070–1077.

Russell, C. (1984). New untouchable class in the U.S. found among mentally ill. *Denver Post,* September 13, 20A.

Salholz, E., Clifton, T., Joseph, N., Beachy, L., Rogers, P., Wilson, L., Glick, D., & King, P. (1990) The Future of gay America. *Newsweek,* March 12, 20–25.

Sampson, H., Messinger, S., & Towne, R. (1961). The mental hospital and marital ties. *Social Problems, 9,* 141–155.

Sampson, H., Messinger, S., & Towne, R. (1962). Family processes and becoming a mental patient. *American Journal of Sociology, 68,* 88–96.

Sarbin, T. R., & Mancuso, J. C. (1980). *Schizophrenia: Medical diagnosis or moral verdict.* New York: Pergamon.

Sargent, M. (1986). *Depressive disorders: Treatments bring new hope.* Rockville, MD: National Institute of Mental Health.

Sargent, M. (1989). *Depressive illness: Treatment brings new hope.* DHHS Publication No. (ADM) 89-1491. Rockville, MD: National Institute of Mental Health.

Schaefer, R. T. (1992). *Sociology* (4th ed.). New York: McGraw-Hill.

Schaefer, R. T. (1990). *Racial and ethnic groups* (4th ed.). Glenview, IL: Scott, Foresman.

Schaefer, R. T., Schaefer, S. L. (1975). Reluctant welcome: U.S. responses to South Vietnamese refugees. *New Community, 4,* 366–370.

Scheff, T. J. (1963). Legitimate, transitional, and illigitimate mental patients in a midwestern state. *American Journal of Psychiatry, 120,* 267–269.

Scheff, T. J. (1974). The labeling theory of mental illness. *American Sociological Review, 39,* 444–452.

Scheff, T. J. (1979). *Catharsis in healing, ritual and drama.* Berkeley: University of California Press.

Scheff, T. J. (1984). *Being mentally ill: A sociological theory* (2nd ed.). New York: Aldine.

Schinke, S. P., Schilling, II, R. F., Gilchrist, L. D., Barth, R. P., Bobo, J. K., Timble, J. E., & Cvetkovich, G. T. (1985). Preventing substance abuse with American Indian youth. *Social Casework, 66,* 213–219.

Schreiber, F. R. (1973). *Sybil.* Chicago: Regnery.

Schulberg, H. C., Saul, M., & McClelland, M. (1985). Assessing depression in primary medical and psychiatric practices. *Archives of General Psychiatry, 12,* 1164–1170.
Schwalbe, M. L., & Staples, C. L. (1991). Gender differences in sources of self-esteem. *Social Psychology Quarterly, 54,* 158–168.
Scully, D., & Marolla, J. (1985). "Riding the bull at Gilley's": Convicted rapists describe the rewards of rape. *Social Problems, 32,* 251–263.
Seidman, L. J. (1990). Neuropsychological dysfunction important in schizophrenia. *The Psychiatric Times, 7* (May), 29–31.
Sheehan, D. V. (1983). *The anxiety disease.* New York: Scribner.
Shapiro, D. H. (1980). *Meditation: Self regulation strategy and altered state of consciousness.* New York: Aldine.
Shapiro, D. H. (1982). Overview: Clinical and physiological comparison of meditation with other self-control strategies. *American Journal of Psychiatry, 139,* 267–274.
Shapiro, L. (1987). Advice-givers strike gold. *Newsweek,* June 1, 64–65.
Shapiro, S., Skinner, E. A., Kessler, L. G., Von Korff, M., German, P. S., Tischler, G. L., Leaf, P. J., Cotler, L., & Regier, D. A. (1984). Utilization of health and mental health services: Three epidemiological catchment area sites. *Archives of General Psychiatry, 41,* 971–978.
Sigvardsson, S., van Knorring, A. L., Bohman, M., & Collinger, R. (1984). An adoption study of somatoform disorders. *Archives of General Psychiatry, 41,* 853–856.
Sizemore, C. C., & Pittilo, E. S. (1977). *I'm Eve.* Garden City, NY: Doubleday.
Skinner, B. F. (1971). *Beyond freedom and dignity.* New York: Knopf.
Skinner, B. F. (1974). *About behaviorism.* New York: Knopf.
Smith, R. M. (1986). The plague among us. *Newsweek,* June 16, 23–28.
Snow, D. A., Baker, S. G., Anderson, L., & Martin, M. (1986). The myth of pervasive mental illness among the homeless. *Social Problems, 33,* 407–423.
Snow, D. A., & Anderson, L. (1987.). Identity work among the homeless: The verbal construction and avowal of personal identities. *American Journal of Sociology, 92,* 1336–1371.
Sobel R., & Ingalls, A. (1964). Resistance to treatment: Explorations of the patient's sick role. *American Journal of Psychotherapy, 18,* 562–573.
Sorenson, S. B., & Golding, J. M. (1988). Suicide ideation and attempts in Hispanics and Non-Hispanic whites: Demographic and psychiatric issue. *Suicide and Life Threatening Behavior, 18,* 205–212.
Spitzer, S. P., & Denzin, N. K. (1968). *The mental patient: Studies in the sociology of deviance.* New York: McGraw-Hill.
Srole, L. (1972). Urbanization and mental health: Some reformulations. *American Scientist, 20,* 576–583.
Srole, L. (1975). Measurements and classifications in socio-psychiatric epidemiology: Midtown Manhattan study I (1954) and Midtown Manhattan study II (1974). *Journal of Health and Social Behavior, 16,* 347–364.
Srole, L., & Langner, T. S. (1969). Protestant, Catholic, and Jew: Comparative psychopathology. In S. C. Plog & R. B. Edgerton (Eds.), *Changing perspectives in mental illness* (pp. 422–440). New York: Holt, Rinehart and Winston.

Srole, L., Langner, T. S., Michael, S. T., Opler, M. K., & Rennie T. A. C. (1962). *Mental health in the metropolis: The Midtown Manhattan study.* New York: McGraw-Hill.
Staines, G. L., Pleck, J. H., Shepard, L. J., & O'Connor, P. (1978). Wives' employment status: Yet another look. *Psychology of Women Quarterly, 3*, 90–120.
Stark, E. (1984). The unspeakable family secret. *Pychology Today,* May, 38–46.
Stephens, R. (1987). *Mood-altering drugs.* Beverly Hills, CA: Sage.
Straus, R. (1976). Alcoholism and problem drinking. In R. K. Merton & R. N. Nisbet (Eds.), *Contemporary social problems* (pp. 181–217, 4th ed.). New York: Harcourt Brace Jovanovich.
Sue, S., & Morishima, J. K. (1982). *Mental health of Asian Americans.* San Francisco: Jossey-Bass.
Suinn, R. M. (1984). *Fundamentals of abnormal psychology.* Chicago: Nelson-Hall.
Sullivan, H. S. (1953). *The interpersonal theory of psychiatry.* New York: Norton.
Sutherland, E. H., & Cressey, D. R. (1978). *Criminology* (10th ed.). New York: Lippincott.
Szasz, T. (1970a). *Ideology and insanity.* New York: Anchor Books.
Szasz, T. (1970b). *The manufacture of madness.* New York: Dell.
Szasz, T. (1970c). The psychiatric justice. *American Psychologist, 15,* 113–180.
Szasz, T. (1974). *The myth of mental illness* (rev. ed.). New York: Harper & Row.
Szasz, T. (1987). *Insanity: The idea and its consequences.* New York: John Wiley & Sons.
Tessler, R., & Mechanic, D. (1978). Psychological distress and perceived health status. *Journal of Health and Social Behavior, 19,* 254–262.
Thigpen, C. H., & Cleckley, H. M. (1957). *Three faces of Eve.* New York: McGraw-Hill.
Thio, A. (1988). *Deviant behavior.* New York: Harper & Row.
Thoits, P. A. (1985). Self-labeling processes in mental illness: The role of emotional deviance. *American Journal of Sociology, 91,* 221–249.
Thomas, M. E., & Hughes, M. (1986). The continuing significance of race: A study of race, class, and quality of life in America, 1972–1985. *American Sociological Review, 51,* 830–841.
Thomas, W. I. (1923). *The unadjusted girl.* Boston: Little, Brown.
Thorman, G. (1988). *Homeless families.* Springfield, IL: Charles C. Thomas.
Torrey, E. F. (1986). *Witch doctors and psychiatrists.* New York: Harper & Row.
Torrey, E. F. (1988a). *Nowhere to go: The tragic odyssey of the homeless mentally ill.* New York: Harper & Row.
Torrey, E. F. (1988b). *Surviving schizophrenia.* New York: Harper & Row.
Tower, C. C. (1989). *Understanding child abuse and neglect.* Boston: Allyn and Bacon.
Townsend, J. M. (1976). Self-concept and institutionalization of mental patients: An overview and critique. *Journal of Health and Social Behavior, 17,* 263–271.
Tschann, J. M., Johnston, J. R., Kline, M., & Wallerstein, J. (1989). Family process and child functioning during divorce. *Journal of Marriage and Family, 51,* 431–444.
Tseng, W. S. (1973). The development of psychiatric concepts in traditional Chinese medicine. *Archives of General Psychiatry 29,* 569–575.

Turque, B., & Underwood, A. (1990). Judgment for the wilders. *Newsweek*, August 27, 39.

Troiden, R. R. (1988). *Gay and lesbian identity: A sociological analysis*. Dix Hills, NY: General Hall.

Tung, T. M. (1980). *Indochinese patients: Cultural aspects of medical and psychiatric care for Indochinese refugees*. Washington, DC: Action for South-East Asians.

Tung, T. M. (1985). Psychiatric care for Southeast Asians: How different is different. In T. C. Owan (Ed.), *Southeast Asian mental health* (pp. 5–40). DHHS Pub. No. (ADM) 85-1399. Rockville, MD: National Institute of Mental Health.

Turner, R. (1978). *The structure of sociological theory*. Homewood, IL: Dorsey Press.

Turner, R. J., & Gartrell, J. W. (1978). Social factors in psychiatric outcome: Toward the resolution of interpretive controversies. *American Sociological Review, 43*, 368–382.

Turner, V. W. (1972). An Ndembu doctor in practice. In A. Kiev (Ed.), *Magic, faith and religion* (pp. 437–444). New York: Free Press.

Turner, V. W. (1973). Symbols in African ritual. *Science, 179*, 1100–1105.

Umberson, D. (1987). Family status and health behaviors: Social control as a dimension of social integration. *Journal of Health and Social Behavior, 28*, 306–319.

U.S. Department of Health and Human Services (Public Health Service: Alcohol, Drug Abuse, and Mental Health Administration). (1988). *The homeless mentally ill: Service needs of the population*. Rockville, MD: National Institute of Mental Health.

U.S. Department of Health and Human Services. (1989). *National Household Survey on Drug Abuse—1988*. Washington, DC: U.S. Government Printing Office.

U.S. Department of Health and Human Services. (1991). *Births, marriages, divorces, and deaths for January 1991*. Monthly Vital Statistics Report, Vol. 40, No. 1: 15.

U.S. General Accounting Office. (1987). *Report to the Congress—Homelessness implementation of food and shelter programs under the McKinney Act*. Washington, DC: U.S. General Accounting Office.

U.S. House of Representatives, Committee on Ways and Means. (1989). *Background material and data on programs within the jurisdiction of the Committee on Ways and Means*. Washington, DC: U.S. Government Printing Office.

U.S. Senate Subcommittee on Aging. (1984). *Aging America: Trends and projections*. Washington, DC: U.S. Government Printing Office.

Vaillant, G. (1983). *The natural history of alcoholism*. Cambridge, MA: Harvard University Press.

Vanyperen, N. W., & Buunk, B. P. (1991). Sex-role attitudes, social comparison and satisfaction with relationships. *Social Psychology Quarterly, 54*, 169–180.

Verbrugge, L. (1982). Sex differences in legal drug use. *Journal of Social Issues, 38*, 59–76.

Veroff, J., Kulka, R. A., & Douvan, E. (1982). *Mental health in America*. New York: Basic Books.

von Zerssen, D., & Weyerer, S. (1982). Sex differences in rates of mental disorders. *International Journal of Mental Health, 11*, 9–45.

Wallerstein, J. S., & Kelly, J. B. (1980). Effects of divorce on the visiting father-child relationships. *American Journal of Psychiatry, 137,* 1534–1539.

Walsh, R. (1989). Asian psychotherapies. In R. J. Corsini & D. Wedding (Eds.), *Current psychotherapies* (pp. 547–559, 4th ed.). Itasca, IL: F. E. Peacock.

Walsh, R., & Shapiro, D. H. (1983). *Beyond health and normality: Explorations of exceptional psychological well-being.* New York: Van Nostrand Reinhold.

Ward, S., Chapman, K., Cohn, E., White, S., & Williams, K. (1991). Acquaintance rape and the college social scene. *Family Relations, 40,* 65–71.

Warheit, G. J., Holzer, C. E., III, & Avery, S. A. (1975). Race and mental illness: An epidemiological update. *Journal of Health and Social Behavior, 16,* 243–256.

Warheit, G. J., Holzer, C. E., III, Bell, R. A., & Avery, S. A. (1976). Sex, marital status, and mental health: A reappraisal. *Social Forces, 55,* 459–470.

Warren, C. A. B. (1987). *Madwives: Schizophrenic women in the 1950s.* New Brunswick, NJ: Rutgers University Press.

Weber, M. (1958). *Protestant ethic and the spirit of capitalism.* (T. Parsons, Trans.) New York: Scribner (original work published 1904).

Weiss, R. S. (1975). *Marital separation.* New York: Basic Books.

Weiss, R. S. (1979). *Going it alone.* New York: Basic Books.

Weitzman, L. (1985). *The divorce revolution: The unexpected social and economic consequences for women and children in America.* New York: Free Press.

Wender, P. H., Kety, S. S., Rosenthal, S. S., Schulsinger, F., & Ortmann, J. (1986). Psychiatric disorders in the biological and adoptive families of adopted individuals with affective disorders. *Archives of General Psychiatry, 43,* 923–929.

Westermeyer, J., & Winthrop, R. (1979). Folk criteria for the diagnosis of mental illness in rural Laos. *American Journal of Psychiatry, 136,* 755–761.

Wheaton, B. (1985). Models for the stress-buffering functions of coping resources. *Journal of Health and Social Behavior, 26,* 352–364.

Whitam, F. L., & Zent, M. (1984). A Cross-cultural assessment of early cross-gender behavior and familial factors in male homosexuality. *Archives of Sexual Behavior, 13,* 427–439.

Whiting, B. (1989). Suspect to forgo jury trial in rental-agent rape cases. *The Arizona Republic,* March 10, C1, C6.

Whitwell, J. R. (1936). *Historical notes on psychiatry.* London: H. K. Lewis Co.

Wickman, P. M. (1986). Deviance. *Encyclopedic Dictionary of Sociology* (pp. 83–85). Guilford, CT: Dushkin.

Wilber, K., Engler, J., & Brown, D. (Eds.). (1986). *Transformation of consciousness: Conventional and contemplative perspectives on development.* Boston: New Science Library.

Wilkinson, G. S. (1975). Patient-audience, social status, and the social construction of psychiatric disorders: Toward a differential frame of reference hypothesis. *Journal of Health and Social Behavior, 16,* 28–38.

Williams, J. B., & Spitzer, R. L. (1983). The issue of sex bias in DSM-III. *American Psychologist, 38,* 793–798.

Willie, C. V. (1979). *The caste and class controversy.* Bayside, NY: General Hall.

Wilson, R. R. (1986). *Don't panic: Taking control of anxiety attacks.* New York: Harper & Row.

Wilson, W. J. (1980). *The declining significance of race: Blacks and changing American institutions* (2nd ed.). Chicago: Universtiy of Chicago Press.

Witteman, P. A. (1991). Lost in America. *Time,* February 11, 76–77.

Witter, R. A., Stock, W. A., Okun, M. A., & Haring, M. J. (1985). Religion and subjective well-being in adulthood: A quantitative synthesis. *Review of Religious Research, 26,* 332–342.

Wolinsky, F. P. (1980). *The sociology of health.* Boston: Little, Brown.

Wright, J. D. (1989). *Address unknown: The homeless in America.* New York: Aldine de Gruyter.

Wright, L., Schaefer, A. B., & Solomon, G. (1979). *Encyclopedia of pediatric psychology.* Baltimore: University Park Press.

Wynne, L. C., Ryckoff, I. M., Day, J., & Hirsch, S. I. (1958). Psuedo-mutuality in the family relations of schizophrenics. *Psychiatry, 21,* 205–220.

Yalom, I. D. (1980). *Existential psychotherapy.* New York: Basic Books.

Zarrow, S. (1988). 21 hints for outstanding sex. *Prevention,* November, 81–87.

Zilboorg, G. (1941). *A history of medical psychology.* New York: W. W. Norton.

Zinberg, N. E. (1984). *Drug, set, and setting.* New Haven, CT: Yale University Press.

Zung, W. W. K., Macdonald, J., & Zung, E. M. (1988). Prevalence of clinically significant depressive symptoms in black and white patients in family practice settings. *American Journal of Psychiatry, 145,* 882–883.

Index

AARP (American Association of Retired Persons), 308
Abadinsky, H., 181–183
Abbey, A. 202
ABC (American Broadcasting Co.), 302, 318
AIDS (Acquired Immunodeficiency Syndrome), 209
Addams, J., 294
Addiction
  cross-addiction, 162
  medical, 162
  sex, 198
  substance, 162
Adjustment disorder, 61, 126
  definition of, 126
  response to stressors, 127
  types of response, 127
Adler, A., 48
Adler, J., 174
Admissions
  by race, 222
  in county and state hospitals, 11
  inpatient, 223
Adolescents, 242–243
Adoption
  studies of schizophrenia, 66–67
Advice-givers, 326, 344
Affective disorders, 117–121
AFL-CIO, 308

Africa, 18–21
Africanus, C., 37, 41
Age and mental disorders, 241–245
Agoraphobia, 115
Albert the Great, 37
Alcohol
  alcohol web, 169
  alcoholic personality, 169
  abuse, 166–170
  dependence, 168
  its place in social life, 166–167
  use among Irish and Jewish Americans, 169
Alcoholics Anonymous, 171, 198, 332
  twelve-step program, 333
Alcoholism
  explanations, 169
  extent of, 168
Alexander, F. G., 36, 39, 52
Alexander of Tralles, 37
Allport, G., 104
Alter, J., 303–305, 317
Altschuler, L. L., 231
Alzheimer's disease, 65
Amato, P. R., 255–257
American Indian, 227–228
APA (American Psychiatric Association), 13, 201, 314
  committee on women, 76
  on homosexuality, 189

Amish, 337
Amok, 19
Amphetamines, 176–177
  side-effects, 177
Anderson, K., 115, 117
Anderson, L., 215
Anderson, N., 298
Andorfer, J. C., 141
Andreasen, N., 66, 68, 78, 138, 157
Anorgasmia, 208
Anorexia nervosa, 19
Antidepressants, 118
Antipathy drugs, 118
Antipsychotic drugs, 70
Antisocial
  personality disorder, 151
Antonovsky, A., 258
Anxiety, 102
  disorders, 111, 112–115
  medications used for, 113
  types, 102–103
Appleby, L., 281
Aquinas, Thomas, 37
Arabic medicine, 22
Arce, A. A., 304
Arenberg, J. K., 140
Aristotle, 36
Ashton-Jones, E., 262
Asi, Rabbi, 33
Asia, 18–23
Asian Americans, 228–229
  Chinese Americans, 230
  Filipino, 229
  Indochinese, 231–232
  Korean, 232–233
  Japanese, 233
Asian therapies, 347–350
  Morita and Naikan 349–350
  underlying themes, 347–348
Asylums, 42–43, 271
Attributional theory, 90
Autism, 132
Avery, S. A., 223, 250
Avicenna, 37
Avoidant
  personality disorder, 149–150
Ayurveda, 22, 34–36, 70
AZT, 210

Babylonia, 32
Baker, S. G., 215
Balance theory, 34
Ball, I., 190
Barbiturates, 177–178
Barnes, D. M., 157
Bart, P., 244
Basham, A. L., 35
Bassuk, E. L., 304
Bateson, G., 145, 346
Bateson, W., 63
Batra, R., 217
Baur, K., 189
Bean, J., 215
Beasley, R., 190, 196, 207, 211, 212
Becker, H. S., 88, 264, 268
Beckman, J. G., 171
Bedlam, 43
Behaviorists, 50, 91
Bell, A. P., 189
Bell, R. R., 189
Benjamin, L. S., 67
Benzodiazepines, 123
Berg, B., 251
Berger, J., 227
Berger, P., 258
Berk, B. B., 230
Berkowitz, D. (Son of Sam), 148, 264, 317
Bernard, V. W., 275
Berne, E., 342
Bernstein, L. H., 140
Bhakti, 348
Bianchi, K. W. (The Hillside Strangler), 125–126, 136, 147, 317
Bible, 192
Biederman, J., 155
Biochemical
  revolution, 53, 69–73
  therapy, 11
Biogenic, factors
  in personality disorders, 155
Biological
  approach, 2, 50, 54
  biomedical and biophysical, 55–56
  determinants of mental disorder, 62–67
  inheritance, 62

Biological *(cont'd.)*
 viewpoint, 55
Birnbaum, H. J., 201
Black, J. L., 75
Black Americans, 224–226
Blame-the-mama theory, 142
Blanchard, R., 203
Bland, R. C., 157
Blau, P. M., 98
Blazer, D., 213, 260
Bleuler, E., 132
Block, J. H., 255
Bono, A., 125
Borderline personality disorder, 149
Borman, K. M., 262
Bourgeoisie, 95
Bowen, M., 144
Braid, J., 44
Brain pathology, 55–55
Brain-mind
 definitions, 2
 controversies, 2–3
Brazil, 222
Brent, D. A., 26
Bridges, K. W., 114, 122
Broman, C. L., 224
Broverman, I. K., 247
Brown, D., 348
Brown, P., 79, 322
Brown, P. L., 332
Bruce, B. K., 75
Buck, C., 201
Buckner, H. T., 194
Buddha, 34
Buddhism, 34, 233, 347
Bumpass, L., 256
Bundy, T., 147–148
Burgess, A. W., 202
Burgess, E. W., 23
Burnham, M. A., 226
Burns, C., 256
Burt, M. R., 306
Burton, R., 41, 43
Busfield, J., 250
Buss, T. F., 322
Butcher, J. N., 140
Buunk, B. P., 251

Caesar, J., 32
Cahalan, D., 183
Calvin, J. 259–260
Campbell, E. G., 255
Cannon, A., 73
Capitalism, 95
Career of mental patient, 272–275
Carnes, P., 198
Carpenter, W. T., 157
Carson, R. C., 140, 316
Carstairs, G. M., 22
Carter, E. B., 98
Castration anxiety, 104
Caspi, A., 255
Catholics, 260
CBS (Columbia Broadcasting System), 300, 316
Center for Epidemiological Studies, 254
Chapman, K., 202
Character disorders. *See* Personality disorders
Charak, 35
Chemotherapy, 266
Cherlin, A. J., 255
Chesler, P., 38
Chiarugi, V., 44
Chicago study, the, 219
Chicanos, 226–227
Child molesters, 198
Children and mental disorders, 255–257
China, 97, 189
Chinese, 34, 350
 immigrants, 172
Chino, A. F., 245
Chlorpromazine, 70
Christianity, 259–261
Cicero, 36, 41
Clark, M., 179, 210
Class, social, 215–217
 categories of, 216–218
 methods of measuring, 216
 and power, 97–99
 and psychiatric disorders, 218–222
Clausen, J. A., 164, 289–292
Clayton, R. R., 173
Cleary, P. D., 122, 265
Cleckley, H. M., 126

Clemmensen, L. H., 203
CNN (Cable News Network), 11
Cocaine, 173–176
  babies, 174
  effects, 175–176
  extent of use and abuse, 173–176
Cockerham, W. C., 7, 30, 40, 226, 230, 264, 296, 314
Coffignon, W. C., 7
Cognitive
  behavior therapy, 70
  consistency, 91
  dissonance, 92
  theory, 91–93
Cohen, A. K., 6
Cohen, B. E., 306
Cohn, E., 202
Coleman, J. C., 140
Coleman, L., 314
Coles, R., 302
Commitment. *See* Institutionalization
Community mental health (CMH), 294–312
  objectives of, 295
  organization of, 296
  philosophy of, 294
  services act, 295
Compadrazgo, 227
Conceptual approaches, 87
Concordance rate, 66
Conditioning, 90
  classical, 90
  conditioned reflex, 90
Conflict
  perspective, 95–96
  theorists, 50
Confucian philosophy, 350
Connolly, K. J., 63
Conrad, J., 27
Conrad, P., 11, 49, 130
Constantino, A., 41
Constantino, G., 226
Conversion hysteria 123
Cooley, C. H., 23, 83–84, 154
Coping
  mechanisms, 111
  process, 98
Corey, G. 340–341

Corsini, R. J., 352
Coughey, K., 189
Counseling. *See* Therapies
Countryman, L. F., 140
Cowley, G., 86, 278, 341
Cox, S., 246
Cox, S. M., 27, 200, 262, 295
Co-conscious personalities, 125
Crack, 173–176
Cressey, D. R., 151
Crime and mental disorder, 318–320
Crocetti, G. M., 275
Chromosomes, 63–65
Crooks, R., 189
Cross-cultural
  studies, 1
  perspective on mental disorders, 18–23
Crow, G., 198
CT (Computed tomography), 139
Cullen, F. T., 288, 291
Cullen, W., 109
Culture and mental disorders, 14
Cultures
  guilt and shame, 110
Culture-specific disorders, 17–18
Cummings, E., 272, 288
Cummings, J., 272, 288
Cunningham, S. C., 313
Curanderos, 21

Dahmer, J., 264, 318
Dangerousness and mental disorders, 320–321
Daniels, R., 233, 238
Datan, N., 244, 248
Davenport, L., 243, 333
Davis, K. E., 90
Davis, M., 71
Decompensation, 141
Defense-mechanism
  related to anxiety disorders, 111
Degler, C. N., 50
Degradation ceremonies, 285
Deinstitutionalization, 279
  decline in resident population, 298
  objectives of, 298
  and public policy, 298

Delinquency, 243
Deliriants, 178–179
DeLong, R., 71
Dementia praecox, 47, 132
Demming, B., 181
Denmark, 94
Dentler, R. A., 85
Denzin, N. K., 6–7, 49, 81, 87, 107, 170, 183, 291, 333
Depersonalization
  disorder, 124
  in the institution, 285
Depo-provera, 202
Depression
  adolescent, 120
  childhood, 120
  elderly, 120
  among women, 46
  definition of, 118–119
  and manic syndromes, 119
  racial differences, 222
  and suicide, 119
  symptoms of, 118–119
Deutsch, A. 294
Deutscher, I., 81
Developmental disorders, 60–62
Deviance, 87, 264–265
  primary, 88, 270
  secondary, 88, 270
Dewey, John, 83
Diagnosis, principal, 265
Diagnostic and Statistical Manual of Mental Disorders (DSM), 12
  anxiety disorders in, 111–114
  classification of mental disorders, 57–62
  biases in, 75
  DSM-I, 57
  DSM-II, 15, 43, 57
  DSM-III, 57
  DSM-III-R, 58, 62, 111–113, 133–135, 145, 150, 193, 201, 230, 245, 335–337
Discordance rate, 66
Dissociative disorders, 124
Divorced, 251–252
Dix, D., 46, 294
Dizygotic twins, 65–67, 138

Dohrenwend, B. S., 79, 93, 218, 236, 241, 245, 254, 262, 283
Dohrenwend, B. P., 79, 93, 218, 236, 241, 243, 247, 264, 275, 283, 295
Dopamine, 68
  hypothesis, 69, 138–139
  L-dopa, 69–70
Double-bind
  theory, 143
Double standard in mental health
  class, ethnicity, and race, 234
  gender, 248
Douvan, E., 268
Down's syndrome, 63–64
Drugs
  illegal, 163
  trade, 163
Drummond, E., 314
DSM. See *Diagnostic and Statistical Manual of Mental Disorders*
Dual-career, 250
Dukakis, M., 15
Dukakis, K., 159
Dunham, H. W., 218–220, 295
Dunn, W., 300
Dupont, family, 216
Durham rule, 315–318
Durkheim, E., 26, 32, 47–48, 85, 94, 258, 325
Dyspareunia, 207
Dysphoria, gender, 203–204

Eagleton, T., 15
Earle, R., 199
Eaton, W. W., 157, 236
Ego, 102–104
Ego-defense mechanisms, 103
Ego-dystonic homosexuality, 203
Egypt, 32, 189
Ehrenwald, J., 42
Eitzen, D. S., 13, 15, 76
Elder, G. H., 255
Elderly, 244–247
Electra complex, 103
ECT (electroconvulsive therapy), 2, 72–73, 328
Elkin, I., 70, 75

Ellis, A., 82
Ellison, C. G., 259
Emery, R. E., 255
Emotions, 81
  classification, 82
  consequences, 82
  role in mental disorders, 81–83
Empedocles, 34
Engler, J., 348
Epidemiological studies, 8, 218–222, 236
  catchment area (ECA), 9, 214, 238
  Chicago study, the, 218
  criticism, 240–241
  New Haven study, the, 219–221
  Midtown Manhattan study, the, 221–222
Erectile dysfunction, 206
Erikson, K. T., 85, 89, 108, 264
Essex, M., 248
Esteem, 216
Ethnic groups, 222–233
  ethnicity and healing, 234–235
Ethnocentrism, 223
Ethnomethodology, 50
Evans, R., 8, 18
Exchange theory, 97–98
Exhibitionism, 193–194
Existentialists, 50
Ex-mental patient experience, 286
Explanations of mental disorders
  Chinese, Greek, and Indian, 34
Eysenck, H. J., 156, 343
Eysenck, S. B. G., 194

Factitious
  disorder, 60
  post-traumatic disorder, 127
Family
  history studies of, 65
  one-parent, 253
  pseudomutuality in , 144
  reactions to mental disorders, 288–290
  two-career, 250
Faraone, S. V., 155
Farber, S., 155
Faris, R. E., 218–219 295
Faris, E., 23

Farmer, V., 237
Farnil, D., 190
Feelings, 81–83
Felix, R. H., 294
Female sexual dysfunctions, 207–208
Family Planning Perspectives, 247
Feminization of mental disorders, 49
Festinger, L., 92
Fetish, 194
Filipino Americans, 229–230
Finkelhor, D., 200
Fixation, 156
Flaherty, A., 71–72
Fleck, S., 143
Foley, D. P., 259
Foley, V. D., 345
Food-mood link, 64
Ford, B. 159
Ford Foundation, 300, 306
Forward, S., 201
Foucault, M., 30, 40, 49, 52, 79
France, 44
Frank, J., 288, 291
Franklin, D., 312
Frazer, J., 98
Freeman, H. E., 287
Free association technique, 49, 102
Free-will, 28
Freud, S. 47–49, 81, 101–104, 108, 140
  concept of id, ego, superego, 102
  psychoanalytical therapy, 339–340
  psychosexual development, 103–104
  religion and obsessional neurosis, 258
  unconscious, 102
Fromm, E., 340–341
Fromm–Reichman, F., 142
Frotteurism, 193
Fugue, psychogenic, 124
Funabiki, D., 245
Functionalists, 50

Gacy, J., 147–148
Gagnon, J. H., 191
Galen, 33
Gall, F.J., 43
Gallagher, B. J., 126, 155, 171, 223, 237, 248–249, 258, 260
Gallup, G., 151, 257

Garfinkel, H., 93, 285
Gartrell, J. W., 249
Gautie, M., 64
Gay, D. A., 259
Gebhard, P. H., 190, 198
Gelberg, L., 307
Gelman, D., 64
Gemeinschaft, 235
Gender
  dysphoria, 203
  identity disorders, 14, 203–204
  mental disorders, 245–248
General medical care system, 112113
  treatment of anxiety disorders, 112-113
Genes, 62–65
  dominant, 63
  recessive, 63
Genetic, 53
  factors in mental disorders, 62–67
  transmission, 62–66
George, L. K., 123
Gerhart, U. C., 141, 143–144, 146, 157
Gerontophobia, 244
Gesselschaft, 235
Glass, T. A., 259
Glasser, W., 128, 344–345
Glick, P. C., 253
Global assessment of functioning, 62
Goffman, E., 17, 84, 89, 130, 272–276, 278 286, 290, 311
Gold, H.R., 33
Goldberg, D. P., 114, 122
Golden Triangle, 172
Goldfried, M. R., 337
Golding, J. M., 226
Goldstein, M. J., 138
Gonzalez, R., 255
Good, B., 1
Goode, E., 162, 163, 175, 178, 182, 211, 221
Goode, W. J., 253
Goodman, A. G., 71
Goodman, L. S., 71
Gook syndrome, 231
Gordon, J., 88
Gordon, L., 200

Gosslin, C. C., 194
Gossnell, M., 212
Gough, H. G., 151
Gove, W. R., 247, 249,251, 289
Great Society idea, 296
Greek, 34–36
Greeley, A. M., 181
Greenberg, N. F., 174
Greenberg, R. S., 255
Greenley, J. R., 265
Greer, S., 155
Gregory, R. L., 78
Greyhound therapy, 308
Griesinger, W., 54–55
Grinker, R. R., 141
Grob, G. N., 295
Groth, A. N., 198, 201
Grusky, D. B., 287
Grusky, O., 108, 287, 290
Guilt, 110–1131
  cultures, 110–111
  neurotic, 110
  real, 110
Gupta, G. R., 200, 263, 305
Guy, R. F., 260

Haessly, L., 319
Hager, M., 179
Haiqing, Q., 232
Halbreich, U., 337
Haley, J., 345
Hall, L. A., 255
Haller, A.V., 54
Hallucinogens, 178
Hamilton, V. L., 224
Hammersmith, S. K., 189–190
Haring, M. J., 259
Harrow, H., 141
Harvard Medical School-Mental Health Letter, 142, 179, 193, 212
Hashish, 167
Hassinger, E. W., 235
Healers, 19–24
Healy, W., 48
Health Maintenance Organization (HMO), 10
Hearst, P., 75

Hebrew, 32
Help seeking
  cross-cultural, 19–24
  involuntary, 270
  and religious affiliation, 259–261
  role of family, relatives, and friends, 267
  self-initiated, 273
  stages in, 266–267
  steps in, 267
  visits to physicians and psychiatrists, 293–294
  voluntary, 265
Hemophilia, 62
Heroin
  abuse, 172
  addiction, 173
  relation with crime, 173
Hester, R. K., 181
Heston, L., 67
Hewitt, J. P., 83
Hidden costs of mental disorders, 279
Hillside strangler. See Bianchi, K. W.
Hinckley, J., 264, 312
Hindu, 34
Hinduism, 189, 346
Hippocrates, 33, 34–36, 41, 123
Hirata, L. C., 230
Hispanic Americans, 85, 226–227, 248
  positive mental health in, 226
Histrionic personality disorder, 149
Hoeper, E. W., 122
Hollingshead, A. B. 15, 144, 219, 283
Hollister, L. D., 123
Holmes, T., 252
Holmstrom, L. L., 201
Holzer, C. E., 223, 251
Homans, G. C., 98, 341
Homeless, 298
  children and families, 307
  classification, 299
  composition of, 302–303, 306
  difficulties in enumeration of, 301–302
  disaffiliation process, 311
  emergency room visits, 301
  number of, 300
  policy issues, 310–312

Homelessness, 240
Homosexuality, 15, 189–190
  in other countries, 189
  prevalence, 189–190
  studies in Denmark, Netherlands, and the United States, 190
Hoover Commission, 294
Hope, M., 299, 322
Hornblower, M., 308
Hospital General, Paris, 40
Hough, R. L., 226
Houpt, J. L., 123
Howard, C. S., 225
Huffine, C. L., 289
Hughes, M., 224
Humanistic perspective, 104–105
Humanitarian reform, 39
  the age of, 39–41, 45
  humanitarian spirit, 45
  moral management, 45
  mental hygiene movement, 46
Humor theory (Greek), 34–35
  Chinese Ying/Yang theory, 34
  Indian *Tridosha* theory, 35
Huntington's disease, 65
Hurh, W. M., 232–233
Hutchinson, J., 174
Hypnos, 46–344
  hypnosis and multiple personalities, 125
Hypochondriasis, 123–124
Hysteria
  conversion type, 123
  neurotic, 123
  origin of, 33, 123

Ice. See Cocaine
Id, 102–104
Imber, S. E., 283
Incest, 199–200
  incestuous fathers, 200
  emotional consequences, 200–201
Income
  by households and race, 217
India, 22, 346
Indochinese, 231
Indonesia, 21
Ingalls, A., 282

Insanity
  categories of, 317
  defense, 312
Instincts
  see Freud, 102
  death instincts, 102
  life instincts, 102
Institutionalization, 276
Institute of Medicine, 322
Institute of Social Research (University of Michigan), 174
Institutions. See Mental health institutions
Interactional, symbolic, 29, 81–85
Interest groups, 12
  power of, 76
International
  classification of diseases (ICD), 57
Interpersonal
  conflict and suicide, 26
  therapy, 129
Intrapsychic conflict, 102
Involuntary help-seeking, 270
  steps in involuntary commitment, 272
Irish Americans, 169
Ishiyama, F., 348
Islam, 22

Jackson, D. D., 345
Jacquet, C. H., 257
James, B., 201
James, W., 83
Japan, 189
Japanese-Americans, 233, 247
Jarvis, E., 245
Jedlicka, D., 166, 188
Jefferson, L., 263
Jeffery, C. R., 201, 314–315, 318
Jellinek, E. M., 169, 317
Jewish
  Americans, 169
  people, 260
Job stress, 9
Johnson, A. B., 300
Johnson, J. S., 254
Johnson, L. B., 296
Johnson, V. E., 204–209, 211
Johnston, J. R., 255

Johnston, L. T., 171
Jones, E. E., 90
Jones, M., 115, 117, 124
Joy, V. D., 287
Judd, Lewis, 15
Julian, R. M., 168
Justice, B., 200
Justice, R., 200

Kakar, S., 22–23, 346
Kamasutra, 189
Kandel, D., 171
Kaplan, B. H., 260
Kaplan, H. I., 37, 43, 52
Kaplan, H. S., 206
Kapur, R. L., 22
Karma, 347
Karyotypes, 63
  see genes, 63
Katon, W., 113–115, 122
Keenan, K., 155
Kelly, H. H., 90
Kelly, J. B., 255
Kempe, C., 200
Kempe, R., 200
Kemper, E., 148
Kemper, T., 83
Kennedy, J. F., 48, 295, 312
Kephart, W. M., 166
Kermis, M. D., 130, 244
Kesey, K., 284
Kessler, R. C., 221, 248
Kety, S. S., 68–69, 100, 138, 157
Khantzian, E. J., 181
Kiev, A., 20, 32, 52
Kim, K. C., 232–233
Kinsey, A. C., 189–190, 204
Kinzie, J. D., 231
Kitano, H. H. L., 233, 238
Kitsunetsuki, 19
Kleptomania, 14
Klerman, G. L., 246
Klienman A., 1, 20, 325, 338, 351
Kline, M., 2555
Kline, N. S., 70
Klinefelter's syndrome, 65
Knee, D., 155
Knight, R., 142

Kolb, L. C., 275
Komarovsky, M., 247
Korean Americans, 232–233
Koro, 19
Kotulak, R., 73–74, 78
Kozal, J., 322
Kraeplin, E., 47, 55, 113
Kreisman, D. E., 287
Kudashin, C., 260
Kulka, R. A., 268
Kupersmidt, J. B., 253
Kuru, 20

Labeling theory, 87
  process, 88, 268
  evaluation and criticism, 105–106
Langer, E., 348
Langner, T. S., 260
Larson, D. B., 260
Lauriat, A., 304
Lazarus, A., 342
Learning, 90–91
  process, 90
  theory, 90
Lebra, W., 20
Leerhsen, C., 245, 332
Leff, J., 262
Lehmann, A.C., 20, 52
Lejeune, J. 64
Lemert, E. M., 270
Lemkau, P. V., 275
Leonard, E. A., 88
Lesbian, 189–190
Lester, D., 211
Levin, J., 244
Levin, W. C., 244
Levine, E. M., 166
Levi-Strauss, C., 98
Levy, L., 218
Lewis, S. D., 243, 332
Lidz, T., 143
Lieb, J., 267
Lieberman, M. A., 252
Liem, J., 221
Liem, R., 221
Life cycle and mental disorders, 241
Link, B. G., 218, 238, 245, 262, 288–291, 295

Lips, H. M., 246, 248
Lithium, 69. 128
Lobotomy, 333
Lombroso, C., 62, 155
Longo, R. E., 198
Loring, B., 224
Los Angeles Times, 190
Lucas, H. L., 148
Luce, C. B., 231
Lund, D. S., 260

Macdonald, J., 223
Machismo, 227
Macrosociology, 79
  macro-level analysis, 79
MRI (Magnetic Resonance Imaging), 73, 141
Maisch, H., 200
Malaysia, 22
Malgady, R. G., 226
Malinowski, B., 98
Malleus Maleficarum, 42
Mancuso, J. C., 67, 138
Manderscheid, R. W., 11, 287
Manic-depression, 117–119
Mann, J. M., 209
Manning, P., 296
MAO inhibitors, 128
Marcuse, P., 306, 309
Marianismo, 227
Marijuana
  costs, 171
  extent of use, 171
  history of use, 170–171
  use and abuse controversies, 171
Marital
  interactions, 143
  marital schism, 143
  marital skew, 143
  status and mental disorders, 247–257
Marlatt, G. A.
Marolla, J., 201
Martin, C. E., 190
Martin, T. C., 256
Marx, K., 95–96, 258
Maser, J. D., 151
Masland, R., 73
Maslow, A., 104

Masochism, 188
Masson, J. M., 340
Masters, W. H., 204–209, 211
Masturbation, 193
Mathews, T., 319
Maton, K. I., 258
Matza, D., 85
Mauss, M., 98
May, P. A., 228
Mayo clinic, 75
McCall, G. J., 108
McCheney, K. Y., 302
McClelland, M., 113, 124
McCready, W. C., 181
McDadniel, A., 225
McFadin, J. B., 198
McGovern, George, 15
McRae, J. A., 248
Mead, G.M., 23–25, 83
Mechanic, D., 265, 283, 294, 322
Medicalization
  of deviance, 11
  of the feelings of women, 49
Medical-biological
  approach, 2, 53
Medications
  for depression, 70
  for psychotic symptoms, 71
  side-effects, 71–72
Meditation, 347–348
Mednick, S. A., 138
Meilan, X., 232
Melancholia, 36
Menaghan, E. G., 252
Mendel, W. M., 258
Meniere's, disease, 142
Mens rea, 314
Mental disorder, 1–2
  becoming mentally ill, 7
  and insanity defense, 312–318
  as myth, 16, 99
  as social status, 93
  stigma of, 15–17
Mental disorders
  axes in *DSM-III-R*, 55
  classification, 57–62
  clinical syndromes, 58–60
  conceptualization of, 83

  in cross-cultural perspective 18–23
  and the law, 312
  managing of, 86
  as spiritual experience, 258
  person-centered approaches, 333
Mental health
  cost, 12
  definition, 2–4
  organizations, 269
Mental health institutions
  (organizations), 269
  institution-centered and patient-
    centered, 281
  patient length of stay, 280
  staff, 280–282
  types, 280–282
Mental illness 1–4
  as myth, 16, 99
  differences between mental and
    physical illness, 100
  problems of living, 99
Mental hygiene movement, 46
Mental patient role, 282
Merton, R. K., 6, 74, 181
Mesmer, F.A., 43
  mesmerism, 43
Mesopotamia, 32
Messinger, S., 49, 267
Meyer, J. M., 285
Microsociology, 79
Middle ages, 37–39
Midtown Manhattan study, the, 221–222
Miller, A., 319
Miller, M., 174
Miller, W. R., 181
Milligan, W. S., 125
Mills, J., 163
Mind
  as superorganic entity, 56
  healing, 74
  mind-brain controversy 2
Minorities, 222–233
  length of stay in institutions, 280
Mirowsky, J., 226
M'Naghten rule, 314–315
  criticism of, 315
Model penal code, 316

Mongoloism, 63
Monoamine oxidase (MAO), 69
Mood-disorders, 109, 117
  bipolar, 117
  unipolar, 117
  See also Depression
Moore, J. W., 227, 238
Moore, M. S., 315–318
Moral causes of insanity, 45
Moral management, 45
Moral treatment, 46
Morbidity, rate, 214
Morganthau, T., 174
Morita, therapy, 348
Morrison, A., 255
Motimer, J., 262
Multiple personality
  disorder, 124–126
Mulvey, A., 254
Munakata, T., 131
Murad, F., 71
Murdock, G. P., 185
Murr, A., 174
Musto, D. F., 182
Mutual help groups, 331–332
Myers, J. E., 20
Myers, J. K., 115, 260
M'Naghten rule, 315

Naikan therapy, 348
Narcissism, 166
Narcissistic personality disorder, 149
Nash, E. H., 285
Nasjleti, M., 201
National Advisory Mental Health
  Council, 242
National Alliance for the Mentally
  Ill, 15
National Center for Health Statistics,
  165, 295
National Coalition for the Homeless,
  300, 302–303, 324
National Institute on Alcohol Abuse &
  Alcoholism, 168
National Institute on Drug Abuse
  (NIDA), 163, 174 181–182

National Institute of Mental Health
  (NIMH), 7, 15, 78, 124, 130, 157,
  214, 222, 223, 239–242, 253, 266–267,
  269, 278–282, 291, 294, 298, 305
  admissions, 222
  admissions by sex and marital status,
    253
  anxiety disorders, 111
  NIMH (ECA) affective disorder
    study, 112
  extent of mental disorders, 7–8,
    patient care episodes, 11
  findings on depression, 75
  mood disorders, 119
  patient care episodes, 278
  selected principal diagnosis, 266
National Man-Boy Love League, 188
Necrostuprum, 197
Nelson, M., 243, 332
Neugebauer, R., 245
Neurology, 55
Neuroscience, 68
  branches of, 68
Neurosis, 109
Neurosurgeons, 73
Neurosurgery, 336
Neurotransmitter, 69
New Haven study, the, 219
Newmann, J. P., 46
Nicotine addiction, 179
Nielson, A. C., 113
Nigeria, 222
Nirvana, 34
Nixon, R., 152
Nixon administration, 296
Norepinephrine, 128
Norton, A. J., 253
Nuthkavihak, 20
Nyczi, G. R., 122

Obsessive-compulsive disorder, 121–122
  definition, 121
  NIMH findings, 121
  and personality disorder, 150
Occupation, 9

O'Connor, P., 251
Oedipus complex, 103
Ohio Department of Mental Health, 299, 305
O'Keefe, P., 200
Okun, M. A., 258
Oldham, S., 190
O'Leary, K. D., 255
Oliven, J., 198
Olson, G. A., 262
O'Malley, P., 171
Omran, A. R., 260
Once-married, 251–254
One-parent families, 253–254
Orgasmic dysfunction, 207
Orleans, C. T., 123
Orn, H., 1557
Ortmann, J., 68
Osanka, F., 320

Pachon, H., 227, 238
Padgett, D. K., 301
Page, L., 314
Panic disorder, 114–115
Papolos, D. F., 72, 78, 119, 130
Papolos, J., 72, 78, 119, 130
Paracelsus, 41
Paradigm shifts, 54
Paradox of normality, 269–270
Personality disorders, 145–152
Paraphilias, 192–204
  See also Sexual
Park, R.E., 23, 110
Parkes, C. M., 252
Parkinson's disease, 68
Parrillo, V. N., 227
Parsons, T., 92, 283
Passive-aggressive personality disorder, 150
Pathogenic families, 165–166
Patient (mental)
  characteristics, 277
  status, 277
  care episodes, 278
Patient-centered institutions. See Mental health institutions
Patterson, C. J., 253
Pattison, E. M., 260

Pearlin, L. I., 254
Pedophile, 197
  pedophilia, 195
Peele, S., 183
Peluso, E., 183
Peluso, L. S., 183
Perkins, R. M., 316
Perls, F. S., 344
Personality
  core or dominant 125
  co-conscious or subpersonalities, 125
Personality disorders, 131, 145–156
  types of, 147–150
Person-centered approach, 80
Personal identity, 84
PET (Positron emission tomography), 139
Peterson, J. L., 255
Peterson, L. A., 259
Peterson, W.P., 35
Pharmaceutical enterprise, 10
Pharmacological advances, 73
Phillips, D. L., 275
Philosophers, 343
Phobic disorders, 115–117
  extent, 115
  primary gain, 117
  secondary gain, 117
  types, 116
Physicians, primary care, 123
Piers, G., 110
Pigache, P., 22
Pinel, P., 44–45, 294
Pittillo, E. S., 126
Plato, 35–36
Pleck, J. H., 251
Pollner, M., 108, 259, 290
Pomeroy, W. B., 190
Pomper, S., 243, 332
Pope, H. G., 134
Porkert, M., 349
Positions, 84
Possession by spirits, 14
Posttraumatic stress disorder (PTSD), 61–62
  definition, 127
  factitious PTSD, 127
Powell, B., 224

Power, 95–97
President's Commission on Organized Crime, 171–172
Presley, E., 159
Press, A., 2255
Prestige, 216
Prevention, primary, 295
Prevalence, rates of mental disorders, 214
Prepatient, 265
Price, S. J., 165
Problems of living, 13, 21
Proletariat, 95
Protestant ethic, 260
Protestants and mental disorders, 260
Prozac, 86
Pseudo-patients, 101
Psychedelics, 167, 170–172, 178
Psychiatric
  approach, 4, 53, 56
  enterprise, 10, 151
  imperialism, 76
  new trends in assessment, 334–335
Psychiatric News, 336
Psychiatric Times, 337
Psychiatrists, 12, 55–57, 328
Psychiatry
  infant, 12
Psychoactive drugs, 2, 10, 335
  antianxiety, 70–71
  antidepressants, 70
  antipsychotic, 70
  commonly abused, 167
  dependency, 337
Psychoanalysis, 48, 333
Psychoanalytical approach, 46–48, 101–105
Psychodynamic approach, 101–105
Psychogenic
  amnesia, types, 124
  fugue, 124
  pain, 123
  somatoform pain disorder, 123
Psychological approach
  abnormal, clinical, pathological, 4
Psychoneuroimmunology, 73
Psychoneuroscience, 68

Psychopath, 150–154
  psychopathic personality, 150–151
Psychosexual development, 103
  See also Freud
Psychosis, 136–145
  explanations, 137–145
  types, 136–137
Psychosocial
  processes, 4–5
  stressors, 61
  therapy, 13
Psychosomatic disorder, 131
Psychosurgery, 333
Psychotherapists, 328–330
Psychotherapy
  Asian, 346–349
  behavior, 342
  cognitive, 340
  existential, 342
  family, 345
  gestalt, 344
  interpersonal, 341
  objectives of, 339
  person-centered, 342
  psychoanalytical, 339–341
  reality, 344–345;
  value conflicts in, 231
Psychotic disorders, 131
Psychotropic drugs. *See* Psychoactive drugs
Purvis, A., 329

Qiang, H., 232
Quick-fix therapies, 329, 334

Rabkin, J. G., 288
Race, 222–233
Radcliffe-Brown, A. R., 98
Radlaff, L. S., 246
Rahe, R., 251
Raine, G., 174
Rall, T. W., 71
Rape, 202
  rapists, 199
Rational emotive therapy, 82
Raymond, M. E., 267
Reagan administration, 297

Reagan, R., 313
Reality therapy, 129
Reconstituted families, 256–257
Redburn, F. S., 322
Redlich, F. C., 14, 144, 219, 283
Reese, M., 210
Reformation, age of, 39–41, 44–46
Reformists, 44–46
Refugees, 228
Regier, D. A., 8, 113, 218
Reid, J. B., 181
Reinforcement, 91
Reinisch, J. M., 190, 196, 205, 210, 211
Reliability
 of mental health figures, 9–10
Religion, 257–261
 religious groups, 257
Renaissance, 42
Rene Guyon Society, 188
Renner, D. S., 224
Reserpine, 70
Residual deviance, 89, 268
Residual rule breaking, 268
Reynolds, B., 15
Riesman, D., 231
Right, J. W., 165
Robbins, K., 88
Roberts, B. H., 260
Robins, L. N. 154, 245
Robinson, I. E., 188
Rodeheaver, D., 244, 248
Roff, J. D., 142
Rogers, C., 104, 343–344
Rogers, P., 319
Rogler, L. H., 226, 326
Role, 84
 master role, 270
 role overload, 252
 role status, 270
 role theory, 92–93
Roman Catholics, 229
Romans, 36
Ropers, R. H., 306, 322
Rosen, G., 52
Rosenberg, M., 234
Rosenhan, D., 101
Rosenthal, D., 67–68
Rosenthal, S. S., 67–68

Ross, C., 226
Rossi, P. H., 299, 3042 307, 322
Rossides, D. W., 216
Roth, D., 305
Rowe, C. J., 114
Rowitz, L., 218
Roy, A., 259
Rubin, L., 304
Rule-breaking, 88
 residual, 89
Runyan, W. K., 140
Rural living, 235–237
Rush, B., 45–46
Russell, C., 305
Russo, J., 113, 115, 122

Sadistic personality disorder, 150
Sadock, B. J., 37, 43
Sampson, H., 49, 267
Sandhya, 34
Sarbin, T. R., 67, 138
Sargent, M., 119, 128–129
Saul, M., 113, 122
Savants, 316
Schaefer, A. B., 65
Schaefer, R. T., 216, 224, 230
Schaefer, S. 230
Scheff, T. J., 28, 52, 79, 82, 88, 93, 108, 266, 268, 289–291, 333
Schinke, S. P., 228
Schizoid personality disorder, 148
Schizophrenia, 66–67, 131
 association with class, 218–222
 definition, 132
 genetic inheritance of, 66–67
 incidence, 134
 process schizophrenia, 132
 reactive type, 132
 symptoms, 132
 treatment, 134
 types, 132, 135
Schizophreniform disorder, 132
Schizotypal personality disorder, 147
Schneider, J. W., 11, 49, 130
Schreiber, F. R.
Schulberg, H. C., 113, 122
Schulsinger, F., 69
Schwalbe, M. L., 251

Scot, R., 42
Scully, D., 201
Second revolution in mental health, 295
Seidman, L. J., 336
Selesnick, S. T., 36, 39, 52
Self-actualization, 105
Self-defeating, 105
  personality disorder, 150
Self-esteem, 105
Self-feeling, 264–265
Self-fulfilling prophecy, 83, 284
Self-fulfillment, 105
Self-help groups, 331–332
Self-labeling, 83, 266
Self-objectification, 83
Self-selection, 237
Senate Committee on the Homeless, the, 308
Separation distress, 252
Serial-killers, 147–148
Serotonin, 128
Sex
  addiction, 198
  assault, 201–202
  bias in defining mental disorders, 12
  therapy, 209–210
Sexual
  changing values, 188
  desire disorders, 208
  deviance, 191
  disorders, 192
  dysfunctions among male, 206–207
  dysfunctions among females, 207–208
  revolution, 204
  sadism, 196
Sexuality
  cross-cultural, 204
  and emotions, 190–191
  procreational, 186
  recreational, 186
Sexualization
  of mental disorders, 49–50
  in hysteria 123
Shambaugh, G. E., 140
Shame cultures, 110–111
Shapiro, D. H., 347, 351
Shapiro, L., 327
Shapiro, S., 8, 113

Shapiro, S. H., 304
Sheehan, D. V., 115
Shepard, L. J., 251
Sherrill, P., 127
Shore, D., 78
Sick role, 114
Side-effects of drugs, 129
Simbionese Liberation Army, 136
Simmel, G., 95, 98
Simmons, J. L., 108
Simmons, O. G., 287
Simon, W., 191
Singapore, 21
Singer, M. B., 110
Situation
  definition of, 83
  meaningful, 83
  problematic, 83
Sizemore, C. C., 126
Skinner, B. F, 91, 342
Slaby, A. E., 267
Smith, R., 332
Smith, R. M., 160, 163
Snow, D., 304–305
Sobel, R. 282
Social construction of mental disorders, 83–85
Social deviance perspective, 85
Social epidemiology
  definition, 213
Social exchange perspective, 97
Social forces, 12
Social learning theory, 90
Socialization, 91
  pathogenic, 142
Social-identity, 84
Social–reaction, 87, 270
  perspective, 93, 145
Social selection, 87, 145
  and class, 93
  perspective, 93
  theory, 93, 249
Social stress, 87
  hypothesis, 145
  perspective, 93
Sociological
  approaches to mental disorders, 79
  findings, 79–80

Sociological *(cont'd.)*
  evaluation, 105
Sociopaths, 151–154
Socrates, 32
Sodomy, in Asia, Africa, Middle East, 190
Soloman, G., 65
Somatic
  therapies, 56
Somatization, 9, 326
  in anxiety disorders, 114
Somatoform disorder, 98
  definition, 122
  process of somatization, 122
Sonnenschein, M.A., 11
Soranus, 36
Sorenson, S. B., 226
Southeast Asia, 14
Speck, R., 65
Spitzer, S. P., 291
Springen, K., 88, 319
Srole, L., 221–222, 260
St. Vitas' dance, 39
Staines, G. L., 251
Staples, C. L., 251
Stark, E., 200
Stark, R., 258
Steiner, B. W., 203
Stephens, R., 183
Stereotypes, 229–233
Stewart B. McKinney Homeless Assistance Act, 299
Stigma, 15–16, 251
  causes, 17
Stimulants, 167
Stock, W. A., 258
Stone, A. R., 283
Straus, R., 166
Stress related disorders, 109
Structural–functional perspective, 94
Struening, E. L., 301
Subpersonalities, 125
Substance abuse
  dependence, 161–162
  factors involved, 161–164
Substances abuse disorders
  explanations of abuse, 180–182
  substance induced, 161

Substantia nigra, 68
Suicide, 26
  interpersonal crisis, 26
  among youth, 26
  in Denmark, England, and France, 94
  among Protestants and Catholics, 94
Suinn, R. M., 155
Sullivan, H. S., 142
Super-ego, 102
Superwoman, 251
Support groups, 331–332
Sutherland, E. H., 151
Sweet, J., 256
Sybil, 126
Symbolic interaction, 23–30
  perspective, 81–83
System-centered approach, 80
Szasz, T. S., 5, 13, 30–31, 40, 52, 76, 78, 79, 99–100, 107, 130, 264–265, 333, 351

Tadlock, M., 304
Tarantism, 39
Tessler, R., 265
Thailand, 22
Theisen, G., 181
Therapists, 328
Therapy
  biochemical, 128, 335–337
  cognitive-behavioral, 128
  genetic, 127
  interpersonal, 128
  neurological, 335–337
  psychological, 338–345
  revolution, 330–331
  short-term or brief, 330
Therapies
  quick-fix, 329–330
  proliferation of, 330–331
Thigpen, C. H., 126
Thio, A., 8
Thoits, P. A., 83, 264
Thomas, M. E., 224
Thomas, W.I., 23, 83, 284
Thorman, G., 305, 322
Thorndike, E. L., 91
Three Faces of Eve, 126

Tierney, K., 287
Timbers, D. N., 226
Torrey, E. F., 13, 30, 65–67, 100, 134, 137–138, 157, 238, 298, 305, 330, 336, 351
Total institution, 275–276
Tourette's syndrome, 316–317
Tower, C. C., 211
Towne, R., 49, 267
Townsend, J. M., 288
Transsexualism, 203
Transvestic fetishism, 194
Treatment
 costs, 243
 of mental disorders, 5
Trephining, 31
Trycyclics, 128
Troiden, R. R., 211
Tschann, J. M., 255
Tseng, W.S., 34
Tsuang, M. T., 1555
Tudor, J., 250
Tuke, W., 45
Tung, T. M., 232
Turner, R., 95
Turner, R. J., 249
Turpin, R., 64
Turque, B., 156
Twins, studies of, 65–66, 137
 fraternal (dizygotic), 65–66
 identical (monozygotic), 65–66
Two-career couples and families, 250

Ulbrich, P., 226
Umberson, D., 258
Underclass, 224
Underwood, A., 156
U.S. Bureau of Census. *See* Bureau of Census
U.S. Department of Health and Human Services (DHHS), 163, 247, 300, 322
U.S. Department of Housing and Urban Development (HUD), 300
U.S. General Accounting Office, 299
U.S. House of Representatives Committee on Ways and Means Report, 217

U.S. National Highway Traffic Administration, 168
 accidents, 168
U.S. Senate Committee on Aging, 244
U.S.S.R. (former), 97
Urban living, 235–237

Vaden, N. A., 253
Vaginismus, 207–208
Vaillant, G., 181
Van Gough, V., 140
Vanyperen, N. W., 251
Vaughn, C., 262
Vedas, 34
Venidad, 33
Verbrugge, L., 246
Vergare, M. J., 304
Vermont study, the, 133
Veroff, J., 268
Visits to physicians, 293
Vitalino, P. P., 115, 117, 124
Volkart, E. H., 283
von Zerssen, D., 248
Voss, H. L., 173
Voyeurism, 198

Wallace, Mike, 10
Wallerstein, J., 255
Walsh, R., 346, 347–348, 351
Ward, S., 202
Warheit, G. J., 223, 250
Warren, C. A. B., 49, 52, 108
Watson, J. B., 90
Weakland, J., 345
Wedding, R. J., 320
Weinberg, M. S., 189–190
Weiner, J., 69
Weiss, R. S., 252–253
Weissman, M. M., 246
Weitzman, L., 255
Wender, P. H., 66–67
Were, 20
Westermeyer, J., 232
Weyer, J., 41–42
Weyerer, S., 248
Wheaton, B., 259
White, S., 202
Whiting, B., 320

Whitwell, J.R., 33
Wilber, K., 347
Williams, C. A., 254
Williams, J.M., 23
Williams, K., 202
Williams, T. A., 113
Willie, C. V., 224
Wilson, W. J., 223, 240
Winthrop, R., 232
Witchcraft, 37
  witches, 37-39
  witch doctors, 37-39
  witch hunts, 37-39
Witter, R. A., 258
Wittman, P. A., 127
Wittiko, 20
Wolinsky, F. P., 213
World Health Organization, 8, 18
Wozniak, J. F., 288, 291

Wright, J. D., 215, 322
Wright, L., 65

Xida, W., 232

Yalom, I. D., 110
Yoga, 346-348
Young, J., 299, 322

Zarrow, S., 187
Zilboorg, G., 34
Zill, N., 255
Zinberg, N. E., 180
Zinn, M. B., 11, 13, 76
Znaniecki, F., 23
Zucker, M., 296
Zung, E. M., 223
Zung, W. W. K., 223